P9-BXW-642

# THE CANADIAN LIVING ENTERTAINING COOKBOOK

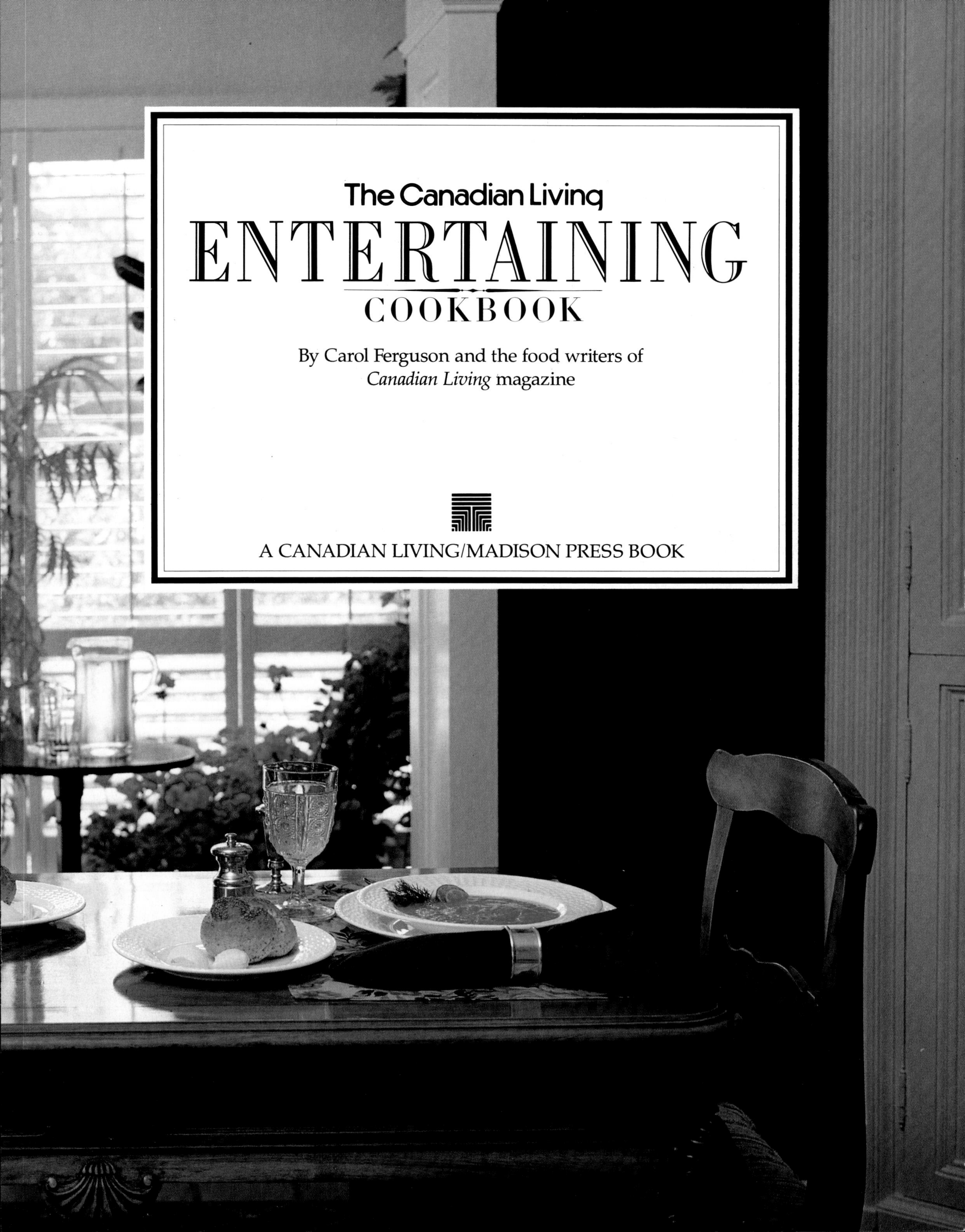

By Carol Ferguson and the food writers of
*Canadian Living* magazine

A CANADIAN LIVING/MADISON PRESS BOOK

Telemedia Publishing Inc.
50 Holly Street
Toronto, Ontario
Canada
M4S 3B3

Canadian Cataloguing in Publication Data

Ferguson, Carol
The Canadian living entertaining cookbook

ISBN 0-394-22153-2

1. Entertaining. 2. Cookery. 3. Cookery, Canadian.
4. Menus. I. Title.

TX731.F47 1990 642′.4 C90-093290-2



**Produced by**
**Madison Press Books**
**40 Madison Avenue**
**Toronto, Ontario**
**Canada**
**M5R 2S1**

*Printed in Italy*

# TABLE OF CONTENTS

# INTRODUCTION

Hospitality is the oldest of Canadian traditions. From the days of our earliest pioneer homesteaders, good company and good food have always welcomed visitors to Canadian homes in every region. Today, that heritage is more relevant than ever to our entertaining styles.

The 1990s have brought a renewed focus on "what's really important," from concern about the environment to a renewed closeness of families and friends. Comfort and casualness are downright fashionable.

And the food we choose matches this mood—sometimes elegant, sometimes homey—but always generous in spirit. We may be more sophisticated in our tastes than ever before, but at the same time we are simplifying our entertaining menus to fit comfortably into contemporary restrictions of time, space and budget. We enjoy an occasional splurge (weddings, anniversaries, holidays) but tend to smaller gatherings. We choose menus with an eye to quality, fast and easy preparation and interesting presentation at the table.

The entertaining styles of the '90s give you plenty of moods and tastes to personalize your own way. The menus in this book are a reflection and sampling of those choices—nostalgic tradition, stylish sophistication, casual coziness, festive elegance. The chapters group the menus into categories of time and occasion, and within each you'll find parties for all seasons, ages, numbers and locations. Whether it's a cozy fireside gathering at the cottage or a spiffy cocktail party before the theatre, a birthday party for a four-year-old or a fund-raiser barbecue for a crowd, we hope you'll find exactly what you had in mind or inspiration for new themes. We've added lots of scene-setting ideas and presentation tips along with beautiful photographs to make your preparation easy and enjoyable. And most of all, we hope you discover a return to the true purpose of entertaining—the mutual pleasure of guests and hosts. Enjoy!

*Carol Ferguson*

# EVENINGS

*Whether it's a cozy little dinner with special friends or a big festive bash for a crowd, we all want our evening entertainments to have a special magic. In this chapter, you'll find a wide variety of interesting menus, some that will be exactly what you had in mind for that special occasion you're planning, others that will inspire a new approach. For small dinner parties, choose "easy and elegant" or add an Italian, Spanish or Oriental flavor theme. The "big" parties are here, too—from a stylish celebration feast for ten to a sensational cocktail party for a crowd. In other chapters, you'll find lots more for evening entertaining—theme parties, international dinners, and menus for family occasions, the Christmas season and holidays throughout the year.*

# A CELEBRATION FEAST

FOR TEN

*Celebrate an extra-special occasion in elegant style with this sumptuous dinner. Each menu item has been designed for make-ahead preparation or quick cooking.*

FRESH OYSTERS

*DILLED SALMON PÂTÉ

*LAMB LOINS WITH MELLOW GARLIC SAUCE

*COUSCOUS PILAF TIMBALES

*TWO-PEPPER, MUSHROOM AND SNOW PEA SAUTÉ

*BELGIAN ENDIVE AND ORANGE SALAD WITH AVOCADO

*BRANDY SNAP TULIPS WITH TWO ICES AND FRESH FRUIT

**Recipes are given for menu items marked with an asterisk.*

## Dilled Salmon Pâté

*Serve with thinly sliced pumpernickel bread and an easy-to-make sauce—just combine sour cream with horseradish and dill to taste.*

| | | |
|---|---|---|
| **1/2 cup** | **dry white wine** | **125 mL** |
| **1/4 cup** | **chicken or fish stock** | **50 mL** |
| **1/4 cup** | **chopped green onion** | **50 mL** |
| **1** | **slice lemon** | **1** |
| **1** | **sprig fresh parsley** | **1** |
| **1-1/2 lb** | **salmon fillets** | **750 g** |
| **2** | **envelopes unflavored gelatin** | **2** |
| **1/3 cup** | **cold water** | **75 mL** |
| **3/4 cup** | **sour cream** | **175 mL** |
| **3/4 cup** | **plain yogurt** | **175 mL** |
| **1/2 cup** | **mayonnaise** | **125 mL** |
| **2 tbsp** | **each chopped fresh dill and parsley** | **25 mL** |
| **2 tbsp** | **lemon juice** | **25 mL** |
| **1 tsp** | **salt** | **5 mL** |
| **1/2 tsp** | **hot pepper sauce** | **2 mL** |
| | **GARNISH:** | |
| | **Fresh dill sprigs and lemon slices** | |

■ In large shallow saucepan, bring wine, stock, half of the onion, lemon slice and parsley sprig to boil. Cover and reduce heat; simmer for 3 minutes. Add salmon. Cover and return to simmer; cook for 8 to 10 minutes or until salmon flakes easily when tested with fork.

■ With slotted spoon, remove salmon; remove and discard skin and bones. Cover and refrigerate until chilled. Strain and reserve cooking liquid.

■ In small saucepan, stir gelatin into cold water; let stand until softened. Add reserved cooking liquid; cook over low heat until gelatin has dissolved.

■ In food processor, process salmon, remaining onion, sour cream, yogurt, mayonnaise, dill, parsley, lemon juice, salt and hot pepper sauce until smooth, scraping down side of bowl as necessary.

*Lamb Loins with Mellow Garlic Sauce; Couscous Pilaf Timbale; Two-Pepper, Mushroom and Snow Pea Sauté; Belgian Endive and Orange Salad with Avocado*

■ Pour in gelatin mixture; process just until blended. Taste and adjust seasoning if necessary. Transfer to greased 8- × 4-inch (1.5 L) loaf pan. Cover and refrigerate for at least 4 hours or up to 2 days.
**GARNISH:** Turn out pâté onto serving platter. Garnish with dill sprigs and lemon slices. Makes 10 servings.

# *Lamb Loins with Mellow Garlic Sauce*

*The simmered garlic mellows into a sweet ingredient which harmonizes well with lamb.*

| | | |
|---|---|---|
| 2-1/2 lb | boneless lamb loins | 1.25 kg |
| 1 tsp | pepper | 5 mL |
| 3/4 tsp | dried thyme | 4 mL |
| 2 tsp | butter | 10 mL |
| 2 tsp | olive oil | 10 mL |
| | GARLIC SAUCE: | |
| 2 | large heads garlic | 2 |
| 1-1/2 cups | chicken stock | 375 mL |
| 3/4 cup | dry white wine | 175 mL |
| 3 tbsp | butter | 50 mL |
| | Salt and pepper | |

■ Trim lamb and pat dry; sprinkle with pepper and thyme. Cover and refrigerate for at least 1 hour or up to 5 hours.
**GARLIC SAUCE:** Meanwhile, separate garlic into cloves but do not peel. Rinse cloves and place in saucepan with enough boiling water to cover; bring to boil. Reduce heat and simmer for 20 to 30 minutes or until softened. Drain and let cool.
■ Squeeze out pulp into food processor; purée until smooth and set aside.
■ Divide butter and oil between 2 large ovenproof skillets; melt over high heat. Cook lamb for 45 to 60 seconds per side or just until browned. Transfer skillets to 400°F (200°C) oven and roast lamb for 6 to 10 minutes or until desired doneness. Remove from skillets; cover and keep warm while finishing sauce.
■ Combine stock and wine; divide evenly between same 2 skillets. Bring to boil, stirring to scrape up any brown bits; cook for 3 to 5 minutes or until sauce is reduced by one-third.
■ Divide reserved garlic purée between skillets and boil for 1 minute; strain into saucepan, pressing garlic through sieve. Chop butter into 6 pieces and swirl one piece at a time into sauce. Season with salt and pepper to taste.
■ Slice lamb diagonally across the grain into thin slices; arrange on warmed plates. Spoon sauce over. Makes 10 servings.

## *Couscous Pilaf Timbales*

*These timbales can be made ahead and reheated just before serving. You can serve this side dish mounded into a bowl instead of packing it into moulds if desired.*

| | | |
|---|---|---|
| **1/4 cup** | **butter** | **50 mL** |
| **1 cup** | **finely chopped shallots, leeks or onions** | **250 mL** |
| **1 cup** | **finely diced carrots** | **250 mL** |
| **2-1/2 cups** | **chicken stock** | **625 mL** |
| **2 cups** | **precooked couscous*** | **500 mL** |
| **1/4 cup** | **pine nuts or slivered almonds, toasted** | **50 mL** |
| | **Salt and pepper** | |

■ In saucepan, melt butter over medium heat; cook shallots and carrots for 5 minutes or until softened. Stir in stock. Cover and bring to simmer; cook for 5 to 8 minutes or just until carrots are tender.

■ Uncover and bring to boil; stir in couscous, nuts, and salt and pepper to taste. Remove from heat; cover and let stand for 5 minutes. Fluff with fork.

■ Grease ten 1/2-cup (125 mL) timbales or custard cups. Line bottoms with rounds of waxed paper; grease waxed paper. Pack couscous mixture into moulds. (Timbales can be prepared ahead and kept warm for up to 40 minutes by setting in roasting pan with enough boiling water to come halfway up sides of moulds and covering with foil. Or refrigerate timbales for up to 4 hours. To reheat, set in roasting pan with boiling water and heat over low heat just until warmed through.) Turn out onto individual plates. Makes 10 servings.

*Available at Middle Eastern and natural food stores and some supermarkets.

## *Two-Pepper, Mushroom and Snow Pea Sauté*

*This last-minute sauté makes a fine accompaniment to the lamb and couscous. If desired, you can substitute shiitake or large brown mushrooms for the oyster variety.*

| | | |
|---|---|---|
| **2** | **large sweet red peppers** | **2** |
| **1** | **large sweet yellow pepper** | **1** |
| **1/2 lb** | **snow peas** | **250 g** |
| **1/3 lb** | **oyster mushrooms** | **175 g** |
| **2 tbsp** | **butter** | **25 mL** |
| **2 tbsp** | **chicken stock** | **25 mL** |
| | **Salt and pepper** | |

***WINE SUGGESTIONS***
***A celebration dinner calls for special wines. Offer a chilled bubbly such as Delapierre from Spain, a fine dry white chablis from Moreau or Jaffelin, or dusty-dry muscadet with the oysters and salmon pâté. Enjoy a velvety red pinot noir from Latour or Chateau des Charmes with the lamb, and finish the meal in style with Pol Roger Brut.***

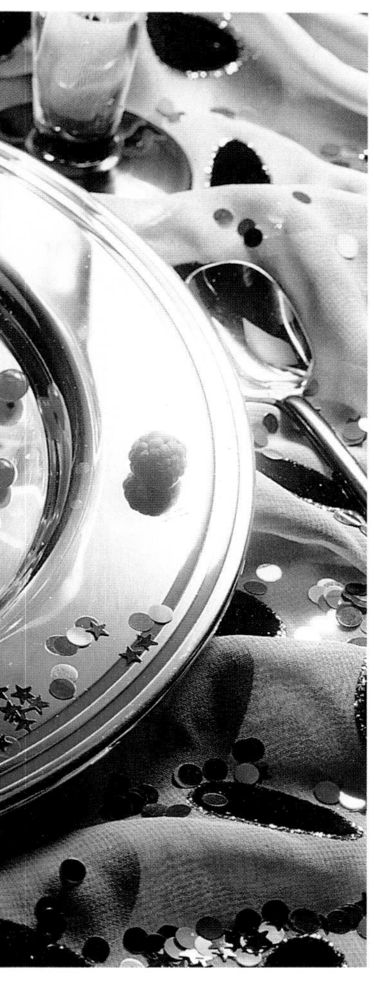

*Brandy Snap Tulip with Two Ices and Fresh Fruit*

■ Halve, core and seed red and yellow peppers. In large saucepan of boiling water, cook peppers for 4 to 5 minutes or until skins are loosened. Drain and let cool slightly; peel and slice peppers into 1-inch (2.5 cm) wide strips.
■ Trim and string snow peas. In large saucepan of boiling water, blanch for 30 seconds. Drain and refresh under cold running water; drain again.
■ Separate mushrooms into 10 pieces. (Vegetables can be prepared ahead, placed in separate containers, covered and refrigerated for up to 4 hours.)
■ In large wok or skillet, melt butter over medium-high heat; stir in peppers, snow peas and mushrooms just until coated with butter. Drizzle in stock; cover and cook for 1 to 2 minutes or just until vegetables are tender-crisp. Season with salt and pepper to taste. Makes 10 servings.

## *Belgian Endive and Orange Salad with Avocado*

*Serve this refreshing composed salad on its own after the main course.*

| | | |
|---|---|---|
| 5 | **large navel oranges** | 5 |
| 6 | **radishes** | 6 |
| 3 | **large Belgian endives** | 3 |
| 1 | **small red onion** | 1 |
| 3 | **avocados** | 3 |
| 30 | **small black olives** | 30 |
| 10 | **sprigs mint** | 10 |
| 1/3 cup | **olive oil** | 75 mL |
| 1 tbsp | **red wine vinegar** | 15 mL |

■ Peel oranges; with sharp knife, remove thin outer membrane. Slice between each section and inner membranes, removing one section at a time; discard membranes and seeds.
■ Trim radishes and slice thinly. Wipe endives; carefully separate leaves. Dice onion. (Recipe can be prepared ahead to this point. Place ingredients in separate containers, cover and refrigerate for up to 2 hours.)
■ At serving time, peel and slice avocados thinly. On each of ten individual plates, fan 4 large endive leaves. In each hollow, nestle slice of avocado; lay orange sections about one-third of the way up each leaf. At base of leaves, arrange slices of radish and 3 olives. Sprinkle onion over orange sections. Garnish with mint sprigs.
■ In small jar, shake together oil and vinegar; drizzle over avocado and oranges. Serve immediately. Makes 10 servings.

## *Brandy Snap Tulips with Two Ices and Fresh Fruit*

*You can make these tulip-shaped cookies up to two days ahead and store in an airtight container. Serve them filled with two scoops of sorbet or ice cream of compatible colors and flavors (such as mango and lemon, or vanilla and raspberry). Garnish with fresh fruit.*

| | | |
|---|---|---|
| 1/2 cup | **packed brown sugar** | 125 mL |
| 1/2 cup | **butter** | 125 mL |
| 1/2 cup | **corn syrup** | 125 mL |
| 3/4 cup | **all-purpose flour** | 175 mL |
| 1/3 cup | **finely chopped brazil nuts** | 75 mL |
| 1 tsp | **brandy or vanilla** | 5 mL |
| | **Ice cream** | |
| | **Sorbet** | |
| | **Fresh fruit** | |

■ In heavy saucepan, combine sugar, butter and corn syrup over medium heat; bring to boil, stirring constantly. Remove from heat. Combine flour with nuts; add to sugar mixture along with brandy and mix well.
■ Drop tablespoons (15 mL) of batter about 4 inches (10 cm) apart onto greased baking sheets. Bake in 350°F (180°C) oven for 6 to 8 minutes, rotating baking sheets if necessary, or until golden brown and bubbles break but do not fill in. Let cool for about 30 seconds or until easily lifted with wide spatula. Immediately drape over inverted custard cups, gently pressing to flute edges. (If cookies become too firm to shape, return to oven just until softened.) Transfer to wire racks; let cool. Fill with ice cream and sorbet; garnish with fruit. Makes about 16 servings.

# A SPECIAL LITTLE DINNER

FOR FOUR

*This reassuringly cozy dinner features comfort food with a light piquant twist. Add soft candlelight flickering in the background and you have a perfect setting for the sharing of memories and good times with the closest of friends.*

*COLD ORANGE-CARROT SOUP

*ROASTED LEMON-DILL CHICKEN

ROAST POTATOES

STEAMED GREEN BEANS WITH TOASTED SESAME SEEDS

BIBB LETTUCE WITH TANGY VINAIGRETTE

*ALMOND CHESTNUT TORTE

## *Cold Orange-Carrot Soup*

*Here's a smooth starter with the refreshing tang of orange.*

| | | |
|---|---|---|
| 2 tbsp | butter | 25 mL |
| 1 | onion, chopped | 1 |
| 1 | clove garlic, minced | 1 |
| 2 cups | thinly sliced carrots | 500 mL |
| 3 cups | chicken stock | 750 mL |
| 1/2 cup | orange juice | 125 mL |
| 1/2 tsp | granulated sugar | 2 mL |
| 1/4 tsp | dried thyme | 1 mL |
| 1/4 tsp | each salt and pepper | 1 mL |
| 3/4 cup | plain yogurt | 175 mL |
| | Nutmeg | |

■ In saucepan, melt butter over medium heat; cook onion, garlic and carrots, stirring, for 3 to 5 minutes or until softened but not browned.

■ Stir in stock, juice, sugar, thyme, salt and pepper; bring to boil over high heat. Reduce heat to low; cover and simmer for 35 to 40 minutes or until carrots are tender. Let cool slightly, then purée in batches in blender or food processor. Refrigerate until chilled or for up to 2 days.

■ Stir in 1/2 cup (125 mL) of the yogurt; season with nutmeg, salt and pepper to taste. Divide among 4 bowls; swirl 1 tbsp (15 mL) of the remaining yogurt into each bowl as garnish. Makes 4 servings.

*Cold Orange-Carrot Soup; Roasted Lemon-Dill Chicken; steamed green beans with toasted sesame seeds*

# Roasted Lemon-Dill Chicken

*The elegant flavor of this dish belies its simple preparation.*

| | | |
|---|---|---|
| 1 | **chicken (about 3-1/2 lb/1.75 kg)** | 1 |
| | **Salt and pepper** | |
| Half | **bunch fresh dill** | Half |
| 1 | **lemon, quartered** | 1 |
| 1 tbsp | **butter** | 15 mL |
| | **Creamy Lemon Sauce (recipe follows)** | |

■ Remove chicken neck and giblets. Rinse and wipe cavity; sprinkle with salt and pepper. Tie dill together in bunch; place in cavity along with lemon. Truss chicken; rub skin lightly with butter. Tuck wing tips behind back; tie legs together.

■ Place breast side up on greased rack in roasting pan. Roast in 350°F (180°C) oven, basting occasionally, for 1-1/4 to 1-3/4 hours or until juices run clear when thigh is pierced with skewer and meat thermometer registers 185°F (85°C). Remove stuffing and discard. Serve chicken with Creamy Lemon Sauce. Makes 4 servings.

| | **CREAMY LEMON SAUCE:** | |
|---|---|---|
| 2 tbsp | **butter** | 25 mL |
| 2 tbsp | **all-purpose flour** | 25 mL |
| 1 cup | **chicken stock** | 250 mL |
| 1/4 cup | **chopped fresh dill** | 50 mL |
| 1/4 cup | **whipping cream** | 50 mL |
| 2 tbsp | **lemon juice** | 25 mL |
| 1 tbsp | **dry vermouth** | 15 mL |
| | **Salt and pepper** | |

■ In saucepan, melt butter over medium heat; stir in flour until blended. Stir in chicken stock; cook, stirring constantly, for about 5 minutes or until sauce boils and thickens.

■ Stir in dill, cream, lemon juice and vermouth. Season with salt and pepper to taste. Makes about 1-1/2 cups (375 mL).

Almond Chestnut Torte

## Almond Chestnut Torte

*Garnish this meringue cake with grated chocolate or sifted icing sugar.*

| | | |
|---|---|---|
| **2 tbsp** | **fine dry bread crumbs** | **25 mL** |
| **1** | **pkg (3-1/2 oz/100 g) ground almonds** | **1** |
| **1 tsp** | **baking powder** | **5 mL** |
| **1/4 tsp** | **salt** | **1 mL** |
| **1/4 cup** | **butter, softened** | **50 mL** |
| **1/2 cup** | **granulated sugar** | **125 mL** |
| **3** | **eggs, separated** | **3** |
| **1/2 tsp** | **almond extract** | **2 mL** |
| **3 tbsp** | **milk** | **50 mL** |
| **1 cup** | **sliced almonds** | **250 mL** |
| | **TOPPING:** | |
| **1 cup** | **chestnut purée** | **250 mL** |
| **1/4 cup** | **sifted icing sugar** | **50 mL** |
| **2 tbsp** | **brandy** | **25 mL** |
| **1 cup** | **whipping cream** | **250 mL** |

■ Combine bread crumbs with 2 tbsp (25 mL) of the ground almonds; divide between two greased 8-inch (20 cm) pie plates. Shake to coat sides and bottoms, letting any extra mixture remain on bottoms. Set aside.

■ Combine remaining 1 cup (250 mL) ground almonds, baking powder and salt; set aside. In mixing bowl, cream butter; add 1/4 cup (50 mL) of the sugar, beating until fluffy. Add egg yolks, one at a time, beating well after each addition. Beat in almond mixture, almond extract and milk. Divide between prepared pie plates; cover and refrigerate until chilled, about 1 hour.

■ In bowl, beat egg whites until soft peaks form; beat in remaining sugar until stiff and glossy. Spread evenly over each torte, then sprinkle 1/2 cup (125 mL) sliced almonds over each one. Bake in 300°F (150°C) oven for 45 to 50 minutes or until cake tester inserted in center comes out clean and meringue is golden. Run knife around edges. Let cool and remove from pans.

**TOPPING:** In large bowl and using electric mixer, beat chestnut purée until smooth. Gradually beat in sugar and brandy. In separate bowl, whip cream; fold into chestnut mixture. Place 1 torte on serving plate; spread with half of the chestnut mixture. Top with second torte; mound remaining chestnut mixture on top. Makes 4 to 6 servings.

***SETTING THE SCENE***

***Use old linen curtains as placemat-runners. Grandma's guest towels make perfect napkins. Loosely tie drapery ropes around napkins and let them drift off the table.***

***Arrange tulips in a low vase. Their fresh light scent doesn't interfere with the food. Scatter votive candles on galax leaves (available at florist shops) around the table. The candles create a soft atmosphere and flatter the guests as well as the food.***

# A FIRESIDE SUPPER

FOR SIX

*Take a break in the middle of a busy week or the hustle-bustle holiday season with a relaxed little supper with friends. This one's easy enough for an impromptu get-together; set out a buffet, let guests help themselves and get comfortable with lap trays by the fire.*

*SPAGHETTINI WITH ITALIAN SAUSAGE

*CARROT AND GREEN PEA SALAD

HOT FRENCH BREAD

*WINTER FRUIT COMPOTE

***DRESSING UP AN IMPROMPTU DINNER***
***Stretch a meal by adding an extra vegetable or salad. Jazz up a dish with a few exotic ingredients—add water chestnuts, artichoke hearts, hearts of palm or olives to a basic salad, or fancy up frozen green beans with garlic or sesame seeds. Stir-fried dishes or pasta are quick to make at the last minute and easy to embellish. Turn plain fruit into a delectable dessert by soaking it in rum, topping with ice cream and nuts, or drizzling with chocolate sauce.***

## *Spaghettini with Italian Sausage*

*Use either hot or sweet (mild) Italian sausage in this quick-to-make, colorful pasta dish.*

| | | |
|---|---|---|
| **1 tbsp** | **vegetable oil** | **15 mL** |
| **1 lb** | **Italian sausages** | **500 g** |
| **1/2 cup** | **water** | **125 mL** |
| **2 tsp** | **dried basil** | **10 mL** |
| **1/2 tsp** | **crushed hot pepper flakes** | **2 mL** |
| **1** | **sweet red pepper, chopped** | **1** |
| **1 cup** | **coarsely chopped fresh parsley** | **250 mL** |
| **3/4 lb** | **spaghettini (or capellini)** | **375 g** |
| **1/3 cup** | **(approx) freshly grated Parmesan cheese** | **75 mL** |

■ In large skillet, heat oil over medium-high heat; cook sausages, turning often, for 5 minutes. Remove from skillet and cut into 1/4-inch (5 mm) thick rounds; return to skillet and cook for 2 minutes.

■ Add water, basil and hot pepper flakes, stirring to scrape up any brown bits from bottom of pan. Add red pepper and parsley.

■ Meanwhile, in large pot of boiling water, cook spaghettini for 3 to 4 minutes or until al dente (tender but firm). Drain and arrange on warm serving platter.

■ Spoon sausage mixture over and sprinkle with cheese. Serve immediately. Pass extra cheese separately if desired. Makes about 6 servings.

# Carrot and Green Pea Salad

*Artichoke hearts liven up everyday vegetables in this salad; hearts of palm or water chestnuts could be substituted.*

| | | |
|---|---|---|
| **1 cup** | **frozen peas** | **250 mL** |
| **1** | **can (14 oz/398 mL) artichoke hearts** | **1** |
| **4** | **carrots, coarsely grated (about 1-1/2 cups/ 375 mL)** | **4** |
| **1/2 cup** | **diced celery** | **125 mL** |
| **2** | **green onions, chopped** | **2** |
| **1/4 cup** | **chopped fresh parsley** | **50 mL** |
| **1/4 cup** | **mayonnaise** | **50 mL** |
| **1/4 cup** | **plain yogurt** | **50 mL** |
| | **Salt and pepper** | |

■ Rinse peas under hot water; dry on paper towels. Drain and quarter artichoke hearts.

■ In small salad bowl, combine peas, artichoke hearts, carrots, celery, green onions, parsley, mayonnaise and yogurt; toss lightly to mix. Season with salt and pepper to taste. Cover and refrigerate until serving or for up to 3 days. Makes about 6 servings.

# Winter Fruit Compote

*Figs, apricots and prunes spiked with rum are a delicious base for an easy compote. Add the fresh fruits suggested here or any you have on hand, such as kiwifruit or pineapple.*

| | | |
|---|---|---|
| **1/2 cup** | **each dried figs, apricots and prunes** | **125 mL** |
| **1-1/2 cups** | **orange juice** | **375 mL** |
| **1/2 cup** | **rum** | **125 mL** |
| **2 cups** | **seedless green grapes** | **500 mL** |
| **1 cup** | **purple or red grapes, halved and seeded** | **250 mL** |
| **1** | **can (10 oz/284 mL) mandarin oranges (undrained)** | **1** |
| **1** | **grapefruit, peeled and sectioned** | **1** |

■ In saucepan, combine dried figs, apricots and prunes; stir in orange juice. Cover and bring to boil; reduce heat and simmer for 10 minutes. Remove pan from heat; add rum and let stand for 20 minutes or until fruit is plump and tender. Let cool.

■ In serving dish, combine fig mixture, green and purple grapes, mandarins and grapefruit. Serve immediately or cover and refrigerate for up to 3 days. Makes 6 to 8 servings.

*Spaghettini with Italian Sausage; Carrot and Green Pea Salad; Winter Fruit Compote*

# A CO-OP BUFFET SUPPER

FOR SIXTEEN

*Consult your guests beforehand and enlist their help in preparing a memorable meal with these menu suggestions. All the dishes can be prepared ahead and are totable, so your guests can share the cooking and the credit for the evening's success. You'll be responsible for only the wine, condiments and dessert.*

*PEPPER CHEESE BISCUITS

*CHICKEN, SAUSAGE AND BEAN RAGOUT

*NOODLES AND RICE WITH PEAS

CARROT AND ZUCCHINI VINAIGRETTE

*RASPBERRY MOUSSE

***PRE-DINNER NIBBLES***

***If you want to add pre-dinner nibbles, arrange a big tray of vegetable crudités and add an assortment of creamy dips spiced with curry or herbs. Include bowls of black and green olives. For an easy but impressive appetizer, make pâté truffles by shaping chicken liver pâté into small balls and rolling in crushed walnuts.***

## *Pepper Cheese Biscuits*

*These zesty little biscuits are a perfect accompaniment to the ragout. Double the recipe to satisfy hearty appetites and freeze any leftovers to serve with cream soups.*

| | | |
|---|---|---|
| **1-1/4 cups** | **all-purpose flour** | **300 mL** |
| **1 cup** | **whole wheat flour** | **250 mL** |
| **1 tbsp** | **baking powder** | **15 mL** |
| **1/2 tsp** | **salt** | **2 mL** |
| **1/4 cup** | **cold butter** | **50 mL** |
| **1/2 cup** | **crumbled feta cheese** | **125 mL** |
| **1 tsp** | **green peppercorns, cracked** | **5 mL** |
| **3/4 cup** | **milk** | **175 mL** |

■ In bowl, combine all-purpose flour, whole wheat flour, baking powder and salt. With pastry blender or 2 knives, cut in butter until mixture resembles coarse crumbs. Cut in feta cheese; stir in peppercorns.

■ Add milk; stir until mixture sticks together. Gather into ball and turn out onto lightly floured surface. Knead about 10 times or until dough is smooth.

■ Roll out dough to 1-inch (2.5 cm) thickness. With 2-inch (5 cm) cookie cutter, cut into rounds (gather, reroll and cut trimmings). Place rounds 2 inches (5 cm) apart on lightly greased or nonstick baking sheets.

■ Bake in 425°F (220°C) oven for 10 to 12 minutes or until lightly browned. (Biscuits can be stored in airtight plastic bags and frozen for up to 6 weeks. To reheat, bake frozen biscuits in 350°F/180°C oven for 10 to 15 minutes or until heated through and crisp on outside.) Makes about 24 biscuits.

# *Chicken, Sausage and Bean Ragout*

*For a party of 16, prepare two batches of this ragout. If the preparation is shared, two guests can make this dish.*

| | | |
|---|---|---|
| 6 | **sweet Italian sausages, sliced** | 6 |
| 1/4 cup | **vegetable oil** | 50 mL |
| 2 tbsp | **butter** | 25 mL |
| 2 | **cloves garlic, minced** | 2 |
| 8 | **chicken breasts, skinned, boned and cut in 1/2-inch (1 cm) strips** | 8 |
| 1 lb | **mushrooms, sliced** | 500 g |
| 3 | **onions, coarsely chopped** | 3 |
| 2 tsp | **dried sage** | 10 mL |
| 1 tsp | **salt** | 5 mL |
| 1/2 cup | **dry white wine** | 125 mL |
| 1 tsp | **grated lemon rind** | 5 mL |
| 2 tbsp | **lemon juice** | 25 mL |
| 2 tsp | **Worcestershire sauce** | 10 mL |
| 1 | **can (28 oz/796 mL) plum tomatoes** | 1 |
| 2 tsp | **granulated sugar** | 10 mL |
| 1 | **can (19 oz/540 mL) white kidney beans** | 1 |
| | **Pepper** | |
| 1/4 cup | **chopped fresh parsley** | 50 mL |

■ In large skillet over medium heat, cook sausages in 1 tbsp (15 mL) of the oil for about 10 minutes or until browned all over. With slotted spoon, transfer to 12-cup (3 L) casserole; discard fat from skillet.

■ In same skillet, heat together butter, garlic and remaining oil; cook chicken in single layer (in batches if necessary) until opaque and lightly browned. With slotted spoon, transfer to casserole.

■ Add mushrooms and onions to fat remaining in skillet. Sprinkle with sage and salt; cook, stirring often, for 5 to 7 minutes or until onions are limp. Transfer to casserole.

■ Stir wine into skillet, scraping up any brown bits. Add lemon rind, lemon juice and Worcestershire; cook for 1 minute. Stir in tomatoes and sugar. Bring to boil; cook, breaking up tomatoes with spoon, for about 25 minutes or until thickened and most of the liquid has evaporated.

■ Mash about half of the beans; stir mashed and whole beans into skillet. Cook for 10 minutes; pour over sausage-chicken mixture and mix well.

■ Bake, covered, in 350°F (180°C) oven for

***CARROT AND ZUCCHINI VINAIGRETTE***
***Thinly slice carrots, zucchini and small white cooking onions; marinate overnight in a zesty vinaigrette. To serve, present the colorful combination in a pretty glass bowl.***

*(Clockwise from top) Noodles and Rice with Peas; carrot and zucchini vinaigrette; Pepper Cheese Biscuits; Chicken, Sausage and Bean Ragout*

30 minutes or until hot and bubbly. (Alternatively, let cool, cover and refrigerate for up to 2 days or freeze for up to 4 weeks. To heat, defrost if frozen, and heat in 375°F/190°C oven for 30 to 40 minutes, stirring occasionally, or until bubbly and heated through.) Season with pepper to taste and garnish with parsley before serving. Makes 8 servings.

## Noodles and Rice with Peas

*Browning the noodles and rice in butter before cooking them in water gives this casserole a roasted flavor and rich golden color.*

| | | |
|---|---|---|
| **2 tbsp** | **butter** | **25 mL** |
| **1-1/2 cups** | **broken fine egg noodles** | **375 mL** |
| **1-1/2 cups** | **long-grain rice** | **375 mL** |
| **4 cups** | **chicken stock** | **1 L** |
| **3 cups** | **frozen peas** | **750 mL** |
| **3/4 cup** | **chopped fresh dill (or 1/4 cup/50 mL dried dillweed)** | **175 mL** |
| | **Salt and pepper** | |

■ In heavy saucepan, melt butter; add noodles and cook over medium heat, stirring constantly, for about 6 minutes or until golden (do not burn butter; lower heat if necessary).

■ Add rice and stir-cook for 1 minute. Pour in stock; bring to boil, cover and simmer gently for about 20 minutes or until liquid is absorbed.

■ Stir in peas, dill, and salt and pepper to taste. If serving immediately, simmer for 5 minutes or until peas are heated through. (Alternatively, transfer to 12-cup/3 L casserole, cover and refrigerate for up to 2 days. To reheat, pour in 1/2 cup/125 mL boiling water; cover and place in 375°F/190°C oven for 20 minutes or until hot; fluff gently with fork and serve.) Makes 16 servings.

## Raspberry Mousse

*To serve 16, make the recipe twice. Garnish with whipped cream and mint.*

| | | |
|---|---|---|
| **4 cups** | **fresh or frozen unsweetened raspberries, thawed** | **1 L** |
| **3/4 cup** | **granulated sugar** | **175 mL** |
| **2 tbsp** | **raspberry liqueur (optional)** | **25 mL** |
| **1 tbsp** | **lemon juice** | **15 mL** |
| **2** | **envelopes unflavored gelatin** | **2** |
| **1/2 cup** | **water** | **125 mL** |
| **1 cup** | **whipping cream** | **250 mL** |
| **2** | **egg whites** | **2** |

■ In food processor or blender, process raspberries until smooth; press through sieve into saucepan to make about 2 cups (500 mL). Add 1/2 cup (125 mL) of the sugar; cook over low heat, stirring, for about 5 minutes or until sugar has dissolved. Stir in liqueur (if using) and lemon juice. Transfer to bowl.

■ Meanwhile, in small saucepan, sprinkle gelatin over water; let stand for 1 minute to soften. Heat over low heat until dissolved; stir into raspberry mixture.

■ Place bowl in larger bowl of ice and water; chill, stirring frequently, for 20 to 30 minutes or until consistency of raw egg whites. Remove from ice water.

■ Whip cream; set aside. In another large bowl, beat egg whites until soft peaks form; gradually beat in remaining sugar until stiff.

■ Whisk one-quarter of the egg whites into raspberry mixture. Fold raspberry mixture and whipped cream into remaining whites. Pour into rinsed but not dried 6-cup (1.5 L) stainless steel, glass or plastic mould. Cover and refrigerate for at least 6 hours or for up to 2 days. To unmould, wrap hot damp tea towel around mould for 1 minute. Using knife, loosen top edge of mousse from mould. Tilt or gently shake mould to loosen mousse. Invert rinsed serving platter on top of mould. Grasp platter and mould; quickly turn over. Shake, using quick downward motion, to release mousse from mould. (If mousse sticks, repeat procedure.) Makes 6 to 8 servings.

# DROP BY FOR TAPAS

FOR SIX TO EIGHT

*Gather your neighbors or office chums together for a decidedly non-traditional after-work party. Even if the weather outside is bleak, the bright and lively colors you choose for your buffet table will get everyone into a party mood, fiesta-style. And the perfect nibbles for this contemporary cocktail party — tapas, olé!*

*EMPANADAS WITH FRESH TOMATO SALSA

*COD AND POTATO CAKES

*MARINATED OLIVES, MUSHROOMS AND ONIONS

*SHRIMP IN SPICY GARLIC OIL

## *Empanadas with Fresh Tomato Salsa*

*These can be made ahead and frozen, baked or unbaked, for up to six weeks. If baked, thaw and reheat in 350°F (180°C) oven for 8 to 10 minutes. If unbaked, do not thaw before baking, but add 10 to 15 minutes to baking time.*

| | | |
|---|---|---|
| | **Pastry for double-crust pie** | |
| **1** | **egg, slightly beaten** | **1** |
| | **Poppy seeds** | |
| | **Fresh Tomato Salsa (recipe follows)** | |
| | **FILLING:** | |
| **1 tsp** | **vegetable oil** | **5 mL** |
| **1/3 lb** | **lean ground beef** | **175 g** |
| **1** | **small onion, finely chopped** | **1** |
| **1/3 cup** | **chopped sweet red or green pepper** | **75 mL** |
| **1/4 cup** | **tomato sauce** | **50 mL** |
| **1 tbsp** | **finely chopped jalapeño pepper** | **15 mL** |
| **6** | **pimiento-stuffed olives, chopped** | **6** |
| **1 tsp** | **packed brown sugar** | **5 mL** |
| **1/2 tsp** | **salt** | **2 mL** |

**FILLING:** In skillet, heat oil over medium-high heat; cook beef with onion for 3 to 5 minutes or until meat is no longer pink. Reduce heat to medium-low; add red pepper, tomato sauce and jalapeño pepper; simmer for 2 to 4 minutes or until thickened slightly. Remove from heat; add olives, sugar and salt. Let cool completely.

■ Roll out pastry to about 1/8-inch (3 mm) thickness; cut into 3-inch (8 cm) rounds. Place heaping teaspoonful of filling on half of each pastry round. Moisten edges with cold water; fold over and seal with fork.

■ Prick empanadas and place on ungreased baking sheet. Brush with beaten egg; sprinkle with poppy seeds. Bake in 425°F (220°C) oven for 15 to 20 minutes or until golden brown. Serve with Fresh Tomato Salsa. Makes about 30 empanadas.

***SETTING THE SCENE***
***Choose vibrant yellows, blues and greens in your plates and serving dishes, striped tablecloth, paper napkins and candles.***

***Carry the Spanish theme through to table decorations: hang straw angels from the branches of a small potted citrus tree and surround the pot with little clay figures; scatter festive folk art ornaments and brightly colored ribbons among the serving dishes. Banish all thoughts of the office by letting guests try their luck at cracking a hanging piñata.***

***Set out the food buffet-style so guests can help themselves. For an authentic Spanish flavor, serve a dry and medium-sweet sherry. Or, for a Mexican accent, serve margaritas along with a variety of fruit juices and punch.***

*(Clockwise from top) Empanadas with Fresh Tomato Salsa; Marinated Olives, Mushrooms and Onions; Cod and Potato Cakes; marinated beans and peppers*

| | **FRESH TOMATO SALSA:** | |
|---|---|---|
| 1/3 cup | **finely chopped cucumber** | 75 mL |
| 2 | **tomatoes, peeled, seeded and finely chopped** | 2 |
| 2 | **green onions, minced** | 2 |
| 1 tbsp | **olive oil** | 15 mL |
| 1/2 tsp | **salt** | 2 mL |
| 1/4 tsp | **hot pepper sauce** | 1 mL |

■ In small bowl, combine cucumber, tomatoes, onions, oil, salt and hot pepper sauce. If necessary, drain before serving. Makes about 1-1/2 cups (375 mL).

# Cod and Potato Cakes

*Salt cod, soaked overnight before cooking, makes a tasty appetizer when shaped into little cakes and served with a mustardy sour cream sauce. This recipe can be doubled.*

| | | |
|---|---|---|
| 1 cup | **mashed potatoes** | 250 mL |
| 3/4 cup | **flaked cooked salt cod (see sidebar)** | 175 mL |
| 2 tbsp | **chopped green onion** | 25 mL |
| 1/2 tsp | **grated lemon rind** | 2 mL |
| 1 tbsp | **lemon juice** | 15 mL |
| 1 | **egg** | 1 |
| | **Pepper** | |
| | **Vegetable oil** | |
| | **SAUCE:** | |
| 1/2 cup | **sour cream** | 125 mL |
| 2 tbsp | **chopped fresh parsley** | 25 mL |
| 1 tbsp | **white wine vinegar** | 15 mL |
| 2 tsp | **Dijon mustard** | 10 mL |

■ Mix together potatoes, cod, onion, lemon rind and juice, egg, and pepper to taste. Cover and refrigerate for 20 minutes or until firm enough to shape.
**SAUCE:** Mix together sour cream, parsley, vinegar and mustard; set aside.
■ Shape potato mixture into 12 patties about 1-1/2 inches (4 cm) in diameter and 1/2-inch (1 cm) thick. Brush with oil. In non-stick skillet, cook patties, in batches if necessary, over medium heat for 3 minutes on each side or until browned and heated through. Serve with sauce. Makes 12 appetizers.

***TO COOK SALT COD***
***Cover cod with cold water; let soak for 24 hours, changing water several times. Drain off water. Cover cod with fresh cold water; bring just to boil. Reduce heat and simmer for 10 to 15 minutes or until tender. (Do not boil.)***

# Marinated Olives, Mushrooms and Onions

*This simple salad is also delicious served with cold meat or on submarine-type sandwiches. It keeps well, covered and refrigerated, for up to four days.*

| | | |
|---|---|---|
| 2 | **large red onions, sliced** | 2 |
| 1/4 cup | **olive oil** | 50 mL |
| 1 | **can (398 mL) pitted black olives** | 1 |
| 1-1/2 cups | **mushrooms, whole button or halved** | 375 mL |
| 1 tbsp | **balsamic or red wine vinegar** | 15 mL |
| 2 tsp | **chopped fresh oregano (or 1/2 tsp/2 mL dried)** | 10 mL |
| 1/2 tsp | **fennel seed (optional)** | 2 mL |
| | **Pepper** | |

■ In skillet, cook onions in oil over medium heat, stirring often, for about 5 minutes or until softened. Do not brown. Remove from heat and add olives, mushrooms, vinegar, oregano and fennel seed; season with pepper to taste.
■ Transfer to nonmetallic container; cover and refrigerate for at least 4 hours, stirring occasionally, or for up to 4 days. Makes about 4 cups (1 L).

# Shrimp in Spicy Garlic Oil

*To serve with other tapas, let guests spoon shrimp, coated with onion and peppers, onto their serving plates. For a finger-food party, drain off oil and remove shrimp from onion/pepper mixture. Serve on cocktail picks.*

| | | |
|---|---|---|
| 1/4 cup | **olive oil** | 50 mL |
| 1 | **small onion, chopped** | 1 |
| 1 | **small sweet green pepper, chopped** | 1 |
| 2 or 3 | **cloves garlic, chopped** | 2 or 3 |
| 1/4 tsp | **hot pepper flakes** | 1 mL |
| 18 | **large shrimp, peeled and deveined** | 18 |

■ In skillet, heat 1 tbsp (15 mL) of the oil over medium-high heat; cook onion, pepper, garlic and hot pepper flakes just until softened.
■ Add shrimp and stir-fry until bright pink and cooked through, 3 to 5 minutes. Add remaining oil; let cool to room temperature. Refrigerate until serving time or overnight. Makes 1-1/2 dozen.

# AN EASY AND ELEGANT DINNER

FOR FOUR

*This light and easy contemporary menu has a touch of indulgence for a special occasion. Each dish has a sophisticated simplicity, with quality ingredients artistically presented.*

*MELON WITH PROSCIUTTO

*SIRLOIN STEAK WITH BÉARNAISE SAUCE

STEAMED GREEN BEANS

SAUTÉED RED PEPPERS AND ONIONS

SALAD GREENS WITH PINE NUTS AND MANDARIN ORANGES

*PEARS WITH GRAND MARNIER

## Melon with Prosciutto

*This is an elegant appetizer that you can prepare in minutes. If prosciutto isn't available, use four medium-to-large cooked shrimp per person and serve on lettuce leaves.*

| | | |
|---|---|---|
| **Half** | **honeydew melon** | **Half** |
| **8** | **paper-thin slices prosciutto** | **8** |
| **2** | **limes** | **2** |
| **4** | **fresh figs (optional)** | **4** |
| | **Pepper** | |

■ Cut melon into four wedges; remove rind. Place on salad plates; arrange prosciutto over melon.

■ Cut limes and figs into quarters and divide among plates. Sprinkle with pepper. Makes 4 servings.

## Sirloin Steak with Béarnaise Sauce

*Arrange strips of thinly sliced steak in a fan shape on each dinner plate. Place sautéed red peppers and onions at the base of the fan and surround the meat and vegetables with steamed green beans.*

| | | |
|---|---|---|
| **2 lb** | **sirloin steak, at least 1 inch (2.5 cm) thick** | **1 kg** |
| **1** | **large clove garlic, halved** | **1** |
| | **Béarnaise Sauce (recipe follows)** | |

■ Rub both sides of steak with garlic. Barbecue or broil about 4 inches (10 cm) from heat for 4 to 6 minutes per side, depending on heat of coals and desired degree of doneness.

■ Cut steak into thin slices and arrange on heated plates. Spoon a little Béarnaise Sauce over meat and pass remaining sauce separately. Makes 4 servings.

| | BÉARNAISE SAUCE: | |
|---|---|---|
| 2 tbsp | white wine or vermouth | 25 mL |
| 2 tbsp | tarragon vinegar or white wine vinegar | 25 mL |
| 2 tbsp | chopped fresh tarragon (or 1 tsp/5 mL dried) | 25 mL |
| 1 tbsp | minced shallot or white part of green onion | 15 mL |
| Pinch | pepper | Pinch |
| 3 | egg yolks | 3 |
| 1/4 tsp | salt | 1 mL |
| 1/2 cup | butter | 125 mL |

■ In small saucepan, bring wine, vinegar, tarragon, shallot and pepper to boil. Boil rapidly until reduced to 2 tbsp (25 mL). Remove from heat.

■ In food processor or blender, combine egg yolks, salt and vinegar mixture; process for 2 seconds to blend thoroughly.

■ In small saucepan or microwave, heat butter until sizzling but not browned. With machine running, add a few drops of sizzling butter through the feed tube, then add butter in thin steady stream and process until blended. Serve warm or at room temperature. Makes about 3/4 cup (175 mL) sauce.

# *Pears with Grand Marnier*

*Classic poached pears flavored with Grand Marnier or other orange liqueur make a simple yet wonderful dessert, especially when teamed with a chocolate truffle or crisp cookie.*

| | | |
|---|---|---|
| 1 cup | water | 250 mL |
| 1/2 cup | granulated sugar | 125 mL |
| 1 | wide strip lemon rind | 1 |
| 4 | firm ripe pears | 4 |
| 1 tbsp | lemon juice | 15 mL |
| 2 tbsp | Grand Marnier | 25 mL |
| 2 tbsp | toasted sliced almonds* | 25 mL |

■ In large saucepan, combine water, sugar and lemon rind; bring to boil and boil for 1 minute.

■ Peel pears; cut in half lengthwise and remove cores. Immediately, brush with lemon juice to prevent darkening. Add to sugar syrup; cover and simmer, turning

*Sirloin Steak with Béarnaise Sauce; steamed green beans; sautéed red peppers and onions; salad greens with pine nuts and mandarin oranges*

pears over once or twice, for 10 to 25 minutes (depending on ripeness of pears) or until tender when pierced with knife. With slotted spoon, remove pears to serving dish; let cool.

■ Boil liquid until reduced to 1/2 cup (125 mL). Let cool slightly, then add Grand Marnier. Pour over pears; cover and refrigerate for up to 2 days. Serve warm or at room temperature. Sprinkle with almonds. Makes 4 servings.

*Toast almonds on baking sheet in 350°F (180°C) oven for 5 minutes or until golden.

# AN EASY ITALIAN DINNER

FOR EIGHT

*The chops, sauce for the pasta appetizer and impressive dessert can all be prepared the day ahead, making this sophisticated menu easy on the cook. For a more budget-minded entrée, substitute boneless chicken breasts for the veal chops.*

*PASTA WITH RED PEPPERS AND EGGPLANT

*VEAL CHOPS SICILIAN-STYLE

FRESH ASPARAGUS OR GREEN BEANS

*FROZEN ZABAGLIONE WITH CHOCOLATE SAUCE

## *Pasta with Red Peppers and Eggplant*

*Salting the eggplant draws out excess moisture and any bitterness. Peel the red peppers with a vegetable peeler for a sweeter taste.*

| | | |
|---|---|---|
| **1** | **small eggplant (about 1/2 lb/250 g)** | **1** |
| **2 tsp** | **salt** | **10 mL** |
| **1/2 cup** | **all-purpose flour** | **125 mL** |
| **1/3 cup** | **(approx) olive oil** | **75 mL** |
| **1** | **red onion, chopped** | **1** |
| **3** | **cloves garlic, minced** | **3** |
| **1/4 tsp** | **hot pepper flakes** | **1 mL** |
| **3** | **sweet red peppers, cut in chunks** | **3** |
| **1** | **can (28 oz/796 mL) tomatoes (undrained)** | **1** |
| **1 lb** | **rigatoni pasta** | **500 g** |
| **1/2 cup** | **freshly grated Parmesan cheese** | **125 mL** |
| **1/4 cup** | **chopped fresh basil or parsley** | **50 mL** |
| | **Salt and pepper** | |

■ Trim eggplant, quarter lengthwise and cut into 1/4-inch (5 mm) thick slices. In sieve, layer slices with salt. Drain for 30 minutes. Rinse and pat dry.

■ Dip eggplant slices into flour, shaking off excess. In large skillet, heat 2 tbsp (25 mL) of the oil over medium-high heat; cook eggplant, in batches, until browned, about 2 minutes per side. Add more oil to pan between batches, if necessary, and heat before adding eggplant. Set eggplant aside.

■ In clean skillet, heat 2 tbsp (25 mL) of the oil over medium heat; cook onion, garlic and hot pepper flakes for about 5 minutes or until tender and fragrant but not browned.

■ Add red peppers; cook for 5 to 10 minutes or until slightly wilted. Add tomatoes, breaking up with spoon; cook for 10 to 15 minutes or until sauce is reduced and slightly thickened. Add browned eggplant; cook for 5 minutes.

■ In large pot of boiling salted water, cook pasta until al dente (tender but firm). Drain well; toss with sauce. Sprinkle with cheese and basil; season with salt and pepper to taste. Toss well and serve immediately. Makes 8 appetizer servings.

*Pasta with Red Peppers and Eggplant; Veal Chops Sicilian-Style; fresh asparagus; Frozen Zabaglione with Chocolate Sauce*

## Veal Chops Sicilian-Style

*This dish can be made ahead and reheated at the last minute.*

| | | |
|---|---|---|
| 1/3 cup | olive oil | 75 mL |
| 1 | onion, finely chopped | 1 |
| 1 | clove garlic, minced | 1 |
| 1-1/2 cups | fresh bread crumbs | 375 mL |
| 1/3 cup | raisins | 75 mL |
| 1/3 cup | pine nuts, toasted | 75 mL |
| 2 tbsp | drained capers | 25 mL |
| 1/4 cup | freshly grated Parmesan cheese | 50 mL |
| 1/4 cup | chopped fresh parsley | 50 mL |
| 1/4 tsp | salt | 1 mL |
| 1/4 tsp | pepper | 1 mL |
| 8 | veal chops (each about 1/2-in/1 cm thick, 6 oz/175 g) | 8 |

■ In skillet, heat 3 tbsp (50 mL) of the oil over medium heat; cook onion and garlic until tender, about 3 minutes. Add bread crumbs, raisins, pine nuts and capers. Stir in cheese, parsley, salt and pepper; set aside.

■ Pat veal dry. In large skillet, heat remaining oil over medium-high heat; cook veal for 3 to 4 minutes on each side or until browned.

■ Arrange veal on baking sheet. Sprinkle crumb mixture over veal and pat on. (Recipe can be prepared to this point, covered and set aside at room temperature for up to 30 minutes or refrigerated for up to 8 hours.)

■ Bake in 400°F (200°C) oven for 10 minutes, or 15 to 20 minutes for meat that has been refrigerated. Makes 8 servings.

## Frozen Zabaglione with Chocolate Sauce

*This frozen dessert, which doesn't even require an ice-cream machine, makes an elegant finale.*

| | | |
|---|---|---|
| 6 | egg yolks | 6 |
| 1/2 cup | granulated sugar | 125 mL |
| 3/4 cup | dry Marsala wine | 175 mL |
| 1/3 cup | coffee liqueur | 75 mL |
| 1-1/2 cups | whipping cream | 375 mL |
| 3 oz | bittersweet or semisweet chocolate, chopped | 90 g |
| 1/2 cup | diced pound cake or sponge cake | 125 mL |
| 1/4 cup | chopped toasted almonds | 50 mL |
| | CHOCOLATE SAUCE: | |
| 8 oz | bittersweet or semisweet chocolate, chopped | 250 g |
| 3/4 cup | extra-strong coffee | 175 mL |
| 1/4 cup | whipping cream | 50 mL |
| 2 tbsp | coffee liqueur | 25 mL |
| 2 tbsp | unsalted butter | 25 mL |
| | GARNISH: | |
| | Fresh strawberries | |
| | Unsweetened cocoa powder | |

■ In large heatproof bowl, beat egg yolks with sugar until pale and thickened, 3 to 5 minutes; stir in Marsala and liqueur.

■ Place bowl over gently simmering water and cook, stirring constantly, just until mixture thickens, about 5 minutes. (If cooked too long or at too-high heat, mixture will curdle.)

■ Set bowl over larger bowl filled with ice water. Let cool completely for 15 to 20 minutes, stirring occasionally.

■ Whip cream; fold into cooled egg mixture. Fold in chocolate, cake and nuts. Spoon mixture into 8- × 4-inch (1.5 L) loaf pan lined with plastic wrap. Wrap well. Freeze for 4 to 5 hours or until firm.

**CHOCOLATE SAUCE:** In saucepan, heat chocolate, coffee, cream and liqueur over medium heat, stirring until mixture is smooth, 3 to 5 minutes. Stir in butter. Remove from heat; let cool to room temperature.

**GARNISH:** Pour some of the sauce onto each plate. Unmould zabaglione; slice. Place slice on top of sauce; garnish with strawberries. Drizzle remaining sauce over top. Dust with cocoa. Makes 8 to 12 servings.

***TOASTING NUTS***

***To toast pine nuts, spread on baking sheet and bake in 350°F (180°C) oven for 5 to 7 minutes or until golden brown.***

***To toast almonds, spread on baking sheet and bake in 350°F (180°C) oven for 5 minutes or until golden.***

# A FARAWAY PLACES DINNER

FOR EIGHT

*This inspired meal goes Oriental, with a twist of tropical in the Piña Colada Mousse, which can be made the day before. Prepare the spectacular soup at the last minute and enjoy the delicious aromas of fresh coriander, mint and gingerroot permeating the house.*

*ORIENTAL LEMON SHRIMP AND NOODLE SOUP

*PORK TENDERLOINS WITH SATAY SAUCE

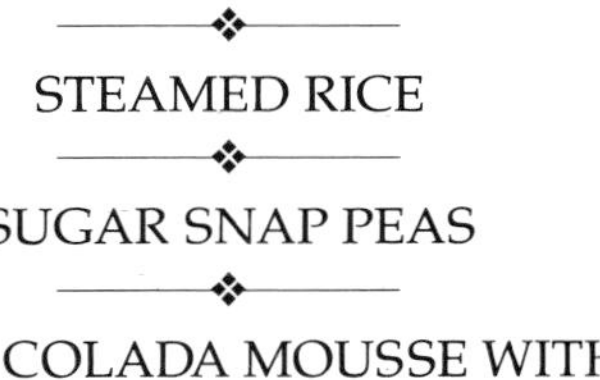

STEAMED RICE

SUGAR SNAP PEAS

*PIÑA COLADA MOUSSE WITH FRESH FRUIT

## *Oriental Lemon Shrimp and Noodle Soup*

*Fresh herbs really make a difference in the exotic taste of this magnificent soup. If available, add 2 tbsp (25 mL) chopped fresh basil to the soup pot. Garnish individual bowls with whole basil and mint leaves and whole shrimp. If you can't find rice vermicelli noodles, use very thin regular (wheat) vermicelli; instead of soaking for 10 minutes, cook for 5 minutes in boiling water, then proceed with recipe.*

| | | |
|---|---|---|
| **3 oz** | **rice vermicelli noodles** | **75 g** |
| **2 tbsp** | **vegetable oil** | **25 mL** |
| **2** | **cloves garlic, minced** | **2** |
| **1 tbsp** | **minced gingerroot** | **15 mL** |
| **1 tsp** | **grated lemon rind** | **5 mL** |
| **Pinch** | **hot pepper flakes** | **Pinch** |
| **4 cups** | **chicken stock** | **1 L** |
| **3 tbsp** | **lemon juice** | **50 mL** |
| **1 tbsp** | **soy sauce** | **15 mL** |
| **3/4 lb** | **shrimp, peeled, deveined and diced** | **375 g** |
| **3** | **green onions, chopped** | **3** |
| **1/3 cup** | **chopped fresh coriander or parsley** | **75 mL** |
| **2 tbsp** | **chopped fresh mint (or 1/2 tsp/2 mL dried)** | **25 mL** |
| **1/2 tsp** | **sesame oil** | **2 mL** |
| | **Salt and pepper** | |

■ Break up noodles into 2-inch (5 cm) lengths. Place in bowl and cover with boiling water; let soak for 10 minutes. Drain well and rinse with cold water. Set aside.

■ Meanwhile, in large saucepan, heat oil over medium heat; cook garlic, ginger, lemon rind and hot pepper flakes for 1 to 2 minutes or until very fragrant but not browned.

■ Add chicken stock, lemon juice and soy sauce; bring to boil. Reduce heat and simmer gently for 5 minutes.

■ Add shrimp and noodles; cook for 3 to 5 minutes or until shrimp turn pink and opaque and noodles are heated through. Stir in green onions, coriander, mint and sesame oil; season with salt and pepper to taste. Makes 8 servings.

## *Pork Tenderloins with Satay Sauce*

*The marinade, which can also be used for chicken breasts or a thick sirloin steak, becomes a wonderful sauce with rich, authentic Eastern flavors.*

| | | |
|---|---|---|
| 2 | **cloves garlic, minced** | 2 |
| 1/3 cup | **chopped fresh coriander or parsley** | 75 mL |
| 1/4 cup | **honey** | 50 mL |
| 1/4 cup | **peanut butter** | 50 mL |
| 2 tbsp | **hoisin sauce** | 25 mL |
| 2 tbsp | **soy sauce** | 25 mL |
| 2 tbsp | **lime juice** | 25 mL |
| 1 tbsp | **frozen orange juice concentrate** | 15 mL |
| 1 tbsp | **chopped gingerroot** | 15 mL |
| 1 tsp | **hot Oriental chili paste (or 1/2 tsp/2 mL hot pepper sauce)** | 5 mL |
| 1 tsp | **sesame oil** | 5 mL |
| 3 lb | **pork tenderloin, trimmed** | 1.5 kg |
| 1/2 cup | **chicken stock** | 125 mL |
| 1/2 cup | **orange juice** | 125 mL |

■ In large bowl, mix together garlic, coriander, honey, peanut butter, hoisin sauce, soy sauce, lime juice, orange juice concentrate, ginger, chili paste and sesame oil until smooth. Add pork; turn to coat well with marinade. Cover and marinate for 2 to 3 hours in refrigerator or overnight.

■ Remove pork from marinade, reserving marinade; place on foil-lined baking sheet. Bake in 350°F (180°C) oven for 45 to 60 minutes or until juices run clear when meat is pierced with skewer and pork is no longer pink inside.

■ Meanwhile, in small saucepan, combine reserved marinade with chicken stock and orange juice. Cook over medium-high heat, stirring constantly, for about 5 minutes or until mixture boils and thickens slightly. Drizzle over pork. Makes 8 servings.

*Oriental Lemon Shrimp and Noodle Soup; steamed rice; Pork Tenderloins with Satay Sauce; sugar snap peas; Pina Colada Mousse*

## *Piña Colada Mousse with Fresh Fruit*

*If canned cream of coconut separates, warm it gently and whisk thoroughly before measuring.*

| | | |
|---|---|---|
| 2 | **cans (each 14 oz/ 398 mL) unsweetened pineapple chunks** | 2 |
| 1/4 cup | **granulated sugar** | 50 mL |
| 1/4 cup | **light rum** | 50 mL |
| 1 | **envelope unflavored gelatin** | 1 |
| 1/4 cup | **cold water** | 50 mL |
| 1 cup | **whipping cream** | 250 mL |
| | **SAUCE:** | |
| 1/2 cup | **canned sweetened cream of coconut** | 125 mL |
| 1/2 cup | **whipping cream** | 125 mL |
| 2 tbsp | **light rum** | 25 mL |
| 3/4 cup | **sour cream** | 175 mL |
| | **GARNISH:** | |
| 8 | **fresh lichees** | 8 |
| 2 | **mangoes, peeled and sliced** | 2 |

■ Line eight 1/2-cup (125 mL) ramekins or custard cups with plastic wrap or parchment paper; set aside.

■ Drain pineapple well; purée in food processor or blender until smooth (makes about 2 cups/500 mL). Blend in sugar and rum.

■ In small saucepan, sprinkle gelatin over water; let soften for 1 minute. Heat gently until gelatin dissolves, about 1 minute; blend into pineapple purée.

■ Whip cream; fold gently into pineapple mixture. Spoon into prepared ramekins; cover with plastic wrap and refrigerate for 2 to 3 hours or until set, or overnight.

**SAUCE:** In small saucepan, heat cream of coconut until clear. Whisk in whipping cream, stirring until smooth. Stir in rum; let cool to room temperature. Whisk in sour cream.

**GARNISH:** Spoon sauce onto each plate. Run knife around edge of each mousse and invert onto sauce. Garnish with lichees and mango slices. Makes 8 servings.

# FIRESIDE DESSERTS AND DRINKS

FOR SIX

*A relaxing dessert party is a welcome break, especially in a busy holiday season. These rich treats are just big enough for a taste of each, and require only a small plate or napkin. They're also perfect for topping off an elegant winter dinner as you linger at the table.*

*GLAZED CHOCOLATE SQUARES

*RUM CAKES

*CHOCOLATE MERINGUES WITH LEMON FILLING

*GROWN-UP HOT CHOCOLATE

*CRÈME DE CACAO NIGHTCAP

*NIGHTCAP COFFEE

*CAFÉ ROMA

## *Glazed Chocolate Squares*

*A simplified version of a rich European-style classic, this dark chocolate cake is filled with apricot jam and topped with a chocolate glaze.*

| | | |
|---|---|---|
| | **CAKE:** | |
| **1/4 cup** | **unsweetened cocoa powder** | **50 mL** |
| **1/2 cup** | **milk** | **125 mL** |
| **1/2 cup** | **hot strong coffee** | **125 mL** |
| **1/2 cup** | **butter** | **125 mL** |
| **1 cup** | **granulated sugar** | **250 mL** |
| **2** | **eggs, separated** | **2** |
| **1 tsp** | **vanilla** | **5 mL** |
| **1 cup** | **all-purpose flour** | **250 mL** |
| **1 tsp** | **baking soda** | **5 mL** |
| **1/2 tsp** | **baking powder** | **2 mL** |
| **1/4 tsp** | **salt** | **1 mL** |
| **1/2 cup** | **apricot jam** | **125 mL** |
| | **GLAZE:** | |
| **1 oz** | **unsweetened chocolate** | **30 g** |
| **1 tbsp** | **butter** | **15 mL** |
| **1/2 cup** | **sifted icing sugar** | **125 mL** |
| **1 tbsp** | **boiling water** | **15 mL** |
| | **GARNISH:** | |
| | **Candied violets or nut halves** | |

**CAKE:** Grease a 15- × 10-inch (2 L) jelly roll pan; line with waxed paper and grease the paper.

■ In heavy saucepan, combine cocoa and milk, stirring with whisk until smooth. Add hot coffee and butter; bring just to boil, stirring to melt butter. Remove from heat and stir in sugar. Pour into mixing bowl and let cool to lukewarm. With whisk, beat in egg yolks and vanilla.

■ Sift or mix together flour, baking soda, baking powder and salt; stir into chocolate mixture until smooth.

■ Beat egg whites until stiff peaks form; fold thoroughly into chocolate mixture.

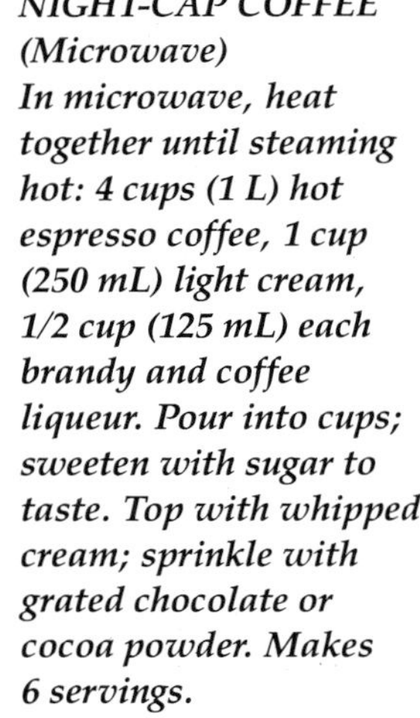

***NIGHT-CAP COFFEE (Microwave)***
***In microwave, heat together until steaming hot: 4 cups (1 L) hot espresso coffee, 1 cup (250 mL) light cream, 1/2 cup (125 mL) each brandy and coffee liqueur. Pour into cups; sweeten with sugar to taste. Top with whipped cream; sprinkle with grated chocolate or cocoa powder. Makes 6 servings.***

Pour into prepared pan, spreading evenly. Bake in 350°F (180°C) oven for 20 minutes or until top springs back when lightly touched. Let cool in pan on wire rack for about 15 minutes, then invert onto sheet of foil. Peel off waxed paper. Let cool completely before assembling.

■ Cut cooled cake in half crosswise to make 2 rectangles. Spread 1 rectangle with jam, then top with second.

**GLAZE:** In small heavy saucepan over very low heat, melt chocolate with butter; remove from heat. Add icing sugar and boiling water, stirring until smooth. If necessary, add a tiny bit more water to give a very thick pourable consistency.

■ Pour glaze immediately over cake and spread evenly.

■ To serve, cut into small squares or rectangles. Top each with a candied violet or nut half. Makes about 25 squares.

## *Rum Cakes*

*These small golden cakes, with a rich sponge-cake texture, are deliciously glazed with a buttery rum syrup.*

| | | |
|---|---|---|
| **3/4 cup** | **pecan halves (optional)** | **175 mL** |
| **1 cup** | **butter** | **250 mL** |
| **1 cup** | **granulated sugar** | **250 mL** |
| **5** | **eggs, separated** | **5** |
| **1 cup** | **all-purpose flour** | **250 mL** |
| **1 tbsp** | **baking powder** | **15 mL** |
| **1/4 cup** | **light or dark rum** | **50 mL** |
| | **RUM SYRUP:** | |
| **1 cup** | **granulated sugar** | **250 mL** |
| **1/2 cup** | **butter** | **125 mL** |
| **1/4 cup** | **water** | **50 mL** |
| **1/2 cup** | **light or dark rum** | **125 mL** |

■ Grease 20 to 24 plain or fluted muffin tins (each about 1/3 cup/75 mL capacity). If desired, arrange 6 to 8 pecan halves in bottom of each.

■ In bowl, cream butter with sugar thoroughly. Add egg yolks and beat well until light and fluffy. Sift or mix together flour and baking powder; add alternately with rum to creamed mixture, beating lightly after each addition.

■ In separate bowl and with clean beaters, beat egg whites until stiff peaks form; stir about one-quarter of the beaten whites into batter to lighten it, then thoroughly fold in remaining whites.

■ Spoon into prepared pans, filling each about two-thirds full. Bake in 350°F (180°C) oven for about 20 minutes or until tops spring back when lightly touched. Let cool in pans for 5 minutes, then loosen cakes by running knife around edges and invert pans onto wire racks. (Bottoms of cakes are now the tops.) Place waxed paper under racks to catch drips from rum syrup.

**RUM SYRUP:** In small saucepan, combine sugar, butter and water. Bring to boil; boil for 5 minutes, stirring occasionally. Remove from heat and stir in rum.

■ Spoon about half over tops and sides of cakes; let it soak in, then gradually spoon remaining syrup over. Let cool completely, then store, covered, in airtight container at room temperature. Makes 20 to 24 cakes.

## *Grown-Up Hot Chocolate*

*This is a rich and warming brew of good chocolate fortified with coffee liqueur.*

| | | |
|---|---|---|
| **4 oz** | **semisweet chocolate*** | **125 g** |
| **2 oz** | **unsweetened chocolate*** | **60 g** |
| **2 tbsp** | **granulated sugar** | **25 mL** |
| **1-1/2 cups** | **boiling water** | **375 mL** |
| **1 cup** | **milk** | **250 mL** |
| **1 cup** | **light cream** | **250 mL** |
| **1/2 cup** | **coffee liqueur** | **125 mL** |
| **1/2 cup** | **whipping cream, whipped** | **125 mL** |

■ In heavy saucepan, combine semisweet and unsweetened chocolate, sugar and boiling water; stir over medium heat until chocolate is completely melted. Add milk and light cream; whisk until completely smooth and very hot but not boiling. Stir in liqueur. Serve in small cups with spoons. Top each serving with whipped cream. Makes 6 servings.

*Six ounces (175 g) good-quality Swiss bittersweet chocolate can be substituted for the semisweet and unsweetened chocolate.

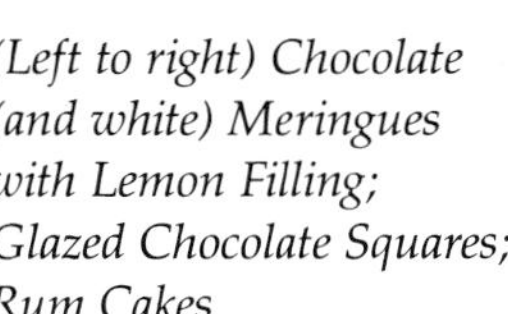

*(Left to right) Chocolate (and white) Meringues with Lemon Filling; Glazed Chocolate Squares; Rum Cakes*

## Chocolate Meringues with Lemon Filling

*Melt-in-your-mouth meringues are delectable and pretty with a tart lemon filling and a drizzle of chocolate. A selection of both white and chocolate meringues is even more attractive. For white meringues, simply omit the cocoa.*

| | | |
|---|---|---|
| | **MERINGUES:** | |
| **3** | **egg whites, at room temperature** | **3** |
| **1/2 tsp** | **cream of tartar** | **2 mL** |
| **3/4 cup** | **fruit/berry sugar** | **175 mL** |
| **1/4 cup** | **unsweetened cocoa powder** | **50 mL** |
| | **LEMON FILLING:** | |
| **1** | **egg** | **1** |
| **3** | **egg yolks** | **3** |
| **1 cup** | **granulated sugar** | **250 mL** |
| **1/2 cup** | **lemon juice** | **125 mL** |
| **1 tbsp** | **grated lemon rind** | **15 mL** |
| **2 tbsp** | **butter** | **25 mL** |
| | **CHOCOLATE DRIZZLE:** | |
| **1 oz** | **semisweet chocolate** | **30 g** |
| **1/4 tsp** | **vegetable oil** | **1 mL** |

■ Line baking sheet with parchment or brown paper. Draw twelve 2-inch (5 cm) circles on paper, at least 1 inch (2.5 cm) apart.

**MERINGUES:** In bowl, beat egg whites with cream of tartar until soft peaks form. Gradually add 1/2 cup (125 mL) of the sugar, beating until stiff and shiny. Combine remaining sugar with cocoa; gradually beat into meringue mixture. (For white meringues, omit cocoa.)

■ Spoon or pipe meringue mixture inside circles, making base about 1/4 inch (5 mm) thick and building up sides to make a rim. If desired, pipe a rim of rosettes with small star tip. (This works best with white meringue; chocolate meringue is a bit softer and will not hold rosette shape as well.)

■ Bake in 275°F (140°C) oven for about 1 hour or until crisp and dry. (If white meringues start to brown, reduce oven temperature.) Remove from oven and let cool a few minutes. Carefully peel off paper and let meringues cool thoroughly.

**LEMON FILLING:** In double boiler or small heavy saucepan, beat egg and egg yolks lightly. Stir in sugar, lemon juice and rind, and butter. Cook over low heat, stirring often, until thickened, about 20 minutes; do not boil. (Mixture will thicken more when cold.) Chill thoroughly. Spoon into meringue shells.

**CHOCOLATE DRIZZLE:** Melt chocolate; stir in oil. Drizzle over filled meringues. Makes 12 meringues.

## Crème de Cacao Nightcap

*Here's a delicious smoothie to serve in espresso cups after dinner.*

| | | |
|---|---|---|
| **2 cups** | **milk** | **500 mL** |
| **1/4 cup** | **crème de cacao** | **50 mL** |
| **1/4 cup** | **brandy** | **50 mL** |
| | **Granulated sugar** | |
| | **TOPPING:** | |
| **1/2 cup** | **whipping cream** | **125 mL** |
| **2 tbsp** | **crème de cacao** | **25 mL** |
| | **Unsweetened cocoa powder** | |

**TOPPING:** Whip cream and beat in crème de cacao.

■ In saucepan, heat milk with crème de cacao and brandy until very hot but not boiling. Pour into cups. Add sugar to taste. Top with flavored whipped cream. Sift cocoa through a small sieve onto cream. Makes 6 demitasse servings.

***CAFÉ ROMA***
***(Microwave)***
***In microwave, heat together until steaming hot: 1/2 cup (125 mL) each brandy and amaretto liqueur, 2 tbsp (25 mL) sugar, 10 whole cloves, 2 sticks cinnamon, pinch of nutmeg and the rinds of 1 lemon and 1 orange. Remove from oven and ignite carefully with long match. Add 5 cups (1.25 L) double-strength hot coffee.***

***Strain into cups, sweeten to taste and top with whipped cream, if desired. Makes 6 servings.***

# A COCKTAIL PARTY

FOR A CROWD

*A few times a year, the entertaining calendar calls for a big, beautiful cocktail party—and this menu makes it elegant but easy. The chic array of interesting tidbits has a sophisticated simplicity that's just right for a holiday open house, or before a charity gala dinner or opening night at the theatre.*

*CHEESE WHEEL WITH PESTO

*STUFFED BAGUETTE

*ROASTED PEPPER-STUFFED MUSHROOMS

*SALMON IN BELGIAN ENDIVE LEAVES

*SKEWERED CHEESE BALLS

SKEWERED SHRIMP WITH FRUIT
(recipe, page 155)

## Cheese Wheel with Pesto

*This appealing appetizer uses an intriguing combination of flavors and colors.*

| | | |
|---|---|---|
| **1-1/2 lb** | **cream cheese** | **750 g** |
| **3 cups** | **shredded old Cheddar cheese** | **750 mL** |
| **1/4 lb** | **blue cheese, crumbled** | **125 g** |
| **1/4 cup** | **milk** | **50 mL** |
| **1/4 cup** | **brandy** | **50 mL** |
| | **Pesto (recipe follows)** | |
| | **Sprigs of fresh herbs** | |

■ Line bottom of 8-inch (20 cm) springform pan with circle of waxed paper cut to fit bottom exactly. Set aside.

■ In food processor or by hand, blend cream cheese, Cheddar and blue cheese. Add milk and brandy; process until smooth. Spoon half of the cheese mixture into prepared pan and spread evenly. Spread pesto evenly over top. Cover with remaining cheese mixture and smooth top. Cover and refrigerate for at least 4 hours or overnight.

■ To serve, remove sides from pan. Invert cheese wheel onto serving plate. Remove pan bottom and waxed paper. Garnish with sprigs of fresh herbs. Serve with crackers. Makes about 30 servings.

| | | |
|---|---|---|
| | **PESTO:** | |
| **1 cup** | **fresh basil leaves** | **250 mL** |
| **2 tbsp** | **toasted pine nuts or walnuts** | **25 mL** |
| **1** | **small clove garlic** | **1** |
| **2 tbsp** | **extra-virgin olive oil** | **25 mL** |
| **2 tbsp** | **freshly grated Parmesan cheese** | **25 mL** |

■ In food processor or blender, combine basil, pine nuts and garlic; process until finely chopped. With motor running, gradually add olive oil; process until mixture forms paste. Stir in cheese. Makes about 1/2 cup (125 mL).

## *Stuffed Baguette*

*Transportable and easy to serve, this loaf makes a particularly attractive presentation when sliced to reveal the filling.*

| | | |
|---|---|---|
| 1 | baguette (French bread) | 1 |
| 2 cups | packed spinach leaves | 500 mL |
| 1/4 lb | cream cheese | 125 g |
| 1/4 cup | chopped fresh dill | 50 mL |
| 1 tbsp | milk or cream | 15 mL |
| 4 cups | minced ham (about 1 lb/500 g) | 1 L |
| 1/3 cup | toasted unsalted pistachios or walnuts, coarsely chopped | 75 mL |
| 1/3 cup | mayonnaise | 75 mL |
| 1 tbsp | Dijon mustard | 15 mL |

(Left to right) Roasted Pepper-Stuffed Mushrooms; Stuffed Baguette; Salmon in Belgian Endive Leaves; Skewered Shrimp; Skewered Cheese Balls; Cheese Wheel with Pesto

■ Slice baguette lengthwise. Hollow out, leaving shell about 1/2 inch (1 cm) thick. (Reserve crumbs for another use; store in freezer.) Wrap loaf in plastic wrap or foil; set aside.
■ Rinse spinach and shake off excess water. In saucepan, cover and cook spinach in just the water clinging to leaves for about 3 minutes or just until wilted. Drain and squeeze dry. Chop finely. In food processor or using electric mixer, process spinach, cream cheese, dill and milk until spreadable; set aside.
■ In bowl, mix together ham, nuts, mayonnaise and mustard; set aside.
■ Completely coat inside surfaces of baguette with cheese mixture, including cut edges that will seal baguette together. Pack ham mixture into hollow of baguette bottom, mounding slightly. Replace top of baguette; wrap tightly in plastic wrap or foil. Refrigerate for at least 2 hours or up to 8 hours. Makes about 30 slices.

## Roasted Pepper-Stuffed Mushrooms

*Choose white, firm mushrooms and simply wipe off any dirt with a paper towel or damp cloth.*

| | | |
|---|---|---|
| 1 | **large sweet red pepper** | 1 |
| 1/4 lb | **cream cheese** | 125 g |
| 1 tsp | **(approx) sour cream or plain yogurt** | 5 mL |
| 24 | **mushrooms, stems removed** | 24 |

■ Halve and seed red pepper. Remove strip and cut into tiny diamonds for garnish; set aside.
■ Broil remaining pepper until skin is completely charred. Place in plastic or paper bag and seal; let stand for 10 minutes. Peel charred skin from pepper. Purée pepper in blender or chop finely by hand. Set aside and let cool.
■ In bowl, cream cheese until soft and fluffy. Add roasted pepper purée and enough sour cream to make texture that can be spooned or piped into mushrooms. Garnish with red pepper diamonds. Makes 24 appetizers.

## Salmon in Belgian Endive Leaves

*If Belgian endive is not available, spread salmon mixture on crackers and garnish with smoked salmon, or serve on chilled steamed artichoke leaves.*

| | | |
|---|---|---|
| 1 | **can (7.5 oz/213 g) red salmon** | 1 |
| 2 | **green onions, finely chopped** | 2 |
| 1 tbsp | **mayonnaise** | 15 mL |
| 1 tsp | **lemon juice** | 5 mL |
| Pinch | **pepper** | Pinch |
| 8 | **slices smoked salmon** | 8 |
| 24 | **Belgian endive leaves** | 24 |
| | **Fresh dill or parsley sprigs** | |

■ Drain salmon; remove bones and skin if necessary. In bowl, mash salmon with fork; mix in onions, mayonnaise, lemon juice and pepper. Chill.
■ At serving time, top each endive leaf with salmon mixture. Garnish with narrow strips of smoked salmon twisted into tiny rose shapes. Top with sprig of fresh dill. Makes 24 appetizers.

## Skewered Cheese Balls

*Flavor the cream cheese with finely chopped chives, dill, or green onions. For a change of pace, use this cream cheese mixture to sandwich together perfect walnut halves.*

| | | |
|---|---|---|
| 1/2 lb | **cream cheese** | 250 g |
| 1/2 cup | **finely chopped fresh parsley*** | 125 mL |

■ Form cheese into 24 balls about 1 inch (2.5 cm) round. Roll in parsley. Skewer on long bamboo picks. Refrigerate on waxed paper-lined tray, covered, for at least 2 hours or overnight. Makes 24 appetizers.
*Substitute finely chopped nuts, a mixture of dill and parsley, or a mixture of equal parts celery seed and coarsely ground black pepper.

# DAYTIME

*Leisurely breakfasts and brunches; sunny summery luncheons; the neighborly warmth of mid-morning coffee; the gentleness of a traditional afternoon tea—there's something especially welcoming about daytime gatherings. In this chapter, you'll find inspiration for every daytime mood—from a casual coffee-and-muffins get-together in a summer garden to a bountiful English breakfast on a cold winter's morn. There are innovative menus that add new flavors to popular occasions (a herb-seasoned Sunday brunch) and others that invite you to try something new (a rose-colored setting for a lighthearted springtime celebration). Most of the recipes are make-ahead or short-order for relaxed daytime enjoyment in every season, indoors or out.*

# AN ENGLISH COUNTRY BREAKFAST

FOR SIX

*The traditional British breakfast comes gloriously into its own on a cold Canadian winter's morning. Recapture the gracious mood of a stately country house where houseguests come leisurely to the dining room sideboard, lifting the lids of silver dishes and helping themselves to the hearty fare that fortified generations of empire-builders.*

BUCK'S FIZZ OR
BLACK VELVET

FRUIT SALAD
OR STEWED PRUNES
WITH CREAM

*KEDGEREE

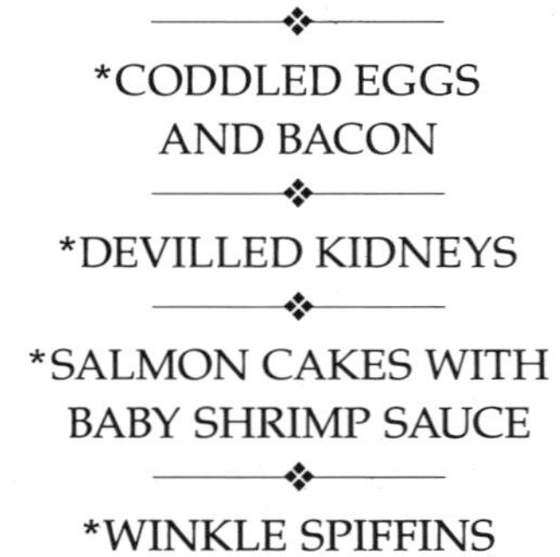

*CODDLED EGGS
AND BACON

*DEVILLED KIDNEYS

*SALMON CAKES WITH
BABY SHRIMP SAUCE

*WINKLE SPIFFINS

**Recipes are given for menu items marked with an asterisk.*

*Coddled Eggs and Bacon; Devilled Kidneys*

## *Kedgeree*

*In the days when England had an empire, the jewel in the crown of the great British breakfast was kedgeree. It was originally an Indian dish, a mixture of beans or lentils, rice and eggs, enlivened with onion and spices; but the old colonials who brought the recipe home with their other trophies replaced the beans or lentils and onion with nuggets of smoked fish.*

| | | |
|---|---|---|
| **1 lb** | **smoked skinned haddock fillets** | **500 g** |
| **1** | **bay leaf** | **1** |
| **1 cup** | **long-grain rice** | **250 mL** |
| **1/4 cup** | **butter** | **50 mL** |
| **2 tbsp** | **(approx) chopped fresh parsley** | **25 mL** |
| **Pinch** | **ground mace** | **Pinch** |
| | **Pepper** | |
| **2** | **hard-cooked eggs** | **2** |
| **1/2 cup** | **light cream** | **125 mL** |

■ In shallow pan over low heat, cover fish with water; add bay leaf and poach for 5 to 10 minutes or until fish flakes easily when tested with knife. Let cool. With slotted spoon, remove fish, draining well; cut into bite-sized pieces and set aside.

■ Remove bay leaf; pour cooking liquid into saucepan and add enough water to make 6 cups (1.5 L). Bring to boil; add rice. Cover, reduce heat and simmer for 20 minutes or until tender. Drain and transfer to greased ovenproof serving dish. Mix in butter, parsley, mace, and pepper to taste.

■ Chop eggs into large pieces; stir into rice mixture along with fish. (Recipe can be prepared to this point, covered and refrigerated for up to 12 hours. To reheat, cover and bake in 350°F/180°C oven for 20 minutes or until heated through.) In heavy saucepan, heat cream until steaming; stir into rice mixture. Garnish with more parsley. Makes 6 servings.

***BREAKFAST BEVERAGES***
***Orange juice, coffee and tea are all suitably stimulating drinks, but there is nothing like champagne to add lustre to a morning, mixed perhaps with orange juice to make Buck's Fizz or with Guinness stout to become Black Velvet.***

# Coddled Eggs and Bacon

*Baked eggs, each in their own little ramekin and concealing pieces of mushroom and bacon, have a certain tidy glamor. A dash of cream can be added with the egg for a moister result.*

| | | |
|---|---|---|
| **1/4 lb** | **lean peameal bacon** | **125 g** |
| **6** | **small mushrooms** | **6** |
| **2 tbsp** | **butter** | **25 mL** |
| | **Salt and pepper** | |
| **6** | **eggs** | **6** |

■ Coarsely chop bacon and mushrooms. In skillet, melt 1 tbsp (15 mL) of the butter over medium heat; cook bacon and mushrooms for 3 to 4 minutes or just until mushrooms are golden.

■ Spoon into six 2/3-cup (150 mL) buttered ramekins. Make well in centers; break egg into each well. Top each yolk with about 1/2 tsp (2 mL) of the remaining butter. Season with salt and pepper to taste.

■ Place ramekins in baking dish large enough to hold them without touching. Pour in enough boiling water to come one-quarter of the way up sides of ramekins. Bake in 400°F (200°C) oven for 12 to 15 minutes or just until eggs are set. Serve immediately. Makes 6 servings.

*Salmon Cakes with Baby Shrimp Sauce*

# Devilled Kidneys

*Devilled kidneys were all the rage in 19th-century England, both as a breakfast dish accompanied by poached eggs, and as a late supper savory. The tangy-sweet sauce should be thick enough to cling to the meat.*

| | | |
|---|---|---|
| 1/3 cup | butter | 75 mL |
| 1 | small onion, finely chopped | 1 |
| 3 | tomatoes, peeled, seeded and chopped | 3 |
| 1-1/4 cups | chicken stock | 300 mL |
| 2 tbsp | chopped fresh parsley | 25 mL |
| 2 tbsp | tomato paste | 25 mL |
| 1 tbsp | lemon juice | 15 mL |
| 4 tsp | Worcestershire sauce | 20 mL |
| 2 tsp | packed brown sugar | 10 mL |
| 2 tsp | wine vinegar | 10 mL |
| | Salt and pepper | |
| 3/4 lb | lamb or veal kidneys | 375 g |
| | All-purpose flour | |
| 4 | slices toast, crusts removed | 4 |

■ In large skillet, melt 1 tbsp (15 mL) of the butter over medium heat; cook onion for 3 to 5 minutes or until softened. Add tomatoes, stock, parsley, tomato paste, lemon juice, Worcestershire sauce, sugar and vinegar; bring to boil over high heat. Reduce heat to medium-high and cook, uncovered, for 10 to 20 minutes or until slightly thickened.

*RISING TO THE OCCASION*
***A well-presented buffet should offer three or four hot hearty dishes in plentiful amounts. In this menu, the kedgeree and fish cakes can be prepared the night before; once reheated, they will wait patiently on the sideboard until guests help themselves. The tangy sauce for the kidneys can also be made in advance. Coddled eggs and winkle spiffins can be brought in on a tray at any time during the party to be eaten at once. The menu can be sweetened with fresh fruit salad or stewed prunes and a jug of cream.***

Season with salt and pepper to taste. For smoother texture, press through sieve or process in blender or food processor. (Recipe can be prepared to this point, covered and refrigerated for up to 12 hours.)

■ Halve and trim lamb kidneys, removing fatty membrane at center. (If using veal kidneys, halve and trim, then cut into 1-inch/2.5 cm pieces.) Place in shallow dish; season with salt and pepper to taste, then dredge with flour.

■ In skillet, melt remaining butter over medium-high heat; fry kidneys for 4 minutes on each side or until golden and no longer pink at center. Remove kidneys to covered shallow casserole and keep warm. Add tomato sauce to skillet. Increase heat to high and cook for about 2 minutes or until heated through; pour over kidneys. Halve toasts diagonally; serve with kidneys. Makes 6 servings.

## *Salmon Cakes with Baby Shrimp Sauce*

*Fish cakes are another venerable treat for the palates of empire builders. A traditional lunchtime dish over Easter week, they are a delicate extravagance for breakfast. If fresh fennel is unavailable, use fresh dill or parsley.*

| | | |
|---|---|---|
| **3** | **potatoes (about 1 lb/500 g)** | **3** |
| **2** | **cans (each 7.5 oz/213 g) salmon** | **2** |
| **1 tbsp** | **chopped fresh fennel leaves** | **15 mL** |
| **1 tbsp** | **lemon juice** | **15 mL** |
| | **Salt and pepper** | |
| **3** | **eggs** | **3** |
| **1-1/2 cups** | **fresh bread crumbs** | **375 mL** |
| **1/4 cup** | **butter** | **50 mL** |
| | **Baby Shrimp Sauce (recipe follows)** | |

■ In saucepan of boiling water, cook potatoes until tender; drain, mash and transfer to bowl. Add salmon, fennel, lemon juice, and salt and pepper to taste. Lightly beat one of the eggs; add to bowl and mix well. Form into 8 firm patties.

■ In shallow dish, lightly beat remaining eggs. Place bread crumbs in another shallow dish. Dip patties into eggs, then dredge with bread crumbs. In skillet, melt butter over medium-high heat; cook patties for 3 to 4 minutes or until browned, turning once. Serve with Baby Shrimp Sauce. Makes 6 to 8 servings.

| | **BABY SHRIMP SAUCE:** | |
|---|---|---|
| **1/4 cup** | **butter** | **50 mL** |
| **1/4 cup** | **all-purpose flour** | **50 mL** |
| **2-1/2 cups** | **milk** | **625 mL** |
| **1/2 lb** | **frozen cooked baby shrimp, thawed and drained** | **250 g** |
| **1 tbsp** | **chopped fresh parsley** | **15 mL** |
| | **Salt and pepper** | |
| **2** | **chopped hard-cooked eggs** | **2** |

■ In saucepan, melt butter over medium heat; stir in flour and cook, stirring constantly, for 1 minute. Gradually whisk in milk; bring to boil. Reduce heat to low and simmer, stirring constantly, for 1 minute or until thickened.

■ Add shrimp, parsley, and salt and pepper to taste; stir to mix. Add eggs and return to boil; remove from heat. Serve hot. Makes 4 cups (1 L) sauce.

## *Winkle Spiffins*

*Sweet dishes most loved by the British usually end up with names from the nursery.*

| | | |
|---|---|---|
| **6** | **slices light rye bread (3/4 inch/2 cm thick)** | **6** |
| **1/2 cup** | **milk** | **125 mL** |
| **1/4 cup** | **butter** | **50 mL** |
| | **Raspberry jam** | |

■ Remove crust from bread; cut slices into squares or diamonds. Brush both sides with milk; let stand for 10 minutes.

■ Meanwhile, in large skillet, melt butter over medium heat; fry bread, turning once, for about 2 minutes on each side or until golden. Reduce heat to medium-low. Top each slice with generous spoonful of jam; heat for 30 seconds or until jam is warmed. Serve immediately. Makes 6 servings.

# A SUMMER SUNDAY BRUNCH

FOR SIX

*Seasoned with fragrant herbs from the garden, this memorable menu is a summer delight. Finish the leisurely feast with an assortment of fresh fruit accompanied by chocolate cookies.*

MIMOSAS OR FUZZY NAVELS

*SMOKED SALMON ON CHEDDAR-FENNEL BISCUITS

*SHIRRED EGGS WITH BASIL OR TARRAGON

CANADIAN BACK BACON

FRESH FRUIT

CHOCOLATE COOKIES

*Smoked Salmon on Cheddar-Fennel Biscuits; Canadian back bacon; Shirred Eggs with Basil or Tarragon*

## *Smoked Salmon on Cheddar-Fennel Biscuits*

*These tempting biscuits can be baked and frozen in advance, if desired.*

| | | |
|---|---|---|
| **2 cups** | **all-purpose flour** | **500 mL** |
| **1-1/2 tsp** | **baking powder** | **7 mL** |
| **1 tsp** | **baking soda** | **5 mL** |
| **Pinch** | **salt** | **Pinch** |
| **1/2 cup** | **packed shredded old Cheddar cheese** | **125 mL** |
| **4 tsp** | **chopped fresh fennel or dill** | **20 mL** |
| **Pinch** | **each cayenne pepper and dry mustard** | **Pinch** |
| **1/3 cup** | **butter** | **75 mL** |
| **2/3 cup** | **(approx) milk** | **150 mL** |
| | **Butter or cream cheese** | |
| **1/2 lb** | **smoked salmon, sliced** | **250 g** |

■ In large bowl, mix together flour, baking powder, baking soda and salt; stir in cheese, fennel, cayenne pepper and mustard. With pastry blender or 2 knives, cut in butter until mixture resembles coarse crumbs. Blend in enough of the milk to make soft, not sticky, dough.

■ Turn out dough onto lightly floured surface and knead gently just until smooth; roll out to 3/4-inch (2 cm) thickness. With 2-1/2-inch (6 cm) cutter, cut out rounds, gathering and rerolling scraps to cut out.

■ Place on greased baking sheet and bake in 425°F (220°C) oven for 10 minutes or until puffed and golden. Let cool on wire rack. Split and spread with butter or cream cheese; top with smoked salmon. Makes 6 to 8 servings.

***BRUNCH BEVERAGES***
***Start with Mimosas (champagne and orange juice) or Fuzzy Navels (peach schnapps and orange juice). End with a choice of herbal tea, coffee or cappuccino.***

# *Shirred Eggs with Basil or Tarragon*

*Fresh herbs lend color and flavor to eggs individually baked in pretty ramekins or custard cups.*

| | | |
|---|---|---|
| **3 tbsp** | **(approx) chopped fresh basil or tarragon** | **50 mL** |
| **6** | **eggs** | **6** |
| **2 tbsp** | **whipping cream** | **25 mL** |
| | **Salt and pepper** | |

■ Lightly butter six 1/2-cup (125 mL) ramekins or custard cups. Evenly sprinkle bottoms with half of the herbs. Break 1 egg into each ramekin; sprinkle with remaining herbs. Spoon 1 tsp (5 mL) whipping cream over each. Season with salt and pepper to taste.

■ Place ramekins in shallow baking dish; pour in enough boiling water to come halfway up sides of ramekins. Bake in 350°F (180°C) oven for about 15 minutes or until eggs are cooked but yolk is still slightly runny. Serve at once in ramekins. Makes 6 servings.

# A SPRINGTIME LUNCHEON

FOR TEN

*In a rose-colored mood for springtime, a pretty table and lighthearted menu bid welcome to a new neighbor or fond adieu to an old one, congratulations to a graduate or "thank-you" to a hard-working committee.*

*PINK STRAWBERRY SOUP

*CHICKEN AND CANTALOUPE SALAD WITH PECANS

WARM CROISSANTS

ASSORTED COOKIES OR SQUARES

*Pink Strawberry Soup; warm croissants; Chicken and Cantaloupe Salad with Pecans*

# *Pink Strawberry Soup*

*Serve glasses or pretty bowls of this chilled soup as an intriguing prelude to the rest of the meal.*

| | | |
|---|---|---|
| **2 cups** | **water** | **500 mL** |
| **1 cup** | **port wine** | **250 mL** |
| **1/3 cup** | **granulated sugar** | **75 mL** |
| **2 tbsp** | **lemon juice** | **25 mL** |
| **1** | **stick cinnamon** | **1** |
| **4 cups** | **strawberries, puréed** | **1 L** |
| **1/4 cup** | **sour cream** | **50 mL** |
| **1/2 cup** | **whipping cream** | **125 mL** |
| **Pinch** | **salt** | **Pinch** |
| | **Fresh mint sprigs** | |

■ In saucepan, stir together water, port, sugar, lemon juice and cinnamon stick. Bring to boil and boil, uncovered, over medium-high heat for 10 minutes, stirring occasionally. Stir in puréed strawberries; reduce heat and simmer for 5 minutes. Discard cinnamon stick and let mixture cool to room temperature.

■ Whisk in sour cream. Beat together cream and salt until stiff; fold into soup. Cover and chill for 4 hours or overnight.

■ Serve in wine glasses, highball glasses or tiny soup bowls. Garnish each serving with sprig of fresh mint. Makes 10 servings.

***A TABLE CENTERPIECE***

***Bring a light, springtime mood to your table with this easy-to-make fantasy grape tree (see photo).***

***Spray bare branches with white or silver paint. Frost small bunches of green grapes by dipping them into beaten egg white, then into granulated sugar. Let grapes dry on a wire rack for 1 to 2 hours.***

***Anchor branches in a tall vase filled with white sand. Hang frosted grapes over the branches. Add velvet bows or single blooms from a stem of fabric flowers (blooms can be attached to branches with white modelling clay).***

# *Chicken and Cantaloupe Salad with Pecans*

*Everyone loves chicken salad. Interesting ingredients give this elegant version extra flavor and color.*

| | | |
|---|---|---|
| **12** | **chicken breasts (about 5 lb/2.2 kg total)** | **12** |
| **1/2 cup** | **cider vinegar** | **125 mL** |
| **1 tsp** | **salt** | **5 mL** |
| **2 cups** | **thinly sliced celery** | **500 mL** |
| **1/2 cup** | **thinly sliced red onion** | **125 mL** |
| **2** | **small cantaloupe** | **2** |
| **1 cup** | **pecan halves** | **250 mL** |
| | **Boston or romaine lettuce leaves** | |
| | **DRESSING:** | |
| **1 cup** | **mayonnaise (preferably homemade)** | **250 mL** |
| **2 tbsp** | **cider vinegar** | **25 mL** |
| **2 tbsp** | **honey** | **25 mL** |
| **1 tsp** | **curry powder** | **5 mL** |
| **1/2 tsp** | **ginger** | **2 mL** |
| | **Salt** | |

■ In large stainless steel or enamelled kettle, combine chicken breasts, cider vinegar and 1 tsp (5 mL) salt; cover with cold water. Gradually bring to boil; reduce heat and simmer, covered, for about 20 minutes or until juices run clear when chicken is pierced with skewer. Let cool for at least 15 minutes in poaching liquid. (Alternatively, cover and refrigerate overnight.)

■ Remove chicken breasts; discard cooking liquid. Remove and discard skin and bones. Cut or shred meat into bite-sized pieces and place in large bowl; add celery and onion.

**DRESSING:** Stir together mayonnaise, cider vinegar, honey, curry powder, ginger, and salt to taste. Pour over chicken mixture and toss lightly to mix. Cover and chill for several hours.

■ Peel cantaloupe. Cut 1 cantaloupe into thin wedges and reserve for garnish. Using melon baller, make tiny balls from second cantaloupe (alternatively, cut into cubes). Cover both with plastic wrap and refrigerate.

■ Just before serving, gently stir cantaloupe balls and 3/4 cup (175 mL) of the pecans into chicken salad. Line large serving platter or individual plates with lettuce leaves. Mound salad in center; surround with cantaloupe wedges and sprinkle with remaining pecans. Makes about 10 servings.

# A MORNING COFFEE PARTY

FOR FOUR TO EIGHT

*"Come for coffee" is an especially neighborly invitation when the welcome includes the fragrance of fresh-brewed coffee and hot-from-the-oven muffins. Add a delectable fruit cup of seasonal berries and melon, and your guests will feel really pampered.*

MELON BALLS AND BLACKBERRIES

*LEMON CURRANT MUFFINS

*ORANGE APRICOT RAISIN BRAN MUFFINS

## Lemon Currant Muffins

*The night before, measure the ingredients for the muffins, grease the muffin pan and mix the streusel topping. Cover lightly with a clean towel. In the morning, mix up a batch of muffins while the oven heats.*

| | | |
|---|---|---|
| **1/4 cup** | **butter** | **50 mL** |
| **2/3 cup** | **granulated sugar** | **150 mL** |
| **1** | **egg** | **1** |
| **1 tsp** | **grated lemon rind** | **5 mL** |
| **2 cups** | **all-purpose flour** | **500 mL** |
| **2 tsp** | **baking powder** | **10 mL** |
| **1/4 tsp** | **salt** | **1 mL** |
| **2/3 cup** | **milk** | **150 mL** |
| **1 cup** | **currants** | **250 mL** |
| | **TOPPING:** | |
| **2 tbsp** | **granulated sugar** | **25 mL** |
| **2 tbsp** | **all-purpose flour** | **25 mL** |
| **1/2 tsp** | **cinnamon** | **2 mL** |
| **2 tbsp** | **butter** | **25 mL** |

**TOPPING:** Combine sugar, flour and cinnamon; work in butter until crumbly. Set aside.

■ In bowl, cream together butter and sugar until light. Beat in egg and lemon rind. Stir together flour, baking powder and salt. Add to creamed mixture alternately with milk, stirring just to mix. (Do not overbeat.) Stir in currants.

■ Spoon into 12 greased muffin cups; sprinkle with topping. Bake in 375°F (190°C) oven for 25 to 30 minutes or until firm to the touch. Makes 12 muffins.

## Orange Apricot Raisin Bran Muffins

*This is a great variation on the bran muffin theme. The orange juice concentrate adds tangy fruit flavor without the bother of grating rind and squeezing juice.*

| | | |
|---|---|---|
| **2 cups** | **all-purpose flour** | **500 mL** |
| **1-1/4 cups** | **packed brown sugar** | **300 mL** |
| **1 cup** | **natural bran** | **250 mL** |
| **2 tsp** | **baking powder** | **10 mL** |

*Lemon Currant Muffins; melon balls and blackberries*

| | | |
|---|---|---|
| 1 tsp | baking soda | 5 mL |
| 1/2 tsp | salt | 2 mL |
| 1 cup | raisins | 250 mL |
| 1/2 cup | chopped dried apricots | 125 mL |
| 1 | egg | 1 |
| 1 cup | sour cream | 250 mL |
| 1/2 cup | vegetable oil | 125 mL |
| 1/2 cup | frozen orange juice concentrate, thawed | 125 mL |

■ In large bowl, mix together flour, sugar, bran, baking powder, baking soda and salt; stir in raisins and apricots.

■ In small bowl, beat egg; stir in sour cream, oil and orange juice concentrate. Stir into dry ingredients just until moistened.

■ Spoon batter into large paper-lined muffin cups, filling each to top of liner. Bake in 375°F (190°C) oven for 20 minutes or until firm to the touch. Makes 16 muffins.

# A TRADITIONAL AFTERNOON TEA

FOR THIRTY

*The gentle art of British teatime is back in vogue. As a form of entertaining, this pleasant, calming ritual adapts beautifully to large or small groups. This menu will serve 30 easily; if you plan to entertain only a few friends, the sandwiches or scones plus one of the sweets would make a lovely tea. Just remember the one essential: perfectly brewed tea, sipped from your prettiest cups and saucers.*

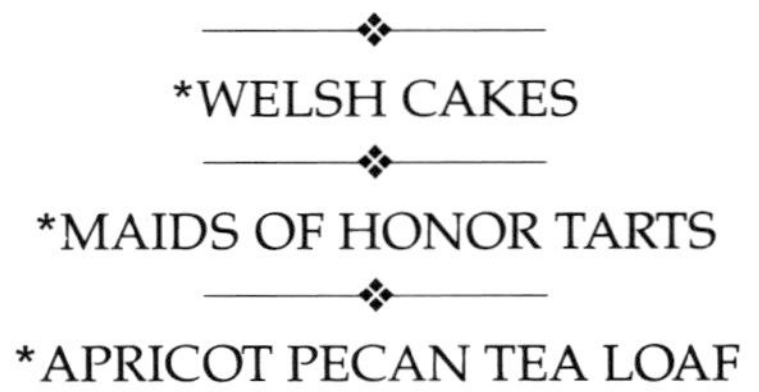

ASSORTED SANDWICHES

*MINIATURE CREAM TEA SCONES

*VICTORIA SANDWICH

*DUNDEE CAKE

*WELSH CAKES

*MAIDS OF HONOR TARTS

*APRICOT PECAN TEA LOAF

***TRADITIONAL BRITISH TEAS***

**The formal afternoon tea** ***(at home, in a hotel or at half-time during a cricket match) always starts with tiny sandwiches followed by a selection of small cakes, slices or tarts.***

***Tea shops and country hotels often specialize in*** **cream teas,** ***where scones are served with fresh strawberries, strawberry jam and cream as rich as butter.***

**Everyday afternoon tea,** ***enjoyed at home with or without guests, is a simple refreshment of tea and plain biscuits or buttered fruitbread. It's an informal occasion, a welcome pause in a busy day.***

**High tea** ***is not, as sometimes thought, a more elaborate version of afternoon tea. It is actually an early supper, usually served between 5 and 6 p.m. The savory course might be poached smoked fish or melted cheese on toast in winter; cold sliced ham, tomatoes and cucumbers in summer. The sweet would be a simple cake or pastry.***

## Miniature Cream Tea Scones

*In the summertime, English tea shops and inns sometimes offer a bowl of fresh strawberries along with thick cream and jam to spread on the scones. For your afternoon tea, halve these miniature versions, spread with whipped cream and top with half a strawberry or a trio of raspberries. For 30 people, make about 3 batches.*

| | | |
|---|---|---|
| **2 cups** | **sifted cake-and-pastry flour** | **500 mL** |
| **1 tbsp** | **granulated sugar** | **15 mL** |
| **1 tbsp** | **baking powder** | **15 mL** |
| **1/2 tsp** | **salt** | **2 mL** |
| **1/4 cup** | **butter** | **50 mL** |
| **1/4 cup** | **shortening** | **50 mL** |
| **1/2 cup** | **sour cream** | **125 mL** |
| **1/2 cup** | **milk** | **125 mL** |
| **1/2 tsp** | **baking soda** | **2 mL** |
| **1** | **egg yolk beaten with 1 tbsp (15 mL) cream or milk** | **1** |

■ In large bowl, stir together flour, sugar, baking powder and salt. With fingertips, rub in butter and shortening until mixture resembles fine crumbs. Combine sour cream, milk and baking soda; add to flour mixture all at once. Using fork, mix with quick light strokes to make soft, somewhat sticky dough.

■ Using spatula, turn out onto well-floured surface; gather into ball and knead gently 4 or 5 times. Sprinkle with flour and pat into 3/4-inch (2 cm) thick circle. With well floured fluted 1-1/2-inch (4 cm) cutter, cut out scones. Place on very lightly greased or nonstick baking sheet 1/4 inch (5 mm) apart. Brush with egg yolk mixture. Bake in 450°F (230°C) oven for 9 to 12 minutes or until tops are golden brown and scones are cooked through. Makes 20 scones.

*Assorted sandwiches; Miniature Cream Tea Scones; Victoria Sandwich*

## *Victoria Sandwich*

*This is a classic teatime layer cake. Good English cooks take pride in producing a Victoria sponge that is fine-textured, high and light. For 30 people, make two cakes.*

| | | |
|---|---|---|
| **1 cup** | **butter** | **250 mL** |
| **1 cup** | **granulated sugar** | **250 mL** |
| **1-3/4 cups** | **sifted cake-and-pastry flour** | **425 mL** |
| **4** | **eggs** | **4** |
| **2 tsp** | **baking powder** | **10 mL** |
| **1/2 tsp** | **salt** | **2 mL** |
| **1-1/2 tsp** | **vanilla** | **7 mL** |
| **1/4 cup** | **raspberry jam** | **50 mL** |
| | **Icing sugar** | |

■ Butter two 8-inch (1.2 L) round cake pans; line bottoms with waxed paper and set aside.

■ In large bowl, beat butter until creamy; gradually beat in sugar until mixture is pale lemon in color and consistency of stiff whipped cream. Sprinkle with about 2 tbsp (25 mL) of the flour; beat until well blended. Beat in 1 of the eggs. Repeat sprinkling with flour and beating in remaining eggs.

■ Sift together remaining flour, baking powder and salt; stir into batter. Stir in vanilla (batter will be stiff). Spread evenly in prepared pans.

■ Bake in 375°F (190°C) oven for 20 to 25 minutes or until cakes pull away slightly from sides of pans and are firm to the touch. Let cool in pans for 5 minutes. Turn out onto wire rack; remove paper and let cool completely. Sandwich together with jam; dust with icing sugar. Makes 12 average or 24 miniature servings.

## Dundee Cake

*This grand Scottish cake with its crown of almonds looks splendid on a glass stand and goes wonderfully with a good cup of tea.*

| | | |
|---|---|---|
| **1-1/2 cups** | **golden raisins** | **375 mL** |
| **1-1/2 cups** | **currants** | **375 mL** |
| **1/3 cup** | **halved candied cherries** | **75 mL** |
| **1/3 cup** | **candied orange peel** | **75 mL** |
| **1 tsp** | **grated orange rind** | **5 mL** |
| **1/2 tsp** | **grated lemon rind** | **2 mL** |
| **2 tbsp** | **lemon juice** | **25 mL** |
| **3/4 cup** | **butter** | **175 mL** |
| **3/4 cup** | **granulated sugar** | **175 mL** |
| **1/2 cup** | **ground almonds** | **125 mL** |
| **2 cups** | **sifted cake-and-pastry flour** | **500 mL** |
| **4** | **eggs** | **4** |
| **1 tsp** | **baking powder** | **5 mL** |
| **1/4 tsp** | **salt** | **1 mL** |
| **1/2 cup** | **halved blanched almonds** | **125 mL** |
| **1 tbsp** | **milk sweetened with 1 tbsp (15 mL) granulated sugar** | **15 mL** |

■ Butter 8-inch (2.5 L) round fruit cake pan at least 3 inches (8 cm) deep; line bottom with waxed paper and set aside.

■ Stir together raisins, currants, cherries, candied peel, orange rind, lemon rind and juice; set aside. In large mixing bowl, beat butter until creamy; gradually beat in sugar until mixture is pale lemon color and consistency of very stiff whipped cream.

■ Stir together ground almonds and 1/4 cup (50 mL) of the flour; sprinkle about one-quarter over butter mixture and beat well. Beat in 1 of the eggs. Repeat with remaining almond mixture and eggs.

■ Stir fruit mixture into batter. Stir together remaining flour, baking powder and salt; add to batter and stir well. Turn into prepared pan; level with spatula. Arrange a few of the split almonds, flat side down, in circle at center. Arrange remaining almonds in two concentric circles around center. Bake in 300°F (150°C) oven for 1 hour and 15 minutes; brush with sweetened milk and bake for 30 to 45 minutes longer or until cake tester inserted in center comes out clean.

■ Let cool in pan on wire rack for 30 minutes. Remove from pan; remove paper and let cool completely before wrapping and storing in cake tin. Store for at least 24 hours before cutting into fingers to serve. Makes about 30 small pieces.

## Welsh Cakes

*These wonderful little cakes (which are rather like very rich scones) are traditionally baked on a bakestone or griddle in Wales.*

| | | |
|---|---|---|
| **2 cups** | **sifted cake-and-pastry flour** | **500 mL** |
| **1/3 cup** | **granulated sugar** | **75 mL** |
| **1 tsp** | **baking powder** | **5 mL** |
| **1/2 tsp** | **salt** | **2 mL** |
| **1/4 tsp** | **nutmeg** | **1 mL** |
| **1/4 cup** | **butter** | **50 mL** |
| **1/4 cup** | **lard** | **50 mL** |
| **1/3 cup** | **currants** | **75 mL** |
| **1** | **egg** | **1** |
| **2 tbsp** | **(approx) milk** | **25 mL** |
| | **Granulated sugar** | |

■ Remove 2 tbsp (25 mL) of the flour and reserve for rolling out dough. In large bowl, stir together remaining flour, sugar, baking powder, salt and nutmeg. With fingertips, rub in butter and lard until mixture resembles fine crumbs. Stir in currants.

■ Beat together egg and milk; with fork, stir into flour mixture just until dry ingredients are moistened, sprinkling with a little more milk if necessary to make firm dough. Gather into ball. On lightly floured surface, roll out to 1/4-inch (1 cm) thickness. With fluted cutter, cut into 2-inch (5 cm) circles.

■ Rub heavy skillet or electric frying pan lightly with lard or shortening. In skillet

***AFTERNOON TEA SANDWICHES***

***• The sandwiches should be small enough to be eaten in two or three bites.***

***• Use fresh, close-textured white or brown bread, thinly sliced.***

***• Whipped butter at room temperature is easy to spread without tearing the bread. Spread it thinly right to edges of bread.***

***• Sandwiches with fillings like ham, chopped egg, smoked salmon or anchovy paste can be made early in the day. Trim crusts within an hour or two of serving.***

***• Hold the sandwich firmly and trim crusts with a sharp knife. Cut into four triangles or three rectangles; cover with dampened tea towel and refrigerate.***

***• To serve a dozen or fewer guests, three varieties are sufficient. For larger occasions, provide about five varieties.***

***TEA FOR THE PARTY***
***Some people suggest making a liquor of strong tea and adding boiling water as a simple method of serving large numbers. But this method lacks the fresh taste that is so important to a good cup of tea. It's better to make freshly brewed tea, allowing two cups per person and replenishing the supply as needed. Tea bags will brew more quickly than if you use loose tea, but be sure to use a good-quality brand.***

**For 25 Cups:**

***Loose tea: Tie 3/4 cup (175 mL) tea in a 20-inch (50 cm) square of cheesecloth; place in large pot and add 16 cups (4 L) boiling water.***
***Tea bags: In large pot, pour 16 cups (4 L) boiling water over 12 tea bags.***

***Let tea steep for 7 to 10 minutes, then pour it into serving teapots that have been heated by half-filling with boiling water and then emptied just before filling with tea.***

**At the Table:**

***Allow 3 cups (750 mL) milk for 25 cups of tea. Provide lemon slices (one medium lemon, very thinly sliced, is enough for 12 cups of tea). Besides jugs of milk, lemon slices and sugar, provide pots of boiling water for those who prefer weaker tea. If using loose tea, strain through a tea strainer and have a small silver or china bowl on which to rest it.***

over medium heat or electric pan at 360°F (185°C), test 1 cake by cooking for about 4 minutes or until golden brown and top is slightly puffed. Turn and cook for about 2 minutes or until browned. Adjust heat if necessary. Cook remaining cakes, transferring to plates and sprinkling with sugar while still warm. Makes about 40 little cakes.

## Maids of Honor Tarts

*Variations of these traditional tarts with a cake-like filling often appear in British tea rooms and bake shops.*

| | | |
|---|---|---|
| **1 cup** | **milk** | **250 mL** |
| **1/2 cup** | **ground almonds** | **125 mL** |
| **1/3 cup** | **fine day-old bread crumbs** | **75 mL** |
| | **Grated rind of 1 lemon** | |
| **1/4 cup** | **butter** | **50 mL** |
| **1/4 cup** | **granulated sugar** | **50 mL** |
| **1** | **egg, beaten** | **1** |
| **1/2 tsp** | **almond extract** | **2 mL** |
| **1/4 cup** | **raspberry jam** | **50 mL** |
| **36** | **2-inch (5 cm) unbaked tart shells** | **36** |

■ In saucepan over medium heat, combine milk, almonds, bread crumbs and lemon rind; bring to boil, stirring constantly. Remove from heat; stir for 1 minute. Let stand for 5 minutes.

■ Beat in butter about 1 tbsp (15 mL) at a time. Beat in sugar, egg and almond extract. Spread 1/4 tsp (1 mL) raspberry jam over bottom of each tart shell. Spoon in filling about three-quarters full. Bake in 425°F (220°C) oven for 15 to 20 minutes or until pastry is golden and filling is puffy and firm. Makes 36 tarts.

## Apricot Pecan Tea Loaf

*Serve in thin slices for an at-home tea, or cut into neat fingers for a larger stand-up occasion. Either way, spread lightly with whipped butter.*

| | | |
|---|---|---|
| **1 cup** | **chopped dried apricots** | **250 mL** |
| **1/4 cup** | **finely chopped crystallized ginger** | **50 mL** |
| **1 tsp** | **grated lemon rind** | **5 mL** |
| **2 tbsp** | **lemon juice** | **25 mL** |
| **1/3 cup** | **butter** | **75 mL** |
| **2/3 cup** | **packed brown sugar** | **150 mL** |
| **2** | **eggs** | **2** |
| **1-1/2 cups** | **all-purpose flour** | **375 mL** |
| **1-1/2 tsp** | **baking powder** | **7 mL** |
| **1/4 tsp** | **salt** | **1 mL** |
| **Pinch** | **mace** | **Pinch** |
| **1/2 cup** | **milk** | **125 mL** |
| **1/3 cup** | **chopped pecans** | **75 mL** |

■ In small bowl, stir together apricots, ginger, lemon rind and juice; set aside.

■ In mixing bowl, cream together butter and sugar; beat in eggs until smooth. Stir together flour, baking powder, salt and mace; stir into creamed mixture alternately with milk. Stir in apricot mixture and pecans.

■ Spoon into greased 8- × 4-inch (1.5 L) loaf pan. Bake in 350°F (180°C) oven for about 1 hour or until golden brown and tester inserted in center comes out clean. Let cool in pan for 10 minutes; turn out onto wire rack to let cool completely. Makes about 30 pieces (15 slices cut in half).

# A GARDENING PARTY

FOR SIXTEEN

*Invite friends or neighbors who enjoy gardening to the first outdoor party of the season. Follow a gardening theme in your choice of dishes, servers, flowers—even the food! (see sidebar below for suggestions)*

CHICKEN LIVER PÂTÉ

COUNTRY LOAF
(recipe, page 140)

HERB GARLIC BUTTER

CRUDITÉS

*GRILLED FLANK STEAK

*CAKESCAPE

FRESH FRUIT

## Grilled Flank Steak

*Well marinated and thinly sliced, flank steak is delicious and economical for large groups. Serve hot on fresh buns with lettuce and a choice of interesting toppings: pepper salsa or relishes, marinated onion rings, assorted mustards.*

| | | |
|---|---|---|
| 4 | flank steaks (about 1-1/4 lb/625 g each) | 4 |
| 1 cup | red wine | 250 mL |
| 1/2 cup | olive oil | 125 mL |
| 1/4 cup | red wine vinegar | 50 mL |
| 2 tbsp | chopped fresh thyme (or 2 tsp/10 mL) dried | 25 mL |
| 1 tsp | pepper | 5 mL |
| 4 | cloves garlic, minced | 4 |
| 2 | bay leaves | 2 |
| | Salt | |

■ Trim excess fat from steaks and score both sides at 2-inch (5 cm) intervals; place in large shallow bowl. Combine wine, oil, vinegar, thyme, pepper, garlic and bay leaves; pour over steaks. Cover and refrigerate for at least 4 hours or overnight, turning occasionally.
■ Drain steaks well, reserving marinade. Cook on greased barbecue grill, 4 to 6 inches (10 to 15 cm) from medium-hot coals or on medium-high setting, brushing often with marinade, for 4 to 6 minutes per side or until cooked to desired doneness. (Steaks may also be broiled in oven.) Transfer steaks to cutting board and let stand for 5 minutes.
■ Season steaks with salt to taste; cut diagonally across the grain into thin slices. Makes 16 to 20 servings.

## Cakescape

*Make this cake for a special birthday or a great ending to a meal. You can substitute pink lemonade or orange juice for the grapefruit juice.*

| | | |
|---|---|---|
| | CAKE: | |
| 4 | eggs | 4 |
| 1 cup | granulated sugar | 250 mL |
| 1 cup | packed brown sugar | 250 mL |
| 1 cup | vegetable oil | 250 mL |
| 2 cups | all-purpose flour | 500 mL |
| 2 tsp | baking powder | 10 mL |

*Grilled Flank Steak*

***SETTING THE SCENE***
***Use rustic everyday items in earthy tones of terra cotta and soft colors like pale green and pink. Present the bread in baskets and the pâté and herb butter in small clay pots. Create a charming still life by combining untrimmed radishes and carrots in a twig basket along with unplanted fresh herbs and flowers. (Leave small scissors on the table for snipping the fresh herbs in the basket.)***

| | | |
|---|---|---|
| 1-1/2 tsp | cinnamon | 7 mL |
| 1 tsp | salt | 5 mL |
| 1/2 tsp | baking soda | 2 mL |
| 1/2 tsp | nutmeg | 2 mL |
| 3 cups | grated raw carrots | 750 mL |
| 1/2 cup | raisins | 125 mL |
| 1/2 cup | finely chopped pecans or walnuts (optional) | 125 mL |
| | GLAZE: | |
| 1 | envelope unflavored gelatin | 1 |
| 1 cup | pink grapefruit juice | 250 mL |
| | Red food coloring (optional) | |
| | DECORATION: | |
| 1 | small fresh rosebud | 1 |
| | Parsley, scented geranium or mint leaves and parsley stems | |
| 1 | thin slice grapefruit or starfruit | 1 |

**CAKE:** Grease and flour 13- × 9-inch (3.5 L) baking dish; line bottom with waxed paper. Pour batter into pan. Bake in 350°F (180°C) oven for 40 to 50 minutes or until cake tester inserted in center comes out clean. Let cool in pan for 10 minutes. Turn out onto rack; turn cake right side up and let cool. Cover cake and refrigerate for about 1 hour or until chilled.

**GLAZE:** In small saucepan, sprinkle gelatin over grapefruit juice and let stand for 2 to 5 minutes or until softened; warm over low heat until gelatin is completely dissolved. Stir in 2 or 3 drops red food coloring (if using). Remove from heat and transfer gelatin mixture to small bowl. Place in larger bowl of ice water. Let stand, stirring frequently, for 20 to 30 minutes or just until slightly thickened.

**ASSEMBLY:** Place cake on serving platter. Tuck pieces of waxed paper underneath cake to collect any drips from glaze. Using pastry brush, spread thin layer of glaze over top and sides of cake. Refrigerate for 10 to 15 minutes or until set. Brush second thin layer of glaze over cake.

**DECORATION:** Meanwhile, separate rosebud into petals. Arrange petals, leaves and parsley stems in floral design over cake. Separate grapefruit slice into 4 to 6 sections and arrange on cake.

■ Carefully spoon remaining glaze over cake decoration. Remove waxed paper. Cover loosely and refrigerate until ready to serve or for up to 6 hours.

*Cakescape*

# A POTLUCK LUNCH

FOR SIX TO TWELVE

*Old-fashioned potluck is back and better than ever. Everyone contributing one dish to the menu is the perfect solution to today's busy schedules. Traditionally popular for club get-togethers, potluck is also the ideal way to see friends and neighbors more often. The following recipes are for 6 servings; for 12 servings, the recipes can be doubled.*

*SCALLOP CASSEROLE AU GRATIN

*BROCCOLI AND CARROT SALAD

*CREAMY LEMON PIE

*Broccoli and Carrot Salad; Scallop Casserole au Gratin; Creamy Lemon Pie*

## *Scallop Casserole au Gratin*

*This delectable scallop dish looks great and is easy to make.*

| | | |
|---|---|---|
| 1 lb | scallops (fresh or frozen) | 500 g |
| | Salt | |
| 1/2 cup | butter | 125 mL |
| 2 cups | sliced mushrooms | 500 mL |
| 1 cup | chopped celery | 250 mL |
| 3/4 cup | chopped onions | 175 mL |
| 3/4 cup | chopped sweet green pepper | 175 mL |
| 1/4 cup | all-purpose flour | 50 mL |
| 1-1/2 cups | milk | 375 mL |
| 1 cup | shredded Swiss cheese | 250 mL |
| | Pepper | |
| | TOPPING: | |
| 1 cup | soft fresh bread crumbs | 250 mL |
| 1/2 cup | chopped cashews or almonds | 125 mL |
| 2 tbsp | butter, melted | 25 mL |

■ Cut any large scallops in half. Sprinkle sparingly with salt and set aside.

■ In large skillet, melt 1/4 cup (50 mL) of the butter over medium-high heat; cook mushrooms, celery, onions and green pepper until tender, about 5 minutes. Set aside.

■ In large saucepan, melt remaining butter and blend in flour; cook for 1 minute. Gradually add milk, stirring constantly; cook until smooth and remove from heat. Stir in cheese, and salt and pepper to taste. Gently fold in vegetables and scallops. Pour into greased 9-inch (2.5 L) square baking dish.

**TOPPING:** Mix together bread crumbs, chopped nuts and melted butter; sprinkle over casserole. Bake in 350°F (180°C) oven for 25 to 30 minutes or until hot and bubbly. Makes about 6 servings.

## *Broccoli and Carrot Salad*

*For this lively dressing, use either regular or coarsely ground Dijon mustard.*

| | | |
|---|---|---|
| 2 lb | broccoli | 1 kg |
| 6 | carrots | 6 |
| 1 | head Boston lettuce | 1 |
| 1/4 cup | sliced green onions | 50 mL |
| 1 cup | shredded mozzarella cheese | 250 mL |

***POTLUCK PLANNING***
***If you're considering this easy solution to entertaining, make sure you organize the menu into categories: appetizers, entrées, salads and desserts. Divide the group evenly and either assign a category or request that people R.S.V.P., indicating the category they prefer. Beverages, paper napkins, bread, butter and condiments***

*are generally provided by the hostess.*

*If you've been asked to contribute to a potluck, make sure the dish you're preparing will travel well, serve easily and divide into many portions. Consider whether it requires oven, refrigerator or freezer space at the party.*

*Try a potluck for your next meeting or party. Inevitably there will be an abundance of tempting dishes, since most cooks tend to deliver their specialties.*

| | **DIJON DRESSING:** | |
|---|---|---|
| **1/2 cup** | **olive or vegetable oil** | **125 mL** |
| **1/4 cup** | **mayonnaise** | **50 mL** |
| **2 tbsp** | **red wine vinegar** | **25 mL** |
| **2 tbsp** | **lemon juice** | **25 mL** |
| **2 tbsp** | **Dijon mustard** | **25 mL** |
| **1** | **clove garlic, minced** | **1** |
| | **Salt and pepper** | |

■ Trim tough ends from broccoli. Peel stalks and cut into uniform diagonal slices; separate head into florets. Steam or microwave until tender-crisp. Drain and immerse in ice-cold water, then drain again.
■ Cut carrots into diagonal slices; cook in small amount of salted water just until tender. Drain and let cool.
**DIJON DRESSING:** Using blender or bowl and wire whisk, mix together oil, mayonnaise, vinegar, lemon juice, mustard, garlic, and salt and pepper to taste.
■ To serve, line salad bowl with lettuce leaves. Top with broccoli, carrots, green onions and cheese. Pour dressing over salad and toss. Makes about 6 servings.

## *Creamy Lemon Pie*

*This smooth and tangy lemon pie is the best ever.*

| | | |
|---|---|---|
| **1** | **baked 9-inch (23 cm) pastry shell** | **1** |
| | **FILLING:** | |
| **1 cup** | **granulated sugar** | **250 mL** |
| **1 cup** | **light cream** | **250 mL** |
| **3 tbsp** | **cornstarch** | **50 mL** |
| **1 tbsp** | **all-purpose flour** | **15 mL** |
| **1 tbsp** | **grated lemon rind** | **15 mL** |
| **1/3 cup** | **lemon juice** | **75 mL** |
| **1/4 cup** | **butter** | **50 mL** |
| **1 cup** | **sour cream** | **250 mL** |
| | **SOUR CREAM TOPPING:** | |
| **1 cup** | **whipping cream** | **250 mL** |
| **1/2 cup** | **sour cream** | **125 mL** |
| **2 tbsp** | **icing sugar** | **25 mL** |
| **1/2 tsp** | **almond extract** | **2 mL** |
| | **Grated lemon rind** | |
| | **Lemon slices** | |

**FILLING:** In saucepan, combine sugar, light cream, cornstarch, flour, lemon rind and juice; bring gradually to boil over medium heat, stirring constantly with wire whisk. Add butter and cook until thick and smooth. Remove from heat and let cool. Stir in sour cream and pour into baked pastry shell. Refrigerate, covered, until chilled.
**SOUR CREAM TOPPING:** Whip cream; fold in sour cream, sugar and almond extract. Spoon over lemon filling. Sprinkle with grated lemon rind and garnish with lemon slices. Makes about 6 servings.

POP
Capitol
HIGH FIDELITY
ATHIS
ORCHESTRA UNDER
THE DIRECTION
OF PERCY FAITH
RICKY
$64,000 Questions:
TV

# PARTIES WITH A DIFFERENCE

*When you really want to liven up the party season, choosing an unusual theme can be the answer. In this chapter, we offer six inventive party menus to choose from. Whether it's a fabulous Fifties snacking menu complete with Bandstand Punch and retro-food, a more unusual zodiac party highlighting recipes to match the various Sun signs, or simply a comforting bistro-style dinner to be shared with close friends, you're sure to find inspiration here. We've supplemented the menus with lots of tips and ideas for planning your event and setting the scene so that even a giant fund-raiser barbecue or a tea-tasting party for twelve will be a breeze to put together. Experiment with these themes and some of your own creations and have a wonderful time!*

# A BISTRO PARTY

FOR SIX

*Soul-warming fare, the glow of good company, and an easy ambience that's romantic in a raffish sort of way—that's bistro. Here's a comforting, classic bistro menu that will evoke memories of Montparnasse and have your guests calling a French travel agent in the morning. Bon appétit!*

*MOUSSE DE FOIES DE VOLAILLE

*POTAGE AU POIREAU

*SALADE FRISÉE AUX NOIX

*POULET AU VIN ROUGE

*PÂTÉ AU CHOCOLAT, CRÈME ANGLAISE

PLATEAU DE FROMAGES

**Recipes are given for menu items marked with an asterisk.*

## Mousse de Foies de Volaille

*This extra-smooth chicken liver pâté is very flavorful and easy to make. Place small ramekins of it on the table for pre-dinner nibbling with toast points or thinly sliced baguette.*

| | | |
|---|---|---|
| **1 lb** | **chicken livers** | **500 g** |
| **1 cup** | **chicken stock** | **250 mL** |
| **3/4 cup** | **chopped onion** | **175 mL** |
| **3** | **cloves garlic, chopped** | **3** |
| **1** | **bay leaf** | **1** |
| **Pinch** | **dried thyme** | **Pinch** |
| **1 cup** | **butter** | **250 mL** |
| | **Salt and pepper** | |
| **1 tbsp** | **water-packed green peppercorns (optional)** | **15 mL** |
| | **Coarsely crushed black peppercorns (optional)** | |

■ In heavy saucepan, combine livers, stock, onion, garlic, bay leaf and thyme; bring to boil. Reduce heat, cover and simmer for about 10 minutes or until livers are just cooked through. Discard bay leaf. Drain and reserve liquid.

■ Transfer liver mixture to blender or food processor; add 3/4 cup (175 mL) reserved liquid and process for a few seconds. Add butter and process until very smooth. Season with salt and pepper to taste.

■ Transfer mixture to bowl; stir in green peppercorns (if using). Refrigerate until cool, stirring once or twice. Spoon into small ramekins. If desired, sprinkle lightly with crushed black peppercorns. Cover with plastic wrap and refrigerate for at least 4 hours or until firm and of spreading consistency. (Pâté can be refrigerated for up to 2 days.) Makes 6 to 8 servings.

## Potage au Poireau

*This leek soup is the rustic, full-flavored kind that's typical bistro food. It may be puréed if desired, and it reheats well.*

| | | |
|---|---|---|
| **1/4 cup** | **butter** | **50 mL** |
| **4 cups** | **sliced leeks* (6 to 8 leeks)** | **1 L** |
| **1** | **small onion** | **1** |
| **5 cups** | **chicken stock** | **1.25 L** |
| **3 cups** | **finely diced peeled potatoes** | **750 mL** |
| **1/2 cup** | **light cream** | **125 mL** |
| | **Salt and pepper** | |

*Poulet au Vin Rouge; Salade Frisée aux Noix*

■ In large heavy saucepan, melt butter over medium heat. Add leeks and onion; cover and cook for 10 minutes or until softened but not browned, stirring often. Add stock and potatoes; cover and cook for 20 minutes or until potatoes are tender.

■ Transfer 2 cups (500 mL) of the soup to food processor or blender; purée until smooth. Return to saucepan; stir in cream and heat through. Season with salt and pepper to taste. Makes 6 to 8 servings.

*To prepare leeks, trim, leaving about 2 inches (5 cm) of green. Halve lengthwise and wash thoroughly under cold running water. Cut crosswise into thin slices.

## Poulet au Vin Rouge

*Nearly every bistro has a comforting chicken dish on the menu—often a* poulet sauté *or* poulet rôti *with a simple sauce flavored with wine, herbs or mustard. This one is a variation of the traditional* coq au vin, *using an oven method to make it easy.*

| | | |
|---|---|---|
| **1/4 lb** | **salt pork or fatty bacon chunk** | **125 g** |
| | **Butter** | |
| **1/2 lb** | **small mushrooms** | **250 g** |
| **18** | **very small onions, peeled** | **18** |
| **6** | **large chicken quarters or small halves** | **6** |
| **1/2 cup** | **chopped onion** | **125 mL** |
| **1 cup** | **dry red wine** | **250 mL** |
| **1 cup** | **beef stock** | **250 mL** |
| **1 tbsp** | **tomato paste (or 6 canned plum tomatoes, crushed)** | **15 mL** |
| **2** | **cloves garlic, minced** | **2** |
| **Pinch** | **dried thyme** | **Pinch** |
| **1** | **bay leaf** | **1** |
| | **Salt and pepper** | |
| **2 tbsp** | **cornstarch** | **25 mL** |
| **2 tbsp** | **water** | **25 mL** |
| | **Chopped fresh parsley** | |

■ Cut pork into 1/2-inch (1 cm) cubes (lardons). Place in saucepan and cover with cold water. Bring to boil and blanch for 2 minutes; drain and dry on paper towels. In large skillet, fry blanched pork until crisp and browned; remove and reserve.

■ Add a little butter to skillet if needed; brown mushrooms lightly. Remove with slotted spoon and set aside. Add whole onions to skillet and brown well all over; remove and set aside. Add chicken to skillet in batches and brown well on all sides, adding more butter as necessary. Transfer chicken to roasting pan or shallow casserole.

■ To skillet, add chopped onion and cook, stirring frequently, until golden. Add wine, stock, tomato paste, garlic, thyme and bay leaf; bring to boil, adding salt and pepper to taste.

■ Pour over chicken. Cover and bake in 350°F (180°C) oven for 30 minutes. Add whole onions and bake for 15 minutes; add mushrooms and bake for 10 to 15 minutes or until chicken is tender and no longer pink inside. Remove bay leaf.

■ Transfer chicken, onions, mushrooms and pork to another pan or platter; keep warm. Skim fat from pan juices; bring to boil over medium-high heat.

■ Blend cornstarch with water; stir into pan juices and cook, stirring constantly, until sauce has thickened. Taste and adjust seasoning.

■ To serve, arrange chicken, onions, mushrooms and pork cubes on serving plates; spoon sauce over and sprinkle with parsley. Makes 6 servings.

## Pâté au Chocolat, Crème Anglaise

*Bistro desserts are often named* délice, mystère *or* fantaisie, *reflecting some whimsy of the chef. This one is sometimes labelled* gateau *because it looks like a cake, but is actually a dense chocolate mousse, just firm enough to slice.* Crème Anglaise *is a light custard sauce.*

| | | |
|---|---|---|
| **4 oz** | **semisweet chocolate** | **125 g** |
| **1/2 cup** | **butter** | **125 mL** |
| **5** | **egg yolks** | **5** |
| **1/2 cup** | **granulated sugar** | **125 mL** |
| **2/3 cup** | **unsweetened cocoa powder** | **150 mL** |
| **1-1/2 cups** | **whipping cream** | **375 mL** |
| | **Crème Anglaise (recipe follows)** | |
| | **Toasted sliced almonds or hazelnuts (optional)** | |

■ Melt chocolate with butter; let cool.

■ In bowl, beat egg yolks with sugar until thick and pale in color; beat in cocoa. Beat in cooled chocolate mixture.

■ Whip cream and fold into chocolate mixture. Turn into 8-×4-inch (1.5 L) loaf pan lined with plastic wrap. Cover and refrigerate for 24 hours.

***SALADE FRISÉE AUX NOIX***

***Serve a simple but interesting* salade verte *before or with the chicken. This one uses a variety of ingredients that are popular in bistro salads.***

***On individual salad plates or large platter, arrange mixture of* frisée *(curly endive) and Boston lettuce. Scatter shreds of Belgian endive on top and arrange sliced cucumber in center. Sprinkle with pine nuts or walnuts. (If using walnuts, use a little walnut oil in dressing, if desired.) Serve with Creamy Vinaigrette.***

***CREAMY VINAIGRETTE***

***Whisk together 1 egg yolk, 1/4 cup (50 mL) white wine vinegar, 1 tsp (5 mL) Dijon mustard, and salt and pepper to taste. Gradually whisk in 3/4 cup (175 mL) oil (half olive, half vegetable). Taste and adjust seasoning, adding a little more oil, salt and pepper to taste if desired. Makes about 1 cup (250 mL).***

*Pâté au Chocolat, Crème Anglaise*

■ To serve, unmould pâté and remove plastic wrap; spoon Crème Anglaise onto dessert plates. Top each with 1/2-inch (1 cm) thick slice of chocolate pâté. Sprinkle with nuts (if using). Makes about 12 servings.

| | **CRÈME ANGLAISE:** | |
|---|---|---|
| **5** | **egg yolks** | **5** |
| **1/3 cup** | **granulated sugar** | **75 mL** |
| **2 cups** | **hot milk** | **500 mL** |
| **1 tsp** | **vanilla** | **5 mL** |

■ In bowl, beat egg yolks with sugar until thick and pale in color; gradually whisk in hot milk.
■ Transfer to very heavy saucepan; cook over medium heat, stirring constantly with wooden spoon, for 5 minutes or until thickened slightly and sauce coats back of spoon. Be careful not to boil.
■ Stir in vanilla. Strain through fine sieve into bowl. Let cool; cover and refrigerate until chilled or for up to 1 day. Makes about 2 cups (500 mL).

# A ZODIAC PARTY

FOR EIGHT

*What's your Sign? That question is sure to start a lively discussion around the dinner table—especially when every dish on the menu has been matched astrologically to the guests.*

*SEVICHE WITH PEPPERS

*FAST PASTA WITH TWO SAUCES

*GARLIC-ROAST LAMB AND VEGETABLES

*TROPICAL FRUIT FLAMBÉ

## Seviche with Peppers

*Creative Water signs enjoy interesting variations of favorite seafood dishes such as this stylish appetizer which "cooks" the fish by marinating in citrus juice.*

| | | |
|---|---|---|
| **2 lb** | **fresh fish fillets or chunks** | **1 kg** |
| **1 cup** | **lime juice** | **250 mL** |
| **1 cup** | **lemon juice** | **250 mL** |
| **1** | **each sweet green, red and yellow pepper** | **1** |
| **Half** | **small hot pepper, minced** | **Half** |
| **1** | **red onion, sliced** | **1** |
| **2** | **cloves garlic, minced** | **2** |
| **1/4 cup** | **chopped fresh coriander or parsley** | **50 mL** |
| **2 tsp** | **packed brown sugar** | **10 mL** |
| **2/3 cup** | **olive oil** | **150 mL** |
| | **Salt and pepper** | |

■ Cut fish into small cubes or strips. Place in large bowl and cover with lime and lemon juices. Cover and refrigerate for at least 5 hours or until fish is opaque. Drain, reserving 1/3 cup (75 mL) of the juice.

■ Cut sweet peppers into strips and add to fish in bowl; add hot pepper, onion, garlic, coriander, sugar, oil and reserved juice; season with salt and pepper to taste. Stir gently but thoroughly. Cover and refrigerate for at least 1 hour or up to 1 day. To serve, remove with slotted spoon to individual plates or small bowls. Makes 8 servings.

*WATER SIGNS*
***Intuitive, mysterious, emotional, sensitive, artistic; generous but need devotion in return; seek security with an edge of excitement; like familiar food with creative touches.***

**Pisces (February 19–March 20):** ***Symbolized by Two Fish, bound together but swimming in opposite directions; full of contrasts, adapting constantly to surroundings; a caring, creative cook: enjoys comfort foods with theatrical finishing touches (creamy soup presented in shimmering sea-blue glass).***

**Cancer (June 21–July 22):** ***Symbolized by the Crab, sensitive inside a protective shell; a comforting, creative Moon Child (ruling planet is the Moon, representing mother, the nourisher); home-loving, generous cook: enjoys traditional foods with interesting variations (lemon meringue trifle, hot seafood salad).***

**Scorpio (October 23–November 22):** ***Symbolized by the fearless Scorpion, also a sign of wisdom and generosity; passionate about everything; adventuresome cook: likes intense colors and assertive seasonings (steak tartare, raw oysters with red hot sauce).***

*AIR SIGNS*
***Idealistic, caring, affectionate, tolerant; liberal but not very practical; social but not very domestic; strong philosophies but non-assertive; adaptable in food choices.***

**Aquarius (January 20–February 18):** ***Symbolized by the Water Bearer, pouring out spiritual enlightenment; philosophical, humanitarian, original thinker rather than doer; will try anything new but favors simple, natural foods (breads, pastas, fruits).***

**Gemini (May 21–June 20):** ***Symbolized by the Twins; dual personality, mercurial nature, easily influenced by environment; artistic, imaginative, charming; likes food fast and interesting (small tidbits, new tastes) and anything reflecting duality (two sauces, textures, colors).***

**Libra (September 23–October 22):** ***Symbolized by the Scales, seeking balance and harmony, swinging from one extreme to another; creative cook: likes balanced flavors, well-proportioned presentations, romantic settings, soft warm foods (especially voluptuous sweets).***

# Fast Pasta with Two Sauces

*With two flavors and colors representing the contrasting natures of Air signs, this makes an interesting first course with both kinds of pasta served together in small portions.*

| | GREEN PASTA WITH WHITE CLAM SAUCE: | |
|---|---|---|
| 1/4 cup | butter | 50 mL |
| 3 | cloves garlic, minced | 3 |
| 1/4 cup | minced onion | 50 mL |
| 1 cup | whipping cream | 250 mL |
| 1/4 cup | chopped fresh parsley | 50 mL |
| 1/4 cup | dry white wine | 50 mL |
| 2 | cans (each 5 oz/142 g) baby clams (undrained) | 2 |
| | Pepper | |
| 1/2 lb | green fettuccine, cooked | 250 g |
| | Freshly grated Parmesan cheese | |

■ In skillet, melt butter over medium heat; cook garlic and onion until softened but not browned. Stir in cream, parsley, wine and 1/4 cup (50 mL) juice drained from clams. Boil gently until thickened slightly, about 5 minutes. Add clams; simmer for 1 minute or until heated through. Season with pepper to taste. Serve over hot, drained green pasta and sprinkle with Parmesan. Makes 8 small servings.

| | WHITE PASTA WITH GREEN PESTO SAUCE: | |
|---|---|---|
| 1/4 cup | butter | 50 mL |
| 2 | cloves garlic, minced | 2 |
| 2 tbsp | pine nuts | 25 mL |
| 1/2 cup | finely chopped fresh basil | 125 mL |
| 1/4 cup | freshly grated Parmesan cheese | 50 mL |
| | Salt and pepper | |
| 1/2 lb | white fettuccine, cooked | 250 g |

■ In small skillet, melt butter over medium heat; cook garlic and pine nuts until garlic is softened but not browned. Stir in basil, cheese, and salt and pepper to taste. Heat through.
■ Pour sauce immediately over hot, drained white pasta and toss well. Makes 8 small servings.

# *Garlic-Roast Lamb and Vegetables*

*This dish has a traditional earthiness plus sensual seasonings to satisfy discriminating Earth signs, who would serve it in splendid style with the best china and a fine red wine.*

| | | |
|---|---|---|
| **4 to 6 lb** | **leg of lamb (bone-in or boneless)** | **2 to 3 kg** |
| **2** | **cloves garlic, slivered** | **2** |
| | **Olive oil** | |
| **1 tsp** | **herbes de Provence (or rosemary and thyme)** | **5 mL** |
| | **Salt and pepper** | |
| **1/2 cup** | **dry red wine** | **125 mL** |
| **1/2 cup** | **beef stock** | **125 mL** |
| | **VEGETABLES:** | |
| | **Potatoes, onions, carrots and rutabaga** | |
| **1/4 cup** | **olive oil** | **50 mL** |
| **4** | **cloves garlic, minced** | **4** |
| **1 tsp** | **herbes de Provence** | **5 mL** |
| | **Salt and pepper** | |

**VEGETABLES:** Prepare enough vegetables for 8 servings using small whole vegetables or large ones cut into chunks. For milder flavor, rutabaga may be parboiled before roasting. Toss vegetables with oil, garlic, herbs, and salt and pepper to taste; place in single layer in baking pan and cover with foil.

■ Cut small slits in fat on lamb; insert garlic into slits. Rub lamb with oil, then herbs, and salt and pepper to taste. (If lamb is butterflied, rub inside surface as well; roll up and tie with string.) Place in roasting pan and roast, uncovered, in 450°F (230°C) oven for 15 minutes; add wine and stock. Reduce heat to 325°F (160°C); place pan of vegetables in oven and roast for 1 hour. Remove foil from vegetables. Roast for 30 minutes longer or until vegetables are tender, and thermometer inserted in center of lamb registers 140°F (60°C) for rare or 160°F (70°C) for medium.

■ To serve, place lamb on large platter and surround with vegetables. In sauceboat, serve pan juices to pour over lamb after slicing. (If desired, sauce may be thickened with a little cornstarch dissolved in cold water; add to pan juices and bring to boil, stirring.) Makes about 8 servings.

*EARTH SIGNS*
***Industrious, practical, serious, perfection-seekers; set high standards for themselves and others; like to be in charge; luxury-loving though frugal when necessary; like food of high quality.***

**Taurus (April 20–May 20):** ***Symbolized by the Bull, known for stubbornness and determination; hard-working but loves luxury and comfort; artistic as well as practical; prefers down-to-earth food of high quality; collects fine china, silver, linens.***

**Capricorn (December 22–January 19):** ***Symbolized by the Mountain Goat, steadfastly plodding upward to lofty goals; pragmatic and practical; responsible and organized; likes traditional foods (like Mom's apple pie) but entertains in fine style with champagne and caviar.***

**Virgo (August 23–September 22):** ***Symbolized by the Virgin; seeks purity and beauty; born perfectionist, fussy about details, disciplined and idealistic; connoisseur of fine food and wine; likes complicated menus and perfect presentations (composed salads and fruit dessert plates).***

*FIRE SIGNS*
***Confident, optimistic, energetic, independent, self-indulgent; broad interests and eclectic tastes; love good company and special occasions; enjoy cooking when in the mood but like eating out even more.***

**Aries (March 21–April 19):** ***Symbolized by the Ram, headstrong and assertive; likes action and adventure, stimulating conversation and food with strong flavors and bright colors (spicy shrimp, curried lamb).***

**Leo (July 23–August 22):** ***Symbolized by the Lion, king of the beasts, head of the table, a glowing sun god personality; generous and gregarious; loves bright, showy food and dramatic presentation (flambéed desserts, barbecued lobster).***

**Sagittarius (November 23–December 21):** ***Symbolized by the Archer, aiming at the skies; free-spirited and freedom-loving; impatient in conservative company; delights in travel and new experiences; expansive nature loves foreign cuisines and high-rising food (soufflés, exotic tall drinks).***

# Tropical Fruit Flambé

*Perfect fare for Fire signs, this glows with exotic color and flavor, and is fast and easy for impatient cooks.*

| | | |
|---|---|---|
| **1/4 cup** | **butter** | **50 mL** |
| **1/2 cup** | **granulated sugar** | **125 mL** |
| **1/2 cup** | **golden rum** | **125 mL** |
| **Pinch** | **allspice** | **Pinch** |
| **1/4 cup** | **cognac** | **50 mL** |
| **4 cups** | **thickly sliced peeled mango, papaya, pineapple, orange or banana (or combination)** | **1 L** |
| | **Mango sorbet or ice cream** | |

■ In large skillet, melt butter over medium heat; stir in sugar. Add sliced fruit to skillet and cook, stirring gently and often, for about 5 minutes or until fruit is tender but still firm. Stir in rum and allspice. Keep warm over low heat or transfer to chafing dish. Just before serving, heat cognac in small saucepan just until starting to steam. Using long match, ignite carefully and pour over fruit while still flaming. Serve over mango sorbet or ice cream. Makes 8 servings.

*PLANNING A ZODIAC PARTY*

***A zodiac party menu is ideal for a potluck group effort with friends, neighbors or dinner club. Assign one sign of the zodiac to each of twelve cooks and let them come up with an appropriate dish.***

***If you're on your own as host, you can present a menu of four courses, instead of twelve dishes, by grouping the Sun signs under their four ruling elements: Water, Air, Earth and Fire. Be sure your guest list includes at least one representative of each group. And give your table setting a different personality with each course, too, by changing place mats, dishes and flowers.***

# A FUND-RAISER BARBECUE

FOR A CROWD

*It's a winning combination—good food for a good cause. Organizing a big fund-raiser barbecue pays off in wonderful fun for all and a satisfying profit for your favorite charity. The following recipes are examples of easy-to-serve interesting food that you'll want to plan for your menu. Large cuts of barbecued beef need only salads and sweets as accompaniment. Multiply the recipes by the number of batches that will feed your crowd.*

BARBECUED BEEF

*NEW POTATO SALAD WITH HERBS

*CRUNCHY SNOW PEA AND CAULIFLOWER SALAD IN CREAMY LEMON DRESSING

*PASTA SALAD WITH PROVOLONE, PEPPERS AND PEPPERONI

*RAW VEGETABLE AND PEANUT SALAD

*ICEBOX SQUARES

*RASPBERRY CHEESECAKE

## *New Potato Salad with Herbs*

*Chopped fresh herbs make potato salad special. When hot potatoes are tossed with dressing, they absorb the flavors well. Use unpeeled red potatoes for extra color.*

| | | |
|---|---|---|
| **8** | **new potatoes (unpeeled)** | **8** |
| | **Sprig of mint or savory** | |
| | **Salt and pepper** | |
| | **VINAIGRETTE DRESSING:** | |
| **1/3 cup** | **white wine vinegar or tarragon vinegar** | **75 mL** |
| **1 tbsp** | **Dijon mustard (or hot homemade mustard)** | **15 mL** |
| **1/2 cup** | **vegetable oil** | **125 mL** |
| **1/3 cup** | **olive oil** | **75 mL** |
| **1 tsp** | **salt** | **5 mL** |
| **1/4 tsp** | **pepper** | **1 mL** |
| **1/4 cup** | **chopped fresh herbs** | **50 mL** |

■ In large saucepan of boiling salted water, cook potatoes with mint sprig for 20 to 25 minutes or until fork-tender; drain.

**VINAIGRETTE DRESSING:** Meanwhile, in large bowl, whisk vinegar with mustard. Gradually whisk in vegetable and olive oils until blended and thickened. Add salt and pepper. Stir in herbs.

■ If desired, peel hot potatoes. Cut potatoes into 1/4-inch (5 mm) thick slices; add to dressing and toss gently. Cover and refrigerate for up to 4 hours. Before serving, toss gently and season with salt and pepper to taste. Makes about 10 servings.

*Barbecued beef; New Potato Salad with Herbs; Pasta Salad with Provolone, Peppers and Pepperoni; Crunchy Snow Pea and Cauliflower Salad in Creamy Lemon Dressing*

***PLAN AHEAD***

***• Six months or more before your fund-raiser, hold a meeting. Decide on the charity or project and the amount of money you want to raise. Check with the organization to verify procedures.***

***• Decide on a theme; a sporting competition such as a golf tournament can precede your barbecue. Pick the date, place and time.***

***• Set an entry fee or ticket price. Base the fee on projected food and rental costs, plus desired profit, divided by the estimated number of participants.***

***• Compile a list of names and addresses. Design and photocopy tickets or entry forms; include all pertinent information and a tear-off section at the bottom for mail-backs. Mail forms. Appoint one person to process forms and fees.***

***• Keep a record of donated prizes, approximate value and donor names. Thank-you cards and/or receipts can be mailed to donors after the event. Post a list of donor names at the prize table.***

## *Crunchy Snow Pea and Cauliflower Salad in Creamy Lemon Dressing*

*This quick colorful salad can be made up to two hours ahead. Garnish with toasted almonds or pine nuts.*

| | | |
|---|---|---|
| 2 | heads cauliflower | 2 |
| 2 cups | snow peas, trimmed | 500 mL |
| 1/4 cup | chopped green onion or chives | 50 mL |
| 1 | sweet red pepper, chopped | 1 |
| 1 | sweet yellow or green pepper, chopped | 1 |
| 1/4 cup | toasted slivered almonds or pine nuts* | 50 mL |
| | CREAMY LEMON DRESSING: | |
| 1/2 cup | vegetable oil | 125 mL |
| 1/3 cup | mayonnaise or sour cream | 75 mL |
| 1/4 cup | lemon juice | 50 mL |
| 1 | clove garlic, minced (optional) | 1 |

■ Cut cauliflower into florets. In saucepan of boiling water, cook cauliflower for 5 to 7 minutes or until tender-crisp. Drain and rinse under cold running water; drain again and place in large bowl.

■ Blanch snow peas in boiling water for 2 to 3 minutes or until tender-crisp. Drain and rinse under cold water; drain and pat dry. Add to cauliflower along with green onion and red and yellow peppers.

**CREAMY LEMON DRESSING:** In small bowl, gradually whisk oil into mayonnaise; whisk in lemon juice. Stir in garlic (if using). Pour over vegetables, stirring to mix. (Salad can be covered and refrigerated for up to 2 hours.)

■ To serve, transfer to salad bowl; sprinkle with almonds. Makes 10 to 12 servings.

*To toast nuts, spread on baking sheet and bake in 350°F (180°C) oven for 5 to 10 minutes or until golden brown and fragrant.

## *Pasta Salad with Provolone, Peppers and Pepperoni*

*For best results, refrigerate this pasta salad overnight to allow the garlic and spice flavors to mature. If fresh herbs are available, use twice as much as the dried.*

| | | |
|---|---|---|
| 1 | pkg (900 g) fusilli | 1 |
| 1 tbsp | olive oil | 15 mL |
| 2 cups | shredded provolone cheese | 500 mL |
| 2 | small zucchini, chopped | 2 |
| 1 | red onion, chopped | 1 |
| 1 | each sweet red and green pepper, chopped | 1 |
| 1/2 lb | pepperoni sausage, chopped | 250 g |
| 1/2 cup | pitted black olives, chopped (optional) | 125 mL |
| | DRESSING: | |
| 1-1/2 cups | olive oil | 375 mL |
| 1/3 cup | red wine vinegar | 75 mL |
| 4 | cloves garlic, minced | 4 |
| 1 tbsp | dried basil | 15 mL |
| 1/2 tsp | dried oregano | 2 mL |

■ In very large pot of boiling salted water, cook pasta until al dente (tender but firm). Drain and rinse under cold running water; drain well and transfer to large bowl.

■ Add oil and toss well. Add cheese, zucchini, onion, red and green peppers, pepperoni, and olives (if using).

**DRESSING:** In jar with lid, shake together oil, vinegar, garlic, basil and oregano until well blended. Pour over pasta mixture and toss well. Refrigerate for several hours or until chilled, stirring often to distribute dressing. (Salad can be covered and refrigerated overnight.) Stir well before serving. Makes about 16 servings.

***LARGE CROWD MENUS***

***• Several months before the event, plan the menu, decide what foods will be purchased and which dishes assigned to volunteers. Take advantage of fresh seasonal produce for marinated cucumbers, pickled beets, sliced tomatoes and tossed salads. Decide which dishes can be frozen and which can be made a few days in advance.***

***• Several weeks before, check food volunteers to ensure all menu items are covered and avoid duplications. Order large items such as hips of beef and ground beef for burgers. Double-check number of participants attending to make sure you will have the right amount of food and beverages.***

***• Several days before, order items such as ice and rolls, which can be bought in advance and frozen or picked up fresh the morning of the event.***

***BEEF TIPS***

***• When barbecuing for a crowd, boneless beef cuts—rolled rib, rump, sirloin tip—are best. Less tender cuts can be used, but require marinating.***

***• Choose an evenly shaped roast with some outer fat to prevent drying. For a very large crowd (up to 200), ask your butcher to cut one***

*or two roasts (35 to 40 lb/16 to 18 kg total) from the rump or hip.*

*• To barbecue on the spit: Season roast as desired with salt, pepper, fresh garlic, rosemary, thyme. Insert spit lengthwise through center of roast, checking balance. Fasten roast securely with spit forks at both ends. Place drip pan below and slightly in front of roast to catch drips and to use for basting.*

*• To barbecue on the grill: Place roast in large shallow sturdy foil (or metal) pan. Season as desired. Place pan on grill over medium-hot coals or medium setting. Cover with barbecue lid. Occasionally baste with pan drippings and turn pan to ensure even cooking.*

*• To determine doneness, roast until meat thermometer inserted into center of roast, away from fat or spit, registers 140°F (60°C) for rare; 160°F (70 °C) for medium; 170°F (75°C) for well-done. Remove roast from barbecue and let stand for 10 to 15 minutes before carving with sharp knife.*

*Note: As outside of meat will be cooked more than inside, cook only until meat thermometer registers rare or medium. That way, you'll ensure a full range of doneness for your guests.*

# Raw Vegetable and Peanut Salad

*This unique combination shows off summer vegetables at their best.*

| | | |
|---|---|---|
| 1 | small head red cabbage, shredded | 1 |
| 1 | small head green cabbage, shredded | 1 |
| 1 | each sweet red, green and yellow pepper, julienned | 1 |
| 1 | small bunch broccoli, cut in florets | 1 |
| 1 | small head cauliflower, cut in florets | 1 |
| 1 cup | salted peanuts | 250 mL |
| | DRESSING: | |
| 1/4 cup | wine vinegar | 50 mL |
| 1 | clove garlic, minced | 1 |
| 1/2 tsp | dried oregano | 2 mL |
| 1/4 tsp | dried thyme | 1 mL |
| 1/4 tsp | salt | 1 mL |
| Pinch | pepper | Pinch |
| Pinch | granulated sugar | Pinch |
| 2/3 cup | olive or vegetable oil | 150 mL |

**DRESSING:** In small bowl, whisk together vinegar, garlic, oregano, thyme, salt, pepper and sugar; gradually whisk in oil.

■ In very large salad bowl or deep rectangular serving dish, toss together red and green cabbage, red, green and yellow peppers, broccoli, cauliflower and dressing. Sprinkle peanuts over top. Makes about 16 servings.

# Icebox Squares

*These Nanaimo-type bars have an appealing bitter chocolate taste; the recipe is crowd-size.*

| | | |
|---|---|---|
| | CRUST: | |
| 1/2 cup | butter | 125 mL |
| 1/4 cup | granulated sugar | 50 mL |
| 1/4 cup | unsweetened cocoa powder | 50 mL |
| 2 cups | graham wafer crumbs | 500 mL |
| 1 cup | unsweetened desiccated coconut | 250 mL |
| 1/2 cup | finely ground walnuts | 125 mL |
| 1 | egg, beaten | 1 |
| 1 tsp | vanilla | 5 mL |
| | FILLING: | |
| 2 cups | icing sugar | 500 mL |
| 1/4 cup | butter, softened | 50 mL |
| 3 tbsp | custard powder | 50 mL |
| Pinch | salt | Pinch |
| 3 tbsp | boiling water | 50 mL |
| | ICING: | |
| 6 oz | unsweetened chocolate | 175 g |
| 1 tbsp | butter | 15 mL |

**CRUST:** In double boiler over hot, not boiling, water, melt together butter, sugar and cocoa, stirring to dissolve. Remove from heat and sprinkle graham wafer crumbs over top. Let stand for 1 minute, then stir to blend. Stir in coconut, walnuts, egg and vanilla.

■ With damp hands, pat crust mixture evenly onto bottom of 15- × 10-inch (2 L) jelly roll pan to form thin crust. Place pan in refrigerator and chill until firm, at least 30 minutes.

**FILLING:** In small bowl and using electric mixer, mix together icing sugar, butter, custard powder and salt until crumbly. Gradually pour in boiling water, beating until smooth and of spreading consistency. Spread evenly over chilled crust. Return to refrigerator and chill for 30 minutes or until filling has chilled and hardened.

**ICING:** In double boiler over hot, not boiling, water, melt chocolate with butter; drizzle over chilled filling and spread evenly with spatula. Refrigerate for at least 15 minutes or until icing is firm. Cut into squares. Makes about forty 2-inch (5 cm) squares.

# Raspberry Cheesecake

*For a spectacular presentation, decorate this cheesecake with whipped cream, fresh raspberries and shaved chocolate.*

| | | |
|---|---|---|
| | **CRUST:** | |
| **1-1/2 cups** | **chocolate wafer crumbs** | **375 mL** |
| **3 tbsp** | **butter, melted** | **50 mL** |
| | **FILLING:** | |
| **3/4 lb** | **cream cheese** | **375 g** |
| **6** | **eggs, separated** | **6** |
| **1 cup** | **granulated sugar** | **250 mL** |
| **1 tbsp** | **lemon juice** | **15 mL** |
| **1 tbsp** | **kirsch (optional)** | **15 mL** |
| | **TOPPING:** | |
| **2 cups** | **sour cream** | **500 mL** |
| **1/4 cup** | **granulated sugar** | **50 mL** |
| **1 tsp** | **vanilla** | **5 mL** |
| | **GARNISH:** | |
| **2 cups** | **whipping cream** | **500 mL** |
| **2 tbsp** | **granulated sugar** | **25 mL** |
| **1 tsp** | **vanilla or kirsch** | **5 mL** |
| **2 cups** | **fresh raspberries** | **500 mL** |
| | **Shaved chocolate (optional)** | |
| | **SAUCE:** | |
| **2 cups** | **fresh or frozen unsweetened raspberries** | **500 mL** |
| **1/4 cup** | **granulated sugar** | **50 mL** |
| **1 tbsp** | **kirsch (optional)** | **15 mL** |

**CRUST:** Combine wafer crumbs with butter. Press onto bottom and part-way up side of 9-1/2-inch (2.5 L) springform pan. Refrigerate while preparing filling.

**FILLING:** In bowl and using electric mixer, beat cream cheese until light. Add egg yolks one at a time, beating well after each addition. Blend in 1/2 cup (125 mL) of the sugar, lemon juice, and kirsch (if using).

■ With clean beaters, beat egg whites until frothy; gradually beat in remaining sugar until stiff peaks form. Gently fold into cheese mixture until blended. Spoon into prepared crust.

■ Bake in 350°F (180°C) oven for 1 hour or until golden and center of cake is barely firm to the touch. Immediately run knife around rim to loosen cake. Let cool on rack for 30 minutes.

**TOPPING:** Combine sour cream, sugar and vanilla; spoon over top of cake, spreading evenly with spatula. Bake in 300°F (150°C) oven for 20 minutes. Let cool, then cover and refrigerate overnight or for up to 2 days.

**GARNISH:** Remove side of pan and place cake on serving plate. Whip cream with sugar and vanilla; spoon into piping bag. Pipe decoratively on side of cake and in spoked-wheel design on top. Arrange raspberries in spaces between spokes. Place shaved chocolate in center (if using).

**SAUCE:** In blender or food processor, purée raspberries. Press through sieve into small saucepan to remove seeds. Stir in sugar, and kirsch (if using); cook over medium-high heat just until mixture comes to a boil and sugar is dissolved. Spoon sauce, warm or at room temperature, on one side of each plate and place wedge of cheesecake alongside. Makes about 12 servings.

***COOKING, SERVING AND CLEAN-UP***

***• Arrange to borrow or rent barbecues, tents, lights, megaphone, prize table, card tables and chairs. Local rent-all rates are usually reasonable and some include delivery. If not, enlist drivers with vans to pick up and return heavy items.***

***• Try to cook ahead of time to avoid heat and congestion in the kitchen. Arrange to use a neighbor's oven, stove or refrigerator, if necessary. Reheat food in a microwave oven or items such as baked beans, lasagna and casseroles on an outdoor barbecue.***

***• Use foil or disposable plastic cooking dishes and plastic utensils and paper plates for easy clean-up. Have large garbage bags handy and enlist children's help in clearing.***

***• Plan on two or more serving areas (outside in food tents or on picnic tables, or in the house) to eliminate long line-ups. Appoint proficient carvers and servers to speed up things.***

***• Set up desserts in a separate area, along with coffee, tea, disposable cups, milk and sugar. (Much of this can be done in advance.)***

***• Ask people to assist in folding rental chairs and tables. After such a happy occasion, you'd be surprised how much everyone wants to pitch in!***

# A FABULOUS FIFTIES PARTY

FOR TWENTY

*Happy days are here again. . . .*
*Dust off the old 45s, dig out the chip-and-dip and get set for the Fifties Revisited. Romancing the past is a popular theme with all ages, whether you're just starting high school or were there for the "real thing." This casual menu adapts to all sorts of special occasions — a Junior High sock hop, a house-party warm-up, the Grad Prom or a nostalgic High School reunion.*

FOR A SNACKING PARTY

*BEVERAGES:
Bandstand Punch
Pink Party Punch

*NIBBLES:
Curry Snack Mix
Herbed Chive Dip
Shrimp Dip
Ham and Cheese Spread

*SANDWICHES:
Mini-Subs or Party Sandwiches

*SWEETS:
Rock 'n' Rollers
Marshmallow Squares
Polka-Dot Bars

OPTIONAL:
Barbecue Burgers or Chili Dogs
Soda Fountain and Milk Shake Bar

***SETTING THE SCENE***
***"Stars of the '50s" is a good theme for setting the mood. Decorate with posters of TV and movie stars (Marilyn Monroe, James Dean, Nanette Fabray). A tabletop jukebox (and your stereo) will bring back Elvis belting out "Heartbreak Hotel," the Platters with "The Great Pretender," and the Five Satins with "In The Still of the Night." Vintage chip-and-dip sets and aluminum serving dishes can usually be unearthed from basement cupboards or flea markets. For background, choose confetti colors like fuchsia or turquoise. And roll up the rug for dancing!***

***For a prom theme party, invite guests to appear in strapless formals, white sports coats and pink carnations. For a casual gathering, it's pony tails, saddle shoes, V-neck pullovers, crinoline skirts and leather jackets.***

*(Clockwise from top right) Pink Party Punch; Mini-Subs; mixed nuts and seeds; Curry Snack Mix; Herbed Chive Dip; Shrimp Dip; Rock'n'Rollers; Marshmallow Squares; Polka-Dot Bars; Ham and Cheese Spread*

## Curry Snack Mix

*Variations of the popular "nuts and bolts" abounded in the '50s.*

| | | |
|---|---|---|
| **2 tbsp** | **butter** | **25 mL** |
| **2 cups** | **Shreddies or similar cereal** | **500 mL** |
| **1 cup** | **small pretzels or pretzel sticks** | **250 mL** |
| **1 cup** | **salted peanuts** | **250 mL** |
| **1/2 cup** | **blanched almonds** | **125 mL** |
| **1/2 cup** | **raisins** | **125 mL** |
| **1 tbsp** | **curry powder** | **15 mL** |
| **1 tsp** | **cinnamon** | **5 mL** |
| **1 tsp** | **salt** | **5 mL** |

■ In large skillet, melt butter over medium heat. Add cereal, pretzels, peanuts, almonds and raisins. Sprinkle with curry powder, cinnamon and salt. Stir until mixed well and heated through; let cool. Makes about 5 cups (1.25 L).

## Herbed Chive Dip

*The '50s marked the dawn of the television age and snacking became a national pastime. House parties also called for a new kind of casual food, and potato chip dips were the answer.*

| | | |
|---|---|---|
| **2 cups** | **sour cream** | **500 mL** |
| **1/2 cup** | **mayonnaise** | **125 mL** |
| **1/4 cup** | **minced chives or green onions** | **50 mL** |
| **1** | **clove garlic, minced** | **1** |
| **1/4 cup** | **chopped fresh parsley** | **50 mL** |
| **1 tbsp** | **dried dillweed** | **15 mL** |
| **1 tbsp** | **lemon juice** | **15 mL** |
| | **Salt and pepper** | |

■ In bowl, blend together sour cream, mayonnaise, chives, garlic, parsley, dillweed, lemon juice, and salt and pepper to taste. Chill for at least 1 hour to blend flavors. Makes about 3 cups (750 mL).

## Shrimp Dip

*Fifties dipping occasionally ventured past sour cream to seafood mixtures like this, which were considered extravagant but low-cal. Today, we'd serve it with vegetable dippers, interesting small crackers or breadsticks.*

| | | |
|---|---|---|
| **2 cups** | **cottage cheese** | **500 mL** |
| **1/2 cup** | **ketchup** | **125 mL** |
| **1/4 cup** | **milk** | **50 mL** |
| **2 tbsp** | **minced onion** | **25 mL** |
| **2 tbsp** | **lemon juice** | **25 mL** |
| **1 tsp** | **prepared horseradish** | **5 mL** |
| **2** | **cans (4 oz/113 g each) tiny shrimp, drained** | **2** |
| | **Salt and pepper** | |

■ In food processor or blender, combine cottage cheese, ketchup, milk, onion, lemon juice and horseradish; process until smooth. Add shrimp; process briefly until finely chopped. Season with salt and pepper to taste. Makes about 4 cups (1 L).

## Ham and Cheese Spread

*Serve this in small pots, with spreading knives, alongside a basket of crackers.*

| | | |
|---|---|---|
| **1 lb** | **cream cheese, softened** | **500 g** |
| **2 cups** | **shredded Cheddar cheese** | **500 mL** |
| **2** | **cans (85 g each) devilled ham** | **2** |
| **1/4 cup** | **chopped green onion** | **50 mL** |
| **1/4 cup** | **(approx) mayonnaise** | **50 mL** |
| | **Salt and pepper** | |

■ In bowl, blend together cream cheese, Cheddar, devilled ham, green onion and mayonnaise. Add more mayonnaise if necessary to give spreading consistency. Season with salt and pepper to taste. Makes about 4 cups (1 L).

***FIFTIES FOOD***
***Fifties food was a celebration of new casual attitudes—barbecues, food drive-ins and takeouts sprouted all over the country. Pizzas and burgers also became synonymous with informal house-party food. In contrast, special occasions such as prom parties meant fancier fare; buffets featured bubbly punch bowls and tiny pastel sandwiches. An array of sweets often reflected the latest rage in recipes using the new "convenience foods" and packaged ingredients. Don't let this audacious stuff offend your purist '90s sensibilities! Whip up a menu of retro-food and enjoy the time warp.***

***BANDSTAND PUNCH***
***In punch bowl, combine 1 can (12 oz/341 mL) each frozen orange juice and lemonade concentrates and 1 can (48 oz/1.36 L) pineapple juice. Just before serving, add ice cubes, 2 bottles (750 mL each) ginger ale and 2 bottles (750 mL each) club soda. Makes about 40 servings (4 oz/125 mL each).***

***PINK PARTY PUNCH***
***In punch bowl, combine 1 can (280 mL) frozen raspberry cocktail concentrate and 1 can (12 oz/341 mL) frozen pink lemonade concentrate. Just before serving, add ice cubes, 1 bottle (750 mL) pink cream soda and 2 bottles (750 mL each) club soda. Makes about 25 servings (4 oz/125 mL each).***

***MINI-SUBS OR PARTY SANDWICHES***
***Tiny sandwiches that look nice and have lots of flavor always disappear quickly from party buffet tables. Traditional fancy shapes are perennially popular; arrange a large tray of '50s-style checkerboard, ribbon or pinwheel sandwiches with fillings of salmon, tuna, cheese, egg salad, minced ham or peanut butter-and-banana.***

***Alternatively, offer mini-versions of the ever-popular Submarines (called Heroes, Poorboys or Dagwoods over the years). The easiest way is to set out a basket of tiny submarine-shaped rolls (split in half), and a tray of small-sized sliced meats, cheeses, tomatoes, pickles, onion rings and coleslaw, along with mustards and mayonnaise; let guests assemble their own.***

## Rock 'n' Rollers

*Rock and roll goes on and on, and so do variations of a popular '50s recipe, Rocky Road Bars.*

| | | |
|---|---|---|
| **1-1/2 cups** | **graham wafer crumbs** | **375 mL** |
| **1/2 cup** | **butter, melted** | **125 mL** |
| **2 cups** | **flaked coconut** | **500 mL** |
| **1 cup** | **chopped walnuts** | **250 mL** |
| **1-1/2 cups** | **miniature marshmallows** | **375 mL** |
| **1** | **can (14 oz/398 mL) sweetened condensed milk** | **1** |
| **1 cup** | **chocolate chips** | **250 mL** |
| **1 tbsp** | **butter** | **15 mL** |

■ In 9-inch (2.5 L) square cake pan (or, for thinner bars, 13-×9-inch/3.5 L pan), combine crumbs and melted butter, mixing with fork. Spread mixture out evenly and press down. Spread coconut evenly over crumbs, then nuts and then marshmallows. Pour condensed milk evenly over top. Bake in 350°F (180°C) oven for about 20 minutes or until browned on top. Let cool (will firm up as it cools).

■ Melt chocolate chips with butter; drizzle evenly over top. Let cool thoroughly and cut into small bars or squares. (If weather is warm, store in refrigerator.) Makes about 3 dozen.

## Marshmallow Squares

*This easy confection has lots of decorating choices—it may be tinted with food coloring or sprinkled while still sticky with a variety of toppings (sliced almonds, chopped nuts, candied cherries or shredded coconut).*

| | | |
|---|---|---|
| **3/4 cup** | **butter** | **175 mL** |
| **1/4 cup** | **packed brown sugar** | **50 mL** |
| **1-1/2 cups** | **all-purpose flour** | **375 mL** |
| **1** | **envelope unflavored gelatin** | **1** |
| **3/4 cup** | **granulated sugar** | **175 mL** |
| **3/4 cup** | **cold water** | **175 mL** |
| **3/4 cup** | **icing sugar** | **175 mL** |
| **3/4 tsp** | **almond extract** | **4 mL** |

■ In bowl, cream together butter and brown sugar; blend in flour until crumbly. Press into 12-×8-inch (3 L) baking dish. Bake in 325°F (160°C) oven for 15 to 20 minutes or until lightly browned.

■ In saucepan, combine gelatin, granulated sugar and cold water; bring to boil and boil for 3 minutes. Remove from heat; stir in icing sugar and almond extract. Pour into mixing bowl and let cool to lukewarm. With electric mixer at high speed, beat until mixture will hold stiff peaks. Spread over baked base. Chill until set. Cut into small squares with dampened knife. Makes about 3 dozen.

## Polka-Dot Bars

*Chewy butterscotch bars have a '50s taste that everyone still likes. Baking gumdrops are usually available in supermarkets; jujubes are easily cut into small pieces with scissors.*

| | | |
|---|---|---|
| **1 cup** | **butterscotch chips** | **250 mL** |
| **1/4 cup** | **butter** | **50 mL** |
| **2** | **eggs** | **2** |
| **1/2 cup** | **packed brown sugar** | **125 mL** |
| **1/2 tsp** | **vanilla** | **2 mL** |
| **3/4 cup** | **all-purpose flour** | **175 mL** |
| **1 tsp** | **baking powder** | **5 mL** |
| **1/4 tsp** | **salt** | **1 mL** |
| **1 cup** | **baking gumdrops or cut-up jujubes** | **250 mL** |
| | **Icing sugar** | |

■ Melt butterscotch chips with butter, stirring until smooth. In bowl, beat eggs; gradually beat in sugar. Blend in vanilla and melted butterscotch mixture. Combine flour, baking powder and salt; add gumdrops and toss to coat. Stir into butterscotch mixture.

■ Spread evenly in greased 9-inch (2.5 L) square cake pan. Bake in 350°F (180°C) oven for 25 to 30 minutes or until tester inserted in center comes out clean. Let cool; sprinkle with icing sugar. Cut into small bars. Makes about 2 dozen.

# AN INTERNATIONAL TEA-TASTING PARTY

FOR TWELVE

*Tea is as complex and adventurous a subject as wine — and an international tea-tasting party is a charming alternative to wine-tasting. Sampling a number of different teas from various countries gives everyone a chance to explore new tastes and flavors. And you can match the tea's country of origin with complementary foods. As most teas come from India and China, here's a sampling of sips and nibbles. For a sweet ending, add a flavored tea (such as apricot) and serve with an apricot pastry or cookie.*

CHINA:

LAPSANG SOUCHONG, GREEN GUNPOWDER AND JASMINE TEAS

*SHRIMP-STUFFED MUSHROOMS

*BARBECUED PORK

INDIA:

DARJEELING AND ASSAM TEAS

*SAMOSAS

*SPICY YOGURT CHICKEN

*CHINESE TEAS*
**Lapsang Souchong (oolong):** *Smoky, full and aromatic. Excellent with barbecued pork or duck.*
**Green Gunpowder (green):** *A clear, fragrant taste with slight astringency and lots of body. Excellent with all Chinese or Japanese food.*
**Jasmine (oolong):** *Smooth, mellow and flowery, with the scent of jasmine flowers.*

*INDIAN TEAS*
**Darjeeling (black):** *A clear muscatel-like flavor. It matches well with the Spicy Yogurt Chicken, or sip after dinner as a digestif.*
**Assam (black):** *Strong, pungent, full-bodied with a distinct malt taste. It complements samosas and is a strong morning pick-me-up.*

*FLAVORED TEA*
**Apricot:** *Ceylon tea infused with the oil of apricots. A refreshing dessert or afternoon tea. Drink without milk.*

*CHILI DIP*
*In small serving bowl, combine 1/4 cup (50 mL) rice vinegar, 2 tbsp (25 mL) soy sauce, 1/2 tsp (2 mL) chili paste and 1/2 tsp (2 mL) sesame oil.*

*Shrimp-Stuffed Mushrooms; Barbecued Pork*

# Shrimp-Stuffed Mushrooms

*This typical Chinese dim sum dish can be made ahead, covered and refrigerated for up to 8 hours, then steamed when needed.*

| | | |
|---|---|---|
| **1/4 cup** | **soy sauce** | **50 mL** |
| **1** | **clove garlic, crushed** | **1** |
| **2 tbsp** | **vegetable oil** | **25 mL** |
| **24** | **large mushroom caps (about 1 lb/500 g)** | **24** |
| **1/4 cup** | **chicken stock** | **50 mL** |
| | **Chili Dip (see sidebar)** | |
| | **SHRIMP PASTE:** | |
| **1/2 lb** | **shrimp, peeled and deveined** | **250 g** |
| **1 tbsp** | **vegetable oil** | **15 mL** |
| **1** | **egg white** | **1** |
| **1 tsp** | **cornstarch** | **5 mL** |
| **1 tsp** | **minced gingerroot** | **5 mL** |
| **Pinch** | **granulated sugar** | **Pinch** |
| **1 tsp** | **sesame oil** | **5 mL** |
| **1 tsp** | **soy sauce** | **5 mL** |
| **1/4 tsp** | **salt** | **1 mL** |
| | **Pepper** | |

■ In large bowl, mix together soy sauce, garlic and oil. Add mushrooms, stirring gently to coat; set aside.
**SHRIMP PASTE:** Meanwhile, in food processor or blender, combine shrimp, vegetable oil, egg white, cornstarch, ginger, sugar, sesame oil, soy sauce, salt, and pepper to taste. Using on-off motion, process until shrimp are finely chopped. Fill each mushroom with shrimp paste, pressing down firmly. Arrange in two 9-inch (23 cm) pie plates; pour in chicken stock.
■ Place round cookie cutter in wok or deep saucepan. Add enough water to come halfway up cutter; bring to boil. Place one pie plate on ring; cover and steam for 5 minutes or until mixture is pink and firm. Repeat with remaining mushrooms. Serve hot or cold with Chili Dip. Makes 24 stuffed mushrooms.

# Barbecued Pork

*If five-spice powder is unavailable, use a pinch each of cinnamon, nutmeg and cloves.*

| | | |
|---|---|---|
| **2 lb** | **boneless pork butt** | **1 kg** |
| **1** | **pkg mini-pita breads, halved** | **1** |
| **1 cup** | **hoisin sauce** | **250 mL** |
| **6** | **green onions, sliced** | **6** |
| | **MARINADE:** | |
| **1/4 cup** | **soy sauce** | **50 mL** |
| **1/4 cup** | **sherry** | **50 mL** |
| **1/4 cup** | **hoisin sauce** | **50 mL** |
| **2 tbsp** | **granulated sugar** | **25 mL** |
| **1/2 tsp** | **five-spice powder** | **2 mL** |
| **3** | **cloves garlic, crushed** | **3** |
| | **GLAZE:** | |
| **1/4 cup** | **honey** | **50 mL** |
| **1 tbsp** | **soy sauce** | **15 mL** |
| **1 tbsp** | **wine vinegar** | **15 mL** |
| **1 tsp** | **sesame oil** | **5 mL** |

■ Trim thin layer of fat from pork. Cut meat into strips 6 inches (15 cm) long, 2 inches (5 cm) wide and 1 inch (2.5 cm) thick.
**MARINADE:** In large bowl, combine soy sauce, sherry, hoisin sauce, sugar, five-spice powder and garlic. Add pork; marinate in refrigerator for at least 6 hours or overnight.
■ Remove meat from marinade and place on rack on foil-lined baking sheet; reserve marinade. Bake in 450°F (230°C) oven for 15 minutes; turn and brush with marinade. Bake for 15 to 20 minutes or until juices run clear when meat is pierced with fork.
**GLAZE:** In saucepan, combine honey, soy sauce, vinegar and sesame oil over medium heat; cook, stirring, for 2 minutes or until honey dissolves. Brush over pork. Let cool. Slice thinly and transfer to platter. Serve with pita bread, small bowls of hoisin sauce and green onions. Makes about 12 servings.

*Samosas; Spicy Yogurt Chicken*

# *Samosas*

*In India, samosas — deep-fried pastries filled with a spicy meat mixture — are usually served at teatime. They can be reheated in a 350°F (180°C) oven for 5 minutes. If you don't want to make pastry, substitute frozen puff pastry; defrost, cut into 3-inch (8 cm) circles, fill and bake in 450°F (230°C) oven for 10 minutes.*

| | | |
|---|---|---|
| | **PASTRY:** | |
| **2 cups** | **all-purpose flour** | **500 mL** |
| **1 tsp** | **salt** | **5 mL** |
| **1/4 cup** | **shortening, melted** | **50 mL** |
| **3/4 cup** | **(approx) plain yogurt** | **175 mL** |
| **1** | **egg white** | **1** |
| | **Vegetable oil for deep-frying** | |
| | **Mint Dipping Sauce (recipe follows)** | |
| | **FILLING:** | |
| **1 tsp** | **each ground coriander and cumin** | **5 mL** |
| **1/2 tsp** | **turmeric** | **2 mL** |
| **1/4 tsp** | **each cloves and nutmeg** | **1 mL** |
| **Half** | **green chili pepper, seeded and finely chopped (or 3/4 tsp/4 mL cayenne pepper)** | **Half** |
| **1 tbsp** | **vegetable oil** | **15 mL** |
| **Half** | **onion, finely chopped** | **Half** |
| **2** | **cloves garlic, minced** | **2** |
| **1 tbsp** | **finely chopped gingerroot** | **15 mL** |
| **1** | **small stick cinnamon** | **1** |
| **Half** | **tomato, chopped** | **Half** |
| **1/2 lb** | **lean ground beef** | **250 mL** |

*MAKING THE TEAS*
***To make the teas, rinse out one teapot with hot water for each type of tea. (If you have pretty Chinese teapots and cups, use them for the Chinese teas.) Add one tea bag or teaspoonful of loose tea per person plus "one for the pot" (using a tea egg makes removal of the leaves easier). Bring fresh water to the boil and pour it over the tea, allowing about 2 cups (500 mL) of water per teaspoonful of tea or tea bag. Let the tea steep for five minutes, remove the tea eggs or tea bags, then serve. Cover the teapots with tea cosies if desired, and let guests help themselves.***

***Serve milk, never cream, and sugar but encourage guests to first taste the teas clear to discover their distinctive flavors. And do try to use china cups – tea definitely tastes better when sipped from china.***

| | | |
|---|---|---|
| **1/2 cup** | **water** | **125 mL** |
| **2 tsp** | **lime juice** | **10 mL** |
| **1** | **bay leaf** | **1** |
| | **Salt and pepper** | |

**PASTRY:** In bowl, stir together flour and salt; mix in shortening. Blend with fingertips until very crumbly. Stir in enough yogurt to make soft dough; gather into ball.

■ On lightly floured surface, knead until smooth and satiny, about 5 minutes. Cover and chill for 30 minutes. Divide dough in half and roll out each half as thinly as possible. Transfer to baking sheet; cover and chill for 1 hour.

**FILLING:** Meanwhile, combine coriander, cumin, turmeric, cloves, nutmeg and chili pepper; set aside. In heavy saucepan, heat oil over medium heat; cook onion for 10 minutes. Add garlic and ginger; cook until softened, about 2 minutes. Stir in spice mixture and cinnamon stick; cook until fragrant, about 1 minute.

■ Stir in tomato and meat; cook, stirring to break up meat, until meat is no longer pink. Add water, lime juice and bay leaf. Bring to boil; reduce heat and simmer, covered, for 1 hour or until thickened and liquid has evaporated. Remove and discard bay leaf and cinnamon stick; season with salt and pepper to taste.

■ Roll out chilled dough to 1/16-inch (1.5 mm) thickness; cut into 3-inch (8 cm) circles. Place 1/2 tsp (2 mL) filling on lower half of each circle; brush lower edge with egg white. Fold in half; pinch edges together to seal.

■ In skillet or deep-fryer, heat oil to 375°F (190°C) or until 1-inch (2.5 cm) cube of white bread turns golden brown in 50 seconds. Cook samosas, in batches, for 1 minute on each side or until golden brown. Drain on rack. Serve with Mint Dipping Sauce. Makes about 24 samosas.

| | | |
|---|---|---|
| | **MINT DIPPING SAUCE:** | |
| **1/2 cup** | **Worcestershire sauce** | **125 mL** |
| **1/2 cup** | **mint sauce** | **125 mL** |

■ In small bowl, mix together Worcestershire and mint sauces. Refrigerate for 2 hours to blend flavors. Makes 1 cup (250 mL).

## *Spicy Yogurt Chicken*

*This moist and flavorful dish is garnished with salted red onions to mollify the strong flavor.*

| | | |
|---|---|---|
| **2 cups** | **plain yogurt** | **500 mL** |
| **3** | **cloves garlic, minced** | **3** |
| **2 tbsp** | **minced gingerroot** | **25 mL** |
| **1 tbsp** | **ground cumin** | **15 mL** |
| **1 tbsp** | **lime juice** | **15 mL** |
| **2 tsp** | **ground coriander** | **10 mL** |
| **1 tsp** | **each ground cardamom, turmeric and cinnamon** | **5 mL** |
| **1/2 tsp** | **each cayenne pepper and ground cloves** | **2 mL** |
| **6** | **boneless skinless chicken breasts** | **6** |
| | **GARNISH:** | |
| **2** | **red onions, thinly sliced** | **2** |
| **1 tsp** | **salt** | **5 mL** |
| **1** | **lime or lemon, cut in wedges** | **1** |

■ In bowl, beat together yogurt, garlic, ginger, cumin, lime juice, coriander, cardamom, turmeric, cinnamon, cayenne and cloves. Add chicken; cover and marinate in refrigerator overnight.

■ Remove chicken from marinade. Arrange on rack on baking sheet. Bake in 400°F (200°C) oven for 30 to 35 minutes or until golden brown and no longer pink inside. Let cool. Cut chicken into 1/2-inch (1 cm) slices. Transfer to serving platter. Cover and refrigerate for up to 2 days.

**GARNISH:** One hour before serving, sprinkle onion slices with salt; let stand. Just before serving, garnish serving platter with lime wedges and onion slices. Makes about 12 servings.

# A DESSERT SAMPLER PARTY

FOR TWELVE

*A dessert-lover's dream come true — a sampling of nine sensational sweets — is also an unusual variation on the dessert-and-coffee theme. Dessert samplers (small portions of different desserts) are popular in fashionable restaurants; they are often served in groups of three on a plate. For a home party, you could offer sampler trios on popular flavor themes. Here we've chosen chocolate, orange and caramel. Present them in flavor groups on a buffet, and invite guests to sample one trio at a time. The preparation of three trios is easily shared by three different cooks; if you're on your own, one trio would be fine for a smaller dessert party or as an elegant ending to a dinner party.*

*ORANGE MOUSSE

*CHOCOLATE CANDIED ORANGE PEEL

*ORANGE-CARDAMOM POUND CAKE

*WHITE-CHOCOLATE CHEESECAKE SQUARES

*MILK-CHOCOLATE MOUSSE IN DARK-CHOCOLATE CUPS

*DARK-CHOCOLATE ROULADE

*CRÈME CARAMEL

*CARAMEL ICE CREAM

*CARAMEL ALMOND BARK

# Orange Mousse

*Light and creamy, these little orange mousses are brimming with refreshing citrus flavor. Nonstick muffin tins make the job of unmoulding easy.*

| | | |
|---|---|---|
| **1** | **envelope unflavored gelatin** | **1** |
| **3 tbsp** | **orange liqueur** | **50 mL** |
| **3** | **egg yolks** | **3** |
| **2/3 cup** | **granulated sugar** | **150 mL** |
| **1/3 cup** | **frozen orange juice concentrate, thawed** | **75 mL** |
| **1/3 cup** | **water** | **75 mL** |
| **1 cup** | **whipping cream** | **250 mL** |
| **12** | **orange segments** | **12** |
| **2 tbsp** | **chopped pistachio nuts** | **25 mL** |

■ In small saucepan, sprinkle gelatin over liqueur; let stand for 5 minutes to soften. Over low heat, warm gelatin until dissolved.

■ In large saucepan, beat egg yolks with sugar until smooth and fluffy. Mix together orange juice concentrate and water; stir into egg yolk mixture. Cook, whisking, over low heat for about 10 minutes or until slightly thickened. Whisk in gelatin mixture.

■ Transfer to large bowl and set over larger bowl of ice and water. Let stand, stirring often, for 10 to 15 minutes or until cool but not set.

■ Meanwhile, whip cream. Gently fold into cooled orange mixture.

■ Line bottoms of 12 muffin cups with circles of parchment or waxed paper. Pat orange segments dry; place one in each muffin cup. Spoon mousse into cups; tap pan gently to remove any air pockets. Cover and refrigerate until set, at least 2 hours or up to 2 days.

■ To unmould, dip muffin tin in warm water for 30 seconds, then run knife around edges of mousses. Invert onto flat platter. Using metal spatula, transfer to individual plates; remove paper. Garnish with sprinkling of pistachios. Makes 12 small servings.

*Orange-Cardamom Pound Cake; Chocolate Candied Orange Peel; Orange Mousse*

# Chocolate Candied Orange Peel

*When removing the peel from the oranges, include the white pithy part under the peel. It tenderizes and sweetens when fully cooked.*

| | | |
|---|---|---|
| 4 | **thick-skinned oranges** | 4 |
| 2 cups | **granulated sugar** | 500 mL |
| 6 oz | **bittersweet or semisweet chocolate** | 175 g |

■ With sharp knife, remove large pieces of peel from oranges including white pith. Cut into 2- × 1/2-inch (5 × 1 cm) strips. Place peel in large pot of water. Bring to boil; reduce heat to medium and cook, covered, for 15 minutes. Drain, add fresh water and repeat cooking. Drain peel.

■ In large saucepan, combine 1 cup (250 mL) of the sugar with 6 cups (1.5 L) water; bring to boil. Add peel and cook, uncovered, over medium-high heat for about 1 hour and 15 minutes or until peel is tender and almost all syrup has been absorbed. Drain peel.

■ Spread remaining sugar in shallow dish. Working with a few pieces at a time, dredge peel with sugar. Transfer to racks set over baking sheets. Let dry overnight.

■ In top of double boiler over hot, not boiling, water, melt chocolate. Dip pieces of peel halfway into chocolate; dry on waxed paper. Makes about 32 pieces.

# Orange-Cardamom Pound Cake

*When wrapped carefully, this cake keeps well for one week at room temperature or in the freezer for up to two months.*

| | | |
|---|---|---|
| 1-1/4 cups | **granulated sugar** | 300 mL |
| 1 cup | **butter** | 250 mL |
| 5 | **eggs, separated** | 5 |
| 2 tbsp | **frozen orange juice concentrate, thawed** | 25 mL |
| 1 tsp | **vanilla** | 5 mL |
| 2 cups | **sifted cake-and-pastry flour** | 500 mL |
| 1 tsp | **ground cardamom** | 5 mL |

■ Line greased 9- × 5-inch (2 L) loaf pan with waxed or parchment paper; grease paper. Set aside.

■ In large bowl, cream together sugar and butter until fluffy. Add egg yolks one at a time, beating well after each addition. Beat in orange juice concentrate, orange rind and vanilla. Stir together flour and cardamom; stir into batter. (Batter will be very stiff.)

■ In large bowl, beat egg whites until stiff peaks form. Stir about one-quarter into batter, then fold in remaining whites.

■ Spoon batter into prepared loaf pan. Bake in 325°F (160°C) oven for 1-1/4 to 1-1/2 hours or until tester inserted in center comes out clean. Let cool in pan on wire rack for 10 minutes. Turn out cake and let cool completely on rack.

# White-Chocolate Cheesecake Squares

*White chocolate makes a cheesecake even smoother and more luscious than usual. This cake freezes well.*

| | | |
|---|---|---|
| | **CRUST:** | |
| 1-1/2 cups | **crushed chocolate wafers** | 375 mL |
| 1/3 cup | **butter, melted** | 75 mL |
| | **FILLING:** | |
| 8 oz | **white chocolate** | 250 g |
| 1 lb | **cream cheese** | 500 g |
| 1/2 cup | **granulated sugar** | 125 mL |
| 3 | **eggs** | 3 |
| 1 cup | **sour cream** | 250 mL |
| 1 tsp | **grated orange rind** | 5 mL |
| 1 tsp | **vanilla** | 5 mL |
| | **TOPPING:** | |
| 1 cup | **sour cream** | 250 mL |
| 1 tbsp | **granulated sugar** | 15 mL |
| 1/2 tsp | **vanilla** | 2 mL |

*Dark-Chocolate Roulade; Milk-Chocolate Mousse in Dark-Chocolate Cup; White-Chocolate Cheesecake Square*

| | GARNISH: | |
|---|---|---|
| | Chocolate curls or drizzle | |
| 1 tbsp | icing sugar | 15 mL |

**CRUST:** Combine wafer crumbs with butter; press into bottom of 8- × 12-inch (3 L) pan.
**FILLING:** Melt white chocolate; let cool for 5 minutes. Meanwhile, in bowl, beat cream cheese with sugar until light; beat in eggs, one at a time. Beat in melted white chocolate, sour cream, orange rind and vanilla. Pour over crumb mixture in pan and bake in 350°F (180°C) oven for 30 to 35 minutes or just until set.
**TOPPING:** Combine sour cream, sugar and vanilla. Spread over hot cake and return to oven for 3 to 5 minutes. Let cool completely.
**GARNISH:** Scatter chocolate curls over cake or drizzle with melted chocolate. Dust lightly with icing sugar. Chill. Cut into squares to serve. Makes about 12 servings.

## Milk-Chocolate Mousse in Dark-Chocolate Cups

*Look for the foil or paper muffin cups that are 1 to 1-1/2 inches (2.5 to 4 cm) in diameter — just the right size for these chocolate cups.*

| | CUPS: | |
|---|---|---|
| 10 oz | bittersweet or semisweet chocolate, chopped | 300 g |
| | MOUSSE: | |
| 8 oz | milk chocolate, chopped | 250 g |
| 1/4 cup | butter | 50 mL |
| 1/4 cup | strongly brewed coffee | 50 mL |
| 1 cup | whipping cream | 250 mL |
| 12 | chocolate coffee beans* | 12 |

**CUPS:** In top of double boiler over hot, not boiling, water, melt bittersweet chocolate; let cool slightly. With small spoon, coat insides of 12 small foil or paper muffin liners. Place on baking sheet and freeze for about 1 hour or until chocolate is firm. Carefully peel off liners. Cover and refrigerate for up to 1 week or freeze for up to 1 month.
**MOUSSE:** Meanwhile, in top of double boiler over hot, not boiling, water, heat milk chocolate with butter and coffee until chocolate has melted; let cool to room temperature.
■ Whip cream; fold into cool milk-chocolate mixture. Pipe or spoon into prepared chocolate cups. Top each mousse with 1 coffee bean. Refrigerate for at least 3 hours or up to 2 days, or wrap and freeze for up to 2 weeks. Makes 12 small servings.
*Available at confectionary and specialty food stores.

## Dark-Chocolate Roulade

*If this roulade cracks while rolling, don't worry since it will be sliced and then arranged on plates. To store the roulade cake in the freezer, freeze on the baking sheet until firm then wrap well in plastic wrap.*

| | | |
|---|---|---|
| **2 oz** | **bittersweet or semisweet chocolate, chopped** | **60 g** |
| **6** | **eggs, separated** | **6** |
| **2/3 cup** | **granulated sugar** | **150 mL** |
| **1/4 cup** | **unsweetened cocoa powder, sifted** | **50 mL** |
| | **Unsweetened cocoa powder** | |
| | **FILLING:** | |
| **1 cup** | **whipping cream** | **250 mL** |
| **4 oz** | **bittersweet or semisweet chocolate, chopped** | **125 g** |

■ Line greased 15- × 10-inch (2 L) jelly-roll pan with waxed or parchment paper; grease and flour paper. Set aside.

■ In top of double boiler over hot, not boiling, water, melt chocolate; let cool slightly and set aside.

■ In bowl and using electric mixer, beat egg yolks with 1/3 cup (75 mL) of the sugar for 2 to 3 minutes or until light and pale in color. Stir in sifted cocoa and melted chocolate.

■ In large bowl, beat egg whites until soft peaks form; beat in remaining sugar until stiff peaks form. Stir about one-quarter into chocolate mixture; fold in remaining whites.

■ Spoon batter into prepared pan and spread evenly. Bake in 350°F (180°C) oven for about 20 minutes or until top of cake springs back lightly when touched. Let cool in pan for 10 minutes.

■ Dust top of cake heavily with cocoa. Loosen edges of cake and invert onto clean tea towel; carefully remove paper. If edges of cake are dry, trim with serrated knife. Starting at one long side, roll up cake in tea towel. Let cool completely, about 20 minutes.

**FILLING:** Meanwhile, heat 1/2 cup (125 mL) of the cream with chocolate over medium heat until chocolate has melted; mix well and let cool. Stir in remaining cream; refrigerate until chilled. Using electric mixer, beat until consistency of whipped cream.

■ Unroll cake; spread evenly with filling. Roll up cake and transfer to baking sheet. (Cake can be covered and refrigerated for up to 2 days or frozen for up to 1 month.) To serve, slice diagonally. Makes 12 small servings.

## Crème Caramel

*Muffin cups are ideal for making sampler-sized caramel custards that unmould easily onto a baking sheet. Small ramekins can also be used.*

| | | |
|---|---|---|
| | **CARAMEL:** | |
| **1 cup** | **granulated sugar** | **250 mL** |
| **1/4 cup** | **cold water** | **50 mL** |
| | **CUSTARD:** | |
| **5** | **egg yolks** | **5** |
| **2** | **eggs** | **2** |
| **1/3 cup** | **granulated sugar** | **75 mL** |
| **1-1/4 cups** | **hot milk** | **300 mL** |
| **1 cup** | **hot whipping cream** | **250 mL** |
| **2 tsp** | **vanilla** | **10 mL** |

**CARAMEL:** In heavy saucepan, stir together sugar and water; bring to boil, stirring. Reduce heat to medium-high and cook, without stirring, for 8 to 12 minutes or until deep caramel color. Using pastry brush, brush down sides of pan with cold water several times during cooking. Pour caramel into 12 muffin cups or ramekins.

**CUSTARD:** In large bowl, beat together egg yolks, whole eggs and sugar. Whisk in milk and cream; stir in vanilla. Strain mixture, discarding any froth on surface.

■ Divide custard among caramel-lined cups. Place in large pan; pour in enough hot water to come halfway up sides of muffin cups. Bake in 325°C (160°C) oven for 35 to 40 minutes or until knife inserted in center of custard comes out clean.

■ Remove cups from water and let cool completely. Refrigerate until chilled, at least 1 hour or up to 2 days.

■ To unmould, run knife around inside edge of cups and invert onto large flat platter. Transfer to individual plates and spoon caramel over. Makes 12 servings.

*Crème Caramel; Caramel Almond Bark; Caramel Ice Cream*

## Caramel Ice Cream

*This is an easy ice cream to make if you don't have an ice-cream maker. For even freezing, use a stainless steel bowl. Or, if you have an ice-cream maker, simply stir the whipping cream (unwhipped) into the caramel mixture and freeze according to the manufacturer's directions.*

| | | |
|---|---|---|
| **3/4 cup** | **granulated sugar** | **175 mL** |
| **3 tbsp** | **water** | **50 mL** |
| **1/2 cup** | **boiling water** | **125 mL** |
| **4** | **egg yolks** | **4** |
| **1-1/2 cups** | **whipping cream** | **375 mL** |

■ In heavy saucepan, stir together sugar and 3 tbsp (50 mL) water; bring to boil, stirring. Reduce heat to medium-high and cook, without stirring, for 8 to 12 minutes or until deep caramel color. Using pastry brush, brush down sides of saucepan with cold water several times during cooking.

■ Remove pan from heat. Very carefully, standing back in case mixture spatters, add 1/2 cup (125 mL) boiling water to caramel. Return to heat and stir until smooth.

■ In large bowl, beat egg yolks. Beating constantly, gradually add caramel; beat for about 5 minutes or until cool and thickened.

■ Whip cream; fold into caramel mixture. Spoon into stainless steel bowl. Cover and freeze until firm, at least 2 hours or up to 4 days.

■ To serve, soften ice cream in refrigerator for 15 minutes. Using oval ice cream scoop or two tablespoons, place 1 scoop on each plate. Makes 12 small servings.

## Caramel Almond Bark

*Little pieces of this chocolate-drizzled candy add delicious crunch to the caramel trio of desserts. Chopped into even smaller bits, the bark is great sprinkled over ice cream.*

| | | |
|---|---|---|
| **1 cup** | **granulated sugar** | **250 mL** |
| **1/4 cup** | **cold water** | **50 mL** |
| **1 cup** | **whole almonds, lightly toasted*** | **250 mL** |
| **2 oz** | **bittersweet or semisweet chocolate, melted** | **60 mL** |

■ In heavy saucepan, stir together sugar and water; bring to boil, stirring. Reduce heat to medium-high and cook, without stirring, for 8 to 12 minutes or until deep caramel color. Using pastry brush, brush down sides of pan with cold water several times during cooking.

■ Stir in almonds; cook, stirring, for 30 to 60 seconds or until well coated. Spread mixture as evenly as possible onto buttered baking sheet. Let cool until hardened, about 1 hour.

■ Drizzle slightly cooled melted chocolate over caramel bark. Let stand at room temperature until chocolate has set. With large knife, cut into about 24 pieces. Makes 12 servings.

*To toast almonds, spread on baking sheet and bake in 350°F (180°C) oven for about 5 minutes or until golden.

# CELEBRATING THE CANADIAN YEAR

*The Canadian holiday calendar marks at least one important date each month that calls for a special feast. Many of our festive days center around a traditional family dinner—such as a beautiful glazed ham with all the trimmings on Easter Sunday. Other dates honor uniquely Canadian celebrations—Canada Day, Victoria Day and Thanksgiving. These three deserve special attention and in this chapter we have chosen menus that celebrate them in splendid style. In between, we have a delightful Maytime breakfast in honor of Mother's Day and a big Father's Day barbecue for June. Earlier in the year, Valentine's Day is a sweet treat for romantics with a heart-shaped dessert party. And last on the list is a magical midnight supper for Halloween. Christmas and New Year celebrations call for so many festive menus that they have a whole chapter to themselves at the end of this book.*

# A PICNIC FOR CANADA DAY

FOR EIGHT

*What better way to celebrate our country's birthday than by gathering family and friends for a festive summer picnic to enjoy the dishes that say Canada best.*

*CHEDDAR SHORTBREAD MAPLE LEAVES

*POACHED SALMON

*CRISPY OVEN-FRIED CHICKEN

*CUCUMBER AND ONION RINGS

TOSSED SALAD

*MARITIME OATMEAL ROLLS

*RHUBARB AND STRAWBERRY FOOL

MERINGUE KISSES
(recipe, page 203)

**Recipes are given for menu items marked with an asterisk.*

***CHEDDAR SHORTBREAD MAPLE LEAVES***
***Strike a holiday note by serving these small shortbreads as appetizers.***

***In bowl, combine 1/2 cup (125 mL) shredded old Cheddar cheese, 1/4 cup (50 mL) freshly grated Parmesan cheese and 1 cup (250 mL) all-purpose flour; cut in 1/3 cup (75 mL) butter until mixture resembles coarse crumbs. Stir in 1/4 tsp (1 mL) salt and pinch of cayenne pepper. Blend 1 egg yolk with 2 tbsp (25 mL) ice water; stir into dry ingredients, adding more water if necessary to make dough hold together. Knead lightly on floured surface just until smooth. Wrap and refrigerate for 30 minutes.***

***On lightly floured surface, roll out dough to 1/8-inch (3 mm) thickness. Using floured 1-1/2-inch (4 cm) cutter, cut into maple leaf shapes. Place on ungreased baking sheets; bake in 350°F (180°C) oven for about 15 minutes or until golden. Let cool on rack. Makes about 4 dozen.***

*Cheddar Shortbread Maple Leaves; tossed salad; Poached Salmon; Cucumber and Onion Rings; Crispy Oven-Fried Chicken*

# Poached Salmon

*Serve the salmon on a bed of leafy lettuce and garnish the platter with cherry tomatoes.*

| | | |
|---|---|---|
| 1 | **whole salmon (about 4 lb/2 kg), cleaned** | 1 |
| 1 cup | **dry white wine** | 250 mL |
| 1/4 cup | **lemon juice** | 50 mL |
| 2 | **large carrots, chopped** | 2 |
| 1 | **large onion, chopped** | 1 |
| Half | **stalk celery, chopped** | Half |
| 8 | **sprigs fresh parsley** | 8 |
| 6 | **whole peppercorns, cracked** | 6 |
| 4 | **sprigs fresh dill** | 4 |
| 2 | **whole cloves** | 2 |
| 1 | **bay leaf** | 1 |
| 2 tsp | **salt** | 10 mL |

■ Place fish in fish poacher or roasting pan. Add enough water to cover. Remove fish and reserve. To pan, add wine, lemon juice, carrots, onion, celery, parsley, peppercorns, dill, cloves, bay leaf and salt; bring to boil. Reduce heat, cover and simmer for 20 minutes.

■ For easy handling, enfold salmon in rinsed cheesecloth large enough to hang over ends of poacher. Using overhang as handles, place salmon in poacher. Return to boil; boil for 2 minutes. Cover with lid; let cool to room temperature in cooking liquid.

■ Remove salmon to serving platter. Fold back cheesecloth; using knife, peel off skin and grey fatty layer. Using handles, carefully flip salmon over; ease away cheesecloth. Peel off skin and fatty layer. Cover and refrigerate for at least 1 hour or up to 1 day. Makes 8 servings.

# Crispy Oven-Fried Chicken

*If toting cooked chicken to a picnic site, be sure it is well chilled and carried in a refrigerator carry-all. It won't be as crisp, but it will be safe to eat.*

| | | |
|---|---|---|
| 8 | **chicken legs, thighs attached (about 4 lb/2 kg)** | 8 |
| 1/2 cup | **lemon juice** | 125 mL |
| 2/3 cup | **cornmeal** | 150 mL |
| 1/3 cup | **freshly grated Parmesan cheese** | 75 mL |
| 1 tsp | **paprika** | 5 mL |
| 1/2 tsp | **pepper** | 2 mL |
| | **Lemon slices** | |

■ Rinse chicken legs and pat dry. In shallow dish, marinate chicken in lemon juice for at least 1 hour or up to 3 hours.

■ Stir together cornmeal, cheese, paprika and pepper. Shake excess lemon juice from chicken; dip in cornmeal mixture, patting gently to coat evenly. Bake in greased shallow baking pan for 45 to 50 minutes or until juices run clear when chicken is pierced with fork. Makes 8 servings.

# Cucumber and Onion Rings

*This salad has its roots in Ontario's Waterloo County where German and Mennonite settlers have taught their neighbors to dress their salads with sour cream.*

| | | |
|---|---|---|
| Half | **English cucumber** | Half |
| 1 | **red onion** | 1 |
| 1 tsp | **salt** | 5 mL |
| 1/2 cup | **sour cream** | 125 mL |
| 2 tbsp | **granulated sugar** | 25 mL |
| 2 tbsp | **chopped chives** | 25 mL |
| 2 tbsp | **cider vinegar** | 25 mL |
| 1/4 tsp | **pepper** | 1 mL |

■ With fork, score cucumber skin lengthwise. Slice cucumber and onion thinly. Layer in colander with salt; weigh down with plate and refrigerate for 1 hour. Rinse under cold running water and drain; pat dry. In bowl, combine sour cream, sugar, half of the chives, vinegar and pepper; mix in cucumber and onion. Transfer to serving bowl; sprinkle with remaining chives. Cover and refrigerate for up to 3 hours. Makes 8 servings.

## Maritime Oatmeal Rolls

*Moist rolls, with molasses or maple syrup for sweetening, add a touch of the Maritimes to a Canada Day celebration.*

| | | |
|---|---|---|
| **2 cups** | **boiling water** | **500 mL** |
| **1 cup** | **rolled oats** | **250 mL** |
| **1/4 cup** | **maple syrup or molasses** | **50 mL** |
| **2 tbsp** | **butter** | **25 mL** |
| **1-1/2 tsp** | **salt** | **7 mL** |
| **1 tsp** | **granulated sugar** | **5 mL** |
| **1/4 cup** | **lukewarm water** | **50 mL** |
| **1** | **pkg active dry yeast (or 1 tbsp/15 mL)** | **1** |
| **3 cups** | **(approx) all-purpose flour** | **750 mL** |
| **1 cup** | **whole wheat flour** | **250 mL** |

■ In large bowl, stir together boiling water, rolled oats, maple syrup, butter and salt until butter has melted. Let cool to lukewarm.

■ Dissolve sugar in lukewarm water; sprinkle in yeast and let stand for 10 minutes until frothy. Stir into oats mixture. Preferably using electric mixer, or by hand, gradually beat in 1 cup (250 mL) of the all-purpose flour and whole wheat flour; beat until smooth, about 3 minutes. With wooden spoon, gradually beat in enough of the remaining all-purpose flour to make soft dough.

■ Knead on lightly floured surface until smooth and elastic, working in all-purpose flour as needed, about 8 minutes. Place in lightly greased bowl, turning to grease all over. Cover with plastic wrap and let rise for 1-1/2 hours or until doubled in bulk.

■ Punch down dough; turn out and form into 12-inch (30 cm) long sausage. Cut into 12 equal pieces and form each into ball; equally space in greased 13- × 9-inch (3.5 L) cake pan. Cover and let rise for 1 hour or until doubled in bulk. Bake in 375°F (190°C) oven for 20 to 25 minutes or until lightly browned and hollow sounding when tapped on bottom. Transfer to rack and let cool. Makes 12 large rolls.

*Meringue Kisses; Rhubarb and Strawberry Fool*

## Rhubarb and Strawberry Fool

*The simplicity and utter deliciousness of summer fruit and whipped cream appealed to Canadians a century ago when "fools" such as this were popular desserts.*

| | | |
|---|---|---|
| **4 cups** | **chopped rhubarb** | **1 L** |
| **1 tsp** | **grated orange rind** | **5 mL** |
| **1 tbsp** | **orange juice** | **15 mL** |
| **1 cup** | **granulated sugar** | **250 mL** |
| **4 cups** | **strawberries** | **1 L** |
| **1-1/2 cups** | **whipping cream** | **375 mL** |

■ In stainless steel or enamel saucepan, combine rhubarb, orange rind and juice. Cover tightly and cook over low heat, stirring occasionally, for about 25 minutes or until rhubarb is tender.

■ Stir in sugar; cook for about 3 minutes or until sugar has dissolved. Let cool; cover and refrigerate for up to 1 week.

■ Up to 3 hours before serving, hull strawberries and reserve half for garnish. Purée remaining strawberries; stir into rhubarb mixture.

■ In large bowl, whip cream; lightly fold in fruit mixture, leaving streak effect. Transfer to glass or crystal serving dish. Slice remaining berries and arrange in overlapping rows around edge of bowl. Cover and chill until serving time. Makes 8 servings.

*CANADA DAY*

***Ever since the first Dominion Day celebrations at the time of Confederation in 1867, July 1st has been the biggest birthday party of the year. A century ago, the holiday was the great picnic occasion of the summer, and today we still gather in the great outdoors with festivals, parades and fireworks.***

***Our heritage picnic in the park updates the classic favorites of the late 1800s and celebrates now, as then, the finest fresh foods of a Canadian summer.***

# A DESSERT PARTY FOR VALENTINE'S DAY

FOR SIX TO TWELVE

*Indulge a group of romantics with a whole bevy of "sweet hearts" — heart-shaped desserts they'll all fall in love with. The recipes each make 4 to 6 regular servings or up to 12 sample servings. For a small group, make two or three desserts; for a large group, make all four or double batches of a favorite.*

*BROWNIE HEART CAKE

*CHOCOLATE COEUR À LA CRÈME

*MERINGUES WITH SUGARED ORANGES

*STRAWBERRY HEARTS WITH COCONUT SAUCE

## *Brownie Heart Cake*

*Rich and elegant, this cake is actually one large moist and delicious brownie.*

| | | |
|---|---|---|
| | **CAKE:** | |
| **1-1/2 cups** | **packed brown sugar** | **375 mL** |
| **3/4 cup** | **butter, melted** | **175 mL** |
| **1 tsp** | **vanilla** | **5 mL** |
| **3** | **eggs** | **3** |
| **3/4 cup** | **all-purpose flour** | **175 mL** |
| **1/2 cup** | **unsweetened cocoa powder** | **125 mL** |
| **1/4 tsp** | **salt** | **1 mL** |
| **3/4 cup** | **toasted chopped almonds** | **175 mL** |
| | **FROSTING:** | |
| **1/4 lb** | **white chocolate** | **125 g** |
| **1 tbsp** | **butter** | **15 mL** |
| **1/2 cup** | **sour cream** | **125 mL** |
| | **GARNISH:** | |
| | **Unsweetened cocoa powder** | |
| | **Sliced almonds** | |

**CAKE:** Grease 5-cup (1.25 L) heart-shaped pan; dust with unsweetened cocoa powder and set aside. In bowl, blend together brown sugar, butter and vanilla; add eggs, one at a time, beating well with wooden spoon after each addition.

■ Sift together flour, cocoa and salt; add all at once to creamed mixture, mixing just until blended. Stir in nuts; spread in prepared pan. Loosely cover tip of heart with foil to prevent from drying out. Bake in 350°F (180°C) oven for 35 to 40 minutes or until just barely firm to the touch. Let cool in pan for 10 minutes; turn out onto rack and let cool completely.

**FROSTING:** In top of double boiler over hot, not boiling, water, melt white chocolate with butter. (Alternatively, in microwaveable dish, microwave at Medium/50% for 1 to 2 minutes or until softened.) Remove from heat and let cool slightly; stir in sour cream until smooth and blended. Refrigerate for 10 minutes; spread smoothly over sides then top of cooled cake.

**GARNISH:** Sprinkle cocoa in attractive pattern on top of cake. Arrange almonds around top edge.

## Chocolate Coeur à la Crème

*This variation of the traditional white coeur à la crème is the perfect choice for chocoholic sweethearts. Unmould the hearts onto a pool of chocolate sauce or serve them simply with crème fraîche or whipped cream.*

| | | |
|---|---|---|
| 1/3 cup | unsweetened cocoa powder | 75 mL |
| 1/2 cup | instant dissolving (fruit/berry) sugar | 125 mL |
| 1-1/2 cups | whipping cream | 375 mL |
| Half | envelope unflavored gelatin | Half |
| 1/2 lb | cream cheese | 250 g |
| 1 tsp | vanilla | 5 mL |
| | Chocolate Sauce (recipe follows) | |

■ In bowl, stir cocoa and 1/4 cup (50 mL) of the sugar into 1 cup (250 mL) of the cream; refrigerate for 1 hour.

■ In small saucepan, sprinkle gelatin over 1/4 cup (50 mL) of the remaining whipping cream; let stand for 1 minute to soften. Heat over low heat until dissolved. Let cool to lukewarm.

■ Meanwhile, line 6 small 3-inch (8 cm) or 1 large 6-inch (15 cm) porcelain heart mould with wet cheesecloth, leaving 2-inch (5 cm) overhang; set aside.

■ In large bowl, beat cream cheese until creamed; add vanilla and remaining whipping cream and sugar. Beat until smooth and softened; blend in dissolved gelatin mixture.

■ Whip cocoa mixture until soft peaks form; fold into cheese mixture gently but thoroughly. Pour into prepared moulds; fold cheesecloth overhang over tops. Set moulds on pan or plate; chill in refrigerator for at least 6 hours or overnight.

■ Pool some of the chocolate sauce onto each dessert plate; unmould each coeur à la crème onto sauce. Drizzle a little sauce over top. Makes 6 servings.

| | CHOCOLATE SAUCE: | |
|---|---|---|
| 2/3 cup | granulated sugar | 150 mL |
| 1/3 cup | cocoa powder | 75 mL |
| 1/3 cup | strong coffee | 75 mL |
| 2 tbsp | butter | 25 mL |
| 1/2 tsp | vanilla | 2 mL |

■ In small saucepan, stir together sugar and cocoa. Blend in coffee. Bring to boil over medium heat, stirring constantly. Reduce heat and boil gently without stirring, for 3 minutes. Remove from heat; stir in butter and vanilla. Cover and cool to room temperature before serving. Store in refrigerator for up to 2 weeks. Makes 3/4 cup (175 mL).

## Meringues with Sugared Oranges

*Simple but impressive, these heart-shaped meringues are filled with sugared orange sections, drizzled with liqueur if desired, then topped with strands of spun sugar.*

| | MERINGUES: | |
|---|---|---|
| 2 | egg whites | 2 |
| Pinch | cream of tartar | Pinch |
| 1/2 cup | instant dissolving (fruit/berry) sugar | 125 mL |
| 1/4 tsp | vanilla | 1 mL |
| | ORANGES: | |
| 4 | oranges, peeled and sectioned | 4 |
| 1/4 cup | orange liqueur (optional) | 50 mL |
| 2 tbsp | packed brown sugar | 25 mL |
| Pinch | cinnamon | Pinch |
| | SPUN SUGAR: | |
| 1 cup | granulated sugar | 250 mL |
| 1/4 cup | water | 50 mL |
| Pinch | cream of tartar | Pinch |

**MERINGUES:** Line baking sheet with parchment paper or foil; draw 4 heart outlines, each about 4 inches (10 cm) wide. Set aside.

■ In bowl, beat egg whites with cream of tartar until soft peaks form; gradually add

*Meringue with Sugared Oranges; Chocolate Coeur à la Crème; Strawberry Heart with Coconut Sauce*

***SPUN SUGAR TIPS***

- ***Cover work surface and floor space with newspaper because making spun sugar can be very messy.***
- ***Watch sugar syrup closely because it can burn quickly. The threads should be a golden color.***
- ***To obtain threadlike strands of caramel, the caramel must be at the right temperature. If***

***threads are not forming, allow mixture to cool a little longer, then try again. If caramel hardens, return saucepan to heat until desired consistency.***
- ***Remove hardened caramel in saucepan with boiling water. Add water to caramel-coated saucepan and boil until caramel dissolves.***
- ***You can make spun sugar ahead of time. Store in cool, dry place but do not refrigerate. In hot, humid weather, do not make spun sugar ahead.***

sugar, beating until stiff shiny peaks form. Beat in vanilla.

■ Using pastry bag or spoon, pipe meringue inside hearts on prepared pan, building up sides to form shells. Bake in 275°F (140°C) oven for 50 to 60 minutes or until lightly browned. Turn oven off and let meringues stand in oven for 1 hour.

**ORANGES:** In bowl, toss oranges with liqueur (if using), sugar and cinnamon; cover and refrigerate for 1 hour or until chilled.

**SPUN SUGAR:** In small heavy saucepan, combine sugar, water and cream of tartar; bring to boil, stirring occasionally. Reduce heat to medium-high and boil, without stirring, for 10 to 12 minutes or until mixture is light caramel. Let cool for 3 minutes. Dip fork into caramel mixture; lift fork and quickly wave back and forth over greased waxed paper. (If threads don't form, let caramel cool for 1 minute longer.) To serve, place meringues on 4 plates. Spoon oranges into meringues; garnish with spun sugar. Makes 4 servings.

# *Strawberry Hearts with Coconut Sauce*

*These strawberry hearts look beautiful garnished with fresh coconut and flowers.*

| | STRAWBERRY HEARTS: | |
|---|---|---|
| 1 | envelope unflavored gelatin | 1 |
| 1/4 cup | cold water | 50 mL |
| 2 cups | fresh strawberries or 1 pkg (425 g) frozen, thawed and drained | 500 mL |
| 2 tbsp | granulated sugar | 25 mL |
| 1 cup | sour cream | 250 mL |
| | COCONUT SAUCE: | |
| 3/4 cup | milk | 175 mL |
| 1/2 cup | sweetened flaked coconut | 125 mL |
| 4 | egg yolks | 4 |
| 1/4 cup | granulated sugar | 50 mL |
| 1 tsp | vanilla (or 1 tbsp/15 mL coconut liqueur) | 5 mL |

**STRAWBERRY HEARTS:** In small saucepan, sprinkle gelatin over cold water; let stand for 1 minute to soften. Heat over low heat until dissolved.

■ In food processor or blender, purée strawberries. Blend in sugar and dissolved gelatin. Gradually whisk in sour cream, blending well. Spoon into six 1/2-cup (125 mL) individual moulds. Refrigerate for at least 4 hours or until set.

**COCONUT SAUCE:** In saucepan, heat milk just until bubbles appear around edge of pan. Stir in coconut to moisten; let stand for 30 minutes. Drain well to make at least 2/3 cup (150 mL) liquid; discard coconut and set liquid aside.

■ In top of double boiler over simmering water, whisk egg yolks with sugar. Add reserved coconut liquid; cook, stirring constantly, for 8 to 10 minutes or until sauce coats back of spoon. Remove from heat; stir in vanilla. Refrigerate until chilled. To serve, pour some of the sauce onto each dessert plate. Run knife around edge of each heart and dip mould into warm water to loosen edge; unmould onto sauce. Makes 6 servings.

# A FAMILY EASTER DINNER

FOR TWELVE

*Easter Sunday brings family and tradition together with the joyful sharing of a fine springtime feast. The menu centers around a classic glazed ham, and the trimmings are all easy-to-prepare favorites.*

*SHRIMP COCKTAIL WITH PINEAPPLE

*BRAISED HAM WITH ORANGE-HONEY GLAZE

*CHAMPAGNE RAISIN SAUCE

*SCALLOPED POTATOES

STEAMED ASPARAGUS OR GREEN BEANS

*MARINATED VEGETABLE SALAD

*LEMON PARFAIT WITH ALMONDS AND STRAWBERRIES

*(Clockwise from top left) Champagne Raisin Sauce; Braised Ham with Orange-Honey Glaze; steamed green beans; Shrimp Cocktail with Pineapple; Marinated Vegetable Salad; Scalloped Potatoes*

*SUGAR COOKIE EGGS*
*Make egg-shaped cookies from your favorite sugar cookie recipe and let your children have fun decorating them. Provide tinted icing, sprinkles and jelly beans and let them do the rest.*

*These delightful cookies make perfect Easter presents for relatives or use them as place cards for the Easter table.*

# Shrimp Cocktail with Pineapple

*Shrimp Cocktail is a popular starter for special family dinners. Combining the shrimp with fruit, such as pineapple, avocado, orange or grapefruit sections, adds flavor and makes the shrimp stretch a bit further.*

| | | |
|---|---|---|
| 2 lb | shrimp (fresh or frozen), cooked, peeled and deveined | 1 kg |
| 2 cups | pineapple cubes (fresh or canned) | 500 mL |
| | Fresh dill sprigs | |
| 2 | lemons, cut in wedges | 2 |
| | COCKTAIL SAUCE: | |
| 3/4 cup | chili sauce | 175 mL |
| 1 tbsp | lemon juice | 15 mL |
| 1 tbsp | prepared horseradish | 15 mL |
| 1 tsp | Worcestershire sauce | 5 mL |
| Dash | hot pepper sauce | Dash |

**COCKTAIL SAUCE:** In small bowl, combine chili sauce, lemon juice, horseradish, Worcestershire and hot pepper sauce; mix well. Cover and refrigerate for up to 2 weeks.

■ Just before serving, arrange shrimp and pineapple in cocktail glasses; garnish each with dill and lemon wedge. Spoon tablespoonful (15 mL) cocktail sauce over each, or pass cocktail sauce separately. Makes 12 servings.

# Braised Ham with Orange-Honey Glaze

*This ham is cooked with a little liquid in the pan to keep it tender and juicy. Serve with Champagne Raisin Sauce.*

| | | |
|---|---|---|
| 8 lb | semi-boneless ready-to-serve ham | 4 kg |
| 15 | whole cloves | 15 |
| 2 cups | orange juice | 500 mL |
| 1 cup | white wine | 250 mL |
| | Grated rind of 1 orange | |
| 2 tbsp | honey | 25 mL |
| 1 tsp | ginger | 5 mL |
| 1 tsp | dry mustard | 5 mL |

■ Trim skin and excess fat from ham, leaving about 1/4-inch (5 mm) covering of fat over ham. Insert cloves into fat side of ham; place in roasting pan, fat side up.

■ Combine orange juice, wine and orange rind; set 1/2 cup (125 mL) aside and pour remaining mixture over ham. Set roasting pan on top of stove and bring liquid to boil, then place in 325°F (160°C) oven for 1-1/2 hours, basting occasionally.

■ Combine reserved liquid, honey, ginger and mustard; stir until smooth. Pour over ham and bake for 30 minutes, basting occasionally. Makes about 12 servings.

# Champagne Raisin Sauce

*Instead of the champagne, you could use half champagne and half white wine or sherry.*

| | | |
|---|---|---|
| 2 cups | champagne | 500 mL |
| 1 cup | raisins | 250 mL |
| 4 tsp | cornstarch | 20 mL |
| 1 cup | granulated sugar | 250 mL |
| 1/4 cup | butter | 50 mL |
| 1/2 tsp | salt | 2 mL |
| 1/4 tsp | each ground cloves and cinnamon | 1 mL |

■ In saucepan, bring 1 cup (250 mL) of the champagne and raisins to boil; reduce heat to low and simmer for 5 minutes.

■ Dissolve cornstarch in remaining champagne; add to saucepan along with sugar, butter, salt, cloves and cinnamon. Cook, stirring, until boiling and slightly thickened, 2 to 3 minutes. Pour into sauceboat. Makes about 3 cups (750 mL), enough for 12 servings.

## Scalloped Potatoes

*Scalloped potatoes made with chicken stock instead of milk have wonderful flavor.*

| | | |
|---|---|---|
| 12 | **potatoes, peeled and thinly sliced** | 12 |
| 3 | **onions, finely chopped** | 3 |
| | **Salt and pepper** | |
| 1/3 cup | **butter** | 75 mL |
| 1/3 cup | **all-purpose flour** | 75 mL |
| 3 cups | **boiling chicken stock** | 750 mL |
| | **Paprika** | |

■ In two shallow well-greased 8-cup (2 L) casseroles, layer potatoes and onions, sprinkling salt and pepper between layers.

■ In saucepan, melt butter over medium heat; stir in flour until well blended. With wire whisk, mix in hot stock; cook, stirring constantly, until boiling and thickened. Pour over potatoes and onions; sprinkle with paprika to taste. Bake, uncovered, in 350°F (180°C) oven for about 50 minutes or until potatoes are tender and golden brown. Makes about 12 servings.

## Marinated Vegetable Salad

*This is a colorful, crunchy make-ahead salad.*

| | | |
|---|---|---|
| 2 | **small zucchini** | 2 |
| 4 | **carrots** | 4 |
| 1 | **head cauliflower** | 1 |
| 1 | **bunch broccoli** | 1 |
| 1 | **bunch green onions, chopped** | 1 |
| 2 cups | **cherry tomatoes** | 500 mL |
| 2 cups | **small mushrooms** | 500 mL |
| 2 | **stalks celery, sliced** | 2 |
| 1/2 cup | **ripe olives, pitted and sliced** | 125 mL |
| | **DRESSING:** | |
| 1/3 cup | **vinegar** | 75 mL |
| 2 | **cloves garlic, minced** | 2 |
| 1 tsp | **each dried basil and oregano** | 5 mL |
| 1/2 tsp | **dry mustard** | 2 mL |
| 1 cup | **vegetable oil** | 250 mL |
| | **Salt and pepper** | |

■ Cut zucchini and carrots into julienne strips; cut cauliflower and broccoli into florets. In plastic bag, combine carrots, zucchini, cauliflower, broccoli, onions, tomatoes, mushrooms, celery and olives.

**DRESSING:** In bowl or food processor, combine vinegar, garlic, basil, oregano and mustard. Using whisk or with machine running, gradually pour in oil, mixing well. Season with salt and pepper to taste.

■ Pour dressing over vegetables; seal bag and refrigerate for 24 hours, turning several times. Drain and serve in glass bowl. Makes about 12 servings.

## Lemon Parfait with Almonds and Strawberries

*Make this in advance and freeze it, if you like.*

| | | |
|---|---|---|
| | **Butter** | |
| 1 cup | **finely chopped blanched almonds** | 250 mL |
| 6 | **eggs, separated** | 6 |
| 1 cup | **granulated sugar** | 250 mL |
| | **Juice and grated rind of 2 lemons** | |
| 2 cups | **whipping cream, whipped** | 500 mL |
| 4 cups | **strawberries** | 1 L |

■ Butter 12-cup (3 L) serving bowl or soufflé dish or 12 parfait glasses. (If using glass dish, butter only halfway up sides.) Sprinkle with almonds, reserving 1/4 cup (50 mL) for garnish.

■ In non-aluminum saucepan or top of double boiler, beat egg yolks with sugar, lemon juice and rind. Cook over medium heat or simmering water, stirring until thickened. Be careful mixture doesn't boil. Let cool. Beat egg whites until stiff; fold into yolk mixture. Fold in whipped cream.

■ Spoon into prepared dish(es); sprinkle with reserved almonds. Refrigerate for up to 1 day or freeze for up to 2 weeks. Garnish with strawberries just before serving. Makes 12 servings.

# A MOTHER'S DAY BREAKFAST

FOR FOUR

*Let Mom decide if she'd like breakfast in bed or a family brunch in the dining room — and then whip up a perfect Mother's Day feast in her honor. This is an easy menu for Dad and the kids to prepare; it looks, smells and tastes delicious. Present it on pretty dishes, and tuck her favorite flower into the napkin.*

RASPBERRY JUICE

*FRENCH TOAST WITH CITRUS BUTTER AND FRESH FRUIT MEDLEY

GRILLED BACK BACON

CAFÉ AU LAIT

## *French Toast with Citrus Butter and Fresh Fruit Medley*

*Here's a snazzy version using egg bread, or challah, that's easy enough for children to make. You can make the citrus butter the day before and, if you like, fry breakfast sausages or bacon separately to serve along with the French toast.*

| | | |
|---|---|---|
| | **CITRUS BUTTER:** | |
| **1/2 cup** | **unsalted butter** | **125 mL** |
| **1 tsp** | **finely grated orange or lemon rind** | **5 mL** |
| **1 tbsp** | **orange or lemon juice** | **15 mL** |
| | **FRESH FRUIT MEDLEY:** | |
| **12** | **large strawberries** | **12** |
| **1** | **kiwifruit** | **1** |
| **Half** | **cantaloupe** | **Half** |
| **1** | **orange** | **1** |
| | **FRENCH TOAST:** | |
| **4** | **eggs** | **4** |
| **1/3 cup** | **light cream** | **75 mL** |
| **1/4 cup** | **maple syrup** | **50 mL** |
| **2 tbsp** | **orange juice** | **25 mL** |
| **1/2 tsp** | **vanilla** | **2 mL** |
| **1/4 tsp** | **nutmeg** | **1 mL** |
| **Pinch** | **cinnamon** | **Pinch** |
| **1/4 cup** | **(approx) butter** | **50 mL** |
| **8** | **slices egg bread or homemade-style bread, each about 3/4 inch (2 cm) thick** | **8** |
| **2 tbsp** | **icing sugar** | **25 mL** |
| | **Mint sprigs (optional)** | |
| | **Mandarin orange sections (optional)** | |
| | **Maple syrup (optional)** | |

**CITRUS BUTTER:** Using fork, mash butter until softened and fluffy; mix in orange or lemon rind and juice. Cover and chill.

**FRESH FRUIT MEDLEY:** Hull strawberries. Peel kiwifruit. Seed cantaloupe and cut away rind. Cut kiwi and cantaloupe into 1/4-inch (5 mm) thick slices. Thinly slice and seed orange. Store fruit separately in refrigerator while preparing toast.

**FRENCH TOAST:** In large bowl, whisk together eggs, cream, 1/4 cup (50 mL) maple syrup, orange juice, vanilla, nutmeg and cinnamon; set aside.

■ In large skillet over medium heat, melt 1 tbsp (15 mL) of the butter. Dip 1 slice of bread at a time into egg mixture, press down and let soak for 10 seconds. Lift out, letting excess egg mixture drip back into bowl.

■ Fry soaked bread, in batches, for 1-1/2 to 2 minutes on each side or until golden brown, adding more butter to skillet as needed. Transfer toast to baking sheet and keep warm in 150°F (70°C) oven while frying remaining bread.

■ Place 2 slices of toast on each plate; garnish with assortment of fruit. Dust with icing sugar and top with dollop of citrus butter. Garnish with mint sprig and orange sections and drizzle with maple syrup (if using). Makes 4 servings.

# A VICTORIAN COUNTRY PICNIC

FOR TWELVE

*Queen Victoria's birthday has been a public holiday in Canada since 1845 and it brings forth a great exodus to the outdoors. Before the evening fireworks, a big picnic feast is the perfect way to celebrate the occasion. Here's a nostalgic menu for Victoria Day that recalls the Victorian era when beautiful, bountiful wicker picnic baskets produced an abundance of tantalizing goodies.*

*PÂTÉ EN CROÛTE

HOMEMADE MELBA TOASTS

*HERB ROASTED CHICKEN

RADISHES

BREAD AND BUTTER PICKLES

*DEVILLED EGGS

STILTON WITH ASSORTED CRACKERS

FRESH FRUIT

*JAM TARTS

# *Pâté en Croûte*

*A savory terrine encased in pastry, this pâté is at its best the day after baking. Like most* pâté en croûte, *this sturdy pastry doesn't shrink when baked.*

| | | |
|---|---|---|
| | **Hot Water Pastry (recipe follows)** | |
| **3/4 lb** | **ground veal** | **375 g** |
| **3/4 lb** | **lean ground pork** | **375 g** |
| **1/2 lb** | **ham, cut in 1/2-inch (1 cm) cubes** | **250 g** |
| **1/4 lb** | **ground pork fat** | **125 g** |
| **1/3 cup** | **sliced green onions** | **75 mL** |
| **2 tbsp** | **chopped fresh dill** | **25 mL** |
| **1 tbsp** | **each chopped fresh tarragon, sage and basil (or 1 tsp/5 mL each dried)** | **15 mL** |
| **3** | **juniper berries, ground (optional)** | **3** |
| **2** | **cloves garlic, minced** | **2** |
| **1 tsp** | **salt** | **5 mL** |
| **1/2 tsp** | **pepper** | **2 mL** |
| **2** | **eggs, beaten** | **2** |
| **1** | **egg yolk, lightly beaten** | **1** |
| | **ASPIC:** | |
| **2-1/4 cups** | **chicken stock** | **550 mL** |
| **1/4 cup** | **Madeira or sherry** | **50 mL** |
| **1-1/2** | **envelopes unflavored gelatin** | **1-1/2** |
| **4 tsp** | **white wine vinegar** | **20 mL** |
| **2** | **egg whites (with shells)** | **2** |

■ Prepare Hot Water Pastry and let stand for 30 minutes. Meanwhile, in large bowl, mix together veal, pork, ham, pork fat and green onions. Stir together dill, tarragon, sage, basil, ground juniper berries (if using), garlic, salt and pepper. Blend into meat mixture along with 2 eggs, using hands to mix well.

■ On lightly floured surface, roll out two-thirds of the Hot Water Pastry and fit into terrine dish or 9- × 5-inch (2 L) loaf pan, leaving at least 1/2-inch (1 cm) overhang. Spoon in meat filling; tap pan lightly on counter to release air pockets.

■ Roll out remaining pastry to fit top of pan. Brush edges of bottom pastry with water; top with remaining pastry, sealing and crimping edges. Cut three 1/2-inch (1 cm) round holes in top of pastry. Garnish top with pastry cutouts if desired.

■ Mix egg yolk with 2 tsp (5 mL) water; brush over pastry. Insert pie birds or funnel-shaped tubes of foil in holes to prevent juices from bubbling onto surface. Bake in 400°F (200°C) oven for 15 minutes. Reduce heat to 350°F (180°C) and bake for 1-1/4 to 1-1/2 hours longer or until metal skewer inserted in center for 30 seconds feels hot. Set pâté on rack and let cool to room temperature.

**ASPIC:** In saucepan, combine stock, Madeira, gelatin, vinegar, egg whites and crumbled shells; bring to boil over high heat, stirring constantly. Reduce heat to medium-low and simmer, uncovered and without stirring, for 5 minutes. Strain through double-thickness cheesecloth-lined sieve. Let cool until syrupy.

■ Using funnel, pour a little aspic at a time through holes in top of pastry, chilling between additions, until aspic fills gap under pastry. Chill for 24 hours before serving in slices. Makes about 12 servings.

| | **HOT WATER PASTRY:** | |
|---|---|---|
| **2-1/2 cups** | **all-purpose flour** | **625 mL** |
| **1/2 tsp** | **salt** | **2 mL** |
| **3/4 cup** | **boiling water** | **175 mL** |
| **6 tbsp** | **shortening, melted** | **100 mL** |
| **1** | **egg yolk, beaten** | **1** |

■ In large bowl, stir together flour and salt. Combine water and shortening; pour over flour mixture and mix well with fork. Blend in egg yolk; form into ball. On lightly floured surface, knead dough gently. Cover with plastic wrap and let stand at room temperature for 30 minutes before rolling out.

***HOMEMADE MELBA TOASTS***
***Remove crusts from thin slices of white or brown bread. Cut into serving-sized pieces. Spread on baking sheet and bake at 275°F (140°C), turning slices over as they brown and crisp, for about 20 minutes.***

*Herb Roasted Chicken; bread and butter pickles; Pâté en Croûte, homemade melba toasts; Devilled Eggs; Stilton cheese; fresh fruit; Jam Tarts*

## Devilled Eggs

*For picnics, parties, salad plates or just for an appetizer, these are simple and tasty.*

| | | |
|---|---|---|
| 6 | **hard-cooked eggs** | 6 |
| 1/4 cup | **mayonnaise** | 50 mL |
| 1/2 tsp | **salt** | 2 mL |
| 1/4 tsp | **pepper** | 1 mL |
| 1/2 tsp | **dry mustard** | 2 mL |
| 1 tbsp | **finely chopped parsley** | 15 mL |
| | **OPTIONAL GARNISHES:** | |
| | **Sprigs of watercress or fresh dill** | |
| | **Cucumber slices** | |

■ Cut hard-cooked eggs in half lengthwise. Slip out yolks into small mixing bowl and mash them with fork. Blend in mayonnaise, salt, pepper, dry mustard and parsley.
■ Refill white with egg yolk mixture, heaping it lightly, or using a pastry bag. Garnish as desired. Makes 12 devilled eggs.

## Herb Roasted Chicken

*A simple roasted chicken flavored with herbs was a Victorian favorite.*

| | | |
|---|---|---|
| 1 | **roasting chicken (about 6 lb/2.75 kg)** | 1 |
| 3 | **lemons or limes** | 3 |
| 6 | **large cloves garlic** | 6 |
| 1 | **bunch fresh thyme*** | 1 |
| 1 tsp | **coarse cracked pepper** | 5 mL |

■ Rinse chicken and pat dry. Cut 2-1/2 lemons or limes into quarters; insert in cavity of chicken along with garlic, half of the thyme and half of the pepper. Truss chicken, skewering cavity closed tightly.
■ Rub chicken all over with cut side of remaining lemon or lime. Sprinkle with remaining pepper; arrange remaining thyme sprigs over chicken.
■ On rack in shallow pan, roast chicken in 325°F (160°C) oven for about 2-1/2 hours, basting twice, or until chicken is golden and meat thermometer inserted in thickest part of thigh registers 185°F (85°C). Discard thyme sprigs and stuffing. Makes 10 to 12 servings.
*If fresh thyme is not available, use fresh parsley and add 1 tsp (5 mL) dried thyme to cavity. Sprinkle additional 1 tsp (5 mL) on outside of chicken.

## Jam Tarts

*Easy to eat on a picnic, these tarts combine a sweet filling with a cake topping. Use cherry, strawberry, raspberry or blackberry jam.*

| | | |
|---|---|---|
| | **Pastry for double-crust pie** | |
| 3/4 cup | **strawberry jam** | 175 mL |
| 1/2 cup | **butter** | 125 mL |
| 1/2 cup | **granulated sugar** | 125 mL |
| 1 | **egg** | 1 |
| 1/2 tsp | **vanilla** | 2 mL |
| 3/4 cup | **all-purpose flour** | 175 mL |
| 1 tsp | **baking powder** | 5 mL |
| 1/4 cup | **milk** | 50 mL |

■ Roll out pastry and line 18 tart shells about 2-1/2 inches (7 cm) in diameter and 1 inch (2.5 cm) deep. Spoon about 2 tsp (10 mL) jam into each shell; set aside.
■ In bowl, cream together butter and sugar; beat in egg and vanilla. Stir together flour and baking powder; gradually add to creamed mixture alternately with milk, beating until smooth. Spoon over jam in tart shells.
■ Bake in 400°F (200°C) oven for 18 to 20 minutes or until tops are browned and set. Makes 18 tarts.

*(Left to right) Whole Wheat Biscuits; Mixed Bean Casserole; Crusty Barbecued Beef with Horseradish Mayonnaise; Make-Ahead Slaw*

# A BACKYARD BARBECUE FOR FATHER'S DAY

FOR TWELVE

*Delegate the cooking and serving to family members and let father be king for a day in his lawn chair (unless head chef position at the barbecue is where he likes to reign). Recipes make about 12 servings. For larger groups, make recipes again rather than simply doubling.*

*CRUSTY BARBECUED BEEF WITH HORSERADISH MAYONNAISE

*PIZZA CHEESE SQUARES

*MIXED BEAN CASSEROLE

*MAKE-AHEAD SLAW

*WHOLE WHEAT BISCUITS

*CHEESECAKE WITH BLACKBERRY SAUCE

# Crusty Barbecued Beef with Horseradish Mayonnaise

*Two 2-inch (5 cm) thick round steaks are quick to barbecue and ample enough for a crowd. Remember that barbecuing times are a guide. Cold weather, wind, humidity, cold food or a lot of food on the grill at once all lengthen cooking times.*

| | | |
|---|---|---|
| 2 | **round steaks (2 lb/1 kg each)** | 2 |
| | **MARINADE:** | |
| 1/2 cup | **red wine vinegar** | 125 mL |
| 1/4 cup | **olive oil** | 50 mL |
| 1 | **onion, chopped** | 1 |
| 2 | **cloves garlic, chopped** | 2 |
| 1/2 tsp | **hot pepper flakes** | 2 mL |
| | **HORSERADISH MAYONNAISE:** | |
| 1 cup | **mayonnaise** | 250 mL |
| 1/3 cup | **chopped fresh chives** | 75 mL |
| 1/3 cup | **chopped fresh parsley** | 75 mL |
| 2 tbsp | **prepared horseradish** | 25 mL |
| | **COATING:** | |
| 2 tbsp | **prepared horseradish** | 25 mL |
| 2 tbsp | **Dijon mustard** | 25 mL |
| 2 tbsp | **mustard seeds** | 25 mL |

**MARINADE:** In large shallow glass dish or heavy plastic bag set in bowl, combine vinegar, oil, onion, garlic and hot pepper flakes. Add steaks, turning to coat all over; cover tightly. Marinate for 24 to 48 hours in refrigerator, turning occasionally.

**HORSERADISH MAYONNAISE:** Combine mayonnaise, chives, parsley and horseradish. Refrigerate until serving time.

**COATING:** Mix together horseradish, mustard and mustard seeds. Remove steaks from marinade; spread half of the coating over one side of each steak. Cook in covered barbecue or covered with tented foil, coated sides up, on greased grill 6 to 8 inches (15 to 20 cm) over medium-hot coals or at medium setting for 12 minutes.

■ Turn meat; spread remaining mustard mixture on cooked side. Barbecue for about 15 minutes or until meat thermometer registers 140°F (60°C) for rare or to desired doneness. Let meat stand for at least 10 minutes before carving into thin slices. Serve with Horseradish Mayonnaise. Makes 12 servings.

# Pizza Cheese Squares

*Whether serving with cold tomato juice or mugs of beer, these appetizers make a nice snack for kids and grown-ups alike.*

| | | |
|---|---|---|
| 1/4 cup | **butter** | 50 mL |
| 1 | **clove garlic, minced** | 1 |
| 1 | **small onion, chopped** | 1 |
| 6 | **eggs** | 6 |
| 2 cups | **sour cream** | 500 mL |
| 1 | **can (7-1/2 oz/213 mL) tomato sauce** | 1 |
| 1 cup | **cornmeal** | 250 mL |
| 1 tsp | **each dried basil, oregano and salt** | 5 mL |
| 2 cups | **shredded Cheddar cheese** | 500 mL |
| 2 cups | **shredded mozzarella cheese** | 500 mL |
| | **TOPPINGS:** | |
| 1/2 cup | **each sliced pepperoni, olives, sliced mushrooms, diced sweet green pepper and quartered drained marinated artichoke hearts** | 125 mL |

■ In skillet, melt butter over medium-high heat; cook garlic and onion for 2 to 3 minutes or until softened. Let cool.

■ In large bowl, beat eggs. Blend in sour cream, tomato sauce, cornmeal, basil, oregano, salt and onion mixture. Stir in Cheddar and mozzarella cheeses. Pour into lightly greased 13- × 9-inch (3.5 L) baking dish. Garnish with rows of toppings.

■ Bake in 350°F (180°C) oven for 40 to 45 minutes or until firm to the touch. Cut into squares and serve immediately or cover, refrigerate overnight, and serve at room temperature. Makes 32 appetizers.

*Pizza Cheese Squares*

# Mixed Bean Casserole

*This satisfying dish is fast and easy—and great for a hungry crowd.*

| | | |
|---|---|---|
| 1 | can (19 oz/540 mL) chick-peas | 1 |
| 1 | can (19 oz/540 mL) red kidney beans | 1 |
| 1 | can (19 oz/540 mL) romano beans | 1 |
| 1 | can (14 oz/398 mL) lima beans | 1 |
| 1 | onion, chopped | 1 |
| 1 cup | tomato juice | 250 mL |
| 1/3 cup | packed brown sugar | 75 mL |
| 1/3 cup | fancy molasses | 75 mL |
| 1/4 cup | chili sauce | 50 mL |
| 2 tsp | dry mustard | 10 mL |
| 1 tsp | ginger | 5 mL |
| 1/2 tsp | salt | 2 mL |
| 1/2 tsp | pepper | 2 mL |
| 8 | slices bacon | 8 |

■ Drain and rinse chick-peas, kidney beans, romano beans and lima beans. In lightly greased bean pot or 12-cup (3 L) casserole, mix together beans and onion.

■ In saucepan, blend tomato juice, brown sugar, molasses, chili sauce, mustard, ginger, salt and pepper; bring to boil. Stir into beans.

■ Partially cook bacon slices to remove excess fat. Chop and add to bean mixture. Bake, covered, in 325°F (160°C) oven for 1-1/4 hours. Makes 12 servings.

# Make-Ahead Slaw

*Cutting cabbage by hand produces a nicer salad than cutting with a food processor, but it takes longer. If you plan to keep this salad for more than eight hours, use all green cabbage because red will color the celery and onion.*

| | | |
|---|---|---|
| 4 cups | each shredded red and green cabbage | 1 L |
| 1/2 cup | thinly sliced celery | 125 mL |
| 1 | Spanish onion, slivered | 1 |
| 1 | sweet red or green pepper, slivered | 1 |
| 1 cup | slivered jicama or white turnip (optional) | 250 mL |
| 1/2 cup | white vinegar | 125 mL |
| 1/2 cup | vegetable oil | 125 mL |
| 1/3 cup | granulated sugar | 75 mL |
| 1 tsp | celery seeds | 5 mL |
| 3/4 tsp | salt | 4 mL |
| 1/2 tsp | dry mustard | 2 mL |
| 1/2 tsp | pepper | 2 mL |

■ In bowl, toss together red and green cabbage, celery, onion, sweet pepper, and jicama (if using).

■ In small saucepan, mix together vinegar, oil, sugar, celery seeds, salt, mustard and pepper. Bring to boil; stir until sugar dissolves.

■ Pour over cabbage mixture. Refrigerate, covered, for at least 4 hours or overnight. Makes 12 servings.

## Whole Wheat Biscuits

*If space permits, warm the biscuits on the edge of the barbecue.*

| | | |
|---|---|---|
| **2 cups** | **whole wheat flour** | **500 mL** |
| **2 cups** | **all-purpose flour** | **500 mL** |
| **3 tbsp** | **baking powder** | **50 mL** |
| **1-1/2 tsp** | **salt** | **7 mL** |
| **1/2 cup** | **shortening** | **125 mL** |
| **1/2 cup** | **butter** | **125 mL** |
| **1-1/2 cups** | **(approx) milk** | **375 mL** |
| **1** | **egg yolk** | **1** |
| **2 tsp** | **cold water** | **10 mL** |
| **1 tbsp** | **poppy seeds** | **15 mL** |

■ In bowl, stir together whole wheat and all-purpose flours, baking powder and salt. Cut in shortening and butter until mixture resembles crumbs.

■ Add milk, stirring with fork just until dry ingredients are moistened. If dough is too dry, add more milk, 1 tbsp (15 mL) at a time.

■ Turn dough out onto lightly floured surface and knead gently 12 times. Roll out dough to 1/2-inch (2 cm) thickness. Using 3-inch (8 cm) cutter, cut out biscuits and place, with sides just touching, on lightly greased baking sheet. Mix egg yolk with water; brush over dough. Sprinkle with poppy seeds.

■ Bake in 425°F (220°C) oven for about 25 minutes or until golden brown. Let cool for 5 minutes; transfer to rack to let cool completely. Makes about 14 biscuits.

## Cheesecake with Blackberry Sauce

*This easy-to-make cheesecake can be frozen for up to four weeks.*

| | | |
|---|---|---|
| | **CRUST:** | |
| **1-1/2 cups** | **graham wafer crumbs** | **375 mL** |
| **1/2 cup** | **rolled oats** | **125 mL** |
| **1/3 cup** | **packed brown sugar** | **75 mL** |
| **1/3 cup** | **butter, melted** | **75 mL** |
| | **FILLING:** | |
| **1 lb** | **cream cheese, softened** | **500 g** |
| **2/3 cup** | **granulated sugar** | **150 mL** |
| **2 tbsp** | **all-purpose flour** | **25 mL** |
| **1 tsp** | **grated lemon rind** | **5 mL** |
| **2 tbsp** | **lemon juice** | **25 mL** |
| **1/2 tsp** | **vanilla** | **2 mL** |
| **2** | **eggs** | **2** |
| | **BLACKBERRY SAUCE:** | |
| **4 cups** | **blackberries or raspberries** | **1 L** |
| **1/2 cup** | **granulated sugar** | **125 mL** |
| **1 tbsp** | **cornstarch** | **15 mL** |
| **1/4 cup** | **frozen raspberry juice concentrate, thawed** | **50 mL** |

**CRUST:** Combine crumbs, rolled oats, sugar and butter. Press into 13- × 9-inch (3.5 L) baking dish. Bake in 325°F (160°C) oven for 10 minutes. Let cool on rack.

**FILLING:** In bowl, cream together cheese, sugar, flour, lemon rind and juice, and vanilla. Add eggs, 1 at a time, beating well after each addition. Pour over crust. Bake in 450°F (230°C) oven for 10 minutes. Reduce heat to 250°F (120°C) and bake for 20 minutes longer or until filling is set. Run knife around edge of cake. Let cool to room temperature.

**BLACKBERRY SAUCE:** In saucepan, mix berries with sugar. Blend cornstarch into concentrate; stir into berry mixture. Cover and cook over medium-high heat for 15 minutes or until thickened, stirring often. Let cool.

■ To serve, cut cheesecake into squares and place on dessert plates; spoon sauce over top. Makes 12 servings.

# A COUNTRY-STYLE THANKSGIVING DINNER

FOR TWELVE

*In the golden splendor of autumn, Canadian families have gathered together for countless generations in an annual renewal of Harvest Home tradition. Here's a country-style feast of thanksgiving befitting our heritage and the bounty of our land.*

*WINTER SOUP

ROAST TURKEY

*SAUSAGE AND APPLE STUFFING

*POTATO PARSNIP GRATIN

*BRAISED BRUSSELS SPROUTS WITH VINEGAR AND DILL

*BAKED RED ONIONS

FRESH CRANBERRY RELISH

*PECAN PUMPKIN PIE

*(Clockwise from center) Roast Turkey with Sausage and Apple Stuffing; Potato Parsnip Gratin; Braised Brussels Sprouts with Vinegar and Dill; Baked Red Onions; Winter Soup; cranberry relish*

## *Winter Soup with Two Flavors*

*Serve this soup as is or divide into 2 portions, then flavor and color each half before pouring, side by side, into the same serving bowl (as was done for our cover photograph). The recipe can be halved for a smaller gathering.*

| | | |
|---|---|---|
| **3 tbsp** | **butter** | **50 mL** |
| **3 cups** | **chopped leeks (white parts only)** | **750 mL** |
| **1-1/2 cups** | **chopped onion** | **375 mL** |
| **6 cups** | **chicken stock** | **1.5 L** |
| **3 cups** | **diced peeled squash** | **750 mL** |
| **3 cups** | **diced peeled potato** | **750 mL** |
| **3/4 tsp** | **(approx) salt** | **4 mL** |
| **1-1/2 cups** | **light cream** | **375 mL** |
| | **White pepper** | |
| | **FOR TWO FLAVORS:** | |
| **1/3 cup** | **Pesto (recipe, page 39)** | **75 mL** |
| **3 tbsp** | **tomato paste** | **50 mL** |
| | **Fresh herb sprigs** | |

■ In large heavy saucepan, heat butter over medium-high heat; cook leeks and onion, covered, for 10 minutes. Do not brown.

■ Add chicken stock; bring to boil. Add squash, potatoes and salt; return to boil. Reduce heat, cover and simmer for 20 minutes or until vegetables are tender.

■ Remove to blender or food processor; purée, in batches, until smooth. Return to saucepan; add cream, and salt and pepper to taste.

**FOR TWO FLAVORS:** Divide between two saucepans over low heat. To one pan, blend in Pesto; taste and adjust seasoning. To second pan, blend in tomato paste. Cook just until heated through; do not boil.

■ Transfer soups to containers with pouring spouts. Pour both soups at the same time into soup bowl, pouring from opposite sides of bowl. Garnish with sprigs of fresh herbs. Makes 12 servings.

## *Sausage and Apple Stuffing*

*This old-fashioned favorite is still a popular choice.*

| | | |
|---|---|---|
| **1 lb** | **sausage meat** | **500 g** |
| **1 cup** | **chopped onion** | **250 mL** |
| **1/2 cup** | **chopped celery** | **125 mL** |
| **2** | **apples, peeled and chopped** | **2** |
| **1 tsp** | **each dried sage, savory and thyme** | **5 mL** |
| **10 cups** | **stale bread cubes or coarse crumbs** | **2.5 L** |
| | **Salt and pepper** | |

■ In large skillet, crumble sausage meat. Add onion and celery; cook over medium heat, stirring often, for about 10 minutes or until sausage meat is cooked. Add apples and herbs. In large bowl, combine contents of skillet with bread; toss well and season with salt and pepper to taste. Stuff and roast turkey (see page 236). Makes enough stuffing for 14- to 16-lb (6 to 7 kg) turkey.

## *Potato Parsnip Gratin*

*Parsnips add a delicate sweetness to this harvesttime casserole.*

| | | |
|---|---|---|
| **8** | **potatoes** | **8** |
| **8** | **parsnips** | **8** |
| **1** | **clove garlic, halved** | **1** |
| **1 tsp** | **thyme** | **5 mL** |
| | **Salt and pepper** | |
| **2 cups** | **(approx) whipping cream** | **500 mL** |

■ Peel and thinly slice potatoes and parsnips. Generously butter 13- × 9-inch (3.5) casserole dish; rub with garlic. Arrange single layer of potatoes in dish. Sprinkle lightly with a little of the thyme, salt and pepper. Cover with layer of parsnips. Sprinkle with seasonings. Repeat layering with remaining vegetables.

■ Pour in enough cream to come three-

***THANKSGIVING IN CANADA***
***Festivals of thanksgiving have been held in Canada since the days of the earliest colonists, but it wasn't until 1879 that Thanksgiving was officially declared a public holiday, and not until 1957 that it settled to the second Monday in October. (November made sense for honoring the arrival of the Pilgrims in America but October is the better time to properly mark our Canadian end-of-harvest season.) In honor of our heritage and agricultural roots, we continue the celebration with fall fairs and festivals, decorate our churches with wheat sheaves and cornucopias overflowing with pumpkins, corn and apples, then gather for traditional country-style feasts that bond us to our land and our history.***

quarters up side of dish. Place on baking sheet and bake, covered, in 375°F (190°C) oven for 30 minutes. Uncover and bake for 30 minutes longer or until top is brown and crusty and potatoes are cooked through. Makes 12 servings.

## Braised Brussels Sprouts with Vinegar and Dill

*Wine vinegar and dill heighten the fall flavor of the first brussels sprouts of the season.*

| | | |
|---|---|---|
| **3 lb** | **brussels sprouts** | **1.5 kg** |
| **1/4 cup** | **chopped fresh dill** | **50 mL** |
| **2 tbsp** | **wine vinegar** | **25 mL** |
| | **Salt and pepper** | |

■ Trim sprouts; halve if desired. In large pot of boiling salted water, cook brussels sprouts for 8 minutes if whole, 6 minutes if halved, or until barely tender. Drain, refresh under cold running water and drain again.
■ In well-greased 13- × 9-inch (3.5 L) casserole, combine sprouts, dill, vinegar, and salt and pepper to taste; mix well. Bake, covered, in 350°F (180°C) oven for 10 minutes. Uncover and bake for 5 minutes longer. Makes 12 servings.

## Baked Red Onions

*The rich color and taste of this dish make it an excellent foil for turkey. If port is unavailable, use sherry or sweet red wine.*

| | | |
|---|---|---|
| **6** | **red onions, halved** | **6** |
| | **Rind of 1 lemon, cut in strips** | |
| **1/2 cup** | **olive oil** | **125 mL** |
| **1 cup** | **raisins** | **250 mL** |
| **1/2 cup** | **port wine** | **125 mL** |
| **1/4 cup** | **cider vinegar** | **50 mL** |
| **1 tbsp** | **packed brown sugar** | **15 mL** |
| | **Pepper** | |

■ In large saucepan, cover onions and lemon rind with water; bring to boil and boil for 5 minutes. Drain; refresh under cold running water and drain again. Discard rind. Peel onions and arrange in 13- × 9-inch (3.5 L) casserole; pour olive oil over.
■ Bake, uncovered, in 375°F (190°C) oven, basting occasionally, for 40 minutes. Add raisins, port, vinegar, sugar, and pepper to taste. Bake for 30 minutes or until juices are syrupy. Makes 12 servings.

## Pecan Pumpkin Pie

*Pecans add a taste of the South to this traditional pumpkin pie. Make two pies to serve 12 people.*

| | | |
|---|---|---|
| **3** | **eggs, beaten** | **3** |
| **1** | **can (14 oz/398 mL) cooked pumpkin purée** | **1** |
| **1 cup** | **packed brown sugar** | **250 mL** |
| **1/2 cup** | **corn syrup** | **125 mL** |
| **1/3 cup** | **butter, melted** | **75 mL** |
| **1 tsp** | **vanilla** | **5 mL** |
| **1/2 tsp** | **cinnamon** | **2 mL** |
| **1/2 tsp** | **nutmeg** | **2 mL** |
| **1/4 tsp** | **salt** | **1 mL** |
| **1** | **unbaked 9-inch (23 cm) pie shell** | **1** |
| **1 cup** | **pecan halves** | **250 mL** |

■ In food processor or blender, combine eggs, pumpkin, sugar, corn syrup, butter, vanilla, cinnamon, nutmeg and salt; process until blended. Pour into pie shell.
■ Arrange pecans in concentric circles over filling. Bake in 350°F (180°C) oven for 45 minutes or until tester inserted in center comes out clean.

# A MIDNIGHT SUPPER FOR HALLOWEEN

FOR SIXTEEN

*The masks come off at midnight, and your Halloween masquerade party turns into a stylishly spooky feast. This bewitching menu uses orange and black in both food and decorations; a cauldron of steaming cider, golden cheese puffs and a dark and savory tart provide just the right tastes and textures for a mysterious midnight feast.*

*HOT SPIKED CIDER IN A CAULDRON

*SPICY CHEESE GOUGÈRES

*RED ONION AND BLACK OLIVE TART

*WATERCRESS AND ROMAINE SALAD WITH ORANGES

*CHOCOLATE-ORANGE PARFAITS

## Hot Spiked Cider in a Cauldron

*A brisk, chilling Halloween calls for a warming libation such as this mulled cider made with Calvados.*

| | | |
|---|---|---|
| 20 | whole cloves | 20 |
| 10 | whole allspice | 10 |
| 10 | cardamom pods | 10 |
| 6 | sticks (3-inch/8 cm) cinnamon | 6 |
| 16 cups | apple cider or apple juice | 4 L |
| 4 | oranges, thinly sliced | 4 |
| 1/4 cup | packed brown sugar (optional) | 50 mL |
| 2 cups | Calvados or brandy | 500 mL |
| | Orange slices | |
| | Whole cloves | |

■ In cheesecloth bag, tie together cloves, allspice, cardamom pods and cinnamon sticks; place in large saucepan. Add cider, oranges, and sugar (if using); bring to boil, stirring occasionally until sugar dissolves.

■ Cover and reduce heat to medium-low; simmer for 25 to 30 minutes or until fragrant and flavors have blended. With slotted spoon, remove and discard oranges; discard cheesecloth bag. (Recipe can be prepared to this point, covered and refrigerated overnight. Reheat before proceeding.)

■ Just before serving, stir in Calvados. Pour into heatproof punch bowl and garnish with orange slices studded with cloves. Makes 16 to 18 servings.

*(Clockwise from top) Hot Spiked Cider in a Cauldron; Watercress and Romaine Salad with Oranges; Red Onion and Black Olive Tart; Spicy Cheese Gougères; Chocolate-Orange Parfaits*

## *Spicy Cheese Gougères*

*Two cheeses add extra flavor to these delicious little puffs.*

| | | |
|---|---|---|
| 1 cup | all-purpose flour | 250 mL |
| 1 tsp | dried mustard | 5 mL |
| 1/2 tsp | salt | 2 mL |
| 1/4 tsp | pepper | 1 mL |
| 1/4 tsp | cayenne pepper | 1 mL |
| 1 cup | chicken stock | 250 mL |
| 1/2 cup | butter | 125 mL |
| 4 | eggs | 4 |
| 3/4 cup | shredded Cheddar cheese | 175 mL |
| 1/2 cup | freshly grated Parmesan cheese | 125 mL |

■ Combine flour, mustard, salt, pepper and cayenne pepper; set aside.

■ In heavy saucepan, combine stock and butter; bring to boil. Remove from heat and immediately add flour mixture all at once; stir vigorously with wooden spoon until dough is smooth and pulls away from side of pan to form ball.

■ Return to low heat and cook, stirring, for 30 seconds to dry mixture. Remove from heat.

■ Add eggs one at a time, beating vigorously with wooden spoon after each addition until dough is smooth and glossy. Stir in Cheddar and Parmesan cheeses.

■ Using rounded teaspoon or pastry bag with 1/2-inch (1 cm) tip, drop spoonfuls of batter onto lightly greased or parchment paper-lined baking sheets. With wet finger, gently press down tips of rounds to eliminate points.

■ Bake one sheet at a time in 400°F (200°C) oven for 20 to 25 minutes or until puffed and golden. Serve immediately. Makes about 6 dozen. (Gougères can be cooled completely, wrapped and frozen for up to 1 month. To reheat, bake frozen gougères in 350°F/180°C oven for 5 to 8 minutes or until heated through.)

## *Red Onion and Black Olive Tart*

*A generous quantity of sweet-tasting sautéed red onion cooked with fresh tomatoes make for a rustic French tart topped with black olives, capers and fresh herbs. To serve a party of 16, make the recipe twice.*

| | | |
|---|---|---|
| 1/3 cup | olive oil | 75 mL |
| 6 cups | sliced red onions (about 2 lb/1 kg) | 1.5 L |
| 4 | tomatoes, peeled, seeded and chopped | 4 |
| 1/2 tsp | each salt and pepper | 2 mL |
| 1 | can (1.75 oz/50 g) anchovies, drained | 1 |
| 3/4 lb | ready-made pizza dough | 375 g |
| 1 tbsp | each chopped fresh rosemary and thyme (or 3/4 tsp/4 mL dried) | 15 mL |
| 16 | black olives, halved | 16 |
| 1 tbsp | drained capers | 15 mL |
| 2 tbsp | chopped fresh basil or parsley | 25 mL |

■ In large heavy saucepan or deep skillet, heat 1/4 cup (50 mL) of the oil over medium-low heat; cook onions, uncovered and stirring often, for 35 minutes or until onions are very tender but not browned.

■ Add tomatoes and cook, stirring occasionally, for 10 to 15 minutes or until most of the liquid has evaporated. Stir in salt and pepper; let cool completely.

■ Meanwhile, cover anchovies with cold water and let stand for 10 minutes; drain well.

■ On lightly floured surface, roll out pizza dough to about 17- × 12-inch (43 × 30 cm) rectangle, 1/8 inch (3 mm) thick. Ease into lightly greased 15- × 10-inch (2 L) jelly-roll pan; flute edges.

■ Spread onion mixture evenly over dough; sprinkle with rosemary and thyme. Arrange olives, capers and anchovies on top; drizzle with remaining olive oil.

■ Place inverted baking sheet on bottom rack of 425°F (220°C) oven; heat until hot. Place pizza pan on inverted baking sheet and bake for 25 to 30 minutes or until crust

***SETTING THE SCENE***
***Who said Halloween is just for kids?! This year, it's the grown-ups' turn to put on the costumes and have some fun! Invite friends to dress up and come to a Halloween midnight supper. Use orange and black colors for invitations, table decorations and china. Drape the buffet table in shimmering black cloth and place candle-lit pumpkins on the table and throughout the room to cast a golden glow. Add autumn corn husks and gourds for seasonal color. Let a cauldron filled with spicy apple cider be the table centerpiece, and provide midnight-black plates and glasses for the feast. End the evening with a séance or with prizes for best costume.***

is crisp and golden on bottom. Sprinkle with basil. Serve hot or at room temperature. Makes 8 servings.

## *Watercress and Romaine Salad with Oranges*

*Orange segments and juice add tangy fruit flavor to this refreshing salad.*

| | | |
|---|---|---|
| 2 | **heads romaine lettuce** | 2 |
| 2 | **bunches watercress, trimmed** | 2 |
| 8 | **oranges, segmented** | 8 |
| 1 cup | **coarsely chopped toasted walnuts*** | 250 mL |
| | **ORANGE DRESSING:** | |
| 1/4 cup | **orange juice** | 50 mL |
| 1 tbsp | **red wine vinegar** | 15 mL |
| 1 | **clove garlic** | 1 |
| 1 tsp | **Dijon mustard** | 5 mL |
| 1/4 cup | **olive oil** | 50 mL |
| 1/4 cup | **vegetable oil** | 50 mL |
| | **Salt and pepper** | |

**ORANGE DRESSING:** In bowl, stir together orange juice, vinegar, garlic and mustard; whisk in olive oil and vegetable oil; season with salt and pepper to taste. (Dressing can be covered and refrigerated for up to 2 days.)

■ Tear lettuce and watercress into bite-sized pieces; place in salad bowl along with oranges. Pour dressing over and toss to coat; sprinkle with walnuts. Makes 16 servings.

*Spread walnuts on baking sheet and toast in 350°F (180°C) oven for 8 to 10 minutes or until fragrant.

*CHOCOLATE CURLS*
*To make chocolate curls, microwave 2 oz (60 g) chocolate at Medium (50%) for about 30 seconds or until slightly softened but not melting. Using sharp vegetable peeler, peel off curls, rewarming chocolate if necessary.*

## *Chocolate-Orange Parfaits*

*Chocolate and orange stripes are easy to make neatly by using a pastry bag.*

| | | |
|---|---|---|
| 3 cups | **whipping cream** | 750 mL |
| | **ORANGE MOUSSE:** | |
| 1-1/2 cups | **granulated sugar** | 375 mL |
| 1 tbsp | **cornstarch** | 15 mL |
| 6 | **eggs, beaten** | 6 |
| 2 tbsp | **grated orange rind** | 25 mL |
| 2/3 cup | **orange juice** | 150 mL |
| 1/4 cup | **lemon juice** | 50 mL |
| 1/2 cup | **butter, cut in pieces** | 125 mL |
| | **Orange food coloring (optional)** | |
| | **CHOCOLATE MOUSSE:** | |
| 7 oz | **semisweet chocolate, chopped** | 210 g |
| 2 oz | **unsweetened chocolate, chopped** | 60 g |
| 1/3 cup | **butter** | 75 mL |
| 4 | **eggs, separated** | 4 |
| 2 tbsp | **orange liqueur (or 2 tsp/10 mL vanilla)** | 25 mL |
| 1/3 cup | **granulated sugar** | 75 mL |

**ORANGE MOUSSE:** In heavy saucepan, combine sugar and cornstarch; stir in eggs, orange rind and juice, lemon juice and butter. Cook over medium-high heat, stirring constantly, for 7 to 8 minutes or until mixture comes to boil. Reduce heat to medium-low and cook, stirring, for 1 to 2 minutes or until thickened. If desired, tint with a few drops food coloring. Pour into large bowl; cover and refrigerate until chilled.

**CHOCOLATE MOUSSE:** In top of double boiler over hot, not boiling, water, melt semisweet and unsweetened chocolate with butter, stirring frequently. Let cool.

■ Add egg yolks one at a time, mixing well after each addition. Stir in liqueur. Set aside.

■ Beat egg whites until soft peaks form; gradually beat in sugar until stiff peaks form. Stir one-quarter into chocolate mixture; fold in remaining whites.

■ Whip cream; fold half into orange mixture and half into chocolate mixture. Alternately spoon layers of orange and chocolate mousses into 1 cup (250 mL) wine or parfait glasses or glass serving bowl. Cover and refrigerate until firm, about 4 hours, or overnight. Decoratively arrange chocolate curls or Halloween candy over parfaits. Makes 16 servings.

Happy Birthday to you!

# VERY SPECIAL OCCASIONS

*Wonderful food has always been an important part of memorable family occasions. The sharing of family food traditions and the annual rituals of birthdays, anniversaries and reunions have always been the gentle bonds that tie families strongly together. Here, you'll find lots of new recipes to add to your traditional fare for family milestones. Our shower and anniversary menus feature interesting updates of popular dishes. And for that very special wedding reception, there's a gorgeous (but make-ahead easy) menu in a garden party setting. Sensational cakes for weddings, anniversaries and birthdays get special attention here, too; easy-to-follow directions help you to create beautiful contemporary cakes in the favorite flavors of the guests-of-honor.*

# A CHILDREN'S BIRTHDAY PARTY

FOR EIGHT

*Happy Birthday To You!*
*The Big Day has arrived, and the party guests are just as excited as the birthday girl or boy. Make the day memorable and fun for them (and easy on you) by keeping it simple. Lots of colorful decorations, some games and presents and a beautiful birthday cake are the essential kid-pleasers. Plan the rest of the menu around simple, familiar foods that can be dressed up to give a special party look.*

*CREAMY YOGURT SHAKES

*HOTDOG SAILBOATS

VEGETABLE STICKS

*KID-STYLE CAKES

**Recipes are given for menu items marked with an asterisk.*

## Creamy Yogurt Shakes

*Serve these naturally good drinks in plastic glasses or cups with brightly colored straws.*

| | | |
|---|---|---|
| **6 cups** | **milk** | **1.5 L** |
| **3 cups** | **vanilla ice cream, softened** | **750 mL** |
| **2 cups** | **plain yogurt** | **500 mL** |
| **1/2 cup** | **liquid honey** | **125 mL** |
| **1 tbsp** | **vanilla** | **15 mL** |

■ In blender (in 2 batches) or with electric mixer, blend milk, ice cream, yogurt, honey and vanilla. Cover and refrigerate until ready to serve. Just before serving, mix or whisk to blend. Makes about 10 cups (2.5 L).

**STRAWBERRY YOGURT SHAKES:**

■ Substitute strawberry ice cream for the vanilla ice cream, and 1/2 cup (125 mL) strawberry jam for the honey. Omit vanilla.

## Hotdog Sailboats

*Children love hotdogs, and this fancy party version is sure to be a hit.*

| | | |
|---|---|---|
| 8 | **wieners** | 8 |
| 8 | **hotdog buns** | 8 |
| 4 | **slices cheese, cut in half diagonally*** | 4 |
| 8 | **cherry tomatoes** | 8 |
| | **Mustard, relish and/or ketchup** | |

■ Simmer or grill wieners. Split buns; toast if desired.

■ To assemble: Place 1 wiener in each bun. Insert 6- to 7-inch (15 to 18 cm) long bamboo skewer through each cheese slice, then through cherry tomato. With tomato on bottom, stand upright in wiener to form sailboat. Serve with mustard, relish and/or ketchup. Makes 8 servings.

*If cheese slices are very thin, double the number and use 2 slices on each skewer. Cheese should be cold.

***KID-PLEASING THEMES***

***Young children will be delighted with Hotdog Sailboats and a simple Sailboat Cake. You could continue the nautical theme with sailor or pirate hats and a treasure hunt; or if it's summertime, have a bathing suit party around the wading pool and set the picnic table with bright paper plates and cups, and raw veggie sticks in small plastic sandpails.***

***Children love Animal theme parties, which can include everything from a visit to a local zoo to a teddy-bear picnic in the park. Zoo Cake could have a surprise favor hiding behind each animal cracker decoration.***

***For a Circus party, get the kids to make clown masks or hats; cut the party sandwiches into clown shapes, and decorate the cake with clown cookies for everyone to take home.***

***PARTY CONE FAVORS***
***(see photo, page 114)***
***Make delightful party favors by filling flat-bottomed ice cream cones with candies. Decorate the outsides by attaching candies with a dab of icing. Or decorate inverted cones, inserting lollipops at the point, and attaching candies with icing. Pipe names on each if desired.***

*Hotdog Sailboats; vegetable sticks; Creamy Yogurt Shakes*

# *Kid-Style Cakes*

*Here's a tasty basic birthday cake recipe plus three easy decorating ideas.*

| | BASIC WHITE CAKE: | |
|---|---|---|
| 2 cups | sifted cake-and-pastry flour | 500 mL |
| 1 cup | granulated sugar | 250 mL |
| 2 tsp | baking powder | 10 mL |
| 1/2 tsp | salt | 2 mL |
| 1/2 cup | butter, softened | 125 mL |
| 2 | eggs | 2 |
| 2/3 cup | milk | 150 mL |
| 1 tsp | vanilla | 5 mL |
| | BUTTER ICING: | |
| 1/3 cup | butter | 75 mL |
| 3 cups | (approx) sifted icing sugar | 750 mL |
| 3 tbsp | (approx) milk | 50 mL |
| 1 tsp | vanilla | 5 mL |

■ In large mixing bowl, stir together flour, sugar, baking powder and salt. With electric mixer, blend in butter, eggs, milk and vanilla at low speed. Increase speed to medium and beat for 2 minutes, scraping down side of bowl occasionally (mixture may appear slightly curdled).

■ Pour into greased and floured 9-inch (2 L) round or 8-inch (2 L) square cake pan, both at least 2 inches (5 cm) deep. Bake in 350°F (180°C) oven for about 40 minutes or until top is golden and tester inserted in center comes out clean. Let cool in pan for 10 minutes; turn out onto wire rack to cool completely.

*Sailboat Cake*

*Zoo Cake*

**BUTTER ICING:** In bowl, cream together butter, 2 cups (500 mL) of the sugar and 2 tbsp (25 mL) of the milk until smooth. Add vanilla and remaining sugar and milk, beating until smooth, creamy and spreadable. If icing is too soft, beat in more sugar, 1 tbsp (15 mL) at a time. If icing is too stiff, beat in a few drops of milk.

### SAILBOAT CAKE:

Cut a 9-inch (23 cm) round of cake in half. Cut 1 half into 2 semi-circles to make sails. On flat tray, lay out cake pieces to resemble sailboat. Frost completely. Use brightly colored icing for trim, if desired. Decorate with candies, a small flag and birthday candles.

### ZOO CAKE:

Frost an 8-inch (20 cm) square cake, any flavor, with your favorite icing. Outline features on animal crackers with melted chocolate. Arrange on top and sides of frosted cake along with birthday candles.

### CIRCUS CAKE:

Split a round cake (see Basic White Cake above) or use 2 layers of your favorite cake; fill and frost completely. Decorate with brightly colored candies and sugar sprinkles. Add clown cookies, a circus canopy made with straws and ribbons, or bunches of miniature balloons.

***GRILLED CHEESE CRITTERS***
***(see photo, page 115)***
***Grilled cheese sandwiches are kids' favorites. Make them special by cutting both bread and cheese slices into animal shapes. Lightly butter bread—remember to spread half of the slices facing one way, half the other—and sandwich with cheese. Brown in frypan until golden and toasted, and cheese is barely melted. Add pickle slices for eyes and parsley for grass if desired.***

# A GARDEN PARTY WEDDING

FOR TWENTY

*The warm summer sun, the scent of fresh flowers, a big green lawn with a pond or gazebo — a backyard garden can make a fairytale setting for that special wedding. Whether it's your own or that of another couple, our garden party suggestions will provide you with a lavish-looking yet budget-conscious alternative to expensive catered affairs. Our menu serves an intimate gathering of 20, but the recipes can be doubled easily. Garnish the platters with ferns, flowers and herbs. For the wedding cake, a light lemon pound cake is a delicious alternative to the traditional fruitcake.*

*BRIDAL FRUIT PUNCH

SPARKLING WHITE WINE

*DILL BREAD WITH HAM SPREAD

*CHEESE AND MELON BALLS

*CHICKEN SATAYS

*CRAB SALAD IN RADICCHIO CUPS

*OPEN-FACED SANDWICH SLICES

FRUIT BASKET

*LEMON TARTLETS

*LEMON WEDDING CAKE

## *Bridal Fruit Punch*

*Offer an alternative to an alcoholic drink with this pink punch. Chill ingredients well and mix just before serving. Garnish the punch bowl with ice cubes and sprigs of fresh mint; for a fancier touch, use a ring mould to make a fruited ice ring.*

| | | |
|---|---|---|
| **4 cups** | **tropical fruit juice or pink lemonade** | **1 L** |
| **1** | **can (280 mL) frozen strawberry juice concentrate** | **1** |
| **3 cups** | **ginger ale** | **750 mL** |
| **2 cups** | **soda water** | **500 mL** |

■ In punch bowl, mix together fruit juice and juice concentrate. Pour ginger ale and soda water down side of bowl to avoid loss of carbonation. Serve over ice. Makes about 10 cups (2.5 L) or about 20 servings.

# Dill Bread with Ham Spread

*This moist, savory, dill-flecked tea bread looks pretty served with Ham Spread.*

| | | |
|---|---|---|
| | **DILL BREAD:** | |
| **2-1/2 cups** | **all-purpose flour** | **625 mL** |
| **1 cup** | **finely chopped fresh dill** | **250 mL** |
| **1/4 cup** | **granulated sugar** | **50 mL** |
| **1 tbsp** | **baking powder** | **15 mL** |
| **1 tsp** | **salt** | **5 mL** |
| **1 tsp** | **grated lemon rind** | **5 mL** |
| **1-1/4 cups** | **milk** | **300 mL** |
| **1/4 cup** | **vegetable oil** | **50 mL** |
| **1** | **egg** | **1** |
| | **HAM SPREAD:** | |
| **1/2 lb** | **minced ham** | **250 g** |
| **1/4 cup** | **sour cream** | **50 mL** |
| **2 tsp** | **Dijon or horseradish mustard** | **10 mL** |
| | **Hot pepper sauce** | |

**DILL BREAD:** In large bowl, stir together flour, dill, sugar, baking powder, salt and lemon rind. Beat together milk, oil and egg; stir into flour mixture, mixing until well blended.

■ Spread batter in greased and floured 6-cup (1.5 L) loaf pan. (Straight-sided pans are best for shape. A 10-1/4 × 3-1/2 × 2-1/2-inch/25 × 9 × 6 cm pan is perfect.) Bake in 300°F (150°C) oven for 40 to 45 minutes or until cake tester inserted in center comes out clean. (Bread does not brown on outside.)

■ Immediately flatten top of loaf by placing paper-towel-covered cake rack on top of bread and inverting pan for 30 seconds. Turn right side up; let cool in pan on rack for 10 minutes. Turn out onto rack to let cool completely.

**HAM SPREAD:** In food processor or blender, combine ham, sour cream, mustard, and hot pepper sauce to taste; process until smooth.

**ASSEMBLY:** Cut loaf into 1/4-inch (5 mm) thick slices. Spread ham mixture on each slice. Makes about 30 slices.

# Cheese and Melon Balls

*Serve these cheese balls rolled in chopped nuts or, for a contrast in color, chopped fresh mint. As accompaniments, alternate honeydew and cantaloupe balls on picks.*

| | | |
|---|---|---|
| **1/2 lb** | **cream goat cheese (chèvre)** | **250 g** |
| **1/2 cup** | **finely chopped nuts or fresh mint or parsley** | **125 mL** |

■ Form cheese into 20 balls, each about 1 inch (2.5 cm) in diameter. Roll in nuts or herbs. Skewer on long cocktail picks or bamboo skewers. Cover and refrigerate on waxed paper-lined trays until serving time. Makes about 20 appetizers.

# Chicken Satays

*These tender morsels of delicately spiced chicken are simple but tasty.*

| | | |
|---|---|---|
| **8** | **boneless skinless chicken breasts (about 2 lb/1 kg)** | **8** |
| **1/4 cup** | **vegetable oil** | **50 mL** |
| **2 tbsp** | **dry sherry** | **25 mL** |
| **2 tbsp** | **soy sauce** | **25 mL** |
| **2 tbsp** | **honey** | **25 mL** |
| **1 tbsp** | **chopped gingerroot** | **15 mL** |
| **1 tsp** | **ground coriander** | **5 mL** |
| **1** | **clove garlic, crushed** | **1** |

■ Cut chicken into eighty 3/4-inch (2 cm) cubes.

■ In bowl, mix together oil, sherry, soy sauce, honey, ginger, coriander and garlic. Add chicken cubes, stirring gently to coat with marinade. Cover and refrigerate overnight, turning occasionally.

■ Soak 40 bamboo skewers in water for 30 minutes. Onto each soaked skewer, thread two pieces of chicken. Broil for 4 minutes. Turn; brush with marinade. Broil for 3 to 4 minutes longer or until no longer pink inside. Serve warm or at room temperature. Makes 40 skewers or about 20 servings.

*Cheese and Melon Balls; Crab Salad in Radicchio Cups and Baked Tart Shells; Dill Bread with Ham Spread; Heart-Shaped Canapés; Chicken Satays; (On far table) Lemon Wedding Cake*

## *Crab Salad in Radicchio Cups*

*Tiny radicchio cups add a dash of color. For a traditional touch, spoon the salad into baked tart shells or toast cups.*

| | | |
|---|---|---|
| **1/2 lb** | **crabmeat** | **250 g** |
| **1/4 cup** | **finely chopped celery** | **50 mL** |
| **2 tsp** | **lemon juice** | **10 mL** |
| **Pinch** | **cayenne pepper** | **Pinch** |
| | **Salt and black pepper** | |
| **1/4 cup** | **mayonnaise** | **50 mL** |
| **1 tbsp** | **seafood cocktail sauce*** | **15 mL** |
| | **Radicchio** | |

■ Flake crabmeat, removing any bits of membrane; press out excess moisture. In bowl, toss crab with celery, lemon juice, cayenne, and salt and black pepper to taste. Blend mayonnaise with seafood sauce; add to crab mixture and toss lightly to mix. Spoon into 24 tiny radicchio cups or 1-1/2-inch (4 cm) tart shells. Makes 2 dozen.
*If you don't have seafood cocktail sauce, mix together 1 tbsp (15 mL) ketchup with 1/2 tsp (2 mL) horseradish.

## Open-Faced Sandwich Slices

*These dainty, open-faced sandwiches are attractive with the red pepper spread suggested below, or top the bread with your favorite egg salad or any cream-cheese-based filling.*

| | | |
|---|---|---|
| 1 | **white or brown sandwich loaf (unsliced)** | 1 |
| 1/2 lb | **cream cheese, softened** | 250 g |
| 1/4 cup | **red pepper jelly** | 50 mL |
| 4 tsp | **finely chopped fresh parsley** | 20 mL |

■ Remove crusts from bread, leaving bottom and 1 end crust attached for easy handling. Slice loaf lengthwise into 8 slices; set 4 aside for another use. Cream together cheese and jelly; spread about 1/4 cup (50 mL) over each slice. Pipe remaining mixture around edges of each slice. Sprinkle with parsley. Cover and refrigerate for up to 24 hours. Using serrated knife, cut each slice into 10 serving-sized triangles. Makes 40 wedges.

## Lemon Tartlets

*This buttery shortbread crust is topped with a refreshing lemon filling.*

| | | |
|---|---|---|
| | **CRUST:** | |
| 1 cup | **all-purpose flour** | 250 mL |
| 1/2 cup | **butter, softened** | 125 mL |
| 1/4 cup | **icing sugar** | 50 mL |
| | **FILLING:** | |
| 2 | **eggs** | 2 |
| 1 cup | **granulated sugar** | 250 mL |
| 2 tbsp | **all-purpose flour** | 25 mL |
| 1 tsp | **grated lemon rind** | 5 mL |
| 1 tbsp | **lemon juice** | 15 mL |
| 1/2 tsp | **baking powder** | 2 mL |
| | **Icing sugar** | |

**CRUST:** In bowl, mix together flour, butter and sugar until well blended. Press about 1 tsp (5 mL) into each tartlet pan (1-1/2 inches/4 cm in diameter, 3/4 inch/2 cm deep). Bake in 350°F (180°C) oven for 10 minutes. Remove from oven; make a slight depression in each tartlet. Return to oven for 5 minutes longer.

**FILLING:** In bowl, beat together eggs, sugar, flour, lemon rind, lemon juice and baking powder. Spoon about 1 tsp (5 mL) into each tartlet. Return to oven for about 20 minutes or until lightly browned and set. Let cool on rack for 10 minutes. Remove tartlets from pan; let cool completely. Store in airtight container. At serving time, sprinkle with icing sugar. Makes 2 dozen.

## Lemon Wedding Cake

*This three-tiered (two layers per tier) pound cake is tinged with the sparkling flavors of apricot and lemon. Since this is a major baking project, you may wish to borrow a heavy-duty mixer if you don't already own one. You can bake the cake in two batches of three layers each or, to speed up the baking, arrange to use a neighbor's oven as well as your own to bake the cake layers all at once. The cake can be baked up to one month ahead and stored, well wrapped, in the freezer. Then assemble and decorate the thawed cake one to two days ahead; refrigerate until shortly before serving. Make two batches of the pound cake for a total of six cake layers to assemble into three tiers. The recipe fits standard set of deep round wedding or Christmas cake pans.*

| | | |
|---|---|---|
| | **POUND CAKE (Make 2 batches):** | |
| 1-1/4 cups | **butter, softened** | 300 mL |
| 3 cups | **granulated sugar** | 750 mL |
| 7 | **eggs** | 7 |
| 2 tsp | **grated lemon rind** | 10 mL |
| 1 tsp | **vanilla** | 5 mL |
| 3-1/2 cups | **sifted cake-and-pastry flour** | 875 mL |
| 1/2 tsp | **salt** | 2 mL |
| 1/2 tsp | **baking soda** | 2 mL |
| 1-1/4 cups | **sour cream** | 300 mL |
| | **APRICOT FILLING:** | |
| 1/2 cup | **dried apricots** | 125 mL |
| 1 cup | **hot water** | 250 mL |

***HEART-SHAPED CANAPÉS***
***To make fancy-looking canapés, use heart-shaped cookie cutters to cut English cucumber or pumpernickel bread slices. Top slices with rosettes of smoked salmon, whipped cream cheese, sour cream or golden caviar. As an alternative to using cookie cutters, you can bake bread loaves in heart-shaped moulds.***

*ALTERNATIVE WEDDING CAKES*
*If you prefer a non-traditional wedding cake that reflects your personal style and taste, try these alternatives—*
**For the sophisticate:** *a two-tiered chocolate cake with chocolate frosting and Candied Roses and Chocolate Rose Leaves (for instructions on making candied roses and leaves, see sidebar on page 134).*
**For the romantics:** *Strawberry Wedding Cake with Buttercream Icing (recipe, page 126).*
**For the casual:** *A classic carrot cake with cream cheese frosting.*

| | | |
|---|---|---|
| **1/2 cup** | **granulated sugar** | **125 mL** |
| **1/4 cup** | **butter** | **50 mL** |
| **1 tsp** | **grated lemon rind** | **5 mL** |
| **2 tbsp** | **lemon juice** | **25 mL** |
| **1** | **egg, lightly beaten** | **1** |
| | **DECORATING FROSTING:** | |
| **1-2/3 cups** | **butter, softened** | **400 mL** |
| **3 lb** | **(approx) icing sugar (about 13-1/2 cups/3 L), sifted** | **1.5 kg** |
| **3/4 cup** | **lemon juice** | **175 mL** |
| **2 tsp** | **vanilla** | **10 mL** |
| **1** | **egg white** | **1** |
| **1/2 cup** | **strained apricot jam** | **125 mL** |

**POUND CAKE:** Grease and flour deep 11-inch (3 L) round cake pan; line base with waxed paper and set aside. Repeat with deep 8-inch (1.75 L) round cake pan and deep 6-inch (1 L) round cake pan.

■ In large bowl, cream together butter and sugar until light and fluffy. Beat in eggs, one at a time. Blend in lemon rind and vanilla.

■ In separate bowl, sift together flour, salt and baking soda; add to butter mixture alternately with sour cream, making 3 additions of flour mixture and 2 additions of sour cream. Beat well after each addition.

■ Divide batter among prepared pans, filling each slightly less than half full. Bake in 350°F (180°C) oven for 40 to 45 minutes or until tops spring back when lightly touched and cake tester inserted in center comes out clean. (If using only one oven, bake 11-inch/3 L pan first. Cover and refrigerate remaining pans of batter until ready for baking.) Let cake cool in pan for 10 minutes. Turn out onto wire rack and let cool completely. Repeat for second batch to make total of six layers.

**APRICOT FILLING:** In small heavy saucepan, cover apricots with hot water; let stand for 2 to 3 hours or until softened. Bring apricots and water to boil; cover and simmer until tender, 10 to 15 minutes. Drain and transfer to food processor or blender; purée apricots.

■ In heavy saucepan, combine apricot purée, sugar, butter, lemon rind and juice. Cook over low heat, stirring frequently, until sugar has dissolved and butter melted; stir into lightly beaten egg. Return to saucepan and cook for 5 to 10 minutes or until curd is thickened and smooth, stirring constantly. Cover and refrigerate until ready to assemble cake. (Filling can be made up to 1 week ahead.)

**DECORATING FROSTING:** In large bowl, cream butter until light and fluffy. Gradually beat in sugar alternately with lemon juice. Add vanilla and egg white; whip until of spreading consistency, adding more sifted icing sugar if necessary.

**ASSEMBLY:** If necessary, using serrated knife, trim tops of cake layers to make them even.

**BOTTOM TIER:** Invert one of the 11-inch (3 L) layers onto serving plate or tray. Slide strips of waxed paper under cake to protect plate from frosting. In small saucepan over low heat, warm apricot jam gently; brush a little (enough to seal) over top of cake. Spread about two-thirds of the apricot filling over apricot jam glaze. Top with second 11-inch (3 L) cake layer. Brush excess crumbs from outside edge of cake. Spread thin layer of frosting to completely cover top and sides of cake layers and seal in crumbs. Ice cake again with enough frosting to cover evenly and smoothly.

**MIDDLE TIER:** Invert one of the 8-inch (1.75 L) cake layers on small round (slightly smaller than cake) of foil-lined cardboard. Brush with apricot jam glaze; top with half of the remaining apricot filling. Top with second 8-inch (1.75 L) cake layer; cover with frosting.

**TOP TIER:** Repeat with 6-inch (1 L) cake layers, using remaining apricot jam and filling, but reserving enough frosting for piping.

■ Invert 8-inch (1.75 L) cake pan over center of 11-inch (3 L) tier; lightly trace outline. Cut 5 plastic straws to exact height of bottom tier to act as supports for middle tier; insert 1 at center of bottom tier. Insert remaining straws, evenly spaced, about 1 inch (2.5 cm) inside marked circle. Using 2 spatulas, center 8-inch (1.75 L) tier on 11-inch (3 L) tier. Repeat procedure to stack 6-inch (1 L) tier on top of 8-inch (1.75 L) tier. Remove waxed paper strips.

■ If desired, run icing comb around sides of cake for decorative effect. Using pastry bag fitted with star tip, pipe remaining frosting around edges in shell pattern. Refrigerate for up to 2 days. Makes 50 to 60 servings.

# A 25TH WEDDING ANNIVERSARY DINNER

FOR TWENTY

*Wedding anniversaries are very special milestones that are celebrated in traditional style through the years — from a romantic dinner for two on the 1st anniversary to a huge reunion of family and friends on the 50th. For the 25th, a relaxed dinner party for close friends and family is often the choice. This menu for 20 is sure to be a hit; popular dishes are updated with interesting flavors and all are suitable for make-ahead or sharing the preparation.*

*ASPARAGUS MIMOSA

*PROVENÇAL BEEF STEW

*MAKE-AHEAD VEGETABLE MEDLEY

NOODLES OR TINY POTATOES

GREEN SALAD

CROISSANTS, CRUSTY BREAD OR ROLLS

*FRESH FRUIT SALAD

*STRAWBERRY WEDDING CAKE WITH BUTTERCREAM ICING

*SETTING THE SCENE*
***The menu is well suited to presentation on a draped buffet table (emphasize the silver theme with lots of gleaming serving dishes, candlelight, white or pastel linens and fresh flowers). Invite guests to be seated at small tables (such as 5 tables of 4), with the first course (Asparagus Mimosas) in place at each setting, then let them help themselves to the main course casserole and accompaniments. The fruit dessert can be served as the guests of honor cut the beautiful anniversary cake.***

*(Clockwise from top) Fresh Fruit Salad; green salad; Provençal Beef Stew; Make-Ahead Vegetable Medley; noodles; croissants*

# *Provençal Beef Stew*

*Sure to be popular with everyone, this richly flavorful dish is also easy to make and serve.*

| | | |
|---|---|---|
| **12 lb** | **blade roast, trimmed and cut in 1-1/2-inch (4 cm) cubes** | **5.5 kg** |
| **1/2 cup** | **(approx) olive oil** | **125 mL** |
| **5** | **onions, diced** | **5** |
| **4** | **large carrots, diced** | **4** |
| **8 cups** | **beef stock** | **2 L** |
| **2** | **cans (each 5-1/2 oz/156 mL) tomato paste** | **2** |
| **1 cup** | **cornstarch** | **250 mL** |
| **2/3 cup** | **cold water** | **150 mL** |
| | **Salt and pepper** | |
| | **GARNISH:** | |
| | **Lemon or orange rind, julienned** | |
| | **Chopped fresh parsley** | |
| | **MARINADE:** | |
| **5 cups** | **dry red wine** | **1.25 L** |
| **3/4 cup** | **olive oil** | **175 mL** |
| **1** | **orange or lemon** | **1** |
| **Half** | **bunch fresh parsley** | **Half** |
| **15** | **cloves garlic** | **15** |
| **5** | **bay leaves** | **5** |
| **1-1/2 tsp** | **juniper berries** | **7 mL** |
| **1-1/2 tsp** | **dried thyme** | **7 mL** |
| **1/2 tsp** | **whole black peppercorns** | **2 mL** |

**MARINADE:** In large 24-cup (8 L) non-aluminum bowl, combine wine and oil. Using vegetable peeler, remove orange rind in strips. In cheesecloth bag, tie together orange strips, parsley, garlic, bay leaves, juniper berries, thyme and peppercorns. Add to wine mixture along with beef. Cover and refrigerate for 8 hours or overnight.

■ Strain beef, reserving marinade and cheesecloth bag. Using paper towels, pat beef dry. In large shallow saucepan or Dutch oven, heat 2 tbsp (25 mL) of the oil over medium-high heat; cook beef, in batches and adding more oil as needed, for 6 to 8 minutes or until well browned, turning occasionally. Transfer browned beef to large roasting pan.

■ Add onions and carrots to saucepan, adding more oil if necessary; cook, stirring, for 5 minutes or until golden. Stir in reserved marinade; bring to boil, stirring with wooden spoon to scrape up any brown bits from bottom of pan and skimming off any foam. Add beef stock and tomato paste, whisking to blend; pour over meat in roasting pan. Tuck reserved cheesecloth bag into meat mixture.

■ On stovetop, heat meat mixture until liquid comes to boil; cover tightly with lid or foil and bake in 350°F (180°C) oven for 2-1/2 hours or until beef is tender and easily pierced with fork.

■ Strain, reserving cooking liquid in large 16 cup (4 L) saucepan. Return beef to roasting pan and keep warm. Discard cheesecloth bag.

■ Skim fat from cooking liquid; bring liquid to boil. In bowl, whisk together cornstarch and water until smooth; whisk about three-quarters of the mixture into cooking liquid and cook, whisking, for 1 to 2 minutes or until glossy and thickened, adding more cornstarch mixture if needed. Season with salt and pepper to taste.

■ Through large sieve, pour sauce over beef. Taste and adjust seasoning. (Stew can be cooled, covered and refrigerated for up to 1 day. To reheat, let stew stand at room temperature for 30 minutes. Heat, covered, in 350°F/180°C oven for 45 to 50 minutes or until heated through.) Transfer to serving platter and garnish with lemon or orange rind and parsley. Makes 20 servings.

## *Make-Ahead Vegetable Medley*

*This is a great method for keeping vegetables fresh-tasting and good-looking.*

| | | |
|---|---|---|
| 6 | **zucchini** | 6 |
| 6 | **young onions with part of stems attached** | 6 |
| 4 | **sweet red peppers** | 4 |
| 2 | **heads cauliflower** | 2 |
| 1/2 cup | **butter** | 125 mL |
| 1/2 tsp | **salt** | 2 mL |
| 1/4 tsp | **pepper** | 1 mL |

■ Cut zucchini into diagonal slices. Slice onions into wedges, keeping root ends intact. Seed red peppers and cut into strips. Divide cauliflower into bite-sized florets.

■ In large pot of boiling water, cook zucchini for 1 minute; immediately plunge into bowl of ice water just until chilled. Drain and pat dry.

■ Repeat with onions, cooking for 4 to 5 minutes, red peppers, cooking for 2 to 3 minutes, and cauliflower, cooking for 5 minutes or just until all vegetables are tender-crisp. Wrap vegetables separately in towels; place in plastic bags or containers and refrigerate until serving time or for up to 8 hours.

■ In large shallow saucepan, melt butter over medium-low heat; add vegetables and toss gently to coat. Cover and heat until steaming hot. Makes 20 servings.

## *Asparagus Mimosa*

*Cooked asparagus dressed in a classic vinaigrette and garnished with fluffy sieved eggs makes an elegant first course for spring. In the fall, substitute fresh leeks, trimmed and simmered for 20 to 30 minutes or until tender.*

| | | |
|---|---|---|
| 5 lb | **asparagus** | 2.2 kg |
| 2 | **heads Boston or Bibb lettuce, separated** | 2 |
| 10 | **hard-cooked eggs, peeled** | 10 |
| | **Chopped fresh parsley** | |
| | **VINAIGRETTE:** | |
| 3 tbsp | **white wine vinegar** | 50 mL |
| 2 tbsp | **minced shallots** | 25 mL |
| 1 tbsp | **Dijon mustard** | 15 mL |
| 1/2 tsp | **salt** | 2 mL |
| 1/4 tsp | **pepper** | 1 mL |
| 3/4 cup | **vegetable oil** | 175 mL |

■ Snap off tough ends of asparagus; peel stems if desired. In large deep skillet or shallow saucepan, cook asparagus, in batches, in boiling water for about 5 minutes or until tender-crisp. Using slotted spoon, immediately transfer asparagus to bowl of ice water; drain and pat dry. (Cooked asparagus can be wrapped in clean tea towel, placed in plastic bag and refrigerated for up to 1 day.)

**VINAIGRETTE:** In small bowl, combine vinegar, shallots, mustard, salt and pepper; gradually whisk in oil. (Dressing can be covered and refrigerated for up to 1 day. Whisk before using.) Combine asparagus with dressing, tossing gently to coat; divide among lettuce-lined plates.

■ Press egg yolks and whites separately through sieve; sprinkle over asparagus. Sprinkle with parsley. Makes 20 servings.

## *Strawberry Wedding Cake with Buttercream Icing*

*A lush, fresh cake veiled in romantic tones of pink icing. Make one batch of the cake recipe for the top tier of the cake and a double batch for the bottom one.*

| | | |
|---|---|---|
| | **GENOISE CAKE:** | |
| 1/4 cup | **butter** | 50 mL |
| 4 | **eggs** | 4 |
| 3/4 cup | **granulated sugar** | 175 mL |
| 1 tsp | **vanilla** | 5 mL |
| 3/4 cup | **all-purpose flour** | 175 mL |
| 1/2 tsp | **baking powder** | 2 mL |
| Pinch | **salt** | Pinch |
| | **Kirsch Syrup (recipe follows)** | |

*FRESH FRUIT SALAD*
***Peel and slice 24 seedless oranges, reserving any juices. In 16-cup (4 L) serving bowl, combine orange slices, juice and 1/3 cup (75 mL) orange liqueur; cover and refrigerate until chilled or for up to 8 hours.***

***Up to 1 hour before serving, add 8 cups (2 L) whole or sliced strawberries and toss well. Makes about 20 servings.***

| | | |
|---|---|---|
| 8 cups | **Strawberry Buttercream Icing (recipe follows)** | 2 L |
| | **GARNISH:** | |
| | **Whole strawberries** | |
| | **Mint or fern leaves** | |

**TOP GENOISE TIER:** Grease and flour 8-inch (2.5 L) round cake pan that is at least 3 inches (8 cm) deep. Line base with waxed paper and set aside.

■ In small saucepan, melt butter over low heat; set aside to let cool to lukewarm.

■ Meanwhile, warm unshelled eggs slightly by covering with warm water for a few minutes. Rinse mixing bowl in hot water and wipe dry. Break eggs into warmed bowl; add sugar and beat at high speed for about 10 minutes or until thickened, pale yellow and batter falls in ribbons when beaters are lifted from bowl. Beat in vanilla.

■ Stir together flour, baking powder and salt; sift one-third of the mixture over egg mixture and using rubber spatula, fold in until blended. Repeat twice with remaining flour mixture. Add butter; fold in until thoroughly blended. Spoon into prepared pan; level surface.

■ Bake in 325°F (160°C) oven for 30 to 40 minutes or until top of cake springs back when lightly touched. Let cool for 5 minutes in pan on wire rack; loosen edges and invert cake onto rack. Peel off paper and let cool completely.

**BOTTOM GENOISE TIER:** Grease and flour 12-inch (6 L) round cake pan that is at least 3 inches (8 cm) deep. Line base with waxed paper and set aside. Double all ingredients in Genoise recipe; prepare as directed, but bake for 40 to 50 minutes.

**ASSEMBLY:** Using string or serrated knife, split each tier in half horizontally. Place base layer of bottom tier on serving platter. Slide strips of waxed paper under cake to protect platter from icing. Place base layer on top tier on slightly smaller round of oil-lined cardboard.

■ Using pastry brush, brush half of the Kirsch Syrup over base layers of each tier; spread each evenly with some of the Strawberry Buttercream. Place top layers of each tier on base layers; brush with remaining Kirsch Syrup. Spread Strawberry Buttercream over top and sides of each tier, reserving enough for piping.

■ Insert plastic straw supports and stack tiers. Using pastry bag fitted with rose tip (No. 103), pipe remaining Buttercream in swags around tiers. Using leaf tip (No. 69), decoratively pipe leaves around edges. Refrigerate for up to 2 days.

**GARNISH:** Just before serving, garnish cake with strawberries and leaves. Makes 25 regular or 50 small servings.

| | **KIRSCH SYRUP:** | |
|---|---|---|
| 1/2 cup | **granulated sugar** | 125 mL |
| 1/2 cup | **water** | 125 mL |
| 1/4 cup | **kirsch or orange liqueur** | 50 mL |

■ In small saucepan, combine sugar with water. Bring to boil, stirring occasionally; cook over medium-high heat for 1 minute without stirring. Remove from heat and stir in kirsch. Let cool completely. Makes about 1 cup (250 mL).

| | **STRAWBERRY BUTTERCREAM ICING (make recipe twice):** | |
|---|---|---|
| 2 cups | **strawberries, hulled** | 500 mL |
| 1 lb | **unsalted butter** | 454 g |
| 1 cup | **granulated sugar** | 250 mL |
| 3/4 cup | **water** | 175 mL |
| 4 | **egg whites** | 4 |
| 2 tbsp | **kirsch or orange liqueur** | 25 mL |

■ In food processor or blender, process strawberries until puréed. Pass through fine sieve; set aside. Beat butter until softened; set aside.

■ In heavy saucepan, combine sugar and water; bring to boil, stirring occasionally. Cook over medium-high heat, without stirring, for 5 to 10 minutes or until syrup registers 234°F (112°C) on candy thermometer and is at soft-ball stage (1/2 tsp/2 mL of syrup dropped into fresh cold water forms ball when pressed together but does not hold its shape).

■ Meanwhile, in large bowl, beat egg whites until soft peaks form. Gradually pour in hot syrup, beating constantly; beat until cool and very stiff, about 10 minutes. Gradually beat in butter until smooth and fluffy. Gradually beat in strawberry purée and kirsch. Makes about 4 cups (1 L).

# A SUMMER FAMILY REUNION

FOR TWENTY

*Summer is traditionally the time for family reunions. Whether a picnic in the park, a barbecue in the backyard or supper on the porch, reunions are usually noisy and happy. Potluck suppers, where everyone brings a favorite dish and the food tastes wonderful, make the event even more memorable.*

COLD MEATS OR BARBECUED MEATS

PICKLED VEGETABLES, MARINATED MUSHROOMS AND ONION RINGS

*BUFFET CHICKEN SALAD

*PASTA VEGETABLE SALAD

*TOMATO, RED ONION AND ZUCCHINI SALAD

*BEST BEAN SALAD

*ORANGE RAISIN CUPCAKES

*OATMEAL CHOCOLATE CHIP COOKIES

*SUMMER BERRY PIE

*LEMON SQUARES

## *Buffet Chicken Salad*

*This is a popular salad for nearly any occasion.*

| | | |
|---|---|---|
| **5 cups** | **chopped cooked chicken** | **1.25 L** |
| **4 cups** | **cantaloupe balls or seedless green grapes, halved** | **1 L** |
| **1 cup** | **slivered almonds** | **250 mL** |
| **1 cup** | **finely chopped celery** | **250 mL** |
| **1/4 cup** | **minced onion** | **50 mL** |
| **1** | **red pepper, chopped** | **1** |
| | **Lettuce leaves** | |
| | **DRESSING:** | |
| **1 cup** | **plain yogurt** | **250 mL** |
| **1 cup** | **mayonnaise** | **250 mL** |
| **1 tbsp** | **lemon juice** | **15 mL** |
| **1 tsp** | **curry powder** | **5 mL** |
| **1 tsp** | **ginger** | **5 mL** |
| | **Salt and pepper** | |

*(Clockwise from bottom right) Buffet Chicken Salad; Pasta Vegetable Salad; Tomato, Red Onion and Zucchini Salad; Oatmeal Chocolate Chip Cookies; Lemon Squares; Orange Raisin Cupcakes; Summer Berry Pie; pickled vegetables; Best Bean Salad; marinated onion rings; shrimp mousse*

■ In salad bowl, combine chicken, cantaloupe, almonds, celery, onion, and red pepper (if using).

**DRESSING:** Combine yogurt, mayonnaise, lemon juice, curry powder, ginger, and salt and pepper to taste; mix well. Pour over salad and toss to mix.

■ Cover and refrigerate for several hours or until chilled and flavors are blended. Serve on lettuce-lined platter. Makes about 10 servings. Recipe can be doubled.

# Pasta Vegetable Salad

*This salad is a reliable favorite to serve with cold meats for summer buffet suppers. The salad can be doubled, but don't double the vinaigrette.*

| | | |
|---|---|---|
| **5 cups** | **cooked spaghetti or other pasta (10 oz/300 g uncooked)*** | **1.25 L** |
| **2** | **large stalks celery, sliced** | **2** |
| **Half** | **each sweet red, yellow and green peppers, diced** | **Half** |
| **Half** | **head cauliflower, cut in florets** | **Half** |
| **3/4 cup** | **pimiento-stuffed green olives** | **175 mL** |
| **1/2 cup** | **chopped fresh parsley** | **125 mL** |
| **1/4 cup** | **chopped green onion** | **50 mL** |
| **2 tbsp** | **chopped fresh basil or dill (or 1 tsp/5 mL dried)** | **25 mL** |
| | **VINAIGRETTE:** | |
| **1/3 cup** | **white vinegar** | **75 mL** |
| **2** | **cloves garlic, minced** | **2** |
| **1 tsp** | **dry mustard** | **5 mL** |
| **1 tsp** | **Italian herb seasoning (oregano, basil and marjoram)** | **5 mL** |
| **1-1/3 cups** | **vegetable oil** | **325 mL** |
| | **Salt and pepper** | |
| | **Basil leaves (optional)** | |

■ In large salad bowl, combine pasta, celery, red, yellow and green peppers, cauliflower, olives, parsley, onion and basil; toss to mix. **VINAIGRETTE:** In food processor, blender or mixing bowl, combine vinegar, garlic, mustard and Italian seasoning; blend well. With motor running or while whisking, add oil and process until well combined. Season with salt and pepper to taste.

■ Pour half of the vinaigrette over salad and toss to mix. Cover and let stand for a few hours or overnight (refrigerate during warm weather but serve at room temperature). Season with salt, pepper and more vinaigrette, if desired. Garnish with basil leaves (if using). Makes about 10 servings. Recipe can be doubled.

*Rinse hot cooked pasta under cold running water to prevent sticking.

# Tomato, Red Onion and Zucchini Salad

*This attractive salad is perfect for picnics or buffets with hamburgers, cold meats, roast turkey or ham.*

| | | |
|---|---|---|
| **6** | **small zucchini (6-inch/15 cm), sliced** | **6** |
| **4** | **tomatoes, cut in chunks** | **4** |
| **2** | **small red onions, sliced and separated in rings** | **2** |
| **2** | **stalks celery, sliced** | **2** |
| **1/2 cup** | **chopped fresh parsley** | **125 mL** |
| | **DRESSING:** | |
| **2 tbsp** | **wine vinegar** | **25 mL** |
| **1** | **large clove garlic, minced** | **1** |
| **1/2 tsp** | **dry mustard** | **2 mL** |
| **1/4 tsp** | **salt** | **1 mL** |
| **1/2 cup** | **olive or vegetable oil** | **125 mL** |
| | **Pepper** | |
| | **Celery leaves (optional)** | |

■ In salad bowl, combine zucchini, tomatoes, onions, celery and parsley. **DRESSING:** In food processor, blender or mixing bowl, combine vinegar, garlic, mustard and salt. With motor running or while whisking, add oil and process until well combined.

■ Pour dressing over salad and toss to mix. Cover and refrigerate for at least 1 hour or overnight. Add pepper to taste; garnish with celery leaves (if using). Makes about 10 servings. Recipe can be doubled.

***SIP A SUMMER FLAVOR***

***Family members of all ages will enjoy a cool, thirst-quenching drink. Serve a well-loved classic like iced lemonade or, for a change, offer fruit spritzers. Just add water or soda to fruit juice concentrates. Top with ice.***

## Best Bean Salad

*Sweet and sour flavors complement a colorful mix of beans.*

| | | |
|---|---|---|
| 1 lb | wax beans | 500 g |
| 1 lb | green beans | 500 g |
| 1 | can (19 oz/540 mL) red kidney beans | 1 |
| 1 | can (19 oz/540 mL) lima or broad beans | 1 |
| 1 | can (19 oz/540 mL) pinto beans | 1 |
| 1 | can (19 oz/540 mL) chick-peas | 1 |
| 2 | sweet green peppers, chopped | 2 |
| 1 | large Spanish onion, thinly sliced and separated in rings | 1 |
| | MARINADE: | |
| 1/2 cup | red wine vinegar | 125 mL |
| 1/4 cup | vegetable oil | 50 mL |
| 1/3 cup | granulated sugar | 75 mL |
| 1/3 cup | packed brown sugar | 75 mL |
| 1 tsp | pepper | 5 mL |
| 1/2 tsp | salt | 2 mL |

■ Snap off ends of wax and green beans; cut into 1-1/2-inch (4 cm) pieces. In saucepan of rapidly boiling water, cook fresh beans for 3 minutes. Drain and plunge into cold water until cool. Drain again and pat dry.

■ Drain canned beans and rinse under cold water; drain well. In salad bowl, combine wax, green, kidney, lima and pinto beans; mix in chick-peas, green peppers and onion.

**MARINADE:** Combine vinegar, oil, granulated and brown sugars, pepper and salt; stir until sugars have dissolved. Pour over bean mixture and mix well. Cover and refrigerate overnight. Makes about 20 servings.

## Orange Raisin Cupcakes

*Old-fashioned frosted cupcakes will please young and old alike.*

| | | |
|---|---|---|
| 1-1/2 cups | raisins | 375 mL |
| 1-1/2 cups | all-purpose flour | 375 mL |
| 1 tsp | baking soda | 5 mL |
| 1 tsp | cinnamon | 5 mL |
| 1/4 tsp | ground cloves | 1 mL |
| 1/4 cup | butter | 50 mL |
| 3/4 cup | granulated sugar | 175 mL |
| 1 | egg, beaten | 1 |
| 1 tbsp | grated orange rind | 15 mL |
| | Frosting (recipe follows) | |

■ In saucepan, cover raisins with water and bring to boil; reduce heat and simmer for 20 minutes. Drain, reserving 1/2 cup (125 mL) liquid; let cool.

■ In bowl, sift together flour, baking soda, cinnamon and cloves. In separate bowl, cream together butter and sugar until well mixed. Add egg and orange rind; beat well. Alternately stir in reserved raisin liquid and sifted dry ingredients, making 2 additions of each. Add cooled raisins and mix until combined.

■ Spoon batter into 12 greased or paper-lined muffin cups; bake in 375°F (190°C) oven for 20 to 25 minutes or until tester inserted in center comes out clean. Remove to wire rack and let cool. Ice with frosting. Makes 12 cupcakes.

| | | |
|---|---|---|
| | FROSTING: | |
| 2/3 cup | icing sugar | 150 mL |
| 2 tbsp | packed brown sugar | 25 mL |
| 2 tbsp | butter | 25 mL |
| 1 tbsp | milk | 15 mL |
| 1/2 tsp | vanilla or maple flavoring | 2 mL |
| Pinch | salt | Pinch |

■ In bowl, beat together icing sugar, brown sugar, butter, milk, vanilla and salt until smooth and creamy.

## Summer Berry Pie

*Use one kind of berry or a combination in this gorgeous glazed pie. For 20 servings, you'll need about 3 pies.*

| | BUTTER PASTRY: | |
|---|---|---|
| 1 cup | all-purpose flour | 250 mL |
| 2 tbsp | granulated sugar | 25 mL |
| 1/2 tsp | baking powder | 2 mL |
| Pinch | salt | Pinch |
| 1/4 cup | butter | 50 mL |
| 1 | egg, beaten with 1 tbsp (15 mL) ice water | 1 |
| | FILLING: | |
| 2 cups | strawberries, sliced | 500 mL |
| 3/4 cup | granulated sugar | 175 mL |
| 1/4 cup | cornstarch | 50 mL |
| Pinch | salt | Pinch |
| 2 cups | raspberries, loganberries, blackberries or blueberries | 500 mL |

**BUTTER PASTRY:** In bowl, combine flour, sugar, baking powder and salt. With pastry blender or 2 knives, cut in butter until mixture resembles coarse crumbs. Add egg mixture and mix lightly; gather into ball.

■ On lightly floured surface, roll out pastry and fit into 8-inch (20 cm) pie plate. (Alternatively, pat pastry into pie plate.) Flute edge, then prick all over with fork. Bake in 375°F (190°C) oven for 20 minutes or until golden. Let cool.

**FILLING:** In bowl, combine strawberries and sugar (if using just strawberries, use 4 cups/1 L); let stand for 2-1/2 hours.* Transfer to colander set over bowl and let drain for 30 minutes. Add enough water to juice to make 1-1/2 cups (375 mL) liquid; set strawberries aside.

■ In saucepan, combine juice mixture, cornstarch and salt; stir until smooth. Cook over medium heat, stirring, until mixture boils and has thickened; reduce heat and simmer for 2 minutes. Remove from heat and let cool to room temperature.

■ Add reserved strawberries and raspberries (or other berries) to cooled mixture; mix lightly. Spoon into baked pie shell and refrigerate for at least 2 hours. Serve at room temperature. Makes 6 to 8 servings.

*This method gives a clear flavorful glaze. But if you are in a hurry, mash 1 cup (250 mL) strawberries and add 1-1/4 cups (300 mL) water. Stir in cornstarch and salt; bring to boil. Boil until thickened and clear. Let cool and add remaining berries; spoon into pie shell.

## Lemon Squares

*Light and tart, these squares disappear quickly at family gatherings.*

| | | |
|---|---|---|
| 1 cup | all-purpose flour | 250 mL |
| 1/2 cup | butter | 125 mL |
| 1/4 cup | granulated sugar | 50 mL |
| | TOPPING: | |
| 1 cup | granulated sugar | 250 mL |
| 2 tbsp | all-purpose flour | 25 mL |
| 1/2 tsp | baking powder | 2 mL |
| 1/4 tsp | salt | 1 mL |
| 2 | eggs, lightly beaten | 2 |
| 2 tsp | grated lemon rind | 10 mL |
| 3 tbsp | lemon juice | 50 mL |
| | Icing sugar | |

■ In food processor or bowl, combine flour, butter and sugar; mix well. Press into greased and floured 8-inch (2 L) square baking pan; bake in 325°F (160°C) oven for 20 minutes or until golden.

**TOPPING:** In food processor or bowl, combine sugar, flour, baking powder, salt, eggs, lemon rind and juice; mix well.

■ Spread over base and return to 325°F (160°C) oven for 20 to 25 minutes or until nearly set. Let cool in pan. Dust with icing sugar. Makes about 20 small squares.

***OATMEAL CHOCOLATE CHIP COOKIES***

***Crisp oatmeal cookies with chocolate chips and raisins are a perennial favorite.***

***In large bowl, cream together 3/4 cup (175 mL) butter, 3/4 cup (175 mL) granulated sugar, 1/2 cup (125 mL) packed brown sugar and 1 egg. Add 1 cup (250 mL) whole wheat flour, 1 cup (250 mL) rolled oats, 1/4 cup (50 mL) wheat germ, and 1 tsp (5 mL) each baking powder and baking soda; mix well. Stir in 1-1/2 cups (375 mL) raisins and 3/4 cup (175 mL) chocolate chips.***

***Drop by heaping spoonfuls onto lightly greased baking sheets; flatten slightly with floured fork. Bake in 350°F (180°C) oven for 12 to 15 minutes or until light golden. Makes about 3 dozen.***

# A BRIDAL OR BABY SHOWER

FOR TWENTY TO TWENTY-FOUR

*Celebrate the good news with a shower featuring foods that are as pretty as they are delicious. Our recipes serve 20 to 24 people at an afternoon or evening party. If it's a luncheon, add salads for a more substantial menu.*

PARTY SANDWICHES

*SMOKED SALMON STUFFED VEGETABLES

*CHOCOLATE HAZELNUT CHEESECAKE WITH CANDIED ROSES

*WHITE AND DARK CHOCOLATE BROWNIES

FRUIT TRAY

***PARTY SANDWICHES***
***Offer a variety of sandwiches, with about four kinds of fillings on different breads: brown for tuna, rye for egg, soft black bread for salmon, French bread for crab — or mix and match. If you're using rye or French bread, buy it presliced with at least 22 slices.***

***Sandwiches are more elegant when the crusts are trimmed off. Cut sandwiches into quarters for easy handling. Place in wicker baskets lined with paper doilies.***

***SETTING THE SCENE***
***Choose a color theme and coordinate the food and decorations accordingly. For a baby shower, you can decorate in pink or blue. If it's a bridal shower, you can use white as a theme or adopt the color scheme the bride is planning for her wedding.***

## *Smoked Salmon Stuffed Vegetables*

*This stuffing can also be used as one of the fillings for the party sandwiches.*

| | | |
|---|---|---|
| | **FILLING:** | |
| **1 lb** | **smoked salmon** | **500 g** |
| **1 lb** | **unsalted butter** | **454 g** |
| **2 tbsp** | **lemon juice** | **25 mL** |
| **1 tbsp** | **prepared horseradish** | **15 mL** |
| **1/2 tsp** | **pepper** | **2 mL** |
| | **VEGETABLES:** | |
| **48** | **snow peas** | **48** |
| **24** | **mushroom caps, 1-1/2 inches (4 cm) in diameter** | **24** |
| **24** | **cherry tomatoes** | **24** |
| | **GARNISH:** | |
| **1** | **jar (3-1/2 oz/100 g) black caviar** | **1** |
| **1** | **jar (3-1/2 oz/100 g) red caviar** | **1** |

**FILLING:** In food processor or blender, purée salmon in batches. (Alternatively, chop finely by hand.) Beat in butter, lemon juice, horseradish and pepper. Taste and adjust seasoning if necessary. (Filling can be refrigerated for up to 2 days, or frozen for longer storage; bring to room temperature before piping into vegetables.)

**VEGETABLES:** Bring large pot of water to boil; remove string from snow peas and cook for 15 seconds. Drain and rinse under cold running water; pat dry. Carefully open top side of each shell to resemble a little boat. Pat dry.

■ Wipe mushrooms with wet paper towels or wash briefly under cold running water (do not soak). Break or cut out stems carefully and pat caps dry.

■ Cut tops off cherry tomatoes and carefully scoop out pulp. Invert onto paper towels to drain.

**GARNISH:** Using piping bag fitted with star tip, pipe filling into vegetables. Spoon a little caviar onto each and arrange attractively on serving platter. To make vegetables "sit up straight," use a little filling to act as "glue" on the bottom if necessary. Makes 96 appetizers.

# *Chocolate Hazelnut Cheesecake with Candied Roses*

*This cake is beautiful to look at, delicious to taste. You can eat the roses as long as they haven't been sprayed with insecticide.*

| | | |
|---|---|---|
| | **CHOCOLATE NUT CRUST:** | |
| **1 cup** | **fine chocolate wafer cookie crumbs** | **250 mL** |
| **1/2 cup** | **finely chopped hazelnuts** | **125 mL** |
| **1/3 cup** | **unsalted butter, melted** | **75 mL** |
| | **FILLING:** | |
| **12 oz** | **bittersweet chocolate** | **375 g** |
| **1-1/2 lb** | **cream cheese** | **750 g** |
| **1 cup** | **granulated sugar** | **250 mL** |
| **3** | **eggs** | **3** |
| **1 cup** | **sour cream** | **250 mL** |
| **2 tbsp** | **hazelnut liqueur (Frangelico) or rum or brandy** | **25 mL** |
| **1-1/2 tsp** | **vanilla** | **7 mL** |
| **1/2 tsp** | **almond extract** | **2 mL** |
| | **CHOCOLATE GLAZE:** | |
| **4 oz** | **bittersweet chocolate** | **125 g** |
| **1/4 cup** | **whipping cream** | **50 mL** |
| **1 tbsp** | **hazelnut liqueur (Frangelico) or rum or brandy** | **15 mL** |
| | **Chocolate Rose Leaves and Candied Roses (see sidebar)** | |

**CHOCOLATE NUT CRUST:** Combine cookie crumbs, nuts and melted butter; pat onto bottom of 9-inch (2.5 L) springform pan. Set aside.
**FILLING:** In top of double boiler, over hot, not boiling, water, melt chocolate; let cool slightly. In mixing bowl, beat cheese until creamy; beat in sugar, then chocolate. Add eggs, one at a time, beating after each addition. Blend in sour cream, liqueur, vanilla and almond extract; pour into crumb crust.

■ Bake in 350°F (180°C) oven for 50 to 60 minutes or until almost completely set. (Cake will firm up when cold.) Let cool to room temperature.
**CHOCOLATE GLAZE:** In top of double boiler over hot, not boiling, water, melt chocolate with cream, stirring until smooth. Remove from heat and stir in liqueur.

■ Remove cake from pan and spread with glaze. (Cake may be prepared to this point and refrigerated for up to three days, or frozen for longer storage.)

■ Arrange roses in center of glazed cake; surround with chocolate leaves. Present on fancy doily on pedestal cake plate for full effect. Refrigerate until serving time. Makes 20 to 24 servings.

# *White and Dark Chocolate Brownies*

*Dress the brownies up with a chocolate glaze and decorate them with the initials of the bride-to-be or newborn baby, then set them out in pretty paper cups.*

| | | |
|---|---|---|
| **4 oz** | **unsweetened chocolate** | **125 g** |
| **6 oz** | **bittersweet chocolate** | **175 g** |
| **1 cup** | **unsalted butter** | **250 mL** |
| **4** | **eggs** | **4** |
| **2 cups** | **granulated sugar** | **500 mL** |
| **2 tsp** | **vanilla** | **10 mL** |
| **1 cup** | **all-purpose flour** | **250 mL** |
| **1 tsp** | **baking powder** | **5 mL** |
| **1 cup** | **chopped white chocolate** | **250 mL** |
| **1 cup** | **chopped toasted walnuts*** | **250 mL** |
| | **GLAZE:** | |
| **8 oz** | **bittersweet chocolate** | **250 g** |
| **1/2 cup** | **whipping cream** | **125 mL** |
| | **DECORATOR ICING** | |
| **1 tbsp** | **(approx) orange liqueur or water** | **15 mL** |
| **1 cup** | **sifted icing sugar** | **250 mL** |
| **1/4 tsp** | **vanilla** | **1 mL** |

*CHOCOLATE ROSE LEAVES*

***In top of double boiler over hot, not boiling, water, melt 4 oz (125 g) bittersweet or compound (enrobing) chocolate; remove from heat and let cool slightly until spreadable but not runny.***

***Working with one fresh rose leaf at a time, spread back of leaf with chocolate; place on waxed-paper-lined baking sheet to set. Freeze until firm, about 1 hour.***

***Working with one leaf at a time, gently peel leaf from chocolate. Discard real leaf and place chocolate leaves in freezer until ready to use. Makes 8 to 16 leaves.***

*CANDIED ROSES*

***Working over waxed paper and using pastry brush, brush lightly beaten egg whites completely over each fresh rose, including each petal. Sprinkle each petal heavily with sugar. Set roses on wire rack to dry. (Two egg whites will cover about 4 roses.)***

*(Clockwise from top) Chocolate Hazelnut Cheesecake with Candied Roses; White and Dark Chocolate Brownies; fruit tray; Party Sandwiches*

■ In top of double boiler over hot, not boiling, water, melt unsweetened and bittersweet chocolate with butter; let cool slightly.

■ In mixing bowl, beat eggs with sugar; stir in vanilla. Beat in chocolate-butter mixture. Mix or sift together flour, baking powder and salt; gently fold into chocolate batter. Stir in white chocolate and nuts. Spoon into foil- or parchment-lined 13- × 9-inch (3.5 L) baking dish. Bake in 350°F (180°C) oven for 35 to 40 minutes or until crusty on top but still very soft underneath. Do not overbake (brownies will firm up as they cool). Let cool slightly; run knife around edge of cake and invert onto wire rack to cool completely.

**GLAZE:** In top of double boiler over hot, not boiling, water, melt chocolate with cream, stirring. Spread over brownies. Cut into squares and place in paper cups.

**DECORATOR ICING:** Mix enough liqueur into icing sugar to make stiff consistency for piping. Stir in vanilla. With piping bag fitted with small plain tip or with tube made from parchment paper, pipe icing into initials on top of each brownie.

■ Store in tightly sealed container in refrigerator or freeze. Makes about 4 dozen.

*To toast walnuts, spread on baking sheet and toast in 350°F (180°C) oven for about 5 minutes or until golden.

# THE GREAT OUTDOORS

*Hooray for summer! Backyard barbecues, beach parties, picnics in the park. From the first long weekend in May to back-to-school time after Labor Day, all Canada moves outdoors in a carefree celebration of sunshine and sandcastles and wonderful things to eat. In this chapter, we entertain with a sunny luncheon on the top deck and barbecue suppers that adapt beautifully to country cottages or city backyards. Whether you're planning poolside cocktails for sixteen or a romantic picnic for two, our menus bring you the very best of the season. But our love affair with the outdoors doesn't end in September. We make the most of a glorious autumn afternoon with a pack-and-go picnic hamper for bikes or car. And many Canadians look forward to wintertime most of all, so we've included a warming repast of hot toddies, hearty soups and fresh-baked breads around a roaring fireplace.*

# A LOAF AND LADLE PARTY

FOR EIGHT

*Welcoming aromas of gently simmering soups and fresh bread greet your friends as they return from the ski trails or a sleighride. Casual, cozy fare is wonderful after outdoor winter fun, and a loaf and ladle party is a joy to host. Start with a full-bodied toddy, some easy nibblies, then move on to hearty soups and rustic breads; toss in a green salad for good measure, if you like. The recipes are all variations on classic dishes and everything can be made ahead and reheated.*

*GINGER-RYE TODDY

*FRENCH ONION SOUP WITH MADEIRA

*FRENCH-CANADIAN MIXED LEGUME SOUP

*THREE-PASTA SOUP

CARAWAY BREAD

*COUNTRY LOAF

*BREADSTICKS WRAPPED IN PROSCIUTTO

*UPSIDE-DOWN APPLE GINGERBREAD

*MAPLE PECAN PIE

**Recipes are given for menu items marked with an asterisk.*

***GINGER-RYE TODDY***

***Wintry days call for warming libations, and this hot toddy, made with apple juice for extra body, certainly does the trick.***

***In large saucepan, combine 8 cups (2 L) apple juice with 2 oz (50 g) sliced peeled gingerroot. Bring to boil, then reduce heat and simmer, uncovered, for 20 to 25 minutes or until reduced to 6 cups (1.5 L).***

***Remove gingerroot. (Recipe can be made ahead to this point, covered and refrigerated overnight. Reheat before proceeding.) Stir in 1 cup (250 mL) Canadian whisky. Serve immediately in warmed mugs with cinnamon stick in each. Makes about 8 servings.***

*Country Loaf; caraway bread; French-Canadian Mixed Legume Soup; Three-Pasta Soup; French Onion Soup with Madeira*

# French Onion Soup with Madeira

*While classic French onion soup needs little introduction and no improvement, this tantalizing version is extra special. Madeira (instead of dry white wine) adds rich sweetness to the broth and the slowly simmered golden onions. A creamy cheese mixture is the crowning glory.*

| | | |
|---|---|---|
| **1/4 cup** | **butter** | **50 mL** |
| **6 cups** | **thinly sliced onions** | **1.5 L** |
| **2** | **cloves garlic, crushed** | **2** |
| **1 tsp** | **salt** | **5 mL** |
| **1/2 tsp** | **granulated sugar** | **2 mL** |
| **1/4 cup** | **all-purpose flour** | **50 mL** |
| **7 cups** | **beef stock** | **1.75 L** |
| **1/2 cup** | **Madeira or sherry** | **125 mL** |
| | **Salt and pepper** | |
| | **TOPPING:** | |
| **16** | **thick slices French stick (baguette)** | **16** |
| **1/4 cup** | **mayonnaise** | **50 mL** |
| **2 tbsp** | **Dijon mustard** | **25 mL** |
| **2 cups** | **shredded Swiss cheese** | **500 mL** |
| | **Freshly grated Parmesan cheese (optional)** | |

■ In large heavy saucepan, melt butter over medium heat; cook onions and garlic, stirring occasionally, for 15 minutes. Add salt and sugar; cook, stirring frequently, for 30 to 40 minutes or until onions are deep golden brown.

■ Stir in flour; cook, stirring, for 2 minutes. Add stock and Madeira; simmer, partially covered, for 30 minutes. Season with salt and pepper to taste.

**TOPPING:** Meanwhile, on baking sheet, bake bread in 325°F (160°C) oven for about 30 minutes or until dry and lightly browned.

■ In bowl, blend mayonnaise with mustard; stir in Swiss cheese. Spread on top of each bread round. Ladle soup into ovenproof bowls. Float 2 bread rounds, cheese side up, in each bowl. Sprinkle with Parmesan (if using). Broil until cheese mixture is bubbly and lightly browned. Makes 8 servings.

# French-Canadian Mixed Legume Soup

*Similar to French-Canadian pea soup, this smooth and creamy split pea and navy bean soup mellows and thickens when made a day ahead. Traditionally, the cooked salt pork would be chopped and returned to the soup or sliced thinly and served separately.*

| | | |
|---|---|---|
| **3/4 cup** | **navy (pea) beans** | **175 mL** |
| **3/4 cup** | **yellow split peas** | **175 mL** |
| **3/4 cup** | **green split peas** | **175 mL** |
| **1** | **piece salt pork (1/4 lb/125 g)** | **1** |
| **1** | **large onion, chopped** | **1** |
| **1** | **bay leaf** | **1** |
| **2 tsp** | **salt** | **10 mL** |
| **1 tsp** | **dried savory** | **5 mL** |
| **1 cup** | **diced celery** | **250 mL** |
| **1 cup** | **diced carrot** | **250 mL** |
| | **Salt and pepper** | |

■ Rinse and sort beans, discarding any blemished ones. Cover with cold water and soak overnight.

■ Drain beans, reserving soaking liquid. Measure liquid; add enough fresh water to make 12 cups (3 L).

■ Pour liquid into large saucepan or Dutch oven; add beans, yellow and green peas, salt pork, onion, bay leaf, salt and savory. Bring to boil; reduce heat and simmer, covered, for 1-1/2 hours. Add celery and carrot; simmer, covered, for 30 minutes or until peas, beans and vegetables are tender. Remove salt pork and bay leaf.

■ Using slotted spoon, remove 2 cups (500 mL) of the vegetables. Mash or purée in blender or food processor, then return to saucepan; cook until heated through. Season with salt and pepper to taste. Makes about 8 servings.

# Three-Pasta Soup

*Saffron and fennel seeds add lovely distinctive flavors to this hearty minestrone. If leeks are unavailable, use an extra onion.*

| | | |
|---|---|---|
| **2 tbsp** | **olive oil** | **25 mL** |
| **2** | **cloves garlic, minced** | **2** |
| **3** | **small leeks, sliced (white parts only)** | **3** |
| **1** | **onion, chopped** | **1** |
| **2** | **stalks celery, sliced** | **2** |
| **2** | **large carrots, quartered lengthwise and sliced** | **2** |
| **8 cups** | **chicken stock** | **2 L** |
| **1-1/2 cups** | **tomato purée*** | **375 mL** |
| **1/2 tsp** | **crushed fennel seeds** | **2 mL** |
| **1/4 tsp** | **(approx) saffron threads** | **1 mL** |
| **1** | **bay leaf** | **1** |
| **1 cup** | **green beans, cut in 1-inch (2.5 cm) pieces** | **250 mL** |
| **1/2 cup** | **tortellini** | **125 mL** |
| **1/2 cup** | **rotini** | **125 mL** |
| **1/2 cup** | **radiatore or other small pasta** | **125 mL** |
| **1/2 cup** | **cooked or canned romano or navy beans** | **125 mL** |
| **1** | **small zucchini, halved lengthwise and sliced** | **1** |
| **2 oz** | **fresh oyster or chanterelle mushrooms, sliced (optional)** | **50 g** |
| | **Salt and pepper** | |
| | **Freshly grated Parmesan cheese** | |

■ In large saucepan or Dutch oven, heat oil over medium heat; cook garlic, leeks, onion, celery and carrots until softened, about 5 minutes.

■ Stir in stock, tomato purée, fennel seeds, saffron and bay leaf. Bring to boil; reduce heat and simmer, covered, for 15 minutes.

■ Add green beans and tortellini; simmer, uncovered, for 5 minutes. Add rotini and radiatore; simmer for 10 minutes. Add romano beans and zucchini; simmer for 5 minutes.

■ Add mushrooms (if using); simmer for 1 minute or until pasta and vegetables are tender. Remove bay leaf. Season with salt and pepper to taste and more saffron if desired. Ladle into soup bowls and pass Parmesan. Makes 8 to 10 servings.

*Use canned crushed tomatoes available at Italian food stores and some supermarkets. Or, drain and seed 1 can (28 oz/796 mL) plum tomatoes; purée in food processor or food mill.

# Country Loaf

*Similar in texture to a sourdough bread, this rustic bread is superb with hearty soups. The baked loaves can be wrapped and frozen for up to one month.*

| | | |
|---|---|---|
| **2** | **small potatoes, peeled (about 1/2 lb/250 g total)** | **2** |
| **1 tsp** | **granulated sugar** | **5 mL** |
| **1/4 cup** | **warm water** | **50 mL** |
| **1** | **pkg active dry yeast (or 1 tbsp/15 mL)** | **1** |
| **1 tbsp** | **salt** | **15 mL** |
| **1 tbsp** | **lard or shortening, melted and cooled** | **15 mL** |
| **3 cups** | **(approx) all-purpose flour** | **750 mL** |
| **2 cups** | **whole wheat flour** | **500 mL** |
| **2 tbsp** | **cornmeal** | **25 mL** |

■ In pot of boiling water, cook potatoes until tender. Drain, reserving 1-1/2 cups (375 mL) of the cooking liquid; mash and set aside.

■ Dissolve sugar in warm water; sprinkle in yeast and let stand for 10 minutes or until frothy.

■ In large bowl, combine mashed potatoes, reserved lukewarm cooking liquid, salt and lard. Stir in yeast mixture and 1 cup (250 mL) of the all-purpose flour. With wooden spoon, gradually stir in whole wheat flour and up to 1-1/2 cups (375 mL) of the remaining all-purpose flour to make dough that holds together but is still soft.

■ Turn out onto lightly floured surface; knead in enough of remaining flour until smooth and elastic, about 10 minutes. Place in greased bowl, turning dough to grease all

***BREADSTICKS WRAPPED IN PROSCIUTTO***

***One thin slice of prosciutto ham spread with a nippy mustard butter wraps nicely around a crisp breadstick. If you're using Westphalian or other similar ham, you may need more than one slice.***

***Beat 1/3 cup (75 mL) butter with 1 tbsp (15 mL) grainy mustard until well blended. Spread about 1 tsp (5 mL) each over 16 very thin slices of prosciutto or Westphalian ham. Wrap one slice around each of 16 breadsticks. Makes 16 appetizers.***

over; cover with plastic wrap. Let rise for 1-1/2 to 2 hours or until doubled in bulk.

■ Punch down dough; turn out onto lightly floured surface. Knead into smooth ball. Divide dough in half and shape into 2 round loaves; dust tops with all-purpose flour if desired.

■ Grease two 6-cup (1.5 L) soufflé dishes or baking sheet; sprinkle with cornmeal. Place dough in dishes and cover loosely with plastic wrap; let rise again until doubled in bulk, about 1 hour.

■ Using serrated knife, carefully make crisscross slashes across top of loaves. Bake in 375°F (190°C) oven for 40 to 45 minutes or until golden brown and bottoms of loaves sound hollow when tapped. Transfer loaves to wire rack and let cool completely. Makes 2 loaves.

## *Upside-Down Apple Gingerbread*

*Caramel-glazed apple (or pear) slices top this wonderfully moist gingerbread cake. Enjoy it at its best—sliced while still warm with dollops of whipped cream.*

| | | |
|---|---|---|
| **1-2/3 cups** | **granulated sugar** | **400 mL** |
| **1/3 cup** | **water** | **75 mL** |
| **3** | **Granny Smith apples, peeled and sliced** | **3** |
| **1-2/3 cups** | **all-purpose flour** | **400 mL** |
| **1-1/2 tsp** | **ginger** | **7 mL** |
| **1 tsp** | **baking soda** | **5 mL** |
| **1 tsp** | **cinnamon** | **5 mL** |
| **1/4 tsp** | **ground cloves** | **1 mL** |
| **1/4 tsp** | **salt** | **1 mL** |
| **1/2 cup** | **shortening** | **125 mL** |
| **1** | **egg** | **1** |
| **3/4 cup** | **buttermilk** | **175 mL** |
| **2 tbsp** | **molasses** | **25 mL** |

■ In heavy saucepan, stir together 2/3 cup (150 mL) of the sugar and water. Bring to boil, stirring occasionally; cook over medium-high heat, without stirring, for 5 to 10 minutes or until syrup is deep amber color. Immediately pour into 8-inch (2 L) square baking pan; arrange overlapping apple slices on top. Set aside.

■ In large bowl, sift together flour, remaining sugar, ginger, baking soda, cinnamon, cloves and salt. Cut in shortening until mixture resembles fine crumbs.

■ In separate bowl, beat together egg, buttermilk and molasses; stir into flour mixture. (Batter will be slightly lumpy.) Pour over apples. Bake in 350°F (180°C) oven for 50 to 60 minutes or until tester inserted in center comes out clean. Run knife around edge, then invert cake onto serving plate. Let cool slightly before serving.

## *Maple Pecan Pie*

*A sweet pie chock-full of pecans and richly flavored with maple syrup is hard to resist.*

| | | |
|---|---|---|
| | **Pastry for 9-inch (23 cm) single-crust pie** | |
| **1-1/2 cups** | **pecan halves** | **375 mL** |
| **4** | **eggs** | **4** |
| **1 cup** | **maple syrup** | **250 mL** |
| **1/2 cup** | **granulated sugar** | **125 mL** |
| **1/2 cup** | **packed brown sugar** | **125 mL** |
| **2 tbsp** | **butter, melted** | **25 mL** |
| **1 tsp** | **vanilla** | **5 mL** |

■ Roll out pastry to 1/8-inch (3 mm) thickness and fit into pie plate; trim excess and flute edges. Arrange pecans over pastry; refrigerate while preparing filling.

■ In bowl, beat together eggs, maple syrup, granulated and brown sugars, butter and vanilla just until blended; spoon into pie shell.

■ Bake in 375°F (190°C) oven for 40 to 45 minutes or until pastry is golden brown and filling is set.

# A ROMANTIC BOAT PICNIC

FOR TWO

*Whether cruising down a lazy river, floating on a tranquil lagoon in the park or moored in a secluded cove in lake country, nothing is more romantic than a picnic for two by the water. It's easy to recreate a carefree 1920s mood with some spiffy vintage outfits (don't forget the boater hats), wicker baskets, lacy napkins and fresh posies.*

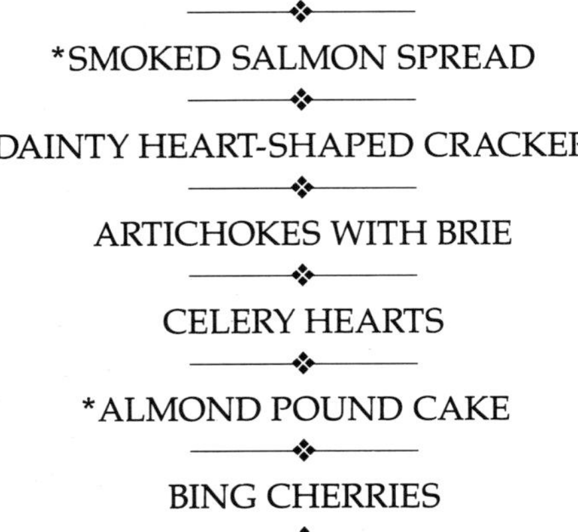

*SMOKED SALMON SPREAD

*DAINTY HEART-SHAPED CRACKERS

ARTICHOKES WITH BRIE

CELERY HEARTS

*ALMOND POUND CAKE

BING CHERRIES

WHITE WINE

## Smoked Salmon Spread

*Garnish this delicately flavored spread with smoked salmon roses. Simply roll up slices of smoked salmon, fanning the edges out to form a rose shape.*

| | | |
|---|---|---|
| **1 cup** | **shredded Cheddar cheese** | **250 mL** |
| **1/4 lb** | **cream cheese** | **125 g** |
| **2 tbsp** | **dry sherry** | **25 mL** |
| **1 tbsp** | **butter** | **15 mL** |
| **1 tbsp** | **lemon juice** | **15 mL** |
| **1/4 lb** | **sliced smoked salmon** | **125 g** |
| | **Salt and pepper** | |

■ In food processor or with electric mixer, cream together Cheddar and cream cheeses, sherry, butter and lemon juice.

■ Reserve 1 or 2 slices salmon for garnish. Chop remaining salmon coarsely and add to processor; process just until blended. Taste and adjust seasoning with salt and pepper if necessary.

■ Pack into crock; cover and refrigerate until serving time. (Can be refrigerated for up to 3 days.) To serve, garnish with remaining salmon slices rolled into rose shape. Makes 1-1/2 cups (375 mL).

## Dainty Heart-Shaped Crackers

*Nibble crisp sesame-seed crackers with the salmon spread.*

| | | |
|---|---|---|
| **1/2 cup** | **whole wheat flour** | **125 mL** |
| **1/2 cup** | **all-purpose flour** | **125 mL** |
| **1/4 cup** | **cornmeal** | **50 mL** |

*(Clockwise from bottom left) Artichokes with Brie; Dainty Heart-Shaped Crackers; celery hearts; Bing cherries; Almond Pound Cake; Smoked Salmon Spread*

***ROMANTIC PICNIC FARE***

***A boat picnic calls for food that's delightfully indulgent yet easy to tote and eat. Our menu suggestions are designed for leisurely nibbling, such as a pretty pot of***

*Smoked Salmon Spread to eat with crispy sesame-seed crackers. Artichokes, too, make great finger food. At home, steam them until tender, then chill and pack for nibbling leaf by leaf along with some perfectly ripe Brie. For a sweet ending, choose a rich little cake that travels well, such as Almond Pound Cake, accompanied with easy-to-eat fruit like Bing cherries.*

| | | |
|---|---|---|
| 1 tbsp | granulated sugar | 15 mL |
| 1/4 tsp | baking soda | 1 mL |
| 1/4 tsp | salt | 1 mL |
| 2 tbsp | butter | 25 mL |
| 1/4 cup | ice-cold water | 50 mL |
| 1 tbsp | vinegar | 15 mL |
| 1 | egg white, lightly beaten | 1 |
| | Sesame seeds | |

■ In bowl, stir together whole wheat and all-purpose flours, cornmeal, sugar, baking soda and salt; cut in butter until mixture resembles coarse crumbs. Add cold water and vinegar; stir until mixture can be gathered into ball. Knead gently just to form pliable dough.

■ On lightly floured surface, roll out dough to about 1/8-inch (3 mm) thickness. Cut into 2-inch (5 cm) heart shapes. Transfer to ungreased baking sheets. Lightly brush dough with egg white; sprinkle with sesame seeds.

■ Bake in 375°F (190°C) oven for 12 to 14 minutes or until faintly browned and crisp. Remove to rack and let cool. Store in airtight container. Makes about 2 dozen.

## Almond Pound Cake

*Mini loaf pans make dainty cakes for a picnic for two, but an 8- × 4-inch (1.5 L) loaf pan can be used instead. Simply add about ten minutes to the baking time.*

| | | |
|---|---|---|
| 1/2 cup | butter | 125 mL |
| 3/4 cup | granulated sugar | 175 mL |
| 2 | eggs | 2 |
| 1/4 tsp | almond extract | 1 mL |
| 1 tbsp | lemon juice | 15 mL |
| 1/2 tsp | grated lemon rind | 2 mL |
| 3/4 cup | cake-and-pastry flour | 175 mL |
| 1/2 cup | ground almonds | 125 mL |
| 1/2 tsp | baking powder | 2 mL |
| 1/4 cup | milk | 50 mL |

■ In bowl, cream together butter and sugar. Add eggs and almond extract; beat until light. Blend in lemon juice and rind. (Batter will appear curdled.)

■ Stir together flour, ground almonds and baking powder. Gradually add to creamed mixture alternately with milk, beating well after each addition.

■ Divide mixture among four greased 1-cup (250 mL) mini loaf pans. Bake in 325°F (160°C) oven for 30 to 35 minutes or until cake tester inserted in center comes out clean. Let cool in pans for 5 minutes, then invert onto racks to let cool completely. Makes 4 mini loaves.

# LUNCH ON THE TOP DECK

FOR FOUR

*Dining on deck is one of summer's greatest pleasures. And whether you're off for a month's cruise up the coast or an afternoon's sail on the lake, good food is a delightful indulgence in the natural ambience of blue skies, sun-sparkled water and good company. In the fresh air, appetites are sure to be hearty, but galley slaves can relax, too—with simple menus geared to the confines of small spaces and limited equipment. This menu is easily adapted to available ingredients; it's also great for a last-day, clean-out-the-galley meal.*

*SKIPPER'S SANGRIA

*BOATERS' BRUSCHETTA

*OYSTERS ON THE BARBECUE

*PASTA AND BEAN SALAD WITH PESTO

*SALMON NIÇOISE SALAD

CRUSTY ROLLS

FRESH FRUIT

## *Pasta and Bean Salad with Pesto*

*Homemade or store-bought pesto sauce is handy to have in a boat galley for hot pastas. For salad dressings, just dilute it with a little oil and vinegar. This recipe produces a chunkier version that can be made on the boat without a food processor. Use it on any available combination of pasta and beans.*

| | | |
|---|---|---|
| **2 cups** | **cooked pasta (such as fusilli)** | **500 mL** |
| **2 cups** | **cooked or canned beans (such as cannellini, white kidney beans)** | **500 mL** |

| | **PESTO DRESSING:** | |
|---|---|---|
| **1-1/2 cups** | **packed fresh basil leaves, minced** | **375 mL** |
| **1/4 cup** | **freshly grated Parmesan cheese** | **50 mL** |
| **1/4 cup** | **pine nuts** | **50 mL** |
| **2** | **cloves garlic, minced** | **2** |
| **1/4 tsp** | **salt** | **1 mL** |
| **1/2 cup** | **olive oil** | **125 mL** |
| **2 tbsp** | **(approx) red wine vinegar** | **25 mL** |

**PESTO DRESSING:** In bowl, mix together basil, cheese, pine nuts, garlic and salt. Gradually blend in oil. Add vinegar to taste. ■ In salad bowl, combine pasta and beans. Toss with enough pesto dressing to coat generously. Makes 4 large servings.

***SKIPPER'S SANGRIA***

***In large pitcher, combine 1 each thinly-sliced small orange, lemon and lime with 1/4 cup (50 mL) each granulated sugar, brandy and orange liqueur. Let marinate for a few minutes. Add 1 bottle (750 mL) chilled dry red or white wine. Chill for at least 1 hour. Just before serving, add ice cubes and soda water to taste. Makes about 6 servings.***

***BOATERS' BRUSCHETTA***

***Season chopped fresh tomatoes generously with salt, crushed garlic, pepper, basil and a little olive oil. Brush more olive oil onto slices of Italian bread. Toast bread, oiled side down, on barbecue or in heavy skillet until golden brown. Spoon tomato mixture onto bread and serve immediately.***

***OYSTERS ON THE BARBECUE***

***Beautifully fresh oysters are an unbeatable treat served raw on the half shell, with just a drizzle of lemon juice or hot pepper sauce. If you're not an expert at opening them with an oyster knife and have a small covered barbecue on deck, place them in the***

***hot barbecue for a few minutes just until they open enough to pry open easily. If you like them lightly cooked, leave them on the grill for a minute or two longer; for fully cooked, 3 to 5 minutes.***

## *Salmon Niçoise Salad*

*Using fresh salmon instead of tuna makes this sunny Mediterranean salad even more delightful. Combine all the ingredients in a large bowl, or arrange them separately on a large platter and let guests assemble their own.*

| | | |
|---|---|---|
| **2 cups** | **diced cooked potatoes** | **500 mL** |
| **2** | **green onions, chopped** | **2** |
| **2 cups** | **cooked salmon in chunks** | **500 mL** |
| **3** | **hard-cooked eggs, sliced** | **3** |
| **1** | **large or 3 small sweet peppers, cut in strips** | **1** |
| **1 cup** | **halved cherry tomatoes** | **250 mL** |
| **12** | **black olives** | **12** |
| **8** | **anchovy fillets (optional)** | **8** |
| | **DRESSING:** | |
| **1/4 cup** | **red wine vinegar** | **50 mL** |
| **1 tsp** | **Dijon mustard** | **5 mL** |
| **1** | **clove garlic, crushed** | **1** |
| **1/2 tsp** | **salt** | **2 mL** |
| **1/4 tsp** | **each dried basil and oregano** | **1 mL** |
| | **Pepper** | |
| **3/4 cup** | **olive oil** | **175 mL** |

**DRESSING:** Whisk together vinegar, mustard, garlic, salt, basil, oregano and generous grinding of pepper. Gradually whisk in oil. Taste and adjust seasoning.

■ Combine potatoes and green onions; toss with enough dressing to moisten. In large bowl, combine potato mixture with salmon, eggs, peppers, tomatoes, olives and anchovies (if using). Toss gently with enough dressing to moisten. Or arrange all ingredients in mounds on platter; drizzle with a little dressing and serve remaining dressing separately. Makes 4 large servings.

*(On large plate) Salmon Niçoise Salad, and Pasta and Bean Salad with Pesto; crusty rolls; fresh fruit*

# AN AUTUMN PICNIC TO GO

FOR FOUR

*It's a glorious day in the golden glow of autumn and the great outdoors is calling. Time for biking, hiking, antiquing or day-tripping with a basket of free-wheeling fare to enjoy in a leafy glade or park. This menu adapts easily to small or large groups, for toting in bike baskets or in big hampers in the car.*

*REFRIGERATOR ANTIPASTO AND CRACKERS

*CORNMEAL CALZONE

BAGUETTES AND ASSORTED CHEESES

GRAPES, PEARS AND APPLES

*GINGERED FRUIT DIP

## Refrigerator Antipasto

*This chunky antipasto of assorted vegetables, olives and tuna in a thick, tomato-chili sauce is perfect served on sturdy crackers or in pre-baked pastry tart shells.*

| | | |
|---|---|---|
| **1/4 cup** | **olive oil** | **50 mL** |
| **2 cups** | **tiny cauliflower florets** | **500 mL** |
| **1** | **sweet red pepper, diced** | **1** |
| **1** | **sweet green pepper, diced** | **1** |
| **1 cup** | **chopped mushrooms** | **250 mL** |
| **1** | **clove garlic, chopped** | **1** |
| **1 cup** | **chili sauce** | **250 mL** |
| **2** | **tomatoes, peeled, seeded and chopped** | **2** |
| **1** | **can (6-1/2 oz/184 g) flaked tuna, drained** | **1** |
| **1/2 cup** | **sweet pickled onions, chopped** | **125 mL** |
| **1/2 cup** | **each stuffed green and black pitted olives, halved** | **125 mL** |
| | **Salt and pepper** | |

■ In large stainless steel or enamelled saucepan, heat oil over medium heat. Add cauliflower, peppers, mushrooms and garlic; cook gently, stirring occasionally, for about 10 minutes or until vegetables are tender.

■ Add chili sauce, tomatoes, tuna, onions and green and black olives. Simmer, stirring constantly, for 10 to 15 minutes or until slightly thickened and flavors are blended. Season with salt and pepper to taste.

■ Transfer to glass bowl or storage container. Refrigerate, covered, for up to 1 week. Makes about 6 cups (1.5 L).

## Cornmeal Calzone

*By using quick-rising yeast, you can eliminate up to one hour of the initial rising time. It's extremely important that the water added to the yeast is hot, not lukewarm. Use an*

***A SELECTION OF CHEESES***
**Semi-Hard/Hard:** ***Old Canadian Cheddar, Swiss Gruyere, Oka, Dutch Gouda***
**Soft:** ***Brie, Camembert, Saint-André, Bel Paese***
**Blue Cheeses:** ***Roquefort (strong-flavored), Gorgonzola (milder and creamier), Stilton***

*instant-read thermometer or your microwave probe to ensure accuracy.*

| | | |
|---|---|---|
| **1-3/4 cups** | **all-purpose flour** | **425 mL** |
| **1/4 cup** | **yellow cornmeal** | **50 mL** |
| **1 tsp** | **each granulated sugar and salt** | **5 mL** |
| **1** | **pkg quick-rising (instant) yeast** | **1** |
| **1/2 cup** | **water** | **125 mL** |
| **1/3 cup** | **(approx) milk** | **75 mL** |
| | **GLAZE:** | |
| **1** | **egg yolk** | **1** |
| **1 tbsp** | **water** | **15 mL** |
| | **FILLING:** | |
| **1/4 lb** | **cream cheese** | **125 g** |
| **1/3 cup** | **cottage cheese** | **75 mL** |
| **1** | **egg** | **1** |
| **1** | **small sweet red pepper, chopped** | **1** |
| **1 cup** | **shredded Cheddar cheese** | **250 mL** |
| **1/2 cup** | **chopped smoked ham (about 2 oz/50 g)** | **125 mL** |
| **2 tbsp** | **chopped green onion** | **25 mL** |
| **1 tsp** | **chili powder** | **5 mL** |
| | **Salt and pepper** | |

*Cornmeal Calzone; Gingered Fruit Dip; Refrigerator Antipasto; baguettes and assorted cheeses; fresh fruit*

**FILLING:** In bowl, beat together cream cheese, cottage cheese and egg; stir in red pepper, Cheddar cheese, ham, green onion and chili powder. Season with salt and pepper to taste; set aside.

■ In food processor, mix together all-purpose flour, cornmeal, sugar, salt and yeast; process for 30 seconds.

■ Heat water until hot, 125 to 130°F (50 to 55°C). With motor running, gradually pour hot water through feed tube of food processor; add just enough milk to make dough form into ball. Process for 1 minute to knead.

■ Remove dough and place on lightly floured surface; cover with plastic wrap and let dough stand for 10 minutes.

■ Divide dough into quarters and roll each into ball; roll out each ball into 8-inch (20 cm) circle. Divide filling into 4 portions; evenly spoon onto half of each circle, then fold dough over and crimp edges.

**GLAZE:** Mix egg yolk with water; lightly brush over each filled calzone.

■ With sharp knife, make several slits in top of each calzone to vent steam. Place 2 inches (5 cm) apart on cornmeal-dusted baking sheet; bake in 450°F (230°C) oven for 15 to 20 minutes or just until golden brown and crisp on bottoms. Makes 4 servings.

## *Gingered Fruit Dip*

*Tote a container of ginger-laced dip to serve with crisp apple or pear wedges and grapes. It's nice spread on crackers, too.*

| | | |
|---|---|---|
| **1/2 lb** | **cream cheese** | **250 g** |
| **2 tbsp** | **icing sugar** | **25 mL** |
| **1 tbsp** | **(approx) milk or cream** | **15 mL** |
| **1/4 cup** | **chopped preserved ginger** | **50 mL** |

■ In bowl, cream cheese with icing sugar until light and fluffy, adding enough milk to give consistency for dipping. Mix in ginger. Makes about 1-1/2 cups (375 mL).

# A BARBECUE BUFFET

FOR TWELVE

*Round up the whole gang for this memorable barbecue party. Adults and kids alike will love the burger sandwiches and side dishes—all are popular favorites with a new twist.*

*SHRIMP AND SPINACH DIP

*GRILLED EGGPLANT AND ONIONS

*PATTY MELTS

*BLACK BEAN SALAD WITH CORN AND RED PEPPERS

*ZUCCHINI AND CARROT COLESLAW

FRESH FRUIT PIES

## Shrimp and Spinach Dip

*Serve this tasty dip with a variety of crackers or black bread and include some corn chips for the kids.*

| | | |
|---|---|---|
| **3/4 cup** | **cream cheese, softened** | **175 mL** |
| **1/2 cup** | **chopped fresh spinach** | **125 mL** |
| **1/4 cup** | **mayonnaise** | **50 mL** |
| **1/4 cup** | **sour cream** | **50 mL** |
| **1/4 cup** | **chopped fresh dill** | **50 mL** |
| **1/4 cup** | **chopped fresh parsley** | **50 mL** |
| **3** | **green onions, chopped** | **3** |
| **2 tbsp** | **lemon juice** | **25 mL** |
| **1** | **clove garlic, minced** | **1** |
| **1/4 tsp** | **pepper** | **1 mL** |
| **1 lb** | **cooked shrimp** | **500 g** |

■ In blender or food processor, blend cream cheese, spinach, mayonnaise, sour cream, dill, parsley, onions, lemon juice, garlic and pepper.

■ Chop shrimp coarsely; add to blender and process until finely chopped but not puréed. Makes 3 cups (750 mL), about 12 appetizer servings.

*(Clockwise from top) Patty Melts; Zucchini and Carrot Coleslaw; Grilled Eggplant and Onions; Black Bean Salad with Corn and Red Peppers*

## Grilled Eggplant and Onions

*These are terrific with the Patty Melts.*

| | | |
|---|---|---|
| **3** | **eggplant** | **3** |
| **1 tbsp** | **salt** | **15 mL** |
| **4** | **red or Spanish onions** | **4** |
| **2/3 cup** | **(approx) olive oil** | **150 mL** |
| **1/3 cup** | **balsamic or red wine vinegar** | **75 mL** |
| **1/4 cup** | **chopped fresh basil** | **50 mL** |
| | **Salt and pepper** | |

■ Cut eggplant crosswise into 1/4-inch thick (5 mm) slices. In colander, toss slices with salt; let drain for 1 hour. Pat dry.

■ Slice onions 1/4 inch (5 mm) thick. Lightly brush eggplant and onion slices with oil. Cook on lightly greased grill over medium-hot coals or at medium setting, brushing with oil occasionally, for about 3 minutes per side or just until eggplant and onion are tender and browned.

■ In large bowl, sprinkle grilled vegetables with vinegar, basil and any remaining oil; season with salt and pepper to taste. Cover and set aside at room temperature for up to 2 hours or in refrigerator overnight. Makes about 12 servings.

## Patty Melts

*Melted cheese holds these unusual barbecued hamburger sandwiches together. Buy thinly sliced Cheddar at the deli or use a cheese slicer.*

| | | |
|---|---|---|
| **2 tbsp** | **vegetable oil** | **25 mL** |
| **1** | **onion, chopped** | **1** |
| **2** | **cloves garlic, minced** | **2** |
| **2** | **eggs** | **2** |
| **2 lb** | **lean ground beef** | **1 kg** |
| **2/3 cup** | **dry bread crumbs** | **150 mL** |
| **1 tsp** | **salt** | **5 mL** |
| **1/4 tsp** | **pepper** | **1 mL** |
| **24** | **thin slices rye bread** | **24** |
| **24** | **thin slices Cheddar cheese (1 lb/500 g)** | **24** |
| **1/4 cup** | **olive oil** | **50 mL** |

■ In skillet, heat vegetable oil over medium heat; cook onion and garlic, stirring, for 3 to 5 minutes or until softened. Let cool.

■ In bowl, beat eggs; mix in beef, bread crumbs, salt, pepper and onion mixture. Shape into 12 patties, each 1/2 inch (1 cm) thick.

■ Cook on greased barbecue grill about 4 inches (10 cm) above medium-hot coals or at medium-high setting for about 5 minutes per side or until no longer pink inside.

■ Meanwhile, trim crusts from bread. Sandwich each cooked patty between 2 slices of cheese and 2 slices of bread. Brush bread with olive oil and grill sandwiches for 1 to 2 minutes on each side or until cheese just starts to melt. Makes 12 servings.

## Black Bean Salad with Corn and Red Peppers

*As a timesaver, two 19-oz (540 mL) cans of black or kidney beans (rinsed and drained) can be substituted for the cooked dried beans in this exotic-flavored salad. If you don't have fresh coriander, use mint, or increase the parsley to 1/2 cup (125 mL).*

| | | |
|---|---|---|
| **1-1/2 cups** | **dried black beans** | **375 mL** |
| **1 cup** | **long-grain rice** | **250 mL** |
| **3/4 cup** | **olive oil** | **175 mL** |
| **2 cups** | **cooked corn** | **500 mL** |
| **2** | **sweet red peppers, diced** | **2** |
| **1/4 cup** | **each chopped fresh coriander and parsley** | **50 mL** |
| **6** | **green onions, chopped** | **6** |
| **1/4 cup** | **red wine vinegar** | **50 mL** |
| **2 tbsp** | **lemon juice** | **25 mL** |
| **1** | **clove garlic, minced** | **1** |
| **1 tbsp** | **chili powder** | **15 mL** |
| **1 tsp** | **salt** | **5 mL** |
| **1/4 tsp** | **pepper** | **1 mL** |

■ In large saucepan, combine beans and 4-1/2 cups (1.125 L) water. Soak overnight (or bring to boil and boil gently for 2 minutes; remove from heat, cover and let stand 1 hour). Drain.

■ Add 4 cups (1 L) cold water to beans and bring to boil. Cover and simmer gently for 1-1/2 to 2 hours or until tender. Drain and rinse with cold water; drain again.

■ Meanwhile, in saucepan, bring 12 cups (3 L) water to boil; add rice and cook for 12 to 14 minutes or until tender. Drain; toss with 1 tsp (15 mL) of the oil.

■ In large bowl, combine beans, rice, corn, peppers, coriander, parsley and onions. Whisk together vinegar, lemon juice, garlic, chili powder, salt and pepper; whisk in remaining oil. Pour over salad and toss. Taste and adjust seasoning. Makes about 12 servings.

***ZUCCHINI AND CARROT COLESLAW***

***Shred 6 large zucchini and 6 large carrots coarsely; place in bowl. Whisk together 1/2 cup (125 mL) rice vinegar, 1/3 cup (75 mL) vegetable oil, 1 tbsp (15 mL) granulated sugar, 1 tsp (5 mL) celery seeds and 1/2 tsp (2 mL) pepper; add 2 tbsp (25 mL) chopped fresh parsley and 2 green onions, chopped. Serve immediately or cover and refrigerate for up to 2 hours. Makes about 12 servings.***

***You can use white wine vinegar instead of rice vinegar, but add a little more sugar to taste.***

# A BEACH BARBECUE PARTY

FOR EIGHT

*Pack up the kids, coolers and hibachis and head for the beach. This food is all easy to make, tote and eat. Most is prepared at home, with the final grilling done at the picnic site. The recipes can easily be doubled or tripled for reunions or cottage gatherings. Be sure to carry all picnic foods in insulated coolers kept cold with freezer packs.*

*CHILLED CANTALOUPE SOUP

*GARLIC-ROSEMARY GRILLED CHICKEN

*WHITE BEANS AND GREENS WITH TARRAGON-LEMON DRESSING

*CONFETTI RICE SALAD

*GARLIC-CHIVE BRUSCHETTA

FRESH FRUIT

*COCONUT-LEMON SQUARES

*Garlic-Rosemary Grilled Chicken; Garlic-Chive Bruschetta; White Beans and Greens with Tarragon- Lemon Dressing*

## Chilled Cantaloupe Soup

*A blender makes a smoother soup, but you can also use a food processor. Carry the soup to the picnic in an insulated container.*

| | | |
|---|---|---|
| 2 | **small cantaloupes (about 3 lb/1.5 kg total)** | 2 |
| 1 cup | **sour cream or plain yogurt** | 250 mL |
| 1/2 cup | **orange juice** | 125 mL |
| 1 tsp | **grated lime rind** | 5 mL |
| 1/4 cup | **lime juice** | 50 mL |
| 2 tbsp | **granulated sugar** | 25 mL |
| 1/2 tsp | **salt** | 2 mL |
| | **Lime slices** | |

■ Cut cantaloupes in half and scoop out seeds; peel. Coarsely chop melon.

■ In large bowl, combine cantaloupe, sour cream, orange juice, lime rind and juice, sugar and salt.

■ In blender, process mixture in batches, blending until smooth. Refrigerate, covered, for several hours or until very cold. Taste and adjust seasoning if necessary. Garnish each serving with lime slices. Makes about 8 servings.

## Garlic-Rosemary Grilled Chicken

*Precook this moist chicken a few hours ahead of time, and then it needs only to be grilled for a short time at the beach.*

| | | |
|---|---|---|
| 4 | **chickens (each about 2 lb/1 kg)** | 4 |
| 6 | **cloves garlic, crushed** | 6 |
| 2 tbsp | **finely chopped fresh rosemary (or 2 tsp/ 10 mL crushed dried)** | 25 mL |
| 1/4 cup | **olive oil** | 50 mL |
| 1 tsp | **grated lemon rind** | 5 mL |
| 1 tbsp | **lemon juice** | 15 mL |
| | **Salt and pepper** | |

■ Cut each chicken in half through breast and backbone, removing tail. Trim off excess fat; discard. Starting at neck end, slip fingers between skin and flesh and, working toward tail end, loosen skin as much as possible around breast, thigh and leg areas without piercing skin.

■ In bowl, mash together garlic and rosemary; gradually whisk in half of the oil, the lemon rind and juice. Spread one-eighth of this mixture evenly under loosened skin of each chicken half. Let stand at room temperature for 20 minutes.

■ Place chicken halves, skin sides up, in 2 large shallow lightly greased baking pans; fold wing tips under. Brush with some of the remaining oil; roast, uncovered, in 350°F (180°C) oven, basting once or twice, for 45 to 55 minutes or until tender and juices run clear. Let stand until chicken stops steaming, about 30 minutes. Refrigerate, covered, for at least 2 hours or until thoroughly chilled.

■ At picnic site, brush chicken lightly with some of the remaining oil; place on greased grill and cook, uncovered, about 4 inches (10 cm) above high heat for 4 to 8 minutes or until chicken is golden brown. Turn; brush with remaining oil. Grill for 4 to 8 minutes longer or until chicken is golden brown. Season with salt and pepper to taste. Makes about 8 servings.

## White Beans and Greens with Tarragon-Lemon Dressing

*This light, lemon-flavored salad is ideal for summertime meals.*

| | | |
|---|---|---|
| 1 | **can (19 oz/540 mL) white kidney beans, drained and rinsed** | 1 |
| 8 cups | **torn leaf lettuce leaves** | 2 L |
| 1 | **small English cucumber, thinly sliced** | 1 |
| 1 | **tomato** | 1 |

| | DRESSING: | |
|---|---|---|
| **2 tbsp** | **tarragon wine vinegar** | **25 mL** |
| **1 tbsp** | **Dijon mustard** | **15 mL** |
| **1 tbsp** | **lemon juice** | **15 mL** |
| **1/4 tsp** | **dried tarragon** | **1 mL** |
| **2** | **shallots or green onions, finely chopped** | **2** |
| **1/3 cup** | **olive oil** | **75 mL** |
| | **Salt and pepper** | |

**DRESSING:** In bowl, combine vinegar, mustard, lemon juice, tarragon and shallots; whisk in olive oil. Season with salt and pepper to taste.

■ Add beans to dressing; refrigerate in plastic airtight container.

■ In separate airtight containers, pack lettuce, cucumber and tomato. Just before serving, slice tomato. Toss lettuce, cucumber, tomato and bean mixture. Makes about 8 servings.

***GARLIC-CHIVE BRUSCHETTA***
***Spread the herb butter on the bread and wrap it before you pack your picnic so the bruschetta will be ready to grill at the beach.***

***In bowl, combine 1/3 cup (75 mL) softened butter, 1 garlic clove (minced) and 2 tbsp (25 mL) chopped fresh chives.***

***Slice bread in half lengthwise. Cut each half into 4 pieces. Spread with herb butter. Grill, cut side down, about 4 inches (10 cm) above medium-high heat for about 2 minutes or until golden brown. Turn and grill, cut sides up, for 30 seconds. Makes 8 servings.***

## Confetti Rice Salad

*This easy salad is full of refreshing flavors and interesting textures.*

| | | |
|---|---|---|
| **4 cups** | **water** | **1 L** |
| **2 cups** | **long-grain rice** | **500 mL** |
| **2-1/2 tsp** | **salt** | **12 mL** |
| **1-1/2 cups** | **plain yogurt** | **375 mL** |
| **1/4 cup** | **white vinegar** | **50 mL** |
| **2 tbsp** | **finely chopped fresh parsley** | **25 mL** |
| **2** | **green onions, finely chopped** | **2** |
| **2 tsp** | **granulated sugar** | **10 mL** |
| **1/2 tsp** | **pepper** | **2 mL** |
| **1/2 cup** | **each diced cucumber, chopped sweet red pepper and grated carrot** | **125 mL** |
| **4** | **hard-cooked eggs, cut in wedges** | **4** |

■ In large pot, bring water to boil; add rice and 1/2 tsp (2 mL) of the salt. Reduce heat to low; cook, covered, for 15 minutes or until rice is tender and water has been absorbed. Let stand for 5 minutes. Using fork, fluff rice; set aside and let cool.

■ In bowl, stir together yogurt, vinegar, parsley, green onions, sugar, pepper and remaining salt. Pour over rice; stir to coat well. Stir in cucumber, red pepper, carrot and eggs. Cover and chill for at least 1 hour before serving. Makes about 8 servings.

## Coconut-Lemon Squares

*Carry these easy-to-make shortbread-based squares right in the pan.*

| | | |
|---|---|---|
| **1 cup** | **all-purpose flour** | **250 mL** |
| **1/4 cup** | **granulated sugar** | **50 mL** |
| **1/2 cup** | **butter** | **125 mL** |
| | **FILLING:** | |
| **2 tsp** | **grated lemon rind** | **10 mL** |
| **1/4 cup** | **lemon juice** | **50 mL** |
| **2 tbsp** | **butter, melted** | **25 mL** |
| **2** | **eggs, beaten** | **2** |
| **1 cup** | **flaked coconut** | **250 mL** |
| **2/3 cup** | **granulated sugar** | **150 mL** |
| **2 tbsp** | **all-purpose flour** | **25 mL** |
| **1/2 tsp** | **baking powder** | **2 mL** |
| **1/2 tsp** | **vanilla** | **2 mL** |
| **Pinch** | **salt** | **Pinch** |

■ In bowl, combine flour with sugar; cut in butter until crumbly. Press into 9-inch (2.5 L) square cake pan; bake in 350°F (180°C) oven for 15 minutes.

**FILLING:** In bowl, mix lemon rind and juice, butter and eggs. Blend in coconut, sugar, flour, baking powder, vanilla and salt; pour over base. Bake in 350°F (180°C) oven for 25 to 30 minutes or until filling is golden and set. Let cool on rack; cut into squares.

# COME FOR COCKTAILS

FOR SIXTEEN

*A sunny summertime gathering at the cottage or by the pool in the backyard calls for colorful, casual finger food to go with cooling drinks. Offer tall glasses of frosty, fruited beverages, wine spritzers or interesting beers and this appetizing array of make-ahead nibbles.*

*CHUNKY AVOCADO DIP

*PEANUTTY BEEF WITH GINGER

*SKEWERED SHRIMP WITH FRUIT

*CRAB CORNUCOPIAS

*DEVILLED EGG DOUBLES

## *Chunky Avocado Dip*

*Surround this multi-colored dip with corn chips or crudités, such as broccoli florets, diagonal carrot slices or sticks of jicama (pronounced hee-cama), a vegetable popular in Mexico. As well as these garnishes, you can use fresh coriander sprigs, stuffed olives and chopped red onions.*

| | | |
|---|---|---|
| 2 | **ripe avocados** | 2 |
| 1/3 cup | **finely chopped onion** | 75 mL |
| 2 tbsp | **chopped fresh coriander** | 25 mL |
| 2 tbsp | **lime juice** | 25 mL |
| 1/4 tsp | **hot pepper flakes** | 1 mL |
| 1 tbsp | **finely chopped jalepeño pepper (optional)** | 15 mL |
| 1 cup | **sour cream** | 250 mL |
| | **GARNISH:** | |
| 1 cup | **shredded Monterey Jack cheese** | 250 mL |
| 1/2 cup | **sliced pitted black olives** | 125 mL |
| 1/3 cup | **sliced green onions** | 75 mL |
| 2 | **tomatoes, seeded and chopped** | 2 |

■ Peel and pit avocado; chop coarsely and place in bowl. Add onion, coriander, lime juice and hot pepper flakes; toss together lightly.

■ Spread in round shallow glass or china dish about 10 inches (25 cm) in diameter and at least 1-1/2 inches (4 cm) deep. Stir jalapeño pepper (if using) into sour cream; spread over avocado mixture, sealing to edge of dish.

**GARNISH:** Sprinkle with cheese, olives, green onions and tomatoes; cover and refrigerate for up to 6 hours. Makes 16 servings.

## *Peanutty Beef with Ginger*

*The peanutty flavor with a hint of ginger makes this dish a crowd pleaser. Serve the beef with slices of bread — rye or multigrain — and Dijon or grainy mustard.*

| | | |
|---|---|---|
| 1 | **eye of round roast (about 2-1/2 lb/1.25 kg)** | 1 |

*(Clockwise from top left) Chunky Avocado Dip; Peanutty Beef with Ginger; Skewered Shrimp with Fruit; Crab Cornucopias; Devilled Egg Doubles*

| | MARINADE: | |
|---|---|---|
| 1/2 cup | peanut butter | 125 mL |
| 1/4 cup | dry sherry | 50 mL |
| 1/4 cup | vegetable oil | 50 mL |
| 2 tbsp | minced gingerroot | 25 mL |
| 2 tbsp | soy sauce | 25 mL |
| 1 tbsp | lemon juice | 15 mL |
| 1 | clove garlic, crushed | 1 |

**MARINADE:** Whisk together peanut butter, sherry, oil, ginger, soy sauce, lemon juice and garlic.

■ Place beef in shallow dish; spread marinade on all sides of beef. Cover tightly with plastic wrap. Marinate in refrigerator overnight, turning occasionally.

■ Barbecue beef over indirect heat (hot charcoal briquettes in two piles, separated by a drip pan) for about 40 minutes or until meat thermometer registers 130 to 140°F (60°C) for rare, 140 to 150°F (65°C) for medium or 150 to 170°F (75°C) for well done. (Alternatively, roast meat on rack in 325°F/160°C oven for about 50 minutes for rare or to desired doneness.) Let meat stand for at least 15 minutes before slicing. Makes enough for about 20 open-faced sandwiches.

## *Skewered Shrimp with Fruit*

*Orange chunks and kiwifruit wedges add color to these marinated shrimp, but you can use anything from cherry tomatoes to mushrooms, black or stuffed olives, green or red pepper squares or bright fresh strawberries to add a flavor difference. These appetizers can be made ahead and served cold, or barbecued at the party and served hot.*

| | | |
|---|---|---|
| 1 lb | large raw shrimp, peeled and deveined (about 25) | 500 g |
| 1/2 cup | lime juice | 125 mL |
| 2 tbsp | vegetable oil | 25 mL |
| 1/2 tsp | hot pepper flakes | 2 mL |
| 25 | (approx) chunks orange | 25 |
| 25 | (approx) wedges kiwifruit | 25 |

■ Place shrimp in heavy plastic bag set in bowl. Pour in lime juice, oil and hot pepper flakes. Tighten bag around shrimp, removing as much air as possible. Turn bag several times to coat shrimp with marinade. Refrigerate for 1 hour.

■ Remove shrimp from marinade; broil or barbecue over medium-high heat for about 3 minutes on each side or until shrimp are opaque and bright pink. Serve hot or cold, skewered on wooden picks with orange and kiwifruit chunks. Makes 25 appetizers.

# Crab Cornucopias

*The influence of the Far East is apparent in this do-it-yourself finger food for a casual patio or deck party. Set out all the makings — crêpes, hoisin sauce, lettuce, onions and crab mixture — and let guests wrap up fillings to eat them on the spot. Make-aheads last longest if you use dampened rice paper (available in Asian food shops) to hold the fillings. Cover the papers on a tray with a damp cloth and refrigerate until serving time.*

| | | |
|---|---|---|
| **4.2 oz** | **frozen or canned crabmeat** | **120 g** |
| | **Salt and pepper** | |
| **3 tbsp** | **(approx) mayonnaise** | **50 mL** |
| **12** | **crêpes (recipe follows) or 7-inch (18 cm) sheets of rice paper** | **12** |
| | **Hoisin sauce** | |
| **6** | **leaves red-tipped lettuce, halved** | **6** |
| **6** | **green onions, halved lengthwise** | **6** |

■ Thaw and drain crabmeat. In bowl, mix crabmeat, salt and pepper to taste and enough mayonnaise for mixture to hold together.
■ Make cornucopias just before serving time. Lightly brush each crêpe or dampened rice paper with hoisin sauce. On upper half of crêpe, place half leaf of lettuce, half green onion and dollop of crab mixture. Fold bottom third of crêpe up and roll from left to right into cornucopia. Secure with wooden picks. Makes 12 cornucopias.

| | | |
|---|---|---|
| | **CRÊPES:** | |
| **1-1/2 cups** | **(approx) milk** | **375 mL** |
| **1-1/4 cups** | **all-purpose flour** | **250 mL** |
| **2** | **eggs** | **2** |
| **1 tbsp** | **granulated sugar** | **15 mL** |
| **1/2 tsp** | **baking powder** | **2 mL** |
| **1/4 tsp** | **salt** | **1 mL** |
| **2 tbsp** | **butter, melted** | **25 mL** |

■ In large mixing bowl, beat milk, flour, eggs, sugar, baking powder and salt. Stir in melted butter. Add more milk if necessary to make batter consistency of whipping cream.
■ For each crêpe, pour about 1/4 cup (50 mL) batter into lightly greased hot crêpe pan. Cook over medium-high heat for about 1 minute or until first side is lightly browned. Turn crêpe; cook second side for about 30 seconds. Stack crêpes on paper towel. (Crêpes can be wrapped in plastic wrap and stored in refrigerator for up to 3 days, or frozen for up to 2 months. Thaw before using.) Makes 12 crêpes.

*Crab Cornucopias; Devilled Egg Doubles*

# Devilled Egg Doubles

*Serve traditional halves or sandwich them together. Black olives add a dramatic garnish.*

| | | |
|---|---|---|
| **8** | **hard-cooked eggs** | **8** |
| **2 tbsp** | **mayonnaise** | **25 mL** |
| **1 tbsp** | **chopped canned green chilies** | **15 mL** |
| **1 tbsp** | **finely minced onion** | **15 mL** |
| **1 tbsp** | **taco sauce** | **15 mL** |
| **Dash** | **hot pepper sauce** | **Dash** |
| | **Salt** | |
| **1/4 cup** | **finely chopped fresh parsley or coriander** | **50 mL** |

■ Cut eggs in half lengthwise or crosswise. Remove yolks; set whites aside.
■ In bowl, mash yolks with fork. Blend in mayonnaise, chilies, onion, taco sauce, hot pepper sauce, and salt to taste.
■ Using fork or piping bag, heap yolk mixture back into whites. Sandwich halves together, pressing gently to leave a ring of filling around edge. Using fingers, gently press chopped parsley onto filling ring. Cover with plastic wrap and refrigerate up to 4 hours. Makes 8 doubles or 16 halves.

*GREEN SALAD SUGGESTIONS*

*A simple green salad composed of several kinds of interesting lettuces and tossed with a homemade dressing is a light, easy and delicious first course.*

*Allow one small head of Boston lettuce for four servings. For six people, use half a head of Boston lettuce and one small head radicchio (or half a head red leaf lettuce) with a few sprigs of watercress, spinach leaves, romaine lettuce, alfalfa sprouts or Belgian endive.*

*Choose as additions:*

- *vegetables (cooked or raw)—as simple as sliced mushrooms or thinly sliced red onion*
- *cheese (grated or cubed)*
- *chopped hard-cooked egg*
- *meat (crumbled cooked bacon or ham cubes)*
- *seafood (tuna, salmon, shrimp, crab, mussels, anchovies, sardines)*
- *fruit (grapes, melon balls, sliced apple, orange wedges)*
- *croutons*

# A COTTAGE SUPPER

FOR EIGHT

*At summer cottages or beachside homes, hearty yet summery fare is called for after a day of sailing, windsurfing or swimming. This sunny menu could be expanded to include barbecued steaks or chicken (bring-your-own if desired).*

*PAELLA WITH SALMON

CRUSTY BREAD OR ROLLS

RAW VEGETABLE PLATTER OR GREEN SALAD

*FROZEN PEACH YOGURT

ASSORTED COOKIES

## Paella with Salmon

*Fresh salmon is a delicious addition to a basic paella.*

| | | |
|---|---|---|
| **1/4 cup** | **olive oil** | **50 mL** |
| **3** | **cloves garlic, minced** | **3** |
| **2 cups** | **parboiled long-grain rice** | **500 mL** |
| **1/2 tsp** | **saffron threads or pinch powdered saffron** | **2 mL** |
| **4 cups** | **hot chicken stock** | **1 L** |
| **1** | **each sweet red and yellow pepper, diced** | **1** |
| **1/2 cup** | **pitted black olives** | **125 mL** |
| **1 cup** | **fresh or frozen peas** | **250 mL** |
| **1 lb** | **fresh salmon fillets, skinned** | **500 g** |
| | **Salt and pepper** | |

■ In large deep ovenproof skillet or Dutch oven, heat oil over medium heat; cook garlic, stirring, for 30 seconds. Stir in rice and cook, stirring frequently, until golden, about 5 minutes.

■ Dissolve saffron in stock; stir into rice mixture along with red and yellow peppers and olives. Bring to boil; cover and bake in 350°F (180°C) oven for about 20 minutes or until rice is tender and liquid is nearly absorbed. (Recipe may be made ahead to this point, covered and refrigerated for up to 1 day. Before proceeding, heat through.)

■ Stir in fresh peas. (For frozen peas, add to pot 5 minutes before end of cooking time.) Cut salmon into 8 or 12 chunks and arrange on top of rice. Cover and bake in 350°F (180°C) oven for 10 to 15 minutes or until salmon flakes easily when tested with fork and peas are tender. Season with salt and pepper to taste. Makes 8 main-course or 12 appetizer servings.

## Frozen Peach Yogurt

*Fast, fresh and fruity, smooth frozen yogurt is a low-calorie indulgence that's bursting with fabulous flavor. Whip up this dessert in minutes using an ice-cream maker, or freeze the fruit and make it in a food processor.*

| | | |
|---|---|---|
| **3 cups** | **sliced peaches (about 1 lb/500 g or 4 medium)** | **750 mL** |
| **1/3 cup** | **instant dissolving fruit/berry sugar** | **75 mL** |
| **1/2 cup** | **plain yogurt** | **125 mL** |
| **1 tbsp** | **lemon juice** | **15 mL** |

**ICE-CREAM MAKER METHOD:** In food processor or blender, process peaches until puréed. Add sugar, yogurt and lemon juice; process until well blended. Freeze in ice-cream maker following manufacturer's instructions.

**FOOD PROCESSOR METHOD:** At least 5 hours before serving, place peaches in single layer on baking sheet; cover and freeze until solid. In food processor, combine frozen peaches with sugar. Using on/off motion, process until coarsely chopped. Stir together yogurt and lemon juice. With machine running, gradually pour in yogurt mixture through feed tube. Process until smooth and creamy, redistributing chunks of fruit if necessary.

■ Serve immediately or transfer to storage container and freeze for up to 1 week. About 30 minutes before serving, transfer yogurt to refrigerator to soften slightly. Makes about 3 cups (750 mL).

# A SEASIDE SUPPER

FOR FOUR

*The sharing of satisfying, casual fare in a cozy beach house brings special warmth to a cool evening. After a lazy afternoon or an all-day outing, this menu can be quickly assembled—in about the time it takes to light the fire and pour a hot toddy or mug of mulled cider.*

*MUSSEL AND SCALLOP STEW

*BIBB LETTUCE AND AVOCADO SALAD

ASSORTED BREADS OR ROLLS

*FRESH FRUIT ON BERRY COULIS

*Mussel and Scallop Stew; assorted breads and rolls*

## *Mussel and Scallop Stew*

*This stew takes only a few minutes to prepare. Serve it with lots of crusty bread for dunking in the sauce.*

| | | |
|---|---|---|
| **2-1/2 lb** | **mussels in the shell** | **1.25 kg** |
| **2 lb** | **scallops** | **1 kg** |
| **1/4 cup** | **butter** | **50 mL** |
| **2** | **small onions, finely chopped** | **2** |
| **2** | **large cloves garlic, minced** | **2** |
| | **Pepper** | |
| **1-1/2 cups** | **dry white wine** | **375 mL** |
| **1-1/2 cups** | **whipping cream** | **375 mL** |
| **1/2 cup** | **chopped fresh parsley** | **125 mL** |

■ Scrub mussels well and remove any hairy beards. Discard any that are not tightly closed. Cut any large scallops in half.
■ In Dutch oven or large heavy saucepan, melt butter; cook onions and garlic until translucent and fragrant, about 2 minutes. Sprinkle with pepper to taste.
■ Add wine and bring to boil; add mussels. Cover and reduce heat to medium; steam for 2 minutes.
■ Add scallops; cover and cook over medium-low heat for 2 to 3 minutes longer or until scallops are tender and mussels open. (Discard any that don't open.)
■ Meanwhile, in small saucepan, bring cream to boil; stir into stew. Spoon stew into tureen or large shallow soup bowls and sprinkle with parsley. Makes 4 servings.

## *Bibb Lettuce and Avocado Salad*

*Serve these attractive salad plates before or after the seafood stew.*

| | | |
|---|---|---|
| **1** | **head Bibb lettuce** | **1** |
| **1** | **large ripe avocado, peeled and sliced** | **1** |
| **1/4 cup** | **chopped toasted pecans** | **50 mL** |
| **1** | **small sweet red pepper, sliced** | **1** |
| **Half** | **red onion, sliced in rings** | **Half** |
| | **DRESSING:** | |
| **2/3 cup** | **vegetable oil** | **150 mL** |
| **3 tbsp** | **lemon juice** | **45 mL** |
| **2 tbsp** | **chopped green onion** | **25 mL** |
| **1 tsp** | **liquid honey** | **5 mL** |
| **1/4 tsp** | **Dijon mustard** | **1 mL** |
| | **Salt and pepper** | |

**DRESSING:** In screwtop jar, combine oil, lemon juice, onion, honey and mustard; shake well. Add salt and pepper to taste. At serving time, arrange lettuce leaves on salad plates. Arrange avocado slices in pinwheel shape on lettuce. Sprinkle with pecans; arrange red pepper strips and onion slices around avocado. Drizzle with dressing. Makes 4 servings.

## *Fresh Fruit on Berry Coulis*

*Use fresh or frozen berries in the sauce, with mixed fruit of your choice on top.*

| | | |
|---|---|---|
| **1 cup** | **strawberries** | **250 mL** |
| **1 cup** | **raspberries** | **250 mL** |
| **2 tbsp** | **(approx) granulated sugar** | **25 mL** |
| **1 tbsp** | **white rum (optional)** | **15 mL** |
| | **Cantaloupe wedges, grapefruit sections, sliced bananas, sliced kiwifruit, green grapes** | |
| | **Icing sugar** | |

■ In food processor or blender, combine strawberries, raspberries, sugar, and rum (if using); purée until smooth. If desired, strain to remove seeds. Taste and add a little more sugar if needed. Chill.
■ At serving time, pool sauce on each dessert plate; arrange fruits on top. Dust lightly with icing sugar. Makes 4 servings.

# INTERNATIONAL FLAVORS

*The flavors of faraway places provide inspiration for all kinds of exciting menus. Host a Bon Voyage party for someone going on a trip; re-create memories of your travels or taste-test a dream destination; celebrate a family heritage with an old-country menu; try your hand at a new cuisine you've tasted in a restaurant or at an ethnic food festival. Many menus here are suitable for a group effort: round up the neighbors for an international celebration, start a dinner club with friends, or focus on one country with your language class (you'll also find Spanish tapas in the Evenings chapter and French bistro fare in Parties with a Difference). And when the snow is piled up around us in mid-winter, who needs a better excuse for a Bahamian feast?*

# STARS OF INDIA

FOR EIGHT

*A profusion of tantalizing fragrances and flavors provides a magic carpet to transport you to a land of complex regional cuisines. This menu provides a delicious sampling. With many East and West Indian food shops now in Canadian cities, it's not difficult to find the ingredients for your feast.*

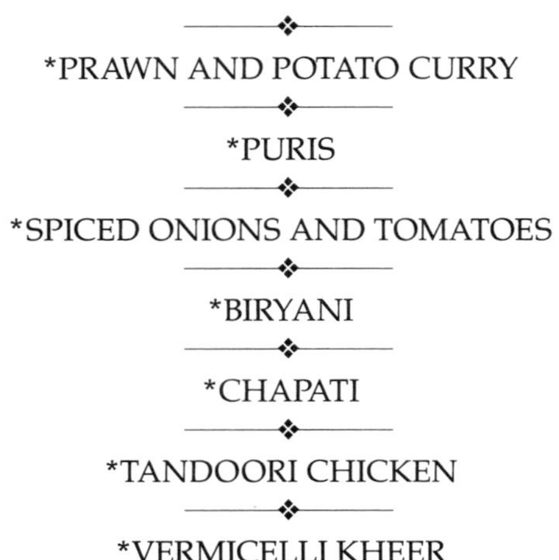

*PRAWN AND POTATO CURRY

*PURIS

*SPICED ONIONS AND TOMATOES

*BIRYANI

*CHAPATI

*TANDOORI CHICKEN

*VERMICELLI KHEER

**Recipes are given for menu items marked with an asterisk.*

## Prawn and Potato Curry

*Although the Indian subcontinent is surrounded by thousands of miles of coastline, most of the population lives inland. Fish and seafood are nevertheless part of the Indian larder and appear in dishes such as this curry. Adjust the amount of chili powder (or omit it altogether) to create a curry that suits your taste buds perfectly.*

| | | |
|---|---|---|
| **2 tbsp** | **shortening** | **25 mL** |
| **2** | **onions, finely chopped** | **2** |
| **1 cup** | **chopped fresh coriander or parsley** | **250 mL** |
| **2 tsp** | **salt** | **10 mL** |
| **2 tsp** | **garam masala (see sidebar, page 164)** | **10 mL** |
| **1 tsp** | **ground turmeric** | **5 mL** |
| **1 tsp** | **chili powder (optional)** | **5 mL** |
| **6** | **tomatoes, sliced** | **6** |
| **1 cup** | **hot water** | **250 mL** |
| **1 lb** | **small new potatoes, scrubbed** | **500 g** |
| **2 lb** | **fresh prawns, peeled and deveined** | **1 kg** |
| **2 tsp** | **lemon juice** | **10 mL** |

■ In large skillet, melt shortening over medium-high heat; cook onions and coriander, stirring, for 2 to 3 minutes or until onions are tender. Add salt, garam masala, turmeric, and chili powder (if using); cook, stirring, for 2 minutes.

■ Add tomatoes; cook for 3 minutes, stirring occasionally and shaking pan. Add hot water; bring to boil. Reduce heat to medium and cook, uncovered, for 15 to 20 minutes or until slightly thickened.

■ Meanwhile, steam potatoes for 10 to 15 minutes or until tender. Add to tomato mixture along with prawns and lemon juice.

■ Increase heat to medium-high and bring to boil; cover and cook for 5 minutes or until prawns are pink. Serve immediately. Makes about 8 servings.

***REGIONAL INDIAN CUISINE***

***As in any of the great gastronomic cultures, such as those of France and China, there is no single Indian cuisine. There are roughly 20 states or territories, each with its own culture and culinary traditions. Ingredients, cooking methods and eating habits are dictated by geography, climate and religion.***

***More than 80 per cent of the people in India are Hindus and eat no beef. In fact, most Indians are vegetarians, either through religious conviction or economic necessity. In Pakistan and Bangladesh, most of the population is Muslim. They eat a lot of beef and lamb (or, more often, mutton or goat).***

***Regional preferences determine which starch accompaniment you are likely to eat along with the main course. In the South, it will usually be rice; in the North, bread. The simplest*** **roti** ***(bread) would be*** **chapati** ***made from whole wheat and rolled out into pancakelike rounds, then cooked on a griddle. Other breads are*** **paratha** ***(also cooked on a griddle but with butter, or*** **ghee*****),*** **puri** ***(like a chapati but deep-fried), and*** **naan** ***(a leavened flatbread traditionally cooked in a tandoori oven).***

Puris; Prawn and Potato Curry

*(Photo, page 160)*
*Tandoori Chicken; Spiced Onions and Tomatoes; Biryani; Chapati*

## Puris

*Use rounds of this deep-fried bread to scoop up mouthfuls of the Prawn and Potato Curry.*

| | | |
|---|---|---|
| 3/4 cup | whole wheat flour | 175 mL |
| 3/4 cup | (approx) all-purpose flour | 175 mL |
| 1 tsp | salt | 5 mL |
| 2 tsp | butter, melted | 10 mL |
| 3/4 cup | warm water | 175 mL |
| 1/3 cup | (approx) vegetable oil | 75 mL |

■ In bowl, combine whole wheat and all-purpose flours and salt. Make a well in center and pour in butter. Stir in water to make soft sticky dough.
■ Turn out onto lightly floured surface and knead for 10 to 15 minutes or until dough is smooth and elastic, adding more all-purpose flour if necessary. Cover and let rest for 15 minutes.
■ Divide dough into 16 equal portions; roll each portion into 4- to 5-inch (10 to 12 cm) round.
■ In skillet, heat oil over medium-high heat just until smoking point; cook 1 round of dough at a time, adding more oil if necessary and basting tops with hot oil to help them puff, for 30 seconds or until puffed. Turn over and cook for 30 seconds longer or until golden brown. Drain on paper towels. Serve warm. Makes 16 puris.

## Spiced Onions and Tomatoes

*Traditionally served as a side dish with a main-course curry, this spicy vegetable mixture goes just as well with Western-style grills or roasts.*

| | | |
|---|---|---|
| 1 tsp | black peppercorns | 5 mL |
| 1 tsp | cumin seeds | 5 mL |
| 2 | whole cloves | 2 |
| 1/2 cup | ghee (see sidebar, page 165) | 125 mL |
| 4 | cloves garlic, minced | 4 |
| 1 tbsp | minced gingerroot | 15 mL |
| 1 tsp | chili powder | 5 mL |
| 1/2 tsp | each ground turmeric, coriander and cumin | 2 mL |
| 4 | onions, quartered | 4 |
| 4 | tomatoes, chopped | 4 |
| | Salt | |
| 1 tsp | lemon juice | 5 mL |
| 1 tbsp | chopped fresh coriander, parsley or spinach | 15 mL |

■ In double-thickness square of cheesecloth, place peppercorns, cumin seeds and cloves; tie securely to form bag.
■ In large skillet, heat ghee over medium-high heat. Add garlic, ginger, chili powder, turmeric, coriander, cumin and spice bag; cook for 2 minutes, stirring constantly.
■ Add onions and tomatoes; cook over medium heat, stirring occasionally, for 10 to 12 minutes or until onions are tender and translucent. Remove spice bag. Season with salt to taste.
■ Transfer to warmed serving dish; sprinkle with lemon juice and garnish with coriander. Makes about 8 servings.

# Biryani

*Biryani, a rice dish, is from Northern India. This richly flavored one-pot version with meat is ideal for entertaining. The spices are tied in a bag for convenience, although in a traditional biryani they would be left loose.*

| | | |
|---|---|---|
| **3 cups** | **long-grain rice** | **750 mL** |
| **6** | **cardamom pods** | **6** |
| **4** | **whole cloves** | **4** |
| **1** | **cinnamon stick, halved** | **1** |
| **1** | **boneless lamb shoulder (about 2 lb/1 kg)** | **1** |
| **3** | **large onions** | **3** |
| **1/2 cup** | **shortening** | **125 mL** |
| **4** | **cloves garlic, minced** | **4** |
| **1 tbsp** | **grated gingerroot** | **15 mL** |
| **1/2 cup** | **plain yogurt** | **125 mL** |
| **2 tsp** | **salt** | **10 mL** |
| **1/2 tsp** | **pepper** | **2 mL** |
| **1/2 cup** | **milk** | **125 mL** |
| **1/2 tsp** | **saffron threads (or pinch powdered saffron)** | **2 mL** |
| **2 tbsp** | **ghee (see sidebar next page)** | **25 mL** |
| **1/2 cup** | **chopped fresh coriander** | **125 mL** |

■ In bowl, cover rice with cold water and let stand for 1 hour; drain well.

■ Meanwhile, evenly divide cardamom pods, cloves and cinnamon stick between 2 double-thickness squares of cheesecloth; tie each securely to form bags. Set aside.

■ Trim fat and membrane from lamb; cut into 1-inch (2.5 cm) cubes. Finely chop 2 of the onions; slice remaining onion.

■ In large skillet, melt shortening over medium-high heat; cook chopped onions for 4 to 5 minutes or until golden. Add lamb, garlic and ginger; cover and cook for 15 minutes, stirring frequently.

■ Stir in yogurt, 1 tsp (5 mL) of the salt, pepper and 2 cups (500 mL) water; add 1 of the cheesecloth bags and bring to boil. Reduce heat to medium-low and cook, covered, for 1 to 1-1/2 hours or until lamb is tender. Discard spice bag.

■ In large saucepan, bring 6 cups (1.5 L) water to boil. Add drained rice, remaining 1 tsp (5 mL) salt and reserved spice bag. Cover and cook over medium heat for 20 minutes or until rice is tender and water is absorbed. Discard spice bag.

■ In 16-cup (4 L) shallow baking dish, spread half of the rice. Top with lamb mixture, then remaining rice. Combine milk and saffron; pour over rice. (Recipe can be prepared to this point, covered and refrigerated for up to 2 days.) Bake, covered, in 350°F (180°C) oven for 20 to 30 minutes or until heated through.

■ In skillet, heat ghee over medium-high heat; cook sliced onion for about 5 minutes or until golden brown. Sprinkle over biryani. Sprinkle coriander over top; mix lightly and serve hot. Makes about 8 servings.

# Chapati

*This simple, unleavened whole wheat bread would be "baked" on a griddle in India. A dry skillet works just as well.*

| | | |
|---|---|---|
| **1 cup** | **whole wheat flour** | **250 mL** |
| **Pinch** | **salt** | **Pinch** |
| | **Melted butter** | |

■ Sift flour and salt onto work surface; make well in center and pour in 1/2 cup (125 mL) water. Using fingers, gradually draw flour into water until soft dough is formed.

■ On clean lightly floured surface, knead dough for about 15 minutes or until smooth and elastic. Make depression in center of dough; gradually add up to 2 tbsp (25 mL) water while kneading for 10 minutes longer or until moist pliable dough is formed that is no longer sticky. Cover with plastic wrap and let stand for 30 minutes.

■ Divide dough into 12 portions. On clean lightly floured surface, roll out each portion into 6-inch (15 cm) round.

■ Heat ungreased skillet over medium-high heat; cook 1 round at a time for 30 to 40 seconds or until bubbles appear on surface. Using spatula, flatten bubbles; turn over and cook for 30 to 40 seconds or until second side is lightly browned. (Chapati can be

***SPICES***

***Spices further divide Indian cuisine. In the South, fresh spices are preferred over dried. They are ground with a liquid such as water, vinegar, lime juice or coconut milk to make a wet* masala *or paste. People in Northern India use more dry spices and pound them to make a powder. They also eat whole wheat breads with their meals and use fewer sauces in their cooking than do the rice eaters of Central, South and East India.***

***Indians like their food tasty and spiced but not always hot. Many of their seasonings are commonly found on any Canadian cook's kitchen shelf—pepper, nutmeg, cloves, bay leaves, cinnamon, mace. For occasional Indian cooking, you can usually get by with these basics plus coriander, cumin, hot chilies, turmeric, cardamom, saffron,* garam masala *(a mixture of hot spices), fresh garlic and gingerroot.***

*SIDE DISHES*
***At most Indian meals, the main dish—in this menu, the Biryani or Tandoori Chicken—would be supplemented with side dishes such as* raita *(sliced or chopped cucumber, onions or other vegetables in yogurt),* dal *(pulses or legumes, the main protein source in Indian food), fresh pickles and perhaps spiced vegetables. There might also be* pakoras *(spiced vegetables coated with chickpea batter, then fried) and* cachumbar *(raw vegetables flavored with fresh herbs) served in small bowls called* katoris, *along with* chapati *and* pappadums *(fried or baked thin disks made with lentil flour) on a* thali *(a big metal platter or tray).***

*GHEE*
***Widely used in Indian cooking,* ghee *is clarified butter. In small saucepan, melt 1 cup (250 mL) butter over low heat. Pour off clear yellow liquid, or clarified butter, leaving white sediment behind. Makes 3/4 cup (175 mL).***

cooled and stored in plastic bag for up to 8 hours. To reheat, place on baking sheet; cover loosely with foil and bake in 350°F/ 180°C oven for 5 to 10 minutes or until heated through.) Serve warm with melted butter. Makes 12 chapati.

## Tandoori Chicken

*An Indian tandoor is a special clay oven used for baking bread, chicken, fish or lamb. With a conventional oven, the smoky flavor is lost but the chicken will be moist and flavorful.*

| | | |
|---|---|---|
| **1 tsp** | **saffron threads (or 1/8 tsp/0.5 mL powdered saffron)** | **5 mL** |
| **3 tbsp** | **boiling water** | **50 mL** |
| **2** | **chickens (each about 3 lb/1.5 kg)** | **2** |
| **1/2 cup** | **lemon juice** | **125 mL** |
| **4 tsp** | **salt** | **20 mL** |
| **2 tsp** | **coriander seeds** | **10 mL** |
| **1 tsp** | **cumin seeds** | **5 mL** |
| **1 cup** | **plain yogurt** | **250 mL** |
| **2** | **cloves garlic, minced** | **2** |
| **1 tbsp** | **minced gingerroot** | **15 mL** |
| **1/2 tsp** | **paprika** | **2 mL** |
| **1/4 tsp** | **chili powder** | **1 mL** |
| **2 tbsp** | **ghee (see sidebar this page)** | **25 mL** |

■ In small bowl, soak saffron in boiling water for 5 minutes.
■ Pat chickens dry inside and out with paper towels; truss securely. With sharp knife, make several 1/2-inch (1 cm) deep cuts in chicken thighs and breasts. Place chickens in 13- x 9-inch (3.5 L) baking dish.
■ Reserve 2 tbsp (25 mL) of the lemon juice. Combine remaining lemon juice with salt and rub over chickens, especially into slits. Pour saffron mixture over chickens and rub in to coat evenly; set aside.
■ In small ungreased skillet, cook coriander and cumin seeds over medium heat, shaking skillet constantly, for 2 to 3 minutes or until golden.
■ Transfer to blender and add 2 tbsp (25 mL) of the yogurt, garlic and ginger; blend until puréed. Stir purée into remaining yogurt along with paprika and chili powder; spread evenly over chickens. Cover and marinate in refrigerator for at least 12 hours or up to 24 hours.
■ Arrange chickens on rack in roasting pan; pour any liquid remaining in dish over chickens. Roast in 400°F (200°C) oven for 15 minutes. Combine ghee and reserved lemon juice; brush over chickens.
■ Reduce heat to 350°F (180°C) and roast for 1-1/4 to 1-1/2 hours or until chickens are golden brown, meat thermometer registers 185°F (85°C) when inserted in thickest part of thigh and juices run clear when chickens are pierced. Makes about 8 servings.

## Vermicelli Kheer

*A delicate creamy dessert like this is perfect after a well-spiced meal.*

| | | |
|---|---|---|
| **2 tsp** | **butter** | **10 mL** |
| **2 cups** | **broken vermicelli or fine egg noodles** | **500 mL** |
| **4 cups** | **milk** | **1 L** |
| **1/2 cup** | **sultana raisins** | **125 mL** |
| **1/2 cup** | **slivered blanched almonds** | **125 mL** |
| **1/2 cup** | **granulated sugar** | **125 mL** |
| **1/2 cup** | **whipping cream** | **125 mL** |
| **Pinch** | **ground cardamom** | **Pinch** |
| **1/4 cup** | **unsalted pistachios, slivered** | **50 mL** |

■ In skillet, heat butter over low heat; cook vermicelli for about 3 minutes or until lightly browned, stirring constantly and breaking up vermicelli as it cooks.
■ In large saucepan, combine vermicelli, milk, raisins and almonds; bring to boil over high heat, stirring occasionally. Boil, stirring constantly, for 5 to 7 minutes or until vermicelli is tender.
■ Add sugar and stir until dissolved; remove from heat. Stir in cream; pour into serving dish. Sprinkle with cardamom; garnish with pistachios. Serve hot or cold. Makes about 8 servings.

# AN IRISH COUNTRY DINNER

FOR EIGHT

*With a menu of authentic gems from the Emerald Isle, you'll honor St. Patrick in fine style or add a little magic to any cozy gathering. This menu celebrates the beloved country-style cooking of Ireland, with traditional dishes sure to warm the hearts of all.*

MUGS OF STOUT OR GUINNESS

*OLD-COUNTRY BROWN BREAD

*POTTED SHRIMP

*SHANAGARRY IRISH STEW

*CHAMP OR STELK

*OLD-FASHIONED SALAD

*WEST COUNTRY APPLE CAKE

*SCALTEEN

## *Old-Country Brown Bread*

*This moist and flavorful loaf is best made with grist mill flour or stone-ground whole wheat flour found at health food stores. The bread is unusual in that it is not kneaded and requires only one rising. It's also delicious toasted.*

| | | |
|---|---|---|
| **2 cups** | **(approx) warm water** | **500 mL** |
| **3 tbsp** | **molasses** | **50 mL** |
| **1** | **pkg active dry yeast (or 1 tbsp/15 mL)** | **1** |
| **3-1/2 cups** | **whole wheat flour** | **875 mL** |
| **1/4 cup** | **wheat germ** | **50 mL** |
| **2 tsp** | **salt** | **10 mL** |
| **1 tbsp** | **sesame seeds** | **15 mL** |

■ Cut 13- x 8-inch (32 x 20 cm) piece of parchment paper; make 3-inch (8 cm) slash into each corner. Fit into greased 9- x 5-inch (2 L) loaf pan; trim excess paper. Set aside.

■ In small bowl, combine 1 cup (250 mL) of the water with molasses; sprinkle in yeast. Let stand for 5 to 10 minutes or until frothy.

■ In large bowl, combine flour, wheat germ and salt. Using wooden spoon, beat in yeast mixture and enough of the remaining water to make sticky dough. In bowl, work with hands for 30 seconds.

■ Transfer dough to prepared pan. Sprinkle with sesame seeds. Cover with tea towel and let rise in warm place for about 20 minutes or just until dough reaches top of pan. Bake in 400°F (200°C) oven for 50 to 60 minutes or until browned and loaf sounds hollow when tapped on bottom. Remove from pan; peel off paper. Turn upside down and return to turned-off oven for 20 minutes. Let cool completely on rack. Makes 1 loaf.

*Old-Country Brown Bread*

# Potted Shrimp

*When packed into tiny pots or jars, this easy appetizer will keep refrigerated for several weeks.*

| | | |
|---|---|---|
| **3/4 cup** | **unsalted butter** | **175 mL** |
| **1** | **clove garlic, minced** | **1** |
| **2 tsp** | **fresh thyme leaves (or 1/2 tsp/2 mL dried)** | **10 mL** |
| **1/2 lb** | **shrimp, peeled and deveined** | **250 g** |
| | **Salt and pepper** | |
| | **Sprig fresh thyme** | |

■ In saucepan, melt butter over medium heat, stirring occasionally, for about 3 minutes or until frothy but not browned. Skim and discard foam; pour off clear liquid, discarding any milky residue. Return liquid to saucepan.

■ Add garlic and thyme leaves; bring to boil, stirring occasionally. Add shrimp; reduce heat and simmer for 3 to 5 minutes or until pink. Add lemon juice, and salt and pepper to taste.

■ Pack into small ramekins or large jar. Pour liquid over. Garnish with sprig of thyme. Makes 1-3/4 cups (425 mL).

# Shanagarry Irish Stew

*Depending on where you eat Irish stew in the Emerald Isle, you will find it with or without carrots, barley and turnip. This version with browned meat, lots of carrots, and potatoes that break up and thicken the stew, is common in the south.*

| | | |
|---|---|---|
| **8** | **shoulder lamb chops, 1-inch (2.5 cm) thick (about 3-1/2 lb/1.75 kg total)** | **8** |
| **6** | **potatoes (about 2-1/2 lb/1.25 kg)** | **6** |
| **8** | **carrots (about 1 lb/500 g)** | **8** |
| **2 tbsp** | **vegetable oil** | **25 mL** |
| **6** | **onions, quartered** | **6** |
| **3/4 cup** | **sliced leeks** | **175 mL** |
| **3-1/2 cups** | **beef stock** | **875 mL** |
| **1-1/2 tsp** | **dried thyme** | **7 mL** |
| **1** | **bay leaf** | **1** |
| **1/4 tsp** | **pepper** | **1 mL** |
| | **Salt** | |
| **1 tbsp** | **all-purpose flour** | **15 mL** |
| **1 tbsp** | **butter** | **15 mL** |
| **1/4 cup** | **coarsely chopped fresh parsley** | **50 mL** |

■ Trim lamb chops and pat dry with paper towels; set aside. Cut potatoes into 1-inch (2.5 cm) chunks; set aside. Cut carrots in half lengthwise, then diagonally into 1-inch (2.5 cm) pieces; set aside.

■ In large saucepan or Dutch oven, heat oil over medium-high heat; cook lamb chops, in batches, for 5 minutes on each side or

***THE POPULAR POTATO***

***With many varieties to choose from, including British Queen, Kerr's Pink and Golden Wonder, the potato stars in many Irish dishes.***

**Boxty:** ***This popular potato bread is baked as a loaf or small cakes.***

**Colcannon:** ***Ireland's national dish is made with potatoes and***

*Shanagarry Irish Stew; Champ or Stelk*

***cabbage. It became known as the festival dish at the Festival of Lugnasa, a harvest celebration to mark the digging of new potatoes.*** **Pratie oaten:** ***A breakfast favorite, it's a tasty combination of potatoes and oatmeal.*** **Potato cakes:** ***Great with bacon and eggs, this is a good way to use up boiled or mashed potatoes.***

until well browned. Remove to plate. Drain off all but 2 tbsp (25 mL) fat. Add onions, leeks and potatoes; cook, stirring constantly, for 3 to 4 minutes or just until vegetables are softened. Remove to bowl.

■ Return chops and accumulated juices to pan. Spread vegetable mixture over chops. Add stock, thyme, bay leaf, pepper, and salt to taste. Reduce heat and simmer, covered, for 35 minutes. Add carrots and simmer, covered, for 45 to 55 minutes or until lamb and vegetables are tender. Taste and adjust seasoning if necessary.

■ Using slotted spoon, transfer lamb and vegetables to heated platter; cover and keep warm. Remove bay leaf and skim any fat from remaining liquid. Knead together flour and butter; whisk into hot pan juices. Cook, whisking constantly, over high heat for 5 to 10 minutes or until sauce has thickened slightly. Stir in parsley. Pour over lamb and vegetables. Makes about 8 servings.

## Champ or Stelk

*Leeks are one of Ireland's oldest recorded vegetables. Simmered in milk, they impart a delicate flavor to this typical mashed potato dish, the perfect partner to Irish stew. Traditionally, champ was served with a well of hot butter in the center. Each spoonful of potato would be dipped into the rich butter.*

| | | |
|---|---|---|
| **3 lb** | **potatoes, quartered (about 8 potatoes)** | **1.5 kg** |
| **1 cup** | **chopped green onions** | **250 mL** |
| **1/4 cup** | **chopped leek** | **50 mL** |
| **1-1/2 cups** | **milk** | **375 mL** |
| **1/4 cup** | **butter, cut in small pieces** | **50 mL** |
| **1/2 tsp** | **salt** | **2 mL** |
| **1/4 tsp** | **pepper** | **1 mL** |

■ In large saucepan, pour enough cold water over potatoes to cover. Bring to boil over medium-high heat; cook, covered, for 20 to 25 minutes or until potatoes are tender. (Do not overcook.)

■ Meanwhile, in small saucepan, combine 3/4 cup (175 mL) of the green onions, leek and milk. Bring to simmer over medium heat; cook for 15 minutes or until softened. Remove from heat and set aside.

■ Drain potatoes and shake over low heat for 1 to 2 minutes to evaporate excess moisture; mash. Beat in butter and enough of the hot milk mixture to make creamy potatoes. Add salt and pepper. Transfer to heated serving bowl. Garnish with remaining green onion. Makes about 8 servings.

## Old-Fashioned Salad

*The light creamy dressing is not tossed with the salad but served separately in a bowl. Sliced cooked beets, quartered hard-cooked eggs and shredded cabbage are optional additions.*

| | | |
|---|---|---|
| **1** | **large head Boston lettuce, separated** | **1** |
| **1** | **bunch watercress** | **1** |
| **Half** | **English cucumber, cut in 1/8-inch (3 mm) slices** | **Half** |
| **8** | **large radishes, cut in 1/8-inch (3 mm) slices** | **8** |
| **16** | **cherry tomatoes, halved** | **16** |
| **8** | **small green onions** | **8** |
| | **DRESSING:** | |
| **6** | **hard-cooked eggs** | **6** |
| **3 tbsp** | **packed brown sugar** | **50 mL** |
| **1-1/2 tsp** | **dry mustard** | **7 mL** |
| **1/4 cup** | **malt vinegar** | **50 mL** |
| **3/4 cup** | **light cream** | **175 mL** |
| | **Salt and pepper** | |

■ Arrange lettuce leaves on large platter. Top with watercress. Arrange, either in group composition or scattered, cucumber, radishes and tomatoes over lettuce.

**DRESSING:** Cut eggs in half lengthwise; scoop out yolks and mash or sieve into bowl. Add sugar and mustard; mash together. Whisk in vinegar, then cream. Season with salt and pepper to taste. Coarsely chop egg whites. Mix about half into dressing; scatter remaining whites evenly over salad. Garnish with green onions. Serve dressing separately. Makes about 8 servings.

*West Country Apple Cake; Scalteen*

# West Country Apple Cake

*Thick cake-like crust enveloping apples, rhubarb or gooseberries is always served warm with whipped cream and brown sugar. As common as the cake is, it varies from house to house but in Ireland, all are made with Bramley apples, which break down into a foamy mass when cooked.*

| | | |
|---|---|---|
| **2 cups** | **all-purpose flour** | **500 mL** |
| **1 tsp** | **baking powder** | **5 mL** |
| **1/2 cup** | **cold unsalted butter, cut in 1/4-inch (5 mm) cubes** | **125 mL** |
| **3/4 cup** | **packed brown sugar** | **175 mL** |
| **1** | **egg, lightly beaten** | **1** |
| **1/4 cup** | **milk** | **50 mL** |
| | **FILLING:** | |
| **3** | **Cortland or Northern Spy apples** | **3** |
| **2 tsp** | **lemon juice** | **10 mL** |
| **1/4 cup** | **raisins** | **50 mL** |
| **1/2 tsp** | **cinnamon** | **2 mL** |
| **1/4 tsp** | **each ground allspice, cloves and nutmeg** | **1 mL** |
| **1 tbsp** | **liquid honey** | **15 mL** |
| | **Whipped cream** | |
| | **Brown sugar** | |

**FILLING:** Peel apples; cut into 1/2-inch (1 cm) pieces. (You should have about 3 cups/750 mL.) In bowl, toss apples with lemon juice. Add raisins, cinnamon, allspice, cloves and nutmeg; stir well. Add honey and mix thoroughly; set aside.

■ In large bowl, sift together flour and baking powder. Using two knives, cut in butter until mixture resembles coarse meal. Stir in sugar. Make well in center; pour in egg and milk. Using fork, stir briskly to make sticky dough; divide in half.

■ Roll out one half between 2 sheets of waxed paper to 1/4-inch (5 mm) thickness. Fit into lightly greased 9-inch (23 cm) pie plate. Spoon filling evenly over dough. Roll out remaining dough; place on top of filling. Press edges together. Using sharp knife, cut small slit in center of pastry top to allow steam to escape.

■ Bake in 350°F (180°C) oven for 45 minutes or until cake is golden brown and firm to the touch and tester inserted in center comes out clean. Cut into 8 wedges while hot. Serve warm. Pass whipped cream and brown sugar separately. Makes about 8 servings.

***SCALTEEN***

***This warming drink is often made with Wexford honey, full of the wildflowers and herbs of the Irish countryside.***

***In saucepan, heat 6 cups (1.5 L) milk over medium-low heat, stirring occasionally, for 5 to 8 minutes or until bubbles start to form around edge of pan.***

***Stir in 1/2 cup (125 mL) honey and 1/4 cup (50 mL) butter (cut in 1/4-inch/5 mm cubes) until butter melts, about 1 minute. Remove from heat. Pour 3 tbsp (50 mL) whiskey into each of 8 mugs, then pour in hot milk mixture. Sprinkle with freshly grated nutmeg. Makes 8 servings.***

# GREEK CLASSICS

FOR EIGHT

*Greece is a land of ancient temples, sparkling blue seas and bountiful food fit for the gods. Good Greek cooking is pure ambrosia, but perhaps the most important ingredient of all is hospitality. When you step inside a Greek home, you enjoy overwhelming attention, good wine and great food. This classic Greek dinner treats your guests to the same warmth and hospitality.*

*TARAMOSALATA
(CARP ROE SPREAD)

*SOUPA AVGOLEMONO
(EGG LEMON SOUP)

GREEK SALAD

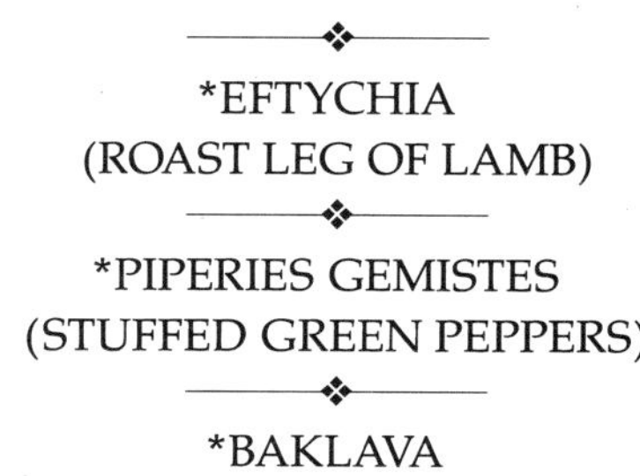

*EFTYCHIA
(ROAST LEG OF LAMB)

*PIPERIES GEMISTES
(STUFFED GREEN PEPPERS)

*BAKLAVA

## *Taramosalata*
### *(Carp Roe Spread)*

*Serve this appetizing dip as a first course on wedges of hot pita bread or use as a dip for vegetables.* Tarama, *or carp roe caviar, is available at Greek food stores.*

| | | |
|---|---|---|
| 4 | **slices white bread** | 4 |
| 1/2 cup | **cold water** | 125 mL |
| 1-1/2 cups | **mashed potatoes** | 375 mL |
| 1/2 cup | **tarama** | 125 mL |
| 1/4 cup | **chopped onion** | 50 mL |
| 1/4 cup | **lemon juice** | 50 mL |
| 3/4 cup | **olive oil** | 175 mL |

■ Remove and discard crusts from bread. Soak in cold water for 5 minutes; squeeze out water.

■ In food processor or blender, combine bread, potatoes and tarama; process for 1-1/2 minutes or until smooth. Add onion and lemon juice; process for 30 seconds.

■ With machine running, gradually pour in oil through feed tube. Transfer to airtight container and refrigerate, covered, for at least 2 hours to allow flavors to blend, or for up to 2 days. Makes about 3 cups (750 mL).

## *Soupa Avgolemono*
### *(Egg Lemon Soup)*

*Lemon is a popular flavoring in Greek dishes.*

| | | |
|---|---|---|
| 8 cups | **chicken stock** | 2 L |
| 2 tbsp | **chopped fresh dill** | 25 mL |
| 1/2 cup | **orzo or rice** | 125 mL |
| 4 | **eggs** | 4 |
| 1/4 cup | **lemon juice** | 50 mL |
| | **Salt and pepper** | |
| | **Lemon slices** | |

■ In large saucepan, combine stock with dill; bring to boil. Add orzo (a rice-shaped pasta); reduce heat and simmer, covered, for 15 to 20 minutes or until al dente (tender but firm).

■ In bowl, beat eggs lightly; stir in about 2 cups (500 mL) of the hot stock mixture. Gradually stir egg mixture back into remaining stock mixture. Increase heat to medium and cook, stirring constantly, for about 5 minutes or until soup is creamy and slightly thickened.

■ Stir in lemon juice; season with salt and pepper to taste. Serve immediately; garnish with lemon slices. Makes about 8 servings.

# *Eftychia*
## *(Roast Leg of Lamb)*

*This dish has the characteristic Greek flavoring of lemon juice, olive oil and cinnamon. Potatoes roasted along with the meat make it an easy meal to prepare.*

| | | |
|---|---|---|
| 1 | **leg of lamb (5 to 6 lb/ 2.5 to 3 kg)** | 1 |
| 1/2 cup | **lemon juice** | 125 mL |
| 1/4 cup | **olive oil** | 50 mL |
| 1/2 tsp | **pepper** | 2 mL |
| 10 | **potatoes, peeled and quartered** | 10 |
| 1/2 tsp | **salt** | 2 mL |
| 1 cup | **water** | 250 mL |
| 1/4 cup | **tomato paste** | 50 mL |
| 1 tsp | **granulated sugar** | 5 mL |
| Pinch | **cinnamon** | Pinch |

■ Trim excess fat from lamb; place in roasting pan. Combine lemon juice with oil; brush half of the mixture over lamb. Sprinkle with pepper. Roast in 450°F (230°C) oven, uncovered, for 20 minutes.
■ Pour remaining lemon juice mixture over lamb. Reduce heat to 325°F (160°C); cover and roast for 30 minutes.
■ Toss potatoes with salt; arrange around lamb. Combine water, tomato paste, sugar and cinnamon; pour over lamb and potatoes. Roast, covered, for 30 minutes.
■ Turn potatoes over and baste meat; roast, uncovered, for about 30 minutes longer or until potatoes are tender and meat thermometer inserted in center of roast registers 140°F (60°C) for rare, 160°F (70°C) for medium or 170°F (75°C) for well-done. Makes about 8 servings.

# *Piperies Gemistes*
## *(Stuffed Green Peppers)*

*Whether raw, stewed or stuffed, sweet peppers are an essential ingredient in Greek fare.*

| | | |
|---|---|---|
| 8 | **sweet green peppers** | 8 |
| 3 tbsp | **olive oil** | 50 mL |
| 1/2 cup | **finely chopped onions** | 125 mL |
| 1-1/4 cups | **long-grain rice** | 300 mL |
| 2 cups | **boiling water** | 500 mL |
| 1/2 cup | **lemon juice** | 125 mL |
| 1/4 cup | **tomato paste** | 50 mL |
| 1/2 tsp | **salt** | 2 mL |
| 1/2 cup | **pine or pistachio nuts** | 125 mL |
| 1/3 cup | **chopped fresh parsley** | 75 mL |
| 1/4 cup | **grated kefalotyri* or Parmesan cheese** | 50 mL |
| 2 tbsp | **fine dry bread crumbs** | 25 mL |

*(Clockwise from top right) Soupa Avgolemono; Taramosalata; Eftychia; greek salad; Piperies Gemistes; assorted olives*

***AT A GREEK TABLE***
***The flavoring of Greek food ranges from robust overtones to subtle nuances, with the predominant flavorings being olive oil,***

*tomatoes, cinnamon, marjoram, oregano and lemon.*

*A Greek meal might start with a glass of ouzo (strong anise-flavored liqueur). This would be accompanied by appetizers* **(orektika)** *such as* **dolmades** *(grape leaves stuffed with rice or minced meat),* **taramosalata** *(tangy pâté of fish roe) or* **tzatziki** *(a blend of yogurt and cucumber). Appetizers like these are also served as snacks throughout the day. Served at the same time would be a salad of tomatoes, cucumbers, feta cheese and one or two kinds of olives. A plate of crusty bread accompanies the meal, but generally there is no butter. And you'll always find cruets of olive oil and vinegar on the table.*

*The most commonly used meats for a main course are lamb, veal and chicken, although Greeks frequently substitute a vegetable dish such as stuffed zucchini, and they also love seafood.*

*Wine is usually served with the meal, and in the country it's homemade. Retsinas (wines flavored with pine resin) are also popular.*

*Honey is a favorite dessert ingredient, together with nuts such as pistachios and walnuts. Paper-thin phyllo pastry is the other main ingredient for a sweet dessert such as baklava.*

■ Cut off and discard 1/2 inch (1 cm) from tops of green peppers. Remove seeds and ribs, being careful not to pierce shells. In large saucepan, cover peppers with boiling water; boil for 5 minutes. Remove and let stand upside down on wire rack to drain.

■ In saucepan, heat oil over medium heat; cook onions for 3 minutes or until translucent but not browned. Stir in rice. Add water, lemon juice, tomato paste and salt; bring to boil. Cover and reduce heat; simmer, stirring occasionally, for 15 minutes or until rice is almost cooked. Stir in nuts and parsley. Taste and adjust seasoning if necessary.

■ Spoon rice mixture evenly into peppers; arrange snugly in greased 11-×7-inch (2 L) baking dish. Sprinkle cheese and bread crumbs evenly over peppers. Cover dish with foil and bake in 350°F (180°C) oven for 30 to 45 minutes or until peppers are tender and rice mixture is heated through. If desired, uncover and broil for 3 to 5 minutes or until golden brown. Makes 8 servings.

*Sheep or goat cheese available at Greek food stores.

## Baklava

*The Greeks, Turks and Russians all lay claim to inventing this syrupy dessert with its golden phyllo layers and nutty filling.*

| | | |
|---|---|---|
| **1** | **pkg (1 lb/454 g) phyllo pastry, thawed** | **1** |
| **1 cup** | **unsalted butter, melted** | **250 mL** |
| | **FILLING:** | |
| **3 cups** | **finely chopped walnuts** | **750 mL** |
| **1/4 cup** | **granulated sugar** | **50 mL** |
| **1 tbsp** | **grated lemon rind** | **15 mL** |
| **1/2 tsp** | **cinnamon** | **2 mL** |

*Baklava*

| | | |
|---|---|---|
| | **SYRUP:** | |
| **1-1/2 cups** | **granulated sugar** | **375 mL** |
| **1 cup** | **water** | **250 mL** |
| **Pinch** | **cream of tartar** | **Pinch** |
| **1/4 cup** | **lemon juice** | **50 mL** |
| **1/4 cup** | **honey** | **50 mL** |

■ Butter shallow 13-×9-inch (3.5 L) baking dish. With scissors, cut stack of phyllo about 2 inches (5 cm) longer and wider than size of dish. Reserve trimmings for another use. While working, keep stack of phyllo covered with damp tea towel to prevent from drying out.

■ Fold 1 sheet of phyllo in half and gently transfer to prepared baking dish. Unfold and press against bottom and sides of pan. Using pastry brush, brush entire surface with a little of the melted butter. Repeat with 6 more sheets of phyllo and some of the remaining butter.

**FILLING:** Combine walnuts, sugar, lemon rind and cinnamon; spoon about half over phyllo, spreading to cover surface. Cover with 7 more sheets of phyllo, pressing each sheet down and brushing with some of the butter.

■ Spread remaining filling over top. Cover with remaining sheets of phyllo, brushing each sheet with remaining butter. Fold pastry under and tuck inside pan, lifting baklava slightly if necessary.

■ With small sharp knife, make diagonal cuts across pastry 1/2 inch (1 cm) deep and 1-1/2 inches (4 cm) apart. Repeat in opposite direction to form diamond shapes. Bake in 350°F (180°C) oven for 30 minutes. Reduce heat to 300°F (150°C) and bake for 45 to 50 minutes longer or until top is crisp and golden brown.

**SYRUP:** Meanwhile, in small saucepan, combine sugar, water and cream of tartar; stir well and add lemon juice. Bring to boil, wiping down sugar crystals from side of pan with wet pastry brush.

■ Boil syrup vigorously, without stirring, for 5 to 10 minutes or until temperature on candy thermometer reaches 230°F (110°C) or until 1/2 tsp (2 mL) of syrup dropped into cold water spins a soft thread. Remove from heat; stir in honey.

■ Pour over hot baklava; let cool to room temperature. Just before serving, cut along scored lines into serving pieces. Makes about 36 pieces.

# A TREASURE OF THAI DELIGHTS

FOR EIGHT

*Exotic and irresistible, the fiery cuisine of Thailand has also become very hot on the North American restaurant scene. A beautifully presented array of spicy dishes, sweets and fruit platters adorned with fresh flowers is traditionally served all at the same time. At home, a Thai buffet dinner is easy on the hosts who can relax and enjoy the flow of courses with their guests.*

*FRESH SPRING ROLLS

*PLUM SWEET SAUCE

*LEMON SHRIMP SOUP

*HOT AND SOUR DIPPING SAUCE

*LAAB ISSAN GAI (NORTHERN-STYLE CHOPPED CHICKEN BREAST)

*STICKY RICE

*MEE GATI (BANGKOK NOODLES)

*SWEET AND SALTY AIR-DRIED BEEF

*TROPICAL JELLIES

*(Clockwise from top) Mee Gati; Lemon Shrimp Soup; Laab Issan Gai; Plum Sweet Sauce; Fresh Spring Rolls; Sweet and Salty Air-Dried Beef; Sticky Rice*

***FLAVORS OF THAILAND***

***Thai cuisine is based on the "five tastes" principle, balancing and blending sweet, piquant, sour, salty and neutral. A well-chosen Thai meal includes a dish to stimulate and satisfy each of these tastes.***

***Rice and noodles are the main staples in Thai cooking, which includes a lot of fish and seafood, chicken and a little pork. These are usually steamed, stir-fried, broiled or grilled over charcoal. The distinctive flavors of Thai cuisine come from garlic, kha root, lemon grass, super-hot fresh chilies, coriander, black pepper and a powerful paste made from dried fermented shrimp. Thai cooks use fish sauce as other Asians use soy sauce.***

***While genuine spicy Thai dishes are almost painfully hot, you can modify your versions so that the other subtle flavors can still be enjoyed. Remove considerable fire from the chilies by taking out the seeds and membranes and by reducing the amount used. Better to begin with a pinch—you can always add more.***

# Fresh Spring Rolls

*These delightful spring rolls, somewhat like a salad wrapped in thin rice pancakes, are served at room temperature. Cut the spring rolls into bite-size pieces and serve with sweet plum sauce and a fiery Thai chili sauce called Sriracha, available bottled in Chinese and southeast Asian food stores.*

*You can tailor these spring rolls to your own taste by adding whatever ingredients appeal to you. Typical Thai additions might include fresh basil or mint leaves, chilies, broccoli (lightly steamed and julienned), Chinese cabbage, bamboo shoots, mushrooms, glass noodles and cucumber. Shredded cooked beef, barbecued pork or duck, ham or bacon can be used instead of chicken.*

| | | |
|---|---|---|
| 8 | **large rice paper crêpes*** | 8 |
| 1 cup | **bean sprouts** | 250 mL |
| 4 | **green onions** | 4 |
| 1/4 cup | **tofu** | 50 mL |
| 8 | **water chestnuts** | 8 |
| 1 tbsp | **vegetable oil** | 15 mL |
| 3 | **eggs, beaten** | 3 |
| 1/2 lb | **boneless chicken breasts, cooked and shredded** | 250 g |
| 1/4 lb | **red Oriental sausage, julienned** | 125 g |
| 1/4 cup | **coriander leaves** | 50 mL |
| 1 | **carrot, grated** | 1 |
| 1 | **egg yolk, lightly beaten (optional)** | 1 |
| | **Lettuce** | |
| | **Carrot and cucumber cutouts (optional)** | |

■ Separate crêpes, then dip into hand-hot water to soften; drain and place on damp tea towel.

■ Remove roots from bean sprouts and discard. Sliver green onions; cut into 1-inch (2.5 cm) lengths. Cut tofu into small cubes or juliennes. Cut water chestnuts into small cubes. Set aside.

■ In skillet, heat oil over medium-high heat. Cook eggs, stirring with fork, for 1 minute; cook, without stirring, for 1 minute longer or just until eggs are set. Slide out of pan and let cool. Cut into thin shreds.

■ On one-third of each crêpe, arrange rows of eggs, chicken, sausage, coriander, grated carrot, bean sprouts, green onions, tofu and water chestnuts. Roll up tightly, tucking in ends. Seal rolls with lightly beaten egg yolk (if using). (Spring rolls can be wrapped in damp tea towel to prevent crêpes from drying out and refrigerated for up to 8 hours.)

■ With very sharp knife and using sawing motion, cut each roll into four bite-size pieces. Serve on bed of lettuce and garnish with carrot and cucumber cutouts (if using). Makes 8 spring rolls.

*Large round rice flour crêpes are available dried at most Oriental grocery stores.

# Plum Sweet Sauce

*The sweetness of this sauce is a matter of personal taste. Thais include the vinegar for bite but feel the sauce should be more sweet than sour. If plums in vinegar are unavailable, use dried plums: cover with hot water and 3 tbsp (50 mL) vinegar and soak until softened; drain. Fresh plums in season will work, but not dried prunes. Pickled crab apples or dried apricots make acceptable alternatives to Chinese plums, although they are not typically Thai. You can also add a little freshly grated gingerroot.*

| | | |
|---|---|---|
| 1 cup | **drained Chinese plums in vinegar** | 250 mL |
| 1/2 cup | **water** | 125 mL |
| 1/4 cup | **(approx) honey** | 50 mL |

■ Rinse plums under cold running water. Cover with cold water for several hours or overnight to remove salt. Drain.

■ In small heavy saucepan, combine plums, water and honey. Bring to boil; cover, reduce heat and simmer gently for 10 minutes. Push through sieve to remove pits. Taste and add up to 1/4 cup (50 mL) more honey if desired. Makes about 1 cup (250 mL).

## Lemon Shrimp Soup

*Thai meals always include a variety of fresh fish and shellfish. For this dish you can use a combination of shellfish—mussels, crab legs, lobster and shrimp—or substitute 2 lb (1 kg) mussels for the shrimp. If you're using dried kha root, which must be soaked first, the soaking liquid can be added to the broth. This soup is served from a large earthenware pot or bowl. The seafood is served first, then the broth is spooned into small bowls to be sipped along with the rest of the meal.*

| | | |
|---|---|---|
| **6 cups** | **chicken stock** | **1.5 L** |
| **1 tsp** | **(approx) Thai chili paste** | **5 mL** |
| **3** | **stalks lemon grass, cut in 1-inch (2.5 cm) sections*** | **3** |
| **5** | **makrood leaves*** | **5** |
| **5** | **slices kha (laos) root*** | **5** |
| **4 tsp** | **fish sauce** | **20 mL** |
| **3/4 lb** | **shrimp, peeled and deveined** | **375 g** |
| **6** | **fresh chilies, finely chopped (optional)** | **6** |
| **12** | **straw mushrooms, cut in half**** | **12** |
| **2 tbsp** | **lime juice** | **25 mL** |
| **2** | **green onions, sliced** | **2** |
| **1** | **stalk fresh coriander** | **1** |

■ In large saucepan, combine stock with chili paste; bring to boil. Add lemon grass, makrood leaves, kha root and fish sauce; return to boil. Add shrimp; cook for about 5 minutes or until shrimp are bright pink. Using slotted spoon, remove shrimp and set aside.

■ Strain soup; discard any tough lemon grass and kha root. Taste and adjust seasoning if necessary, adding more chili paste to taste. To increase saltiness, add more fish sauce. Add chilies (if using) to make soup fiery hot.

■ Return soup to saucepan. Add straw mushrooms; reheat gently. Just before serving, return shrimp to soup and add lime juice. Garnish with onions and coriander leaves. Makes 8 servings.

*See Glossary, this page.

**You can substitute fresh mushrooms for straw mushrooms; add at beginning of recipe.

## Hot and Sour Dipping Sauce

*You can use this clear dipping sauce with spring rolls, all types of seafood or any dish that lacks the fiery bite the Thais love. Before chopping the chilies and garlic, pound the chilies to release the pungent oil of capsaicin, and pound the garlic to release more flavor. The lime provides the sour taste, fish sauce the salty taste.*

| | | |
|---|---|---|
| | **Juice of 2 limes** | |
| **2 tbsp** | **fish sauce** | **25 mL** |
| **4** | **fresh chilies, finely chopped** | **4** |
| **2** | **cloves garlic, chopped** | **2** |

■ Combine lime juice, fish sauce, chilies and garlic. Let stand for at least 30 minutes to allow flavors to develop. Makes about 2/3 cup (150 mL).

## Laab Issan Gai
### (Northern-Style Chopped Chicken Breast)

*This dish earns a "three chilies" rating at Bangkok Garden in Toronto, so you know it's fiery hot, but you can adjust amount of chilies to your own taste. The true northern Thai Laab calls for uncooked beef, a Thai version of steak tartare.*

| | | |
|---|---|---|
| **1/3 cup** | **long-grain rice** | **75 mL** |
| **1-1/2 lb** | **boneless skinless chicken breasts, finely chopped** | **750 g** |
| **1/3 cup** | **lime juice** | **75 mL** |
| **1/4 cup** | **chopped fresh mint leaves** | **50 mL** |
| **3 tbsp** | **fish sauce** | **50 mL** |
| **1 tsp** | **finely chopped fresh chilies** | **5 mL** |

***GLOSSARY OF THAI INGREDIENTS***

- **Agar-agar** ***is used in place of gelatin. It does not break down or melt in warm temperatures. Will set without refrigeration.***
- **Tofu** ***is also known as bean curd.***
- **Canned salted soya beans** ***are available at southeast Asian food stores.***
- **Coconut milk** ***is the liquid pressed from a mixture of shredded fresh coconut and water. (It is not the watery liquid inside a fresh coconut, nor the sweet canned mixture used for drinks.) Available in Oriental and southeast Asian food stores.***
- **Fish sauce (nam pla)** ***looks like soy sauce and is used in Thai cooking much like soy sauce is used in Chinese cooking.***
- **Fresh coriander** ***is often called cilantro or Chinese parsley.***
- **Kha (laos) root,** ***a member of the ginger family, adds a peppery-ginger flavor. Soak in warm water if using the dried version.***
- **Lemon grass** ***must be soaked in hot water before using. If not available, substitute grated lemon rind.***
- **Chilies** ***can cause skin irritation and should always be handled with rubber gloves.***
- **Makrood leaves,** ***from the kaffir lime plant, add a distinct lime flavor. Usually available at Oriental food stores. Or***

*substitute grated or slivered lime rind.*
• **Pandanus, jasmine** *and* **rose-water** *are flavorings available in Oriental food stores.*
• **Straw mushrooms,** *usually canned, are available in Oriental food stores.*
• **Thai chili paste (nam prik pau)** *is available in southeast Asian food stores. You can substitute a Thai chili sauce* **(nam prik)** *or Sriracha sauce, a fiery Thai chili sauce, available in Chinese and southeast Asian food stores. If none of these are available, use* **sambal oelek,** *an Indonesian chili sauce.*
• **Glutinous rice** *is a special variety of rice that becomes sticky when cooked. It's often eaten with the fingers.*

*STICKY RICE*
*Cover 2 cups (500 mL) glutinous rice with cold water and let stand overnight. Drain, then rinse thoroughly under cold running water.*
*In rice steamer or heavy saucepan with tight-fitting lid, combine rice with 4 cups (1 L) water; cook for about 20 minutes or until water is absorbed. Makes 8 servings.*

| | | |
|---|---|---|
| 8 | **shallots, finely chopped** | 8 |
| 2 tbsp | **chopped fresh coriander** | 25 mL |
| 6 | **green onions, finely chopped** | 6 |
| | **Sticky Rice (see sidebar)** | |

■ In skillet or wok (without oil), stir-fry long-grain rice over medium-high heat, stirring constantly, until golden brown, 3 to 5 minutes. Transfer to food processor or blender and process until consistency of coarsely ground pepper. Set aside.
■ Place chicken in strainer, then into pot of rapidly boiling water; cook for 2 to 3 minutes or until chicken is white. Drain and transfer to bowl.
■ Stir in ground rice, lime juice, mint, fish sauce, chilies, shallots, coriander and onions. Stir until well mixed. Taste and adjust seasoning if necessary. (Flavor should be hot, sour and salty.) Serve with Sticky Rice. Makes 8 servings.

## *Mee Gati*
### *(Bangkok Noodles)*

*Thai rice vermicelli is available in many Thai, Chinese, Vietnamese or southeast Asian food stores. Thick unsweetened coconut milk is available at Oriental and southeast Asian food stores, or you can make your own.*

| | | |
|---|---|---|
| 3/4 lb | **Thai rice vermicelli** | 375 g |
| 1/4 cup | **vegetable oil** | 50 mL |
| 6 | **shallots, sliced in thin wedges** | 6 |
| 1 cup | **bean sprouts** | 250 mL |
| 1 tbsp | **fish sauce** | 15 mL |
| 1 tsp | **chopped fresh chives** | 5 mL |
| | **SAUCE:** | |
| 1-1/2 cups | **unsweetened coconut milk*** | 375 mL |
| 1/4 lb | **ground pork** | 125 g |
| 1/4 lb | **peeled deveined shrimp, chopped** | 125 mL |
| 1 | **small clove garlic, chopped** | 1 |
| 1 tbsp | **canned salted soya beans** | 15 mL |
| 1 tsp | **granulated sugar** | 5 mL |
| 1 tsp | **fish sauce** | 5 mL |
| 1 tsp | **lemon juice or tamarind sauce** | 5 mL |
| 1 | **egg, lightly beaten** | 1 |
| | **GARNISH:** | |
| | **A selection of fresh coriander, lime or lemon wedges, chopped fresh green or red chilies, fresh garlic, chopped chives or chopped green onions** | |

**SAUCE:** In saucepan over medium-low heat, bring coconut milk gradually to boil, stirring constantly. Add pork and shrimp; cook for 3 minutes, stirring constantly.
■ Reduce heat to low. Add garlic, soya beans, sugar, fish sauce and lemon juice; cook for 10 minutes, stirring occasionally. Add egg; stir until blended. (Sauce can be covered and refrigerated for up to 3 days. Before serving, bring mixture slowly to boil, stirring constantly. Immediately remove from heat. Serve warm or at room temperature.)
■ Meanwhile, cover vermicelli with hot water; let stand for 10 minutes. Drain well.
■ In wok or large skillet, heat oil over medium-high heat. Add vermicelli; stir and toss to coat with oil. Stir in shallots, bean sprouts, fish sauce and chives. Toss together for 4 to 5 minutes or until noodles are softened and mixture is well blended.
**GARNISH:** Arrange noodle mixture on lettuce-lined platter. Pour sauce over. Garnish. Makes 8 servings.
*Available at Oriental and southeast Asian food stores, or you can make your own by covering 1-1/2 cups (375 mL) freshly shredded coconut or dried unsweetened coconut (flaked or desiccated) with 3 cups (750 mL) hot water. Let stand for 30 minutes. In food processor or blender, process mixture until puréed, 2 to 3 minutes. Let purée drain into bowl through dampened cheesecloth-lined sieve for 5 minutes. Press with spoon to extract all liquid. Makes 1-1/2 cups (375 mL).

# *Sweet and Salty Air-Dried Beef*

*In this dish, the Thais like the meat to be chewy. Choose meat that has a little bit of marbling if possible. If you prefer a more tender meat, use top round or sirloin. This dish is best eaten within 24 hours. Serve along with peanuts.*

| | | |
|---|---|---|
| **1 lb** | **flank steak** | **500 g** |
| **1/4 cup** | **(approx) instant dissolving (fruit/berry) sugar** | **50 mL** |
| **1/4 cup** | **(approx) fish sauce** | **50 mL** |
| **2 tsp** | **vegetable oil** | **10 mL** |
| **2 tbsp** | **coriander seeds** | **25 mL** |
| | **Vegetable oil for cooking** | |

■ Slice steak thinly across the grain; place in large bowl. Combine sugar, fish sauce and oil; pour over beef and toss.

■ To test flavor of dish, fry small piece of meat and taste for sweetness and saltiness; flavor at this point should be just a little less sweet than you want finished dish to be. To increase sweetness, add more sugar; to increase saltiness, add more fish sauce.

■ Pound or crush coriander seeds until coarse; add to beef mixture and stir well. Spread beef slices on wire racks. Place racks in 350°F (180°C) oven; turn off oven. Let meat stand in oven overnight to dry.

■ To serve, lightly broil meat for very dry beef or deep-fry in vegetable oil for moister beef. Drain on paper towels to remove excess oil. Serve at room temperature. Makes 8 servings.

*Tropical Jellies*

# *Tropical Jellies*

*These jellies are made with agar-agar, a sea product that does not break down or dissolve in the excessive heat of the tropics, and sets without refrigeration. Concentrations vary from brand to brand, so try to purchase agar-agar that has instructions on the label. This double-layered dessert has a colored, flavored layer and a jellied coconut cream layer.*

| | | |
|---|---|---|
| | **COLORED LAYER:** | |
| **2 tsp** | **agar-agar** | **10 mL** |
| **2 cups** | **water** | **500 mL** |
| **1/3 cup** | **granulated sugar** | **75 mL** |
| **1 tsp** | **pandanus, jasmine or rosewater** | **5 mL** |
| | **COCONUT CREAM LAYER:** | |
| **1 cup** | **coconut milk** | **250 mL** |
| **1 tsp** | **agar-agar** | **5 mL** |
| **2 tbsp** | **granulated sugar** | **25 mL** |

**COLORED LAYER:** In saucepan, sprinkle agar-agar over water. Bring gradually to boil over medium heat, stirring until agar-agar has dissolved, about 5 minutes. Stir in sugar until dissolved.

■ Add pandanus and one or two drops food coloring. Pour into rinsed, but not dried, 8-inch (2 L) square cake pan. Set aside to set.

**COCONUT CREAM LAYER:** Meanwhile, in small saucepan over low heat, stir together coconut milk and agar-agar. Bring gradually to boil over medium heat, stirring until agar-agar has dissolved, about 5 minutes. Stir in sugar until dissolved. Gently pour over set colored layer. (Mixture will set without refrigeration, but in summer, chilled jelly is more refreshing.) To serve, cut into small squares. Makes 8 servings.

# A BAHAMIAN FEAST

FOR SIX

*A balmy breeze, the fragrance of jasmine, a crimson sunset, a seaside terrace and a long buffet table laden with fresh hibiscus blossoms amid colorful platters of seafood and salads. . . .*

*Dreaming of a tropical vacation in mid-winter? Why not re-create a taste of the Islands in your own living room? Of course, a soft summer evening would do nicely, too, especially if your party has a poolside, lakefront or flowery garden view.*

*All recipes in this menu are for six servings but can easily be doubled or tripled.*

*FRESH FRUIT DAIQUIRI

*BAHAMA MAMA

*GOOMBAY SMASH

*ISLAND SALAD

*CRABMEAT AND AVOCADO SALAD

*BAKED GROUPER NASSAU-STYLE

*PEAS AND RICE

*BAHAMIAN JOHNNYCAKE

*PINEAPPLE TART

*(Clockwise from top left) Island Salad; Baked Grouper Nassau-Style; Crabmeat and Avocado Salad; Peas and Rice; Bahamian Johnnycake*

***SETTING THE SCENE***

***Create a colorful, casual Bahamian mood by decorating the table with fresh flowers and tropical fruit. Then set out all the food platters buffet-style or, if the group isn't too large, down the center of a long table that everyone can sit around. Set up the bar separately and let the bartender treat your guests to exotic creations.***

***If you want to add a meat dish to our menu, curried or fried chicken makes a nice addition. In the Bahamas, this menu would probably include side dishes of cooked green vegetables, fried plantain or candied sweet potatoes. Or you could add a big green salad for variety.***

# Island Salad

*Marinating scallops in lime juice for several hours has the same effect as cooking.*

| | | |
|---|---|---|
| 1 lb | **fresh scallops** | 500 g |
| | **Lime juice** | |
| 1/2 cup | **chopped onion** | 125 mL |
| 1/2 cup | **diced sweet green pepper** | 125 mL |
| 1/2 cup | **diced celery** | 125 mL |
| 1/2 cup | **diced cucumber** | 125 mL |
| 2 | **tomatoes, chopped** | 2 |
| | **Salt and pepper** | |

■ Cut scallops into small cubes; place in bowl. Pour in enough lime juice to cover. Marinate, refrigerated, for about 8 hours or until opaque.
■ Add onion, green pepper, celery, cucumber, tomatoes, and salt and pepper to taste; mix together. Marinate for a few minutes or up to several hours. Makes about 6 servings.

# Crabmeat and Avocado Salad

*This easy-to-make salad is attractive served on lettuce on a large platter or individual salad plates.*

| | | |
|---|---|---|
| 3/4 lb | **cooked crabmeat** | 375 g |
| 1 cup | **finely chopped celery** | 250 mL |
| 6 | **hard-cooked eggs, chopped** | 6 |
| 4 | **green onions, coarsely chopped** | 4 |
| 1/2 cup | **(approx) mayonnaise** | 125 mL |
| | **Lime juice** | |
| | **Salt and pepper** | |
| | **Lettuce leaves** | |
| 2 | **avocados, peeled and sliced** | 2 |
| | **Lime twists** | |

■ Reserve a few of the best crab pieces for garnish. Gently combine remaining crabmeat, celery, eggs and onions; add enough of the mayonnaise to moisten. Add lime juice, salt and pepper to taste; mix gently. Spoon onto lettuce leaves.
■ Dip avocado slices into lime juice; arrange around salad. Garnish with reserved crab pieces and lime twists. Makes about 6 servings.

# Baked Grouper Nassau-Style

*Grouper is a popular Bahamian fish which is cooked in a variety of ways, from pan-fried fillets to peppery chowders. If grouper is unavailable, sea bass or snapper is excellent too.*

| | | |
|---|---|---|
| 4 lb | **grouper (whole or piece)** | 2 kg |
| 2 | **small hot peppers, minced** | 2 |
| 1 tbsp | **salt** | 15 mL |
| 2 | **limes** | 2 |
| 2 tbsp | **Worcestershire sauce** | 25 mL |
| 1 cup | **stewed or canned tomatoes, drained and chopped** | 250 mL |
| 1 | **onion, sliced** | 1 |
| 1 | **stalk celery, chopped** | 1 |
| 1 | **small sweet green pepper, diced** | 1 |
| 1/4 cup | **dry bread crumbs** | 50 mL |

■ Wash fish thoroughly. Mash hot peppers into salt; rub over fish. (Wear rubber gloves to avoid irritating skin.) Squeeze juice from limes over fish; let stand for 2 hours.
■ Place fish in shallow baking pan; sprinkle with Worcestershire. Spread tomatoes, onion, celery and green pepper on top; sprinkle with bread crumbs. Cover with foil; bake in 400°F (200°C) oven for 30 minutes. Remove foil. Baste fish with pan juices. Bake for 15 minutes longer or just until fish flakes easily with fork. Makes about 6 servings.

***FRESH FRUIT DAIQUIRI***
***Delicious frosty daiquiris can be made with fruit such as mango, papaya, banana, pineapple, strawberries or soursop. For tall glasses, double the recipe and garnish with fresh fruit.***

***In blender, combine 1/4 cup (50 mL) coarsely chopped fresh fruit, 1/3 cup (75 mL) crushed ice, 1-1/2 oz (45 mL) golden rum, 1/2 oz (15 mL) apricot or other fruit brandy if desired and 1/2 oz (15 mL) lime juice. Add a dash of Simple Syrup (recipe follows) and blend at low speed for 15 seconds. Serve in saucer-shaped stemmed glass. Makes 1 serving.***

***BAHAMA MAMA***
***In cocktail shaker, combine 3 oz (90 mL) each orange and pineapple juices, 1 oz (30 mL) each lemon juice, golden rum and crème de cassis, dash each grenadine and angostura bitters and pinch of nutmeg.***

***Shake well and pour into tall glass over crushed ice. Garnish with pineapple chunk, lemon slice and fresh flower. Makes 1 serving.***

*GOOMBAY SMASH*
***In cocktail shaker, combine 3 oz (90 mL) pineapple juice, 1 oz (30 mL) each lemon juice, golden rum and coconut rum and 1/2 oz (15 mL) orange liqueur.***
***Add a dash of Simple Syrup (recipe follows) and shake well. Serve in tall glass with crushed ice. Garnish with orange slice and cherry. Makes 1 serving.***

*SIMPLE SYRUP*
***Use this syrup to sweeten drinks.***
***In small saucepan, bring 1 cup (250 mL) each granulated sugar and water to boil. Reduce heat and simmer for 3 minutes.***
***Let cool, then store, covered, in clean jar in refrigerator. Makes about 1-1/3 cups (325 mL).***

# Peas and Rice

*All over the Bahamas and the Caribbean, each island has its own version of "peas and rice." This Bahamian recipe uses pigeon peas.*

| | | |
|---|---|---|
| **1/4 lb** | **salt pork, diced** | **125 g** |
| **2 tbsp** | **vegetable oil** | **25 mL** |
| **1** | **small onion, chopped** | **1** |
| **1** | **stalk celery, chopped** | **1** |
| **1/4 cup** | **tomato paste** | **50 mL** |
| **1/2 tsp** | **dried thyme** | **2 mL** |
| **3 cups** | **water** | **750 mL** |
| **2 cups** | **cooked pigeon peas or 1 can (19 oz/540 mL), drained** | **500 mL** |
| | **Salt and pepper** | |
| **2 cups** | **rice** | **500 mL** |

■ In large heavy saucepan, cook salt pork until fat has melted. Pour in oil. Add onion and celery; cook until softened. Stir in tomato paste and thyme; simmer for 5 minutes.

■ Add water, peas, and salt and pepper to taste. Bring to boil; add rice. Cover and cook over medium heat for about 20 minutes or until rice is tender and liquid absorbed. Makes 6 to 8 servings.

# Bahamian Johnnycake

*Freshly baked johnnycake, served warm and spread with butter, is the traditional bread. Not to be confused with cornbread, this johnnycake is more like a large soft tea biscuit.*

| | | |
|---|---|---|
| **2 cups** | **all-purpose flour** | **500 mL** |
| **1/4 cup** | **granulated sugar** | **50 mL** |
| **1 tbsp** | **baking powder** | **15 mL** |
| **1 tsp** | **salt** | **5 mL** |
| **1/3 cup** | **shortening** | **75 mL** |
| **3/4 cup** | **milk** | **175 mL** |

■ In bowl, mix together flour, sugar, baking powder and salt. Using pastry blender or two knives, cut in shortening until mixture resembles fine crumbs. Add milk, stirring with fork to make soft dough. Gather into ball.

■ On lightly floured surface, knead dough several times until smooth; roll out to 9-inch (23 cm) circle. Place in greased 9-inch (1.5 L) round cake pan. Bake in 425°F (220°C) oven for 15 to 20 minutes or until tester inserted in center comes out clean. Cut into wedges and serve warm. Makes about 6 servings.

*Pineapple Tart*

# Pineapple Tart

*Bake this fresh-tasting pie in a pie plate or in a flan pan, and add a lattice-top crust.*

| | | |
|---|---|---|
| **4 cups** | **crushed fresh pineapple or 2 cans (each 19 oz/540 mL) unsweetened, well-drained** | **1 L** |
| **1-1/2 cups** | **granulated sugar** | **375 mL** |
| | **Pastry for 9-inch (23 cm) double-crust pie** | |

■ In heavy saucepan, combine pineapple and sugar; bring to boil, stirring often. Boil, uncovered, for about 20 minutes or until most of the liquid has evaporated. Let cool.

■ On lightly floured surface, roll out half of the pastry and fit into pan. Spoon in pineapple filling. Roll out remaining pastry and cut into strips; form lattice over filling. Seal and flute edges. Bake in 375°F (190°C) oven for about 40 minutes or until pastry is golden brown. Let cool before serving.

# A MEXICAN FIESTA

FOR EIGHT

*Authentic Mexican food is good, earthy, aromatic fare. Much more than tacos, nachos and enchiladas, it's exciting and complex and captivates the senses immediately. The noon meal,* comida, *is the main meal of the day in Mexico. Traditionally, it's served in five or more small courses. Our menu is streamlined for ease of preparation and is a delicious way to discover some of the intriguing and enduring flavors of Mexican cuisine. This menu makes a great supper party, or serve it in the traditional way at noon — and enjoy an afternoon siesta!*

*SOPA DE AGUACATE
(AVOCADO SOUP)

*CAMARONES À LA VERACRUZANA
(SHRIMP VERACRUZ-STYLE)

*CHILAQUILES

*ARROZ VERDE
(GREEN RICE)

*FRIJOLES NEGROS
(REFRIED BLACK BEANS)

*CALABAZA GUISADA CON PUERCO
(SQUASH WITH PORK)

*MARGARITA PIE

*CAFÉ MEXICANO

## *Sopa de Aguacate*
## *(Avocado Soup)*

*The buttery yellowish flesh of Mexican or Californian avocados makes superb guacamole as well as many other Mexican dishes, including this smooth soup.*

| | | |
|---|---|---|
| 3 | **ripe avocados** | 3 |
| 1 | **tomato, peeled and seeded** | 1 |
| 1 | **small onion** | 1 |
| 1 | **small clove garlic** | 1 |
| 1 tbsp | **lime juice** | 15 mL |
| 3 cups | **hot chicken stock** | 750 mL |
| | **Salt** | |
| 1/2 cup | **sour cream** | 125 mL |
| | **Crisp tortillas** | |

■ Cut avocados in half; remove pit and scoop pulp into food processor or blender. Add tomato, onion, garlic and lime juice; process for about 2 minutes or until smooth and creamy. Transfer to large bowl. (Soup can be made ahead to this point, covered and set aside at room temperature for up to 3 hours.)

■ Just before serving, blend in hot stock; season with salt to taste. Ladle warm soup into small bowls. Swirl sour cream into each bowl. Garnish with triangles of crisp tortillas. Makes about 5 cups (1.25 L).

## *Camarones à la Veracruzana*
## *(Shrimp Veracruz-Style)*

*Fish and shellfish are plentiful in the coastal and gulf regions of Mexico.*

| | | |
|---|---|---|
| 1/4 cup | **vegetable oil** | 50 mL |
| 1-1/2 lb | **shrimp, shelled and deveined** | 750 g |
| 2 tbsp | **lime juice** | 25 mL |

*MEXICAN FOODS AND INGREDIENTS*

- **Chayotes** *are light green, pear-shaped squash with inedible peel.*
- **Chorizo** *are highly seasoned sausages made from pork or beef.*
- **Cilantro,** *or fresh coriander, looks like flat-leaf parsley, is often called Chinese parsley and is usually available in Chinese markets.*
- **Jicama** *is a large white root vegetable that is eaten raw. It looks like a turnip with brown skin and crisp flesh.*
- **Tequila** *is a spirit distilled from the juice of the agave plant.*
- **Masa** *is the dough used to make tortillas. It is made from* **masa harina,** *corn flour.*
- **Mole** *is a sauce or paste (made from chilies, chocolate and nuts) used for meat and poultry dishes.*
- **Pepitas** *are pumpkin or squash seeds. They are ground for sauces and salted for snacks.*
- **Tomatillos** *are small green tomatoes with a parchment-like husk covering the stem end. They're used fresh or canned and add an acidic flavor to sauces.*
- **Tortillas** *are the national bread of Mexico. Flat, like thin unleavened pancakes, they're made from masa or wheat flour dough. They're cooked on an ungreased griddle and can be eaten when fresh and pliable. They're eaten as bread or used*

*to wrap other foods.*
- **Burritos** *are large tortillas wrapped around fillings like refried beans or beef. They can be eaten in your hand or cooked in a sauce.*
- **Enchiladas** *are tortillas rolled around fillings, baked in a sauce and served with salsas and garnishes.*
- **Tacos** *are tortillas folded in half and fried crisp. Fillings of meat, beans or other food are spooned into the tacos, then topped with fresh garnishes such as tomatoes, onion, lettuce and shredded cheese.*
- **Tostaditos** *are crisp-fried tortillas with beans, meat and garnishes.*
- **Totopos** *are small crisp-fried pieces of tortillas, similar to corn chips, used as snacks or appetizers and served with salsa and dips.*
- **Nachos** *are small pieces of crisp tortillas topped with refried beans, cheese, chopped tomatoes and peppers and then heated in the oven until the cheese melts.*
- **Quesadillas** *are deep-fried turnover-like packages. Fresh, uncooked tortillas are folded in half over a filling that usually includes cheese; the edges are pressed together and then they're deep-fried.*
- **Salsas** *are mild or hot sauces.* **Salsa roja** *is hot;* **salsa verde** *is green and usually made with tomatillos.*

| | | |
|---|---|---|
| 1 | **small onion, coarsely chopped** | 1 |
| 1 | **each small sweet red and green pepper, coarsely chopped** | 1 |
| 1 | **tomato, peeled, seeded and coarsely chopped** | 1 |
| 16 | **pimiento-stuffed olives, halved** | 16 |
| 2 tsp | **capers** | 10 mL |
| 1/2 tsp | **salt** | 2 mL |
| 1/2 tsp | **granulated sugar** | 2 mL |
| | **Fresh parsley or cilantro (coriander) sprigs** | |

■ In large skillet, heat half of the oil over medium-high heat; stir-fry shrimp for 2 minutes. Sprinkle with lime juice; stir-fry for 2 minutes longer or until shrimp are pink and liquid has evaporated. Remove to warm dish.

■ Add remaining oil to skillet and heat; stir-fry onion and red and green peppers for 5 minutes or until tender.

■ Add tomato, olives, capers and shrimp; cook, stirring, for 1 minute or until shrimp are hot. Season with salt and sugar. Serve immediately. (Alternatively, transfer to bowl; cover, refrigerate and serve chilled.) Garnish each serving with sprig of parsley. Makes 8 servings.

# *Chilaquiles*

*Crispy fried tortilla strips and shredded chicken bake in a piquant tomato sauce in this easy dish. In the photograph, the baked dish is garnished with additional tortilla strips and Cheddar cheese.*

| | | |
|---|---|---|
| 4 | **chicken breasts (1-1/2 lb/750 g total)** | 4 |
| 3 cups | **water** | 750 mL |
| 3 | **cloves garlic** | 3 |
| 1 | **bay leaf** | 1 |
| Half | **onion** | Half |
| 1 tsp | **salt** | 5 mL |
| 6 | **peppercorns** | 6 |
| 1 | **can (28 oz/796 mL) tomatoes (undrained)** | 1 |
| 1 | **small onion, halved** | 1 |
| 1/2 cup | **fresh cilantro (coriander) leaves or parsley** | 125 mL |
| 1 tsp | **chopped jalapeño pepper** | 5 mL |
| 1/2 tsp | **salt** | 2 mL |
| | **Vegetable oil for frying** | |
| 6 | **large or 12 small corn tortillas** | 6 |
| 1 cup | **sour cream** | 250 mL |
| 1 cup | **shredded Cheddar cheese** | 250 mL |

■ In saucepan, combine chicken breasts, water, 2 garlic cloves, bay leaf, onion half, 1 tsp (5 mL) salt and peppercorns. Bring to boil; reduce heat and simmer, covered, for 35 to 40 minutes or until chicken is tender. Let chicken cool in liquid. Remove chicken; strain and reserve stock. Remove and discard skin and bones. With 2 forks, shred chicken; cover and set aside.

■ In food processor or blender, combine tomatoes, onion, cilantro, jalapeño pepper, 1/2 tsp (2 mL) salt and remaining garlic; process for 1 to 2 minutes or until puréed. Pour into clean saucepan. Add 1 cup (250 mL) reserved stock. Bring to boil; reduce heat and simmer for about 20 minutes or until slightly thickened. Keep warm.

■ Meanwhile, pour 1/4 inch (5 mm) of oil into large skillet and heat to 375°F (190°C) or until 1-inch (2.5 cm) cube of white bread turns golden brown in 50 seconds. Using scissors, cut each tortilla into 8 strips. (If using large tortillas, cut in half first, then into strips.) Fry strips in oil just until crisp and lightly browned, about 15 seconds each side. Drain on paper towels.

■ In 13- × 9-inch (3 L) baking dish, mix tortilla strips with shredded chicken; pour hot sauce over. Top with sour cream, then sprinkle with cheese. Bake in 400°F (200°C) oven for 20 minutes or until heated through and cheese has melted. Makes 8 servings.

# *Arroz Verde*
## *(Green Rice)*

*Cilantro adds a unique flavor to this fragrant rice dish but parsley works as a substitute. Sizzling the rice in hot oil before simmering it in stock maximizes the flavor.*

| | | |
|---|---|---|
| **1-1/2 cups** | **long-grain rice** | **375 mL** |
| **2 tbsp** | **vegetable oil** | **25 mL** |
| **3** | **green onions** | **3** |
| **1** | **sweet green pepper** | **1** |
| **1** | **clove garlic** | **1** |
| **1/2 cup** | **chopped fresh parsley** | **125 mL** |
| **2 tbsp** | **chopped fresh cilantro (coriander) or parsley** | **25 mL** |
| **1 tsp** | **chopped jalapeño pepper** | **5 mL** |
| **3 cups** | **chicken stock** | **750 mL** |
| | **Salt and pepper** | |

■ Soak rice in cold water for 15 minutes; drain. In large saucepan, heat oil over medium heat; cook rice, stirring, for about 2 minutes or until golden but not browned.

■ In food processor or by hand, finely chop green onions, green pepper, garlic, parsley, cilantro and jalapeño pepper. Add to saucepan; cook, stirring, for about 2 minutes or until vegetables are softened.

■ Pour in chicken stock; bring to boil. Reduce heat, cover and simmer for about 40 minutes or until rice is tender. Season with salt and pepper to taste. Makes 8 servings.

# *Frijoles Negros*
## *(Refried Black Beans)*

*These mashed beans are well-fried until they are nearly dry.*

| | | |
|---|---|---|
| **1-1/2 cups** | **dried black beans** | **375 mL** |
| **1** | **clove garlic, halved** | **1** |
| **1** | **small onion, halved** | **1** |
| **1** | **slice bacon, chopped** | **1** |
| **1 tsp** | **salt** | **5 mL** |
| **2 tbsp** | **lard or vegetable oil** | **25 mL** |

■ Sort beans and rinse under cold running water. In large saucepan, combine beans with enough water to cover; bring to boil and boil for 2 minutes. Remove from heat; let stand for 2 hours. Drain.

■ Add enough fresh hot water to generously cover beans. Add garlic, onion and bacon; bring to boil. Reduce heat, cover and simmer for 2 hours. Add salt; cover and simmer for 1-1/2 hours longer or until beans are tender, adding more water as needed to keep beans covered. Drain beans, reserving 1 cup (250 mL) cooking liquid.

■ In large skillet, heat lard over medium heat; add drained beans. With back of fork or potato masher, mash most of the beans, leaving a few whole. Add up to 1 cup (250 mL) of the reserved cooking liquid as desired; cook over low heat, stirring frequently, for about 20 minutes or until thickened. Makes 8 servings.

***CAFÉ MEXICANO***

***In coffee cup, stir 2 tbsp (25 mL) coffee liqueur, 1 tsp (5 mL) unsweetened cocoa powder and 1 tsp (5 mL) granulated sugar until smooth. Pour in 3/4 cup (175 mL) hot coffee. Top with 2 tbsp (25 mL) whipped cream and sprinkle with cinnamon. Makes 1 cup (250 mL).***

*(Clockwise from top right) Arroz Verde; Calabaza Guisada con Puerco; Frijoles Negros; Sopa de Aguacate; Camarones à la Veracruzana; Chilaquiles*

# Calabaza Guisada con Puerco
## (Squash with Pork)

*Some Mexican cooks call this classic stew* manchamanteles, *which means tablecloth stainer.*

| | | |
|---|---|---|
| 3 lb | country-style pork spareribs | 1.5 kg |
| 4 | cloves garlic | 4 |
| Half | small onion | Half |
| 2 tsp | salt | 10 mL |
| 1 | tomato | 1 |
| 1 | onion | 1 |
| 2 tbsp | vegetable oil | 25 mL |
| 2 cups | whole kernel corn (fresh or frozen) | 500 mL |
| 1 | can (14 oz/398 mL) pineapple chunks, drained | 1 |
| 2 tsp | chopped jalapeño peppers | 10 mL |
| 1/2 tsp | ground cumin | 2 mL |
| 6 | small zucchini | 6 |
| 2 | plantains | 2 |

■ Cut spareribs into 8 even portions. Coarsely chop 2 garlic cloves and onion half; place in large saucepan or Dutch oven.
■ Add meat and 1 tsp (5 mL) of the salt; cover with cold water. Bring to boil; reduce heat and simmer, uncovered, for about 45 minutes or until meat is tender. Remove meat and set aside; strain stock and reserve 1 cup (250 mL).
■ Peel, seed and coarsely chop tomato. Coarsely chop onion and remaining garlic. In same saucepan, heat oil over medium heat; sauté tomato, onion and garlic for 5 minutes or until onion is tender.
■ Add corn, pineapple, jalapeño peppers, cumin and reserved stock; cook for 5 minutes. Cut zucchini crosswise into 3/4-inch (2 cm) slices. Add to saucepan; cook for 5 minutes. Cut plantain crosswise into 3/4-inch (2 cm) slices. Add along with reserved meat and remaining salt to saucepan; cover and cook, stirring occasionally, for 15 minutes or until heated through. Makes 8 servings.

# Margarita Pie

*Combine lime and lemon juice for the mellow taste you get from the little yellowish-green lemons found in Mexico. Garnish with chocolate curls or grated chocolate, if you like.*

| | | |
|---|---|---|
| | **CRUST:** | |
| 1 cup | pretzel crumbs | 250 mL |
| 1/3 cup | butter | 75 mL |
| 1/4 cup | packed brown sugar | 50 mL |
| | **FILLING:** | |
| 1 | envelope unflavored gelatin | 1 |
| 1/4 cup | lemon juice | 50 mL |
| | Grated rind of 1 lime | |
| 1/4 cup | lime juice | 50 mL |
| 4 | eggs, separated | 4 |
| 1 cup | granulated sugar | 250 mL |
| 1/4 tsp | salt | 1 mL |
| 1/4 cup | tequila | 50 mL |
| 2 tbsp | orange liqueur | 25 mL |

**CRUST:** In food processor, process pretzel crumbs, butter and brown sugar until mixture begins to stick together. (Alternatively, mix together in bowl.)
■ Press onto sides and bottom of 9-inch (23 cm) pie plate. Bake in 400°F (200°C) oven for 8 minutes or until golden brown. Set aside to let cool.
**FILLING:** Sprinkle gelatin over lemon juice; let stand for 5 minutes to soften.
■ Meanwhile, in top of double boiler over simmering water, combine lime rind, lime juice, egg yolks, 1/2 cup (125 mL) of the sugar and salt; cook, stirring, for about 5 minutes or until mixture is thick enough to coat metal spoon. Remove from heat.
■ Stir in gelatin mixture, tequila and liqueur. Pour into bowl; cover and refrigerate for about 30 minutes or until partially set and consistency of unbeaten egg whites.
■ Beat egg whites until frothy; gradually beat in remaining sugar until stiff peaks form. Fold about 1 cup (250 mL) into gelatin mixture; fold in remainder until mixture is evenly colored. Pour into pie shell, swirling on top. Refrigerate for at least 3 hours or until filling is firm.

# A MOROCCAN DINNER

FOR EIGHT

*Morocco is a land of wonderful tastes and smells—the essence of orange blossom, the spicy smell of curried lamb kabobs sizzling on a brazier, the aroma of bread baking in communal bakeries and the smell of roasted black coffee wafting through the crowded street. In the market, the piquant smell of olives blends with cinnamon, rose petals, lavender, peppercorns, cumin, coriander and aniseed. These spices and seasonings are what really set Moroccan food apart. Classic Moroccan dishes, resplendent with root vegetables and warming stews, are perfect for our Canadian winter.*

*LAMB KABOBS WITH FRESH CORIANDER

*CUCUMBER SALAD WITH FRESH MINT

*BEET AND ORANGE SALAD

ASSORTED OLIVES

*TAGINE OF FISH, TOMATOES, PEPPERS AND POTATOES

*ROUND MOROCCAN LOAVES

*CLEMENTINE TARTS

## Lamb Kabobs with Fresh Coriander

*Set out bowls of chopped fresh coriander and ground cumin for guests to dip kabobs.*

| | | |
|---|---|---|
| **2 lb** | **ground lamb shoulder** | **1 kg** |
| **1 cup** | **finely chopped onion** | **250 mL** |
| **2** | **cloves garlic, minced** | **2** |
| **1/4 cup** | **finely chopped fresh mint** | **50 mL** |
| **2 tbsp** | **each finely chopped fresh coriander and parsley** | **25 mL** |
| **2 tsp** | **paprika** | **10 mL** |
| **1 tsp** | **each salt and ground cumin** | **5 mL** |
| **1/4 tsp** | **each cinnamon, ginger and cayenne pepper** | **1 mL** |
| **Pinch** | **dried marjoram** | **Pinch** |

■ In large bowl and using hands, mix together lamb, onion, garlic, mint, coriander, parsley, paprika, salt, cumin, cinnamon, ginger, cayenne and marjoram until well combined. (Recipe can be prepared to this point, covered and refrigerated for up to 8 hours.)

■ Divide mixture into 16 portions. Form into sausage shapes about 2 inches (5 cm) long; thread 2 each lengthwise onto flat metal skewers, pressing meat firmly onto skewers. Grill or broil about 4 inches (10 cm) from heat, turning occasionally, for 8 to 10 minutes or until well browned and crispy on outside and juicy inside. Serve immediately. Makes 8 appetizers.

*(Clockwise from bottom) Tagine of Fish, Tomatoes, Peppers and Potatoes; olives; Cucumber Salad with Fresh Mint; Round Moroccan Loaves*

# Cucumber Salad with Fresh Mint

*The refreshing flavor of mint perks up cucumber slices.*

| | | |
|---|---|---|
| **2** | **medium cucumbers, peeled** | **2** |
| **1/2 tsp** | **salt** | **2 mL** |
| **1/3 cup** | **thinly sliced green onions** | **75 mL** |
| **2 tbsp** | **finely chopped fresh mint** | **25 mL** |
| **2 tbsp** | **lemon juice** | **25 mL** |
| **2 tbsp** | **olive oil** | **25 mL** |
| **1 tsp** | **white wine vinegar** | **5 mL** |

■ Halve cucumbers lengthwise; remove seeds and slice thinly. In sieve, sprinkle cucumbers with salt; let stand for 30 minutes. Rinse under cold running water and pat dry with paper towels.

■ In bowl, toss cucumbers with onions, mint, lemon juice, oil and vinegar. Taste and adjust seasoning. Makes 8 servings.

# Beet and Orange Salad

*Essence of orange blossoms, or orange-flower water, gives this salad an aromatic lift.*

| | | |
|---|---|---|
| **1 lb** | **beets** | **500 g** |
| **2 tbsp** | **orange juice** | **25 mL** |
| **1 tbsp** | **orange-flower water* or lemon juice** | **15 mL** |
| **1 tsp** | **granulated sugar** | **5 mL** |
| **1/4 tsp** | **cinnamon** | **1 mL** |

■ Scrub beets; trim stems 1 inch (2.5 cm) from bulb. In saucepan of boiling salted water, cook beets for 30 to 40 minutes or until tender. Drain and slip off skins. Cut into 1/4-inch (5 mm) slices and place in bowl.

■ Stir together orange juice, orange-flower water, sugar and cinnamon; drizzle over beets and toss lightly. Let cool to room temperature. Taste and adjust seasoning. Makes 8 servings.

*Available at Middle Eastern food stores.

# Tagine of Fish, Tomatoes, Peppers and Potatoes

*This flavorful tagine can be prepared ahead and popped in the oven just before guests arrive.*

| | | |
|---|---|---|
| **2 lb** | **monkfish, snapper or grouper fillets** | **1 kg** |
| **1** | **small Spanish onion, thinly sliced** | **1** |
| | **Salt and pepper** | |
| **2** | **large potatoes, peeled and thinly sliced** | **2** |
| **1** | **sweet green pepper, thinly sliced in rings** | **1** |
| **3** | **large tomatoes, sliced or 2 cans (each 28 oz/796 mL) tomatoes, drained and sliced** | **3** |
| **1/3 cup** | **finely chopped fresh parsley** | **75 mL** |
| | **SAUCE:** | |
| **1/4 cup** | **olive oil** | **50 mL** |
| **2 cups** | **sliced onions** | **500 mL** |
| **1 cup** | **chopped sweet green peppers** | **250 mL** |
| **4** | **large cloves garlic, slivered** | **4** |
| **4 cups** | **chopped peeled tomatoes or 2 cans (each 28 oz/796 mL) tomatoes, drained and chopped** | **1 L** |
| **1 tsp** | **salt** | **5 mL** |
| **1/2 tsp** | **pepper** | **2 mL** |
| **1 tsp** | **saffron threads (or 1/2 tsp/2 mL powdered saffron)** | **5 mL** |
| **3/4 cup** | **water** | **175 mL** |

**SAUCE:** In large shallow heatproof casserole, heat half of the oil over medium heat; cook onions, green peppers and garlic for 5 to 8 minutes or until softened, stirring occasionally. Add tomatoes, salt and pepper; cook, stirring occasionally, for 8 minutes.

■ Meanwhile, soak saffron threads in water for 5 minutes; pour into casserole and simmer for 10 to 12 minutes or just until vegetables are tender and sauce has thickened slightly. Taste and adjust seasoning. (Sauce can be prepared ahead, covered and refrigerated for up to 2 days.) Remove 1 cup (250 mL) sauce; stir in remaining olive oil and set aside.

■ Trim membrane from monkfish. Cut fish into 8 portions and nestle into sauce in casserole. Arrange onion over fish mixture, overlapping slices if necessary; spoon one-third of the reserved sauce over and season with salt and pepper to taste. Repeat with potatoes and green pepper. Spoon tomatoes over top.

■ Bake in 375°F (190°C) oven, covered, for 45 minutes. Uncover and bake, basting often with sauce, for 45 to 60 minutes or until vegetables are tender and sauce is thickened. Sprinkle parsley over tagine. Cut through layers to serve. Makes 8 servings.

# Round Moroccan Loaves

*This aniseed-speckled bread is made with whole wheat and unbleached flours.*

| | | |
|---|---|---|
| **1 tsp** | **granulated sugar** | **5 mL** |
| **2 cups** | **lukewarm water** | **500 mL** |
| **1** | **pkg active dry yeast (or 1 tbsp/15 mL)** | **1** |
| **1 cup** | **whole wheat flour** | **250 mL** |
| **1/4 cup** | **olive oil** | **50 mL** |
| **1 tbsp** | **aniseed** | **15 mL** |
| **2 tsp** | **salt** | **10 mL** |
| **1 tsp** | **sesame seeds** | **5 mL** |
| **4 cups** | **(approx) unbleached all-purpose flour** | **1 L** |
| | **Cornmeal** | |

■ Dissolve sugar in water; sprinkle in yeast and let stand for 10 minutes or until frothy.

■ Stir yeast mixture and pour into large bowl; beat in whole wheat flour, oil, aniseed, salt and sesame seeds. Beat in 2 cups (500 mL) of the all-purpose flour, 1/2 cup (125 mL) at a time.

■ With wooden spoon, gradually stir in enough of the remaining flour to make stiff dough. Turn out onto lightly floured surface and knead for 10 minutes or until smooth and elastic.

***COUSCOUS***

***Couscous is the name of both the national dish of Morocco and pellets or granules of finely cracked durum wheat or coarse semolina.***

***Couscous (the ingredient) comes in fine, medium and coarse pellets, in long-cooking and precooked versions. You can buy couscous at Middle Eastern and natural food stores and some supermarkets.***

***Couscous can be served as you would rice, noodles or potatoes. Serve the couscous hot, or cold in salads. It makes a delicious stuffing for poultry and can be sweetened and served for a dessert like rice pudding.***

***A traditional couscous is made by steaming the grain in a*** **couscousière** ***(a two-layered pot) over the lamb or chicken stew it's served with. A hot sauce,*** **harissa**, ***is often served with the couscous and stew. In Morocco, couscous is usually served for lunch on Fridays, but at*** **diffas** ***(lavish feasts), it is the last dish served in a quantity large enough to ensure that no one goes home hungry.***

*CLEMENTINES*
***Aptly named candy fruit, sweet, easy-to-peel clementines are virtually seedless. They are believed to be a chance cross between the tart Seville orange and the zipper-skinned mandarin.***
***From November until the end of February, Moroccan clementines are shipped across the Atlantic to us.***
***When buying clementines, look for fruit with a smooth glossy skin and an invitingly zesty fragrance. The fruit should feel firm and heavy for its size. Enjoy clementines as a snack or dessert, or use them in recipes calling for oranges or tangerines.***

■ Transfer dough to lightly greased bowl, turning to grease all over. Cover with tea towel and let rise for about 1-1/2 hours or until doubled in bulk. Punch down dough and divide in half; form each half into ball. Let rest for 5 to 10 minutes if dough is too elastic to roll.

■ On floured surface, roll out each half into rounds about 3/4 inch (2 cm) thick. Sprinkle 2 baking sheets with cornmeal and place one round on each. Cover with tea towel and let rise for 45 to 60 minutes or until doubled in bulk. Prick rounds with fork in 4 spots around edge. Bake in 400°F (200°C) oven for 10 minutes; reduce heat to 325°F (160°C) and bake for about 25 minutes longer or until golden and loaves sound hollow when tapped on bottoms. Let cool on racks. Makes 2 loaves.

## Clementine Tarts

*In Casablanca, the pastry shops do a brisk trade in these glazed tarts.*

| | | |
|---|---|---|
| | **PASTRY:** | |
| **1-1/4 cups** | **all-purpose flour** | **300 mL** |
| **1/4 cup** | **granulated sugar** | **50 mL** |
| **1/4 tsp** | **finely grated clementine rind** | **1 mL** |
| **Pinch** | **salt** | **Pinch** |
| **1/3 cup** | **butter** | **75 mL** |
| **1/4 cup** | **shortening** | **50 mL** |
| **1** | **egg yolk** | **1** |
| **2 tbsp** | **(approx) cold water** | **25 mL** |
| | **CLEMENTINE PASTRY CREAM:** | |
| **2** | **egg yolks** | **2** |
| **1 cup** | **milk** | **250 mL** |
| **1/3 cup** | **granulated sugar** | **75 mL** |
| **Pinch** | **salt** | **Pinch** |
| **3 tbsp** | **all-purpose flour** | **50 mL** |
| **1/4 cup** | **clementine juice** | **50 mL** |
| **1/4 tsp** | **finely grated clementine rind** | **1 mL** |
| **1 tbsp** | **butter** | **15 mL** |
| **1 tbsp** | **orange or mandarin liqueur** | **15 mL** |
| **1 tsp** | **vanilla** | **5 mL** |
| | **TOPPING AND GLAZE:** | |
| **3** | **clementines** | **3** |
| **1/3 cup** | **orange or mandarin marmalade** | **75 mL** |

**PASTRY:** In large bowl, stir together flour, sugar, clementine rind and salt. Cut in butter and shortening until mixture resembles coarse crumbs.

■ Stir together egg yolk and water; gradually pour into dry ingredients, stirring briskly. Add more water if necessary to form dough that holds together. Press into ball and flatten slightly. (Dough can be wrapped and chilled for up to 3 days. Bring to room temperature before continuing with recipe.)

■ On lightly floured pastry cloth and using stockinette-covered rolling pin, roll out dough to slightly less than 1/4-inch (5 mm) thickness. Cut out sixteen 3-1/2-inch (9 cm) rounds. Ease into muffin tins, allowing 1/2 inch (1 cm) to come up sides. Prick bottom and sides. (Shells can be wrapped and refrigerated for up to 1 day.) Bake in 400°F (200°C) oven for 8 to 10 minutes or until golden. Remove from tins; let cool on racks.

**CLEMENTINE PASTRY CREAM:** Meanwhile, in heavy saucepan, whisk together egg yolks, milk, sugar and salt. Blend in flour and bring to simmer over medium heat, whisking constantly, until thickened and smooth.

■ Blend in clementine juice and rind; reduce heat to low and simmer gently, whisking constantly, for 3 minutes. Remove from heat and stir in butter, liqueur and vanilla.

■ Transfer to heatproof bowl and cover surface with buttered waxed paper; refrigerate until chilled, about 1 hour, or for up to 1 day.

**TOPPING AND GLAZE:** Spoon cream into pastry shells. Refrigerate for up to 2 hours. Peel clementines; with sharp knife, remove thin outer membrane and cut out segments. Transfer to sieve and let drain until serving time. Pat dry and divide among tarts. Heat marmalade until melted; strain and brush lightly over tarts. Makes 16 tarts.

# COAST-TO-COAST FAVORITES

*From coast to coast, each region of Canada has produced its own distinctive culinary blend of old-country traditions, new-world influences and local ingredients. No one visiting the Prairies will forget the hearty satisfaction of a good old-fashioned farm dinner. The West Coast is famous for stylish informality and wonderfully fresh local ingredients, and the seaside salmon barbecue here provides the best of both. Seafood is always a reason for culinary celebration on the East Coast, too. We go to the far North for a memorable picnic brunch under the Midnight Sun. Two other menus are seasonal specialties right across Canada: an old-time Strawberry Social and an exuberant Oktoberfest. Our après-ski buffet party would be equally at home in Quebec's Laurentians, in the Rockies or ski country anywhere. And an Indian Summer gathering reminds us of our very earliest Canadian culinary tradition, our heritage of native Indian foods.*

# AN APRÈS-SKI BUFFET

FOR SIX

*In every region of Canada, avid skiers revel in the glories of our great winter wonderland. After an invigorating day on the slopes or cross-country trails, they look forward to the relaxing pleasures of a warm-up feast by the fireside. Here's one that will welcome them with a satisfying array of savory dishes, starting with steaming drinks and ending with a snowy sweet.*

*MULLED CIDER WITH RUM

CRUDITÉS AND SOUR CREAM

FRENCH-CANADIAN MIXED LEGUME SOUP
(recipe, page 139)

*APRÈS-SKI MEATBALLS

*MARINATED CUCUMBERS WITH DILL

*HOT SEAFOOD MOUSSE WITH SHRIMP SAUCE

RYE BREAD

*MOULDED STRAWBERRY SNOW

**Recipes are given for menu items marked with an asterisk.*

*(Clockwise from top) Mulled Cider with Rum; Marinated Cucumbers with Dill; Après-Ski Meatballs; crudités and sour cream; rye bread; Hot Seafood Mousse with Shrimp Sauce; French-Canadian Mixed Legume Soup*

## Après-Ski Meatballs

*Assemble and freeze these meatballs ahead of time, if you wish. Defrost, then bake at party time. Serve plain or with a seasoned tomato sauce for dipping.*

| | | |
|---|---|---|
| **1 lb** | **lean ground beef** | **500 g** |
| **1/2 lb** | **ground pork** | **250 g** |
| **1** | **onion, finely chopped** | **1** |
| **1** | **egg** | **1** |
| **1 cup** | **fresh bread crumbs*** | **250 mL** |
| **2 tbsp** | **chopped fresh parsley** | **25 mL** |
| **1/2 tsp** | **each salt, dried basil and oregano** | **2 mL** |
| **1/4 tsp** | **pepper** | **1 mL** |

■ In bowl, mix together beef, pork, onion, egg, bread crumbs, parsley, salt, basil, oregano and pepper; shape into 1-inch (2.5 cm) balls. Arrange in single layer in lightly greased shallow baking dish. Bake in 400°F (200°C) oven, turning meatballs once, for 25 to 30 minutes or until browned and cooked through. Makes about 50 meatballs.
*2 slices fresh bread makes about 1 cup (250 mL) fresh bread crumbs in blender or food processor.

## Marinated Cucumbers With Dill

*An easy salad to have on hand, this can be made the day before and kept refrigerated until party time.*

| | | |
|---|---|---|
| **2** | **large English (seedless) cucumbers** | **2** |
| **1 tsp** | **salt** | **5 mL** |
| **1** | **Bermuda or Spanish onion, sliced** | **1** |
| **2 tbsp** | **chopped fresh dill** | **25 mL** |
| **3/4 cup** | **white vinegar** | **175 mL** |
| **1 tbsp** | **packed brown sugar** | **15 mL** |
| | **Pepper** | |
| | **Lettuce leaves (optional)** | |

■ Cut unpeeled cucumber into paper-thin slices; place in bowl. Sprinkle with salt and weigh down with plate; let stand at room temperature for 2 hours. Drain thoroughly; rinse with cold water. Drain again, preferably on paper towels.

■ Place cucumber and onion slices in glass or porcelain bowl (not metal or wooden). Sprinkle with dill. Stir together vinegar, sugar, and pepper to taste. Pour over cucumber mixture and chill for at least 3 hours or up to 24 hours.

■ At serving time, drain off liquid. Serve on lettuce-lined plate if desired. Makes about 8 servings.

## *Hot Seafood Mousse With Shrimp Sauce*

*You can make this mousse with any boneless white fish—halibut, bluefish, cod or sole—instead of scallops.*

| | | |
|---|---|---|
| **1 lb** | **scallops (thawed if frozen)** | **500 g** |
| **2 tbsp** | **butter, melted** | **25 mL** |
| **1 tbsp** | **all-purpose flour** | **15 mL** |
| **1** | **egg, lightly beaten** | **1** |
| **3/4 tsp** | **salt** | **4 mL** |
| **1/4 tsp** | **white pepper** | **1 mL** |
| **Pinch** | **nutmeg** | **Pinch** |
| **2 cups** | **light cream** | **500 mL** |
| | **Shrimp Sauce (recipe follows)** | |
| | **Lemon slices** | |

■ In food processor, chop scallops finely. Add butter, flour, egg, salt, pepper and nutmeg; process for 30 seconds. With machine running, gradually pour in cream.

■ Transfer to greased 4-cup (1 L) mould; cover with lid or foil. Place in small roasting pan; pour enough boiling water into pan to come halfway up side of mould. Bake in 350°F (180°C) oven for 1 hour or until firm to the touch and toothpick inserted in center comes out clean, adding more water to pan if necessary to maintain level.

■ Remove mould from water; let stand for 10 minutes. Loosen edges of mousse with point of sharp knife; invert heated platter over top and unmould. Pour half of the Shrimp Sauce over and garnish with lemon slices. Serve immediately and pass remaining sauce separately. Makes 6 to 8 servings.

| | | |
|---|---|---|
| | **SHRIMP SAUCE:** | |
| **1/4 cup** | **butter** | **50 mL** |
| **1/4 cup** | **all-purpose flour** | **50 mL** |
| **2-1/4 cups** | **milk** | **550 mL** |
| **4 tsp** | **lemon juice** | **20 mL** |
| | **White pepper** | |
| **1 cup** | **cooked salad shrimp*** | **250 mL** |

■ In saucepan, melt butter over medium heat; stir in flour and cook, stirring, for 1 minute. Whisk in milk; bring to boil, stirring constantly. Reduce heat to medium-low; cook, stirring, for 5 minutes or until smooth and sauce coats back of spoon. Stir in lemon juice, and pepper to taste. Add shrimp and heat through. Makes about 3 cups (750 mL) sauce.

*You can substitute 2 cans (4 oz/113 g each) shrimp, drained.

## *Moulded Strawberry Snow*

*Make the dessert in a ring mould or pour it into stemmed glasses.*

| | | |
|---|---|---|
| **2** | **pkg (300 g each) frozen unsweetened strawberries, thawed** | **2** |
| **1/2 cup** | **granulated sugar** | **125 mL** |
| **2** | **envelopes unflavored gelatin** | **2** |
| **2/3 cup** | **whipping cream** | **150 mL** |
| **4** | **egg whites** | **4** |
| **1/4 tsp** | **salt** | **1 mL** |

■ Drain strawberries and add enough water to make 1/2 cup (125 mL) juice; set aside. In blender or food processor, purée strawberries; press through sieve into saucepan. Add 1/3 cup (75 mL) of the sugar; cook over low heat for 5 minutes or until sugar dissolves. Transfer to bowl and set aside.

■ In small saucepan, sprinkle gelatin over reserved juice; let stand for 1 minute. Heat over low heat until dissolved; add to strawberry mixture. Place bowl in larger bowl of ice and water; chill, stirring frequently, for 15 to 25 minutes or until consistency of raw egg whites. Remove from ice water.

■ Whip cream; set aside. In large bowl, beat egg whites with salt until soft peaks form; gradually add remaining sugar, beating until stiff peaks form. Whisk one-quarter of the whites into strawberry mixture; fold in remaining whites. Fold in whipped cream. Pour into rinsed 8-cup (2 L) stainless steel, glass or plastic mould. Refrigerate until firm, at least 4 hours. To serve, unmould onto serving plate. Makes 6 to 8 servings.

***MULLED CIDER WITH RUM***

***In large saucepan, combine 8 cups (2 L) apple cider, 1 sliced lemon, 1 sliced orange, 2 cinnamon sticks, 8 whole allspice and 8 whole cloves. Simmer about 15 minutes; remove fruit and spices. Stir in 1 cup (250 mL) dark rum, and sugar to taste. Serve in large or small mugs. Makes 6 to 12 servings.***

***WINE SUGGESTIONS***

***Serve a full-bodied Italian Corvo or Canadian Seyval Blanc with the soup. A Sadias red from Portugal, a Rhône-Villages or a Canadian Pinot Noir goes well with the meatballs. Finish the meal with the strawberry snow and a glass of ruby port by the fire.***

# A WEST COAST BARBECUE

FOR EIGHT

*Freshness, flavor, informality and a gorgeous view add up to unbeatable outdoor entertaining, West Coast style. In the glow of sunset over the sea, a beautiful fresh salmon cooks to simple perfection on a beachside barbecue. Local gardens provide a bountiful choice of seasonal vegetables for grilling or salads and a profusion of summer berries for a delectable dessert.*

*WHOLE GRILLED SALMON

*DILL TARTAR SAUCE

*NEW POTATOES IN GARLIC BUTTER

STEAMED GREEN PEAS WITH MINT

VEGETABLE CRUDITÉS OR TOSSED SALAD

*SPONGE CAKE FRUIT FLAN

*New Potatoes in Garlic Butter; Dill Tartar Sauce; Whole Grilled Salmon*

## Whole Grilled Salmon

*If you don't have a fish basket, improvise by placing fish between two well-greased wire cake racks and securing with thin wire.*

| | | |
|---|---|---|
| 1 | **whole salmon, cleaned (about 5 lb./2.2 kg)** | 1 |
| 1 tsp | **salt** | 5 mL |
| | **Dill sprigs** | |
| | **MARINADE:** | |
| 1/3 cup | **olive or vegetable oil** | 75 mL |
| 1/4 cup | **lemon juice** | 50 mL |
| 1 | **clove garlic, minced** | 1 |
| 4 tsp | **chopped fresh dill (or 2 tsp/10 mL dried)** | 20 mL |

**MARINADE:** Whisk together oil, lemon juice, garlic and dill; set aside.

■ Rinse fish; pat dry inside and out with paper towels. Using scissors, remove all fins and trim tail. Remove head by slicing firmly through backbone.

■ Using sharp knife, cut diagonal scores about 4 inches (10 cm) long and 2 inches (5 cm) apart on each side of fish. Sprinkle fish inside and out with salt. Stuff cavity with dill sprigs. Loosely skewer base of fish closed.

■ Place fish in shallow porcelain or glass dish. Pour marinade over and turn fish to coat evenly. Cover and marinate for 30 minutes at room temperature or for up to 2 hours in refrigerator, turning occasionally.

■ Place fish in greased fish basket, reserving marinade. Place basket on greased grill 4 to 8 inches (10 to 15 cm) from medium-hot coals or on medium-high setting on gas barbecue. Cover with lid or tent with foil; grill fish for 10 minutes per inch (2.5 cm) of thickness or until fish flakes easily when tested with fork, basting occasionally with reserved marinade and turning fish over halfway through cooking time.

■ Carefully transfer fish to serving platter; remove skewers. To serve, cut 1/4-inch (5 mm) deep slit along backbone. Cut top fillet crosswise into serving portions. Carefully lift each portion away from bones. Discard bones and dill sprigs; cut lower fillet into serving portions. Makes 8 servings.

## Dill Tartar Sauce

*Here's the perfect sauce to accompany Whole Grilled Salmon.*

| | | |
|---|---|---|
| 1 cup | **mayonnaise** | 250 mL |
| 2 tbsp | **finely chopped fresh dill** | 25 mL |
| 1 tbsp | **chopped green onion** | 15 mL |
| 1 tbsp | **chopped drained capers** | 15 mL |
| 1 | **hard-cooked egg, finely chopped** | 1 |
| 1 tsp | **Dijon mustard** | 5 mL |
| 1 tsp | **lemon juice** | 5 mL |
| | **Salt and pepper** | |

■ In small bowl, combine mayonnaise, dill, green onion, capers, egg, mustard, lemon juice, and salt and pepper to taste. Makes about 1-1/2 cups (375 mL).

## New Potatoes in Garlic Butter

*New potatoes bathed in garlic butter cook to perfection on the grill.*

| | | |
|---|---|---|
| 1/2 cup | **butter, softened** | 125 mL |
| 2 | **cloves garlic, minced** | 2 |
| 24 | **small new potatoes (about 3 lb/1.5 kg)** | 24 |
| | **Salt and pepper** | |

■ Stir together butter and garlic. Arrange half of the potatoes in single layer on square of double-thickness heavy-duty foil. Dot potatoes evenly with half of the butter mixture; season with salt and pepper to taste. Seal package securely. Repeat with remaining potatoes.

■ Roast directly on hot coals or on grill at High setting for 40 to 45 minutes or until tender, turning packages occasionally. Makes 8 servings.

***BARBECUING FISH***

***• Compensate for the lack of natural fat in fish by using marinades and basting sauces to prevent drying out. These can be as simple as lemon juice and oil or melted butter.***

***• Oil barbecue surfaces, especially if cooking fish directly on grill. Baste fish frequently and keep a glass of water nearby to douse flare-ups when basting oil hits coals.***

***• Don't overcook fish. Winds and outside temperature will affect cooking time but a general rule is to barbecue fish over hot coals or at high setting for 10 minutes per inch (2.5 cm) of thickness, measured at thickest point of fish.***

***• Fish is naturally tender and breaks easily when cooked so handle it carefully when serving.***

# Sponge Cake Fruit Flan

*Arrange your favorite fresh fruit over a pastry cream filling in a delicate sponge cake flan. Brushed lightly with a glaze, it makes a fine ending to a summer meal.*

| | | |
|---|---|---|
| 2 | **eggs (at room temperature)** | 2 |
| **2/3 cup** | **granulated sugar** | **150 mL** |
| **1/3 cup** | **warm water** | **75 mL** |
| **1 tsp** | **vanilla** | **5 mL** |
| **1 cup** | **all-purpose flour** | **250 mL** |
| **2 tsp** | **baking powder** | **10 mL** |
| **Pinch** | **salt** | **Pinch** |
| | PASTRY CREAM FILLING: | |
| 3 | **egg yolks** | 3 |
| **1/4 cup** | **granulated sugar** | **50 mL** |
| **2 tbsp** | **all-purpose flour** | **25 mL** |
| **1 cup** | **milk** | **250 mL** |
| **1 tsp** | **vanilla** | **5 mL** |
| **1/2 cup** | **whipping cream** | **125 mL** |
| | TOPPING: | |
| **3 cups** | **mixed fresh fruit (strawberries, blueberries, raspberries or sliced peaches, kiwifruit or bananas)** | **750 mL** |
| **2 tbsp** | **apple or red currant jelly** | **25 mL** |

■ Grease 11-inch (1.2 L) flan pan with raised center. Dust with flour; place round of parchment or waxed paper in raised center. Set aside.

■ In mixing bowl, beat eggs, sugar and water with electric mixer for 10 minutes or until batter leaves ribbon trail when beaters are lifted. Blend in vanilla.

■ In separate small bowl, stir together flour, baking powder and salt. Sift half of the flour mixture over egg mixture; fold in until blended. Repeat with remaining flour mixture.

■ Pour batter into prepared pan and spread evenly to edge. Bake in 350°F (180°C) oven for 20 to 30 minutes or until top springs back when lightly touched. Let cool in pan for 5 minutes. Loosen edges and invert onto wire cake rack. Peel away parchment paper and let cool completely.

**PASTRY CREAM FILLING:** In bowl, whisk together egg yolks, sugar, flour and 1/4 cup (50 mL) of the milk. In heavy saucepan, heat remaining milk just until bubbles form around edge of pan; gradually whisk into egg mixture. Return to saucepan; cook over medium heat, whisking constantly, for 3 minutes or until thickened and bubbly.

■ Transfer custard to bowl; stir in vanilla. Place waxed paper or plastic wrap directly on surface of custard. Let cool completely. Whip cream; whisk one-quarter into cooled custard until smooth. Fold in remaining whipped cream. Spread evenly over indented part of cake.

**TOPPING:** Arrange fruit over filling. In small saucepan, heat apple jelly over low heat until melted. Using pastry brush, brush jelly glaze over fruit. Serve immediately or refrigerate for up to 2 hours. Makes 8 servings.

# A PRAIRIE HARVEST DINNER

FOR TWELVE

*Whether it's Thanksgiving dinner, a Sunday gathering on the family farm or a community fall supper, the traditional feasts of a Prairie autumn are sure to be generous in both substance and spirit. There's always a bountiful table of perennial favorites: roast turkey or chicken, lots of homegrown vegetables, old-fashioned salads and homemade buns. Good Prairie cooks happily add interesting new variations to their menus (like the inside-out stuffing in this turkey) but you can always depend on a wonderful old-time dessert.*

SEASONAL SOUP

*TURKEY WITH INSIDE-OUT STUFFING

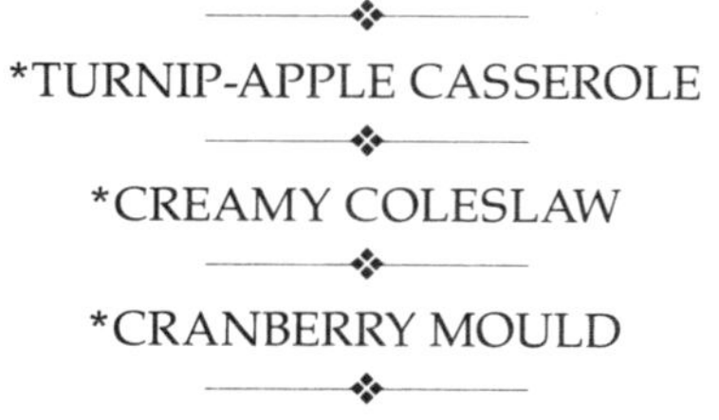

*BAKED CARROT RING WITH GREEN PEAS

*TURNIP-APPLE CASSEROLE

*CREAMY COLESLAW

*CRANBERRY MOULD

*OLD-TIME PUMPKIN PIE

## Turkey with Inside-Out Stuffing

*Inside-out dressing was invented when busy homemakers discovered that the turkey dressing always ran out before the turkey did. So they simply doubled the dressing by putting it under the skin as well as in the cavities. It turned out that the stuffing under the skin was particularly good, so the recipe below, developed by Jean Hoare, author of* Best Little Cookbook in the West, *puts the stuffing under the skin only.*

| | | |
|---|---|---|
| 1 | **turkey (12 to 14 lb/ 5 to 6 kg)** | 1 |
| 2 | **small apples, peeled and quartered** | 2 |
| 3 | **onions, quartered** | 3 |
| 1/4 cup | **vegetable oil** | 50 mL |

| | **STUFFING:** | |
|---|---|---|
| 1 | **loaf day-old white bread** | 1 |
| 1/2 lb | **ground beef** | 250 g |
| 1 | **large onion, chopped** | 1 |
| 1/2 cup | **butter, melted** | 125 mL |
| 8 | **(approx) eggs** | 8 |
| 1/4 cup | **chopped fresh parsley** | 50 mL |
| 1 tbsp | **crumbled dried sage** | 15 mL |
| 1/2 tsp | **each salt and pepper** | 2 mL |

■ Remove neck and giblets from turkey; reserve for stock or gravy, if desired. Wipe turkey inside and out with damp cloth. Keep chilled.

**STUFFING:** Cut bread into cubes (you should have about 18 cups/4.5 L). In large bowl, combine bread, beef, onion and butter. Add eggs and with hands, mix well (it should be gooey). Add 1 more egg if necessary to moisten mixture. Add parsley, sage, salt and pepper.

■ Starting from area around turkey cavity, carefully loosen and lift skin in hip, breast

*Turkey with Inside-Out Stuffing; Cranberry Mould; Creamy Coleslaw; Baked Carrot Ring with Green Peas*

and neck areas, trying not to break skin. Pack dressing between skin and meat, not packing too tightly. (If you have dressing left over, lift more areas of skin and pack lightly.)

■ Draw neck skin over dressing and fasten to body with skewer. Place apples and onions in cavity; sew or skewer closed. Tie legs together and wings close to body.

■ Place turkey, breast side up, in greased roasting pan; brush with oil. Tent loosely with foil, shiny side in. Roast in 350°F (180°C) oven for about 20 minutes per lb (500 g) or until meat thermometer inserted in thickest part of thigh, not touching bone, registers 185°F (85°C) and meat on thickest part of drumstick feels soft when pinched. Remove foil during last 30 minutes of cooking and baste occasionally with pan juices.

■ To serve, slice turkey, including piece of stuffing with each slice of meat. Makes about 12 servings.

# *Baked Carrot Ring with Green Peas*

*This is a new way of serving up the old Thanksgiving favorites —peas and carrots. The carrots are baked into a ring and then the peas piled into the center.*

| | | |
|---|---|---|
| **2 lb** | **carrots, chopped** | **1 kg** |
| **2** | **eggs** | **2** |
| **1 cup** | **milk** | **250 mL** |
| **1 cup** | **crushed soda crackers** | **250 mL** |
| **3/4 cup** | **shredded Cheddar cheese** | **175 mL** |
| **1/2 cup** | **butter, softened** | **125 mL** |
| **1/4 cup** | **minced onion** | **50 mL** |
| **1/4 tsp** | **black pepper** | **1 mL** |
| **Pinch** | **cayenne pepper** | **Pinch** |
| **2 cups** | **frozen peas** | **500 mL** |
| **1 tbsp** | **butter** | **15 mL** |
| | **Salt and pepper** | |
| | **Italian parsley and carrot flowers (optional)** | |

■ In saucepan of boiling salted water, cook carrots until tender, about 10 minutes; drain. Using potato masher, mash carrots. (Alternatively, process carrots in food processor until smooth.)

■ In large bowl, beat eggs with milk. Add carrots, crackers, cheese, softened butter, onion, and black and cayenne peppers; mix well. Transfer to well-greased 6-cup (1.5 L) ring mould. Bake in 325°F (160°C) oven for 50 to 60 minutes or until browned and firm to touch.

■ Meanwhile, in small saucepan, bring to boil enough water to cover peas; add frozen peas. Return to boil; reduce heat and simmer for about 3 minutes or just until tender. Drain peas; toss with 1 tbsp (15 mL) butter, and salt and pepper to taste.

■ Invert carrot ring onto serving platter and remove mould. Fill center with peas. Garnish with parsley and carrot flowers (if using). Makes about 12 servings.

# *Turnip-Apple Casserole*

*Many people still refer to rutabagas as turnips. Whatever they're called, they're an essential part of any Prairie harvest dinner. In this easy make-ahead casserole, rutabagas are sweetened with apples and crowned with a crisp topping.*

| | | |
|---|---|---|
| **1** | **large rutabaga (about 3 lb/1.5 kg)** | **1** |
| **1/4 cup** | **butter** | **50 mL** |
| **4** | **apples** | **4** |
| **2/3 cup** | **packed brown sugar** | **150 mL** |
| **1 tsp** | **cinnamon** | **5 mL** |
| **1/3 cup** | **all-purpose flour** | **75 mL** |

■ Peel rutabaga; cut into cubes. In large saucepan of boiling salted water, cook rutabaga for 10 to 15 minutes or until tender; drain. Using potato masher, mash well. Add 2 tbsp (25 mL) of the butter; set aside.

■ Peel and core apples; slice thinly into bowl. Combine 1/2 cup (125 mL) of the sugar with cinnamon; sprinkle over apples and toss.

■ Spread one-third of the rutabaga mixture in greased 12-cup (3 L) casserole; spread with half of the apple mixture. Repeat layers, ending with layer of rutabaga. (Dish can be prepared ahead to this point, covered and refrigerated overnight.)

■ Combine flour with remaining sugar. Using pastry blender or 2 knives, cut in remaining butter until mixture resembles coarse crumbs. Sprinkle over rutabaga mixture.

■ Bake in 350°F (180°C) oven for 1 hour or until apples are tender and mixture is cooked through. Makes about 12 servings.

## Creamy Coleslaw

*Here's a salad that's always a favorite. For a large gathering, just double the recipe.*

| | | |
|---|---|---|
| **4 cups** | **shredded cabbage** | **1 L** |
| **1/2 cup** | **sliced celery** | **125 mL** |
| **1/4 cup** | **chopped green onions** | **50 mL** |
| **1** | **large apple (unpeeled), chopped** | **1** |
| **1/4 cup** | **mayonnaise** | **50 mL** |
| **1/4 cup** | **plain yogurt** | **50 mL** |
| **1 tbsp** | **vinegar** | **15 mL** |
| **2 tsp** | **granulated sugar** | **10 mL** |
| **1/2 tsp** | **prepared mustard** | **2 mL** |
| **1/2 tsp** | **celery seed** | **2 mL** |
| **1/2 tsp** | **salt** | **2 mL** |
| **1/4 tsp** | **pepper** | **1 mL** |

■ In large bowl, combine cabbage, celery, onions and apple.
■ Mix together mayonnaise, yogurt, vinegar, sugar, mustard, celery seed, salt and pepper; add to bowl and toss thoroughly. Taste and adjust seasoning. Cover and refrigerate until chilled. Makes 6 to 8 servings.

## Cranberry Mould

*Here's the perfect accompaniment to roast turkey.*

| | | |
|---|---|---|
| **2 cups** | **fresh or frozen cranberries** | **500 mL** |
| **2 cups** | **cranberry cocktail juice** | **500 mL** |
| **1 cup** | **water** | **250 mL** |
| **2** | **envelopes unflavored gelatin** | **2** |
| **3/4 cup** | **granulated sugar** | **175 mL** |
| **1 tbsp** | **grated orange rind** | **15 mL** |
| **1 cup** | **ginger ale** | **250 mL** |

■ In heavy saucepan, combine cranberries, cranberry cocktail juice and 1/2 cup (125 mL) of the water; bring to boil. Reduce heat and simmer for 5 to 7 minutes or until cranberries pop and soften.
■ Meanwhile, sprinkle gelatin into remaining water; let stand for 1 minute to soften. Add to cranberry mixture along with sugar and orange rind; stir until gelatin and sugar have dissolved, about 1 minute. Remove from heat. Stir in ginger ale.
■ Chill, stirring occasionally, until slightly thickened and consistency of raw egg whites. Pour into rinsed but not dried 6-cup (1.5 L) mould; refrigerate for about 4 hours or until set, or overnight. To serve, unmould onto serving plate. Makes about 12 servings.

*START WITH SOUP*
***A smooth soup made with seasonal vegetables is an inviting start to an autumn feast. Our cover soup (recipe, page 108) is a good basic recipe that adapts to many variations and is equally tasty if you use pumpkin, carrots or broccoli instead of squash. For an attractive presentation, dress up your soup with:***
- ***chopped fresh herbs such as parsley, chives, tarragon, mint or basil***
- ***roasted sunflower, sesame or celery seeds***
- ***toasted nuts***
- ***shredded cheeses or freshly grated Parmesan***
- ***dollops of whipped or sour cream or crème fraîche***
- ***spices such as freshly grated nutmeg, coarsely ground pepper or red pepper flakes.***

## Old-Time Pumpkin Pie

*This pie is also very good with cooked mashed carrots instead of pumpkin. For 12 servings, make 2 pies.*

| | | |
|---|---|---|
| | **Pastry for 9-inch (23 cm) single-crust pie** | |
| **2 cups** | **cooked or canned pumpkin** | **500 mL** |
| **1 cup** | **milk** | **250 mL** |
| **3** | **eggs, separated** | **3** |
| **1 cup** | **granulated sugar** | **250 mL** |
| **1/2 tsp** | **cinnamon** | **2 mL** |
| **1/4 tsp** | **cloves** | **1 mL** |
| **1/4 tsp** | **nutmeg** | **1 mL** |
| | **Whipped cream** | |

■ On lightly floured surface, roll out pastry and line pie plate, leaving high rim of dough around edge.
■ In large bowl, mix pumpkin with milk. Beat egg yolks well and add to pumpkin mixture. Combine sugar, cinnamon, cloves and nutmeg; stir into pumpkin mixture.
■ In separate bowl, beat egg whites until stiff peaks form; fold into pumpkin mixture. Pour into pie shell and bake in 350°F (180°C) oven for about 45 minutes or until knife inserted in center comes out clean. Serve with whipped cream.

# A STRAWBERRY SOCIAL

FOR A CROWD

*Canada's most popular berry has been the star attraction at strawberry socials ever since pioneer days. This endearing get-together remains a tradition coast-to-coast in Canada. Whether you're involved in planning a strawberry feast for a crowd of hundreds or just a dozen friends in your own backyard, it's the ultimate celebration of a Canadian summer.*

*Recipes are for 8 to 12 servings; make the number of batches needed to serve your group.*

*OLD-FASHIONED STRAWBERRY SHORTCAKE

*MERINGUE KISSES

*CHOCOLATE PECAN STRAWBERRY TART

*STRAWBERRY CHEESECAKE TRIFLE

CHOCOLATE-DIPPED STRAWBERRIES

## Old-Fashioned Strawberry Shortcake

*With shortcake, freshness counts; plan to serve this exceptionally good old-fashioned cake while it's still warm from the oven.*

| | | |
|---|---|---|
| **6 cups** | **strawberries** | **1.5 L** |
| **2 tbsp** | **granulated sugar** | **25 mL** |
| **1 tbsp** | **raspberry liqueur (framboise) or frozen raspberry juice concentrate (optional)** | **15 mL** |
| **1-1/2 cups** | **whipping cream** | **375 mL** |
| | **SHORTCAKE:** | |
| **1-1/2 cups** | **milk** | **375 mL** |
| **2 tsp** | **white vinegar** | **10 mL** |
| **3 cups** | **all-purpose flour** | **750 mL** |
| **3/4 cup** | **granulated sugar** | **175 mL** |
| **4 tsp** | **baking powder** | **20 mL** |
| **3/4 tsp** | **baking soda** | **4 mL** |
| **3/4 tsp** | **salt** | **4 mL** |
| **3/4 cup** | **shortening** | **175 mL** |

**SHORTCAKE:** Stir together milk and vinegar; let stand at room temperature for 20 minutes.

■ Meanwhile, in large bowl, combine flour, all but 1 tsp (5 mL) of the sugar, the baking powder, baking soda and salt. Using pastry blender or 2 knives, cut in shortening until crumbly. Stir milk mixture; drizzle over dry ingredients, tossing with fork to make moist dough.

■ Transfer to greased 9-inch (2.5 L) springform pan. Smooth top; sprinkle with remaining sugar. Bake in 400°F (200°C) oven for 40 to 45 minutes or until golden brown and tester inserted in center comes out clean. Remove sides of pan; let cool for 5 minutes before lifting carefully off base of pan. Let cool on wire rack.

■ In food processor or blender, purée 2 cups (500 mL) of the strawberries. Transfer to bowl; stir in sugar, and liqueur (if using). Reserve 5 berries for garnish. Slice remaining berries and stir into purée. Whip cream.

■ Halve cake horizontally. Place bottom half of cake on serving plate; spread with 2 cups (500 mL) of the berry mixture. Top with some of the whipped cream; cover with top half of cake. Spoon remaining berry mixture and whipped cream attractively over top; garnish with reserved berries. Makes 8 to 10 servings.

*(Clockwise from center) Old-Fashioned Strawberry Shortcake; Chocolate Pecan Strawberry Tart; Meringue Kisses; chocolate-dipped strawberries; Strawberry Cheesecake Trifle*

## Meringue Kisses

*Add a dollop of whipped cream or Creamy Filling to hold a strawberry if you wish.*

| | | |
|---|---|---|
| **4** | **egg whites** | **4** |
| **Pinch** | **cream of tartar** | **Pinch** |
| **1 cup** | **granulated sugar** | **250 mL** |
| **1 tsp** | **vanilla** | **5 mL** |
| | **Creamy Filling (recipe follows)** | |
| **32** | **(approx) strawberries** | **32** |

■ Line 2 large baking sheets with foil or parchment paper.

■ In large bowl, beat egg whites with cream of tartar until soft peaks form; gradually beat in sugar and vanilla until stiff glossy peaks form.

■ With spoon or piping bag fitted with 1/4-inch (5 mm) star tip, form "nests" 1-1/2 inches (4 cm) in diameter on baking sheets. Bake in 225°F (110°C) oven for 1 to 1-1/4 hours or until crisp but not browned. If not completely dry inside, loosen meringues with lifter and return to oven; turn off heat and let dry until oven is cool, about 1 hour. (Meringues can be stored in airtight container for up to 2 weeks.)

■ To serve, top with generous dollop of Creamy Filling and berry. Makes about 32.

| | | |
|---|---|---|
| | **CREAMY FILLING:** | |
| **3/4 cup** | **cream cheese** | **175 mL** |
| **4 tsp** | **icing sugar** | **20 mL** |
| **1/3 cup** | **whipping cream** | **75 mL** |
| **1/2 tsp** | **vanilla** | **2 mL** |

■ In bowl, blend together cream cheese and sugar; gradually beat in cream until smooth. Stir in vanilla. Refrigerate for at least 30 minutes or until chilled. Makes about 1-1/3 cups (325 mL).

## *Chocolate Pecan Strawberry Tart*

*This pecan pastry is as easy to make as cookies, and the filling is simply a layer of melted chocolate brushed over the crust, topped with whole strawberries and a drizzle of chocolate.*

| | | |
|---|---|---|
| | **PECAN PASTRY:** | |
| **1 cup** | **all-purpose flour** | **250 mL** |
| **1/4 cup** | **ground pecans** | **50 mL** |
| **2 tbsp** | **granulated sugar** | **25 mL** |
| **Pinch** | **salt** | **Pinch** |
| **1/4 tsp** | **grated orange rind** | **1 mL** |
| **1/2 cup** | **butter, softened** | **125 mL** |
| **1** | **egg yolk** | **1** |
| **4 tsp** | **orange juice** | **20 mL** |
| | **FILLING:** | |
| **3 oz** | **semisweet, milk or white chocolate** | **90 g** |
| **4 cups** | **strawberries** | **1 L** |

**PECAN PASTRY:** In bowl or food processor, mix together flour, pecans, sugar, salt and orange rind. Cut in butter until crumbly.

■ Stir together egg yolk and orange juice; drizzle over crumbs. Toss or process with on/off motion until mixture holds together. Press into ball and flatten; wrap and chill for at least 20 minutes.

■ On lightly floured pastry cloth and using stockinette-covered rolling pin, or between 2 sheets of waxed paper, roll out pastry to 1/4-inch (5 mm) thickness to fit either 13- × 4-inch (1 L) or 9-inch (23 cm) flan pans with removable bottom. Trim edges; prick at 1/2-inch (1 cm) intervals. Chill for 30 minutes.

■ Line pastry shell with foil and fill with pie weights or dried beans; bake in 400°F (200°C) oven for 10 minutes. Lift out foil and weights; prick pastry again if puffed and return to oven for 10 to 12 minutes longer or until crisp and golden brown. Shield edges with foil if pastry is browning too much. Let cool on wire rack. Remove sides of pan.

**FILLING:** In double boiler over hot, not boiling, water, melt chocolate; spread about two-thirds in shell. Attractively arrange strawberries, tips up, on chocolate; drizzle with remaining chocolate. Refrigerate until firm, about 30 minutes. Let stand at room temperature for 10 to 15 minutes before serving.

## *Strawberry Cheesecake Trifle*

*Fresh berries add a delicious new twist to* tiramisu, *an impressive Italian dessert that can be made ahead.*

| | | |
|---|---|---|
| **4 cups** | **strawberries** | **1 L** |
| **3 tbsp** | **lemon juice** | **50 mL** |
| **2 tbsp** | **water** | **25 mL** |
| **40** | **(approx) amaretti cookies (7 oz/200 g pkg)** | **40** |
| **5** | **eggs, separated** | **5** |
| **1/3 cup** | **granulated sugar** | **75 mL** |
| **1 lb** | **mascarpone or cream cheese, cubed** | **500 g** |
| **1 tsp** | **vanilla** | **5 mL** |
| **1/2 cup** | **whipping cream** | **125 mL** |

■ Reserve 1/2 cup (125 mL) of the berries for garnish; slice remaining berries and set aside.

■ In small bowl, combine lemon juice and water. Dip cookies into juice mixture; arrange about half in bottom of 10-cup (2.5 L) glass bowl or soufflé dish. Set remaining cookies aside.

■ In large bowl, beat egg yolks with half of the sugar until thick and pale yellow. Beat cheese into yolk mixture until smooth and light. Add vanilla.

■ In separate bowl, beat egg whites until soft peaks form. Gradually beat in remaining sugar until stiff peaks form; stir about one-quarter into cheese mixture. Fold in remaining egg whites.

■ Spoon one-quarter of the cheese mixture over cookies in bowl. Neatly layer half of the sliced berries, one-quarter of the cheese mixture, remaining cookies, one-quarter of the cheese mixture and remaining sliced berries and cheese mixture. Cover and refrigerate until firm, about 4 hours.

■ To serve, whip cream and pipe or spoon attractively over tiramisu. Garnish with whole berries. Makes 12 servings.

# AN INDIAN SUMMER FEAST

FOR TEN

*Late autumn in Canada brings a special blessing — a brief return to warm, sunny days after the first chilling frost. It's a mellow, soul-warming respite before another long winter. It's also a reminder of our native Indian tradition of "gathering" — the stocking of wild berries and other foods for winter.*

*CORN SOUP

*FRIED BREAD

*BRAISED LEG OF VENISON

*THREE SISTERS VEGETABLES

*WILD RICE TARTS

CRANBERRY SAUCE

*CRANBERRY FOOL

***NATIVE INDIAN COOKING***
***This is the original Canadian home-cooking, an authentic taste of history. It can be sampled at fall fairs, ceremonies and celebrations within native communities, and at a few restaurants scattered across the country.***

***The food reflects the produce of each region. Along the Pacific coast, salmon is king, and native cooking is rich in seafood. Across the North, game and freshwater fish predominate. On the Prairies, buffalo and bannock are prevalent. In Central and Eastern Canada, home of the Eastern Woodland Indians, the distinguishing ingredient is corn.***

## *Corn Soup*

*Use regular yellow corn if hominy corn is not available.*

| | | |
|---|---|---|
| **1 cup** | **dried red kidney or navy beans** | **250 mL** |
| **2** | **cans (19 oz/540 mL) white hominy corn** | **2** |
| **1/4 lb** | **lean salt pork** | **125 g** |
| **6 cups** | **(approx) water** | **1.5 L** |
| **1/4 cup** | **chopped fresh parsley** | **50 mL** |

■ In small saucepan, cover beans with water; bring to boil and boil for 2 minutes. Cover and let stand for 1 hour; drain and rinse under cold running water. Place in large saucepan.

■ Drain corn, adding liquid to beans; set corn aside. Chop salt pork into 1/4-inch (5 mm) cubes; add to saucepan along with 6 cups (1.5 L) water. Cover and bring to boil; reduce heat and simmer for about 1 hour or until beans are tender.

■ Stir in reserved corn and return to simmer; cook gently for 20 minutes to blend flavors. Add more water if desired. Serve sprinkled with parsley. Makes 10 to 12 servings.

## *Fried Bread*

*Close to bannock in ingredients, fried bread has a delicious crisp golden crust. Serve hot with a meal or as a snack with butter and jam.*

| | | |
|---|---|---|
| **2 cups** | **all-purpose flour** | **500 mL** |
| **1-1/2 tsp** | **baking powder** | **7 mL** |
| **1/2 tsp** | **salt** | **2 mL** |
| **Pinch** | **baking soda** | **Pinch** |
| **1-1/3 cups** | **(approx) buttermilk** | **325 mL** |
| | **Vegetable oil** | |

■ In large bowl, stir together flour, baking powder, salt and soda. Gradually pour in buttermilk, stirring constantly and adding more buttermilk if necessary to make soft but not sticky dough.

■ Turn out onto lightly floured surface and knead several times. Roll out into 1/2-inch (1 cm) thickness; cut into 3-inch (8 cm) rounds or squares.

■ Pour oil into large skillet to depth of 1 inch (2.5 cm); heat over medium heat. Cook rounds, one layer at a time, for 5 to 6 minutes per side or until golden, crisp and cooked through. Makes about 12 rounds.

## Braised Leg of Venison

*Because venison is so lean, it needs to be marinated for a long time. This marinade complements the meat's rich flavor and adds its savor to the serving sauce. You will find venison at a growing number of butcher shops and German delicatessens. For our photograph, we used a bone-in roast. The version in the recipe is an easy-to-carve boned leg, which is referred to as a top and bottom round. Marinate the meat for 2 to 3 days, then tie into a neat cylindrical roast just before cooking.*

| | | |
|---|---|---|
| **1** | **boned top and bottom venison round (about 5 lb/2.5 kg)** | **1** |
| **2 cups** | **chicken stock** | **500 mL** |
| | **Salt** | |
| **5 tsp** | **cornstarch** | **25 mL** |
| | **MARINADE:** | |
| **2/3 cup** | **vegetable oil** | **150 mL** |
| **1/3 cup** | **cider vinegar** | **75 mL** |
| **2** | **onions, chopped** | **2** |
| **2** | **carrots, chopped** | **2** |
| **1** | **stalk celery, chopped** | **1** |
| **1/4 cup** | **chopped fresh parsley** | **50 mL** |
| **1** | **clove garlic, minced** | **1** |
| **2** | **bay leaves** | **2** |
| **1/2 tsp** | **pepper** | **2 mL** |
| **1/4 tsp** | **ground cloves** | **1 mL** |

■ Wipe meat and trim if necessary; place in large plastic bag.

**MARINADE:** Combine 1/2 cup (125 mL) of the oil, vinegar, onions, carrots, celery, parsley, garlic, bay leaves, pepper and cloves; pour over meat and work into all crevices. Seal bag and set in large bowl; refrigerate for at least 2 or up to 3 days, turning and rubbing in marinade occasionally.

■ Remove meat and pat dry, reserving marinade; tie into cylindrical roast. Pour remaining oil into Dutch oven or casserole large enough to leave 2-inch (5 cm) space around roast; heat over high heat. Brown roast well all over, using 2 wooden spoons to turn meat.

■ Add reserved marinade; pour in 1-3/4 cups (425 mL) of the chicken stock. Cover and cook in 325°F (160°C) oven, turning once, for 2-1/2 to 3 hours or until meat thermometer registers 150 to 160°F (65 to 70°C). Remove meat and place on warmed platter; untie and season lightly with salt to taste. Cover with foil and let stand in warm place for 15 minutes.

■ Meanwhile, strain pan juices into large saucepan, pressing vegetables to extract as much juice as possible. Boil hard over high heat, stirring often, for 5 to 8 minutes or until reduced to about 3 cups (750 mL). Mix cornstarch with remaining 1/4 cup (50 mL) stock; stir into boiling sauce and cook until thickened. Taste and adjust seasoning if desired. Pour into warmed sauceboat and serve with roast. Makes 10 to 12 servings.

## Three Sisters Vegetables

*The three sisters — squash, corn and beans — were traditionally planted together and eaten together.*

| | | |
|---|---|---|
| **1** | **butternut squash (about 2-1/2 lb/1.25 kg)** | **1** |
| **1/2 lb** | **green beans** | **250 g** |
| **4** | **ears corn** | **4** |
| **3/4 cup** | **(approx) water** | **175 mL** |
| **2 tbsp** | **butter** | **25 mL** |
| **1/2 tsp** | **salt** | **2 mL** |
| | **Pepper** | |

■ Peel, seed and cut squash into bite-sized cubes. Trim beans; cut into 1-inch (2.5 cm) lengths. Remove husks and silk from corn; cut off kernels.

■ In large heavy saucepan, combine water and squash; cover and bring to boil. Reduce heat to low and simmer for 15 minutes or just until squash begins to soften, adding more water if necessary. Add beans and cook for 5 to 8 minutes or until bright green but still tendercrisp.

■ Add corn, butter, salt, and pepper to taste, adding a little more water if necessary. Cook, covered, for 3 to 5 minutes or until vegetables are tender and liquid has been absorbed. Taste and adjust seasoning if necessary. Makes 10 to 12 servings.

*Braised Leg of Venison; Wild Rice Tarts; Fried Bread; Three Sisters Vegetables*

## Wild Rice Tarts

*This is a recipe from Phyllis Lickers who does all the baking for The Village Inn on the Six Nations Reserve in Ontario. Serve these savory tarts with venison.*

| | | |
|---|---|---|
| **1/2 cup** | **wild rice (about 3 oz/85 g)** | **125 mL** |
| **2 tbsp** | **butter** | **25 mL** |
| **3/4 cup** | **finely chopped mushrooms** | **175 mL** |
| **1/3 cup** | **finely chopped onion** | **75 mL** |
| **1-1/3 cups** | **(approx) chicken stock** | **325 mL** |
| **Pinch** | **each salt, pepper, dried sage, basil, and crushed aniseed** | **Pinch** |
| **16** | **baked 3-inch (8 cm) tart shells** | **16** |

■ Rinse rice; cover with cold water and let soak overnight. Drain and set aside.

■ In small heavy saucepan, melt butter over medium heat; cook mushrooms and onion, stirring, for about 4 minutes or until tender. Stir in rice; cook for 2 minutes.

■ Pour in stock; add salt, pepper, sage, basil and aniseed. Cover and bring to boil; reduce heat to low and simmer for about 1 hour or until rice is tender and liquid has been absorbed, adding more stock if necessary to keep rice moist. Taste and adjust seasoning if necessary. (Filling can be cooled, covered and refrigerated for up to 2 days. Reheat before continuing with recipe.) Spoon hot rice mixture into warmed tart shells. Makes 16 tarts.

## Cranberry Fool

*This easy, elegant dessert spotlights a berry native to Canada.*

| | | |
|---|---|---|
| **2 cups** | **boiling water** | **500 mL** |
| **2/3 cup** | **slivered orange rind** | **150 mL** |
| **3 cups** | **granulated sugar** | **750 mL** |
| **1 cup** | **orange juice** | **250 mL** |
| **6 cups** | **cranberries** | **1.5 L** |
| **2 tbsp** | **orange liqueur (optional)** | **25 mL** |
| **2 cups** | **whipping cream** | **500 mL** |

■ In saucepan of boiling water, simmer orange rind until tender, about 15 minutes. Drain through sieve into 2 cup (500 mL) measure; set rind aside. Add enough water to liquid to make 1-1/3 cups (325 mL).

■ In large heavy saucepan, combine reserved liquid, sugar and orange juice; bring to boil. Reduce heat and simmer, covered, for 5 minutes. Stir in cranberries and reserved rind; increase heat to high and boil, stirring often, until cranberries have popped and formed sauce, about 7 minutes. (Cranberry sauce mixture can be covered and refrigerated for up to 2 weeks.)

■ Up to 4 hours before serving, pick out and reserve 12 of the best-looking berries from sauce. Transfer remaining cranberry mixture to large bowl; stir in orange liqueur (if using). Whip cream; fold into cranberry mixture, leaving streaks. Spoon into fruit nappies or stemmed glasses. Garnish each serving with reserved berry. Makes 12 servings.

# A MIDNIGHT SUN PICNIC

FOR TWELVE

*If you're lucky enough to live in or visit the Yukon or Northwest Territories in midsummer, a picnic brunch with a lakeside setting in the lingering daylight near midnight would be an unforgettable feast. The North is a very special place of unique flavors and hospitable people; a lot of socializing is done over generous tables. This memorable menu will bring some of that Northern spirit to a Southern picnic too, whether it's at midnight or high noon.*

*BERRY SPRITZERS

*SCRAMBLED EGGS WITH SALMON CAVIAR

*CRÊPES WITH SMOKED TROUT

MULTIGRAIN BREADS AND ROLLS

MINCEMEAT PIE

*BERRY TARTS

*(Clockwise from top) Multigrain breads and rolls; mincemeat pie; Scrambled Eggs with Salmon Caviar; wild raspberry jam; yogurt; Crêpes with Smoked Trout; Berry Spritzers*

## *Scrambled Eggs with Salmon Caviar*

*If red salmon caviar isn't available, substitute golden caviar from whitefish.*

| | | |
|---|---|---|
| 18 | **eggs** | 18 |
| 1/2 tsp | **salt** | 2 mL |
| 1/4 tsp | **pepper** | 1 mL |
| 1/4 cup | **butter** | 50 mL |
| 1/3 cup | **whipping cream** | 75 mL |
| 1/3 cup | **chopped fresh parsley (optional)** | 50 mL |
| 1/4 cup | **salmon caviar** | 50 mL |

■ In bowl, whisk eggs with salt and pepper. In large heavy skillet, melt butter over medium-low heat; cook eggs, stirring almost constantly, for 6 to 8 minutes or until thickened.

■ Stir in cream, and parsley, if using; cook for 2 to 4 minutes or until eggs set but are still moist. Transfer to warm platter. Form hollow in top; spoon in caviar. Makes 12 servings.

## *Crêpes with Smoked Trout*

*Fold a crêpe around pieces of smoked trout and top with Lemon Dill Yogurt Sauce.*

| | | |
|---|---|---|
| 3 | **smoked trout** | 3 |
| | **CRÊPES:** | |
| 4 | **eggs** | 4 |
| 1 cup | **all-purpose flour** | 250 mL |
| 1 cup | **milk** | 250 mL |
| 1/4 cup | **water** | 50 mL |
| 2 tbsp | **butter, melted** | 25 mL |
| 1/4 tsp | **salt** | 1 mL |
| 1/4 tsp | **grated lemon rind** | 1 mL |
| | **LEMON DILL YOGURT SAUCE:** | |
| 2 cups | **plain yogurt** | 500 mL |
| 1/4 cup | **chopped fresh dill** | 50 mL |
| 1 tbsp | **Russian-style mustard** | 15 mL |
| 1/2 tsp | **lemon juice** | 2 mL |
| | **Salt and pepper** | |

**CRÊPES:** In food processor or blender, process eggs, flour, milk, water, butter, salt and lemon rind until smooth and creamy. Refrigerate, covered, for at least 30 minutes

***BERRY SPRITZERS***

***Use either lingonberries or cranberries to make this refreshing drink. You can also combine the concentrate with an equal amount of water and heat it until steaming for a delicious wintertime berry tea.***

***In large saucepan, cook 6 cups (1.5 L) cranberries and 5 cups (1.25 L) water over medium-high heat, stirring occasionally, until berries pop. Crush with potato masher; cook for 3 minutes longer. Strain through***

*cheesecloth-lined sieve or dampened jelly bag. (There should be about 3 cups/750 mL concentrate.) In saucepan, heat concentrate with 1/2 cup (125 mL) granulated sugar until sugar dissolves, stirring. Transfer to covered jar and store in refrigerator for up to 1 week.*

*To serve, fill glasses with ice cubes. Half-fill with concentrate; top with sparkling water. Makes 10 to 12 drinks.*

or up to 1 day.

■ Lightly grease 7-inch (18 cm) crêpe pan or nonstick skillet; heat over medium-high heat. Stir crêpe batter and spoon about 3 tbsp (50 mL) into pan to thinly cover bottom. Cook until bottom is golden and top is no longer shiny, about 45 seconds. Flip and cook until bottom is speckled with brown, about 30 seconds. Let cool on paper-towel-lined baking sheets. (Crêpes can be wrapped and refrigerated for up to 3 days or frozen for up to 2 months.)

**LEMON DILL YOGURT SAUCE:** In cheesecloth-lined sieve set over bowl, drain yogurt for 8 hours or overnight. Stir dill, mustard, lemon juice, and salt and pepper to taste into bowl.

■ To assemble: skin trout; discard head and tail. Lift trout off bones in wide "V" shapes. Place bowl of sauce in center of large platter. Surround with trout and crêpes folded in quarters. Makes about 12 servings.

## Berry Tarts

*Wild berries add a true taste of the North to these creamy treats. The recipe is inspired by similar tarts from the Alpine Bakery in Whitehorse.*

| | SWEET PASTRY: | |
|---|---|---|
| 2 cups | all-purpose flour | 500 mL |
| 3/4 cup | granulated sugar | 175 mL |
| 1 tsp | grated orange or lemon rind | 5 mL |
| 1/4 tsp | salt | 1 mL |
| 2/3 cup | cold butter | 150 mL |
| 2 | eggs | 2 |
| 1 tbsp | ice water | 15 mL |
| 1 tsp | lemon juice | 5 mL |
| | FILLING: | |
| 3/4 cup | granulated sugar | 175 mL |
| 1/4 cup | all-purpose flour | 50 mL |
| 1 tsp | grated orange or lemon rind | 5 mL |
| 1-1/2 cups | sour cream | 375 mL |
| 1 | egg yolk | 1 |
| 2 cups | mossberries or wild blueberries | 500 mL |

**SWEET PASTRY:** In large bowl, stir together flour, sugar, orange rind and salt. With pastry blender or 2 knives, cut in butter until crumbly.

■ Whisk together eggs, water and lemon juice; drizzle over flour mixture, tossing with fork until moist enough to shape into ball (dough will be slightly sticky). Flatten into disc; wrap and refrigerate for 30 minutes or up to 3 days. Let soften to room temperature before rolling.

■ On generously floured pastry cloth and using stockinette-covered rolling pin, roll out half of the pastry at a time to 1/8-inch (3 mm) thickness. Cut into 3-1/2-inch (9 cm) rounds; ease into shallow 2-3/4-inch (7 cm) tart shells. Refrigerate for 30 minutes.

■ Line each tart shell with foil; fill with pie weights or dry beans. Bake in 400°F (200°C) oven for about 10 minutes or until light golden and firm. Remove foil and weights; let cool.

**FILLING:** In bowl, combine sugar, flour and orange rind; blend in sour cream and egg yolk. Spoon about 1 tbsp (15 mL) berries into each tart shell; cover with about 1 tbsp (15 mL) filling and top with 3 or 4 berries. Bake in 350°F (180°C) oven for about 20 minutes or until pastry is golden and filling is set. Let stand for 1 minute. Remove from pan and let cool on racks. Makes about 24 tarts.

# OKTOBERFEST

FOR EIGHT

*At folk festivals and food fairs, in restaurants and home kitchens, a world of international cooking now flavors the Canadian culinary scene. One of our most popular adopted traditions, Oktoberfest, heralds the start of autumn in Canada. In the many German-heritage areas across the country, Oktoberfest brings an annual celebration of song and dance, parades and oompah bands, sausages and sauerkraut and beer. Launch the festivities in your area (or start your own annual tradition) with a feast of hearty German fare. Shopping for the ingredients at a local farmers' market or fall fair will get you into the mood of the season.*

*ROULADEN

*SAUSAGES IN BEER

*SCHNITZEL

*PIGS' TAILS

*BAVARIAN CABBAGE

*POTATO DUMPLINGS

SAUERKRAUT

*APPLE TORTE

## Rouladen
### (Braised Stuffed Beef Rolls)

*These delicious beef rolls are permeated with the distinctive flavor of bacon and dill pickle filling.*

| | | |
|---|---|---|
| 1 | **boneless round steak, 1/2 inch (1 cm) thick (about 2 lb/1 kg)** | 1 |
| 2 tbsp | **German-style mustard** | 25 mL |
| 4 | **slices bacon, chopped** | 4 |
| 1 | **onion, chopped** | 1 |
| 1/4 cup | **chopped fresh parsley** | 50 mL |
| 2 | **dill pickles, quartered lengthwise** | 2 |
| 1/4 cup | **vegetable oil** | 50 mL |
| 1 cup | **beef stock** | 250 mL |
| 1 cup | **dry red wine** | 250 mL |
| 1/2 tsp | **salt** | 2 mL |
| 1/4 tsp | **pepper** | 1 mL |
| 1 tbsp | **all-purpose flour** | 15 mL |

■ Place steak between 2 pieces of waxed paper; pound to half its original thickness. Cut into 8 serving portions about 7- × 4-inches (18 × 10 cm) each.

■ Spread each piece with mustard; sprinkle evenly with bacon, onion and parsley. Place pickle quarter on narrow end of each; roll up and fasten with wooden toothpicks or skewers, or tie with string.

■ In large ovenproof saucepan, heat oil over medium heat; cook rolls until browned on all sides. Add stock, wine, salt and pepper. Heat to boiling; reduce heat and simmer, covered, or braise in 325°F (160°C) oven for 1-1/4 to 1-1/2 hours or until tender.

■ Remove rolls to warm platter and keep warm. Add enough water to pan liquid to make 1 cup (250 mL). Place flour and 2 tbsp (25 mL) water in tightly covered container and shake until smooth; stir gradually into pan liquid. Heat to boiling, stirring constantly; boil for 1 minute until thickened. Spoon over rolls and serve. Makes 8 servings.

*(Clockwise from top) Bavarian Cabbage; Sausages in Beer; sauerkraut; Rouladen; Schnitzel; Potato Dumplings; glazed carrots; Pigs' Tails*

## Sausages in Beer
### *(Wurst im Bierosse)*

*Thick, pleasantly spicy German-style sausages or wursts are available in most meat markets.*

| | | |
|---|---|---|
| **2 lb** | **German-style sausages** | **1 kg** |
| **2 tbsp** | **butter** | **25 mL** |
| **1** | **small onion, chopped** | **1** |
| **2 tsp** | **granulated sugar** | **10 mL** |
| **1** | **can (12 oz/341 mL) light beer** | **1** |
| **1/2 cup** | **dark rye bread crumbs** | **125 mL** |
| | **Salt and pepper** | |

■ In saucepan, pour boiling water over sausages and simmer for about 5 minutes; drain.

■ In skillet, heat butter; brown sausages on all sides. Remove and set aside. Add onion and sugar to pan; cook gently, stirring, for about 4 minutes or until sugar caramelizes. Pour in beer; add bread crumbs and season lightly with salt and pepper. Return sausages to pan; cover and simmer for 20 minutes. Makes 8 servings.

## Schnitzel
### *(Breaded Boneless Pork)*

*Here's a favorite recipe of Mennonite cooks across Canada. Traditionally, Wiener Schnitzel is made with veal but since it is expensive, pork makes a good substitute.*

| | | |
|---|---|---|
| 8 | **slices boneless pork, 1/4 inch (5 mm) thick (from leg, shoulder or loin)** | 8 |
| 1 cup | **all-purpose flour** | 250 mL |
| 2 | **eggs, lightly beaten with 1 tbsp (15 mL) water** | 2 |
| 2 cups | **dry bread crumbs** | 500 mL |
| 1/4 tsp | **pepper** | 1 mL |
| 1/2 cup | **butter** | 125 mL |
| 2 tbsp | **vegetable oil** | 25 mL |
| 1/2 cup | **drained capers (optional)** | 125 mL |
| | **Chopped fresh parsley** | |

■ With mallet, pound pork lightly to flatten. Dredge thoroughly with flour. Dip floured slices into egg mixture, then coat with crumbs seasoned with pepper. Place pork on wire rack and refrigerate for 1 hour to dry crumb coating and prevent it from falling off during cooking.

■ In large skillet, heat together butter and oil; sauté pork quickly, turning once or twice, for about 5 minutes until golden brown and cooked through. On heated serving platter, arrange slices; sprinkle with capers (if using) and parsley. Makes 8 servings.

## Pigs' Tails
### *(Schweine Schwantz)*

*If pigs' tails are not always available, your local butcher can usually get them for you if you order them a few days in advance.*

| | | |
|---|---|---|
| 16 | **pigs' tails** | 16 |
| 2 | **cloves garlic, minced** | 2 |
| 1/2 cup | **soy sauce** | 125 mL |
| 1 cup | **tomato sauce** | 250 mL |
| 1/4 cup | **packed brown sugar** | 50 mL |
| 1 tsp | **Worcestershire sauce** | 5 mL |
| 2 | **drops hot pepper sauce** | 2 |

■ Scrub pigs' tails; rinse and pat dry.

■ In large saucepan, cover tails with water. Add garlic and 1/4 cup (50 mL) of the soy sauce; bring to boil. Skim off foam, then reduce heat; cover and simmer for 2 hours or until fork-tender. (Or pressure-cook for 45 minutes.) Drain and place tails on rack in shallow roasting pan.

■ In small bowl, mix together remaining soy sauce, tomato sauce, sugar, Worcestershire and hot pepper sauce; brush over tails to coat completely. Bake, uncovered, in 350°F (180°C) oven for about 45 minutes until tails begin to brown. Makes 8 servings.

## Bavarian Cabbage

*The reddish-purple color and sour-sweet taste of this dish make it a delicious accompaniment for Schnitzel or Rouladen. For best results, cook the cabbage the day before, then reheat before serving.*

| | | |
|---|---|---|
| 2 tbsp | **butter** | 25 mL |
| 2 | **tart red apples. sliced** | 2 |
| 1 | **head red cabbage, coarsely shredded (8 cups/2 L)** | 1 |
| 1 | **bay leaf** | 1 |
| 1/4 cup | **water** | 50 mL |
| 2 tbsp | **packed brown sugar** | 25 mL |
| 2 tbsp | **red wine vinegar** | 25 mL |
| 1 tsp | **salt** | 5 mL |
| 1/4 tsp | **pepper** | 1 mL |

■ In large saucepan or Dutch oven, over medium heat, melt butter; stir-cook apples for about 3 minutes or until just tender. Add cabbage, bay leaf, water, sugar, vinegar, salt and pepper; stir well. Heat to boiling; reduce heat, cover and simmer for 35 to 40 minutes or until cabbage is tender. Remove bay leaf. Makes 8 servings.

***SAUERKRAUT SIDE DISH***

***Here's a versatile recipe for sauerkraut. It can be heated and served as a side dish or topped with sausages, or served cold as a relish with meats or on its own as a salad. You can also use it to stuff a chicken before roasting or as a bed for roasting a loin of pork.***

***Combine 1 can (14 oz/398 mL) drained and rinsed sauerkraut, 1/2 cup (125 mL) finely chopped onions, 2 tbsp (25 mL) cider vinegar, 2 tsp (10 mL) brown sugar, 2 tsp (10 mL) vegetable oil, 1 tsp (5 mL) caraway seed, 1 small diced red or green pepper and hot pepper flakes to taste (optional).***

***Store in covered container in refrigerator for up to 4 days. Makes about 3-1/2 cups (875 mL).***

## *Potato Dumplings*
### *(Kartoffel Knepp)*

*This dish is better if the potatoes are cooked and mashed the day before preparing these dumplings. It's handier and the mashed potatoes firm up overnight.*

| | | |
|---|---|---|
| **4** | **potatoes (unpeeled)** | **4** |
| **2** | **slices bread** | **2** |
| **2 tbsp** | **butter** | **25 mL** |
| **1** | **egg, lightly beaten** | **1** |
| **1/2 cup** | **all-purpose flour** | **125 mL** |
| **2 tbsp** | **cornstarch** | **25 mL** |
| **1/2 tsp** | **salt** | **2 mL** |
| **1/4 tsp** | **pepper** | **1 mL** |
| **Pinch** | **mace** | **Pinch** |
| **1/2 cup** | **buttered bread crumbs** | **125 mL** |

■ In saucepan of lightly salted boiling water, cook potatoes for 15 to 20 minutes or until tender. Drain and peel; mash (or put through potato ricer) to measure 2 cups (500 mL). Let stand, uncovered, for several hours, preferably overnight.
■ Cut bread into small cubes. In skillet, heat butter; add bread cubes and fry until golden brown. Drain on paper towels.
■ To potatoes, add egg, flour, cornstarch, salt, pepper and mace; mix well and shape into 16 balls about 1-1/2 inches (4 cm) in diameter. Press 2 or 3 bread cubes into center of each ball, then reroll to cover bread completely.
■ In pot of simmering salted water cook dumplings, uncovered and in batches if necessary to avoid crowding, for 12 to 15 minutes or until no longer sticky, turning occasionally. With slotted spoon, remove dumplings and drain well. Sprinkle with bread crumbs and serve hot. Makes 8 servings.

## *Apple Torte*
### *(Krümmeltorte)*

*German cooks boast dozens of versions of apple tortes and kuchens. The pastry for this one is easy enough for novice cooks to make.*

| | | |
|---|---|---|
| | **FILLING:** | |
| **2 lb** | **cooking apples** | **1 kg** |
| **3/4 cup** | **granulated sugar** | **175 mL** |
| | **PASTRY:** | |
| **1 cup** | **all-purpose flour** | **250 mL** |
| **2 tbsp** | **granulated sugar** | **25 mL** |
| **1/2 tsp** | **baking powder** | **2 mL** |
| **1/4 tsp** | **salt** | **1 mL** |
| **1/2 cup** | **butter** | **125 mL** |
| **1** | **egg** | **1** |
| **1 tsp** | **vanilla** | **5 mL** |
| | **GARNISH:** | |
| | **Whipped cream** | |

**FILLING:** Peel, core and quarter apples; cut each quarter crosswise into 5 or 6 pieces. In saucepan, combine apples and 1/2 cup (125 mL) of the sugar. Cover and simmer for 7 minutes or until apples are partially cooked. Drain in sieve.
**PASTRY:** In bowl, combine flour, sugar, baking powder and salt; cut in butter until mixture resembles fine crumbs. Lightly beat together egg and vanilla. Stir into flour mixture until ball of soft dough forms. (If dough seems too stiff, add a few drops of water.)
■ On lightly floured surface, roll out half of the pastry to about 1/8-inch (3 mm) thickness; cut to fit bottom of lightly greased 8-inch (20 cm) springform pan. Spread apples over pastry, leaving 1/2-inch (1 cm) space between apples and inside edge of pan.
■ Crumble remaining pastry into currant-sized crumbs. Drop half of the crumbs into the space between apples and edge of pan. Flatten surface of apples; sprinkle with remaining crumbs. Sprinkle with remaining sugar.
■ Bake in 425°F (220°C) oven for 25 to 30 minutes or until well browned. Remove side of pan and serve warm, garnished with whipped cream. Makes 8 servings.

# AN EAST COAST SEAFOOD CELEBRATION

FOR EIGHT

*The Atlantic provinces of Canada are blessed with the finest quality and variety of seafood in the world. And east-coasters are equally famous for their warm-hearted down-home hospitality. This menu celebrates both. A sampling of four sensational seafood dishes is accompanied by two traditional homegrown favorites.*

*SMOKED FISH PÂTÉ WITH HORSERADISH

*OYSTER STEW

*LOBSTER ROLLS

*MUSSEL AND POTATO SALAD

*POTATO BANNOCK

*BLUEBERRY BUCKLE

## *Smoked Fish Pâté with Horseradish*

*Either smoked trout or mackerel can be used in this pleasing spread. Surround with rye melba toast.*

| | | |
|---|---|---|
| **1/4 lb** | **smoked mackerel or trout** | **125 g** |
| **1/4 lb** | **firm cream cheese** | **125 g** |
| **2 tsp** | **finely chopped chives or green onion** | **10 mL** |
| **2 tsp** | **lemon juice** | **10 mL** |
| **1-1/2 tsp** | **prepared horseradish** | **7 mL** |
| **Pinch** | **each salt and pepper** | **Pinch** |
| | **Chopped fresh parsley or toasted almonds (optional)** | |

■ Remove skin and any bones from fish. Scrape off fat along skinned side, if necessary. Break into chunks.

■ In food processor or blender, process fish until smooth. Add cream cheese, chives, lemon juice, horseradish, salt and pepper; process until well blended and smooth, scraping down sides of bowl when necessary. Taste and adjust seasoning.

■ Transfer to bowl and smooth top. Cover and refrigerate for up to 2 days. Before serving, garnish with parsley (if using). Makes about 1 cup (250 mL).

*(Clockwise from top) Oyster Stew; Mussel and Potato Salad; Smoked Fish Pâté with Horseradish; Lobster Rolls*

## Oyster Stew

*Serve with whole wheat rolls and sweet butter.*

| | | |
|---|---|---|
| 3/4 cup | unsalted butter | 175 mL |
| 1 cup | finely chopped celery | 250 mL |
| 1 cup | thinly sliced leeks | 250 mL |
| 1 cup | finely grated carrots | 250 mL |
| 1 | onion, finely chopped | 1 |
| 1/2 cup | whole wheat flour | 125 mL |
| 2 cups | light cream | 500 mL |
| 2 cups | milk | 500 mL |
| 1 cup | minced clams with liquor (about 5 large clams) | 250 mL |
| 2 cups | shucked oysters with liquor (about 30 oysters) | 500 mL |
| | Pepper | |
| | Fresh coriander or parsley sprigs | |

■ In large saucepan, heat 1/2 cup (125 mL) of the butter; stir in celery, leeks, carrots and onion. Cover tightly and cook over low heat for 30 minutes, stirring occasionally.
■ Meanwhile, in separate saucepan, heat remaining butter over medium heat; whisk in flour and cook for 2 to 3 minutes. Do not brown. Remove from heat and gradually whisk in cream and milk. Return to heat and cook until smooth and thickened, whisking constantly. Stir sauce into vegetables.
■ In another saucepan, combine clams and oysters; cook, uncovered, over low heat for 10 minutes or until oysters just start to curl. Add to vegetable mixture and heat through. Season with pepper to taste; garnish each serving with coriander or parsley. Makes about 8 servings.

## Lobster Rolls

*This tasty lobster salad in a bun is a hearty and refreshing change to tuna or salmon.*

| | | |
|---|---|---|
| 2 cups | cubed cooked lobster (about 4 lobsters) | 500 mL |
| 1 cup | mayonnaise (preferably homemade) | 250 mL |
| 1/4 cup | finely chopped celery (optional) | 50 mL |
| 2 tsp | finely chopped green onion or chives | 10 mL |
| 2 tsp | lemon juice | 10 mL |
| | Salt and pepper | |
| 8 | buttered, halved large crusty rolls (preferably homemade) | 8 |
| | Lettuce | |

■ Shell lobster and chop into 1/2-inch (1 cm) cubes (makes about 2 cups/500 mL).
■ In small bowl, combine lobster, mayonnaise, celery (if using), green onion, lemon juice, and salt and pepper to taste.
■ Line half of each roll with lettuce. Scoop lobster mixture on top. Cover with remaining halves. Makes 8 servings.

## Mussel and Potato Salad

*Here's a tasty variation of a popular favorite.*

| | | |
|---|---|---|
| 4 lb | mussels, steamed and shucked | 2 kg |
| 1/4 cup | chopped fresh parsley | 50 mL |
| 1/4 cup | lemon juice | 50 mL |
| 2 tbsp | finely chopped shallots | 25 mL |
| 1-1/2 lb | new potatoes | 750 g |
| 2 tbsp | dry white wine | 25 mL |
| 2/3 cup | olive or vegetable oil | 150 mL |
| | Salt and pepper | |
| 1 | egg | 1 |
| 1 tbsp | white wine vinegar | 15 mL |
| 1-1/2 tsp | finely chopped fresh oregano (or 1/2 tsp/ 2 mL dried) | 7 mL |
| 1-1/2 tsp | Dijon mustard | 7 mL |

***CLEANING AND OPENING FRESH SHELLFISH***

**Oysters**

***Scrub oysters under cold running water to remove any mud or grit. To shuck them, you will need an oyster knife with a short strong blade, pointed tip and handguard. (To ease opening, they can be microwaved, 3 or 4 at a time, on High for 1 minute.)***

- ***Hold the oyster in a heavy cloth or protective glove with the deeper half of the shell on the bottom to catch as much of the liquor as possible. Insert the blade near the hinge and twist to pry the shells apart.***
- ***Run the blade along the inside of the top shell to sever the muscle holding the meat to the shell. Remove the top shell.***
- ***Slide the knife under the oyster and sever the muscle underneath. Remove any particles of shell.***

**Mussels**

***Discard any mussels with broken shells or shells that don't close when touched.***
***• Scrub mussels with a stiff brush under cold running water to remove any barnacles. Pull out the byssus (black beard) attached to the shell.***
***• Mussels can be opened before cooking with a knife between the shells to pry them apart, but are most frequently poached or steamed in the shells until opened. Discard any shells that don't open.***

| | | |
|---|---|---|
| **1/2 tsp** | **dry mustard** | **2 mL** |
| | **GARNISH:** | |
| | **Oak or other leaf lettuce** | |
| **2** | **hard-cooked eggs, cut in wedges** | **2** |
| | **Chopped fresh parsley** | |

■ In large bowl, combine mussels, half of the parsley, lemon juice and shallots; cover and refrigerate for 1 hour.
■ Scrub potatoes. In saucepan of boiling salted water, cook potatoes until tender but firm; drain and peel. If large, cut in quarters; if tiny, leave whole.
■ In bowl, combine warm potatoes with wine, 2 tbsp (25 mL) of the oil, remaining parsley, and salt and pepper to taste. Set aside and let marinate at room temperature for 30 to 60 minutes.
■ In blender or food processor, combine egg, vinegar, oregano, Dijon and dry mustards, and salt and pepper to taste. With machine running, gradually add remaining oil, a drop at a time at first, then in thin stream as dressing thickens.
■ Combine mussel mixture, potato mixture and dressing; stir gently. Cover and refrigerate for about 2 hours to blend flavors.
■ To serve, line individual plates with lettuce and mound salad on top. Garnish with egg wedges and parsley. Makes about 8 servings.

# *Potato Bannock*

*Serve this moist quick bread hot or cold with chowders and stews.*

| | | |
|---|---|---|
| **2-1/2 cups** | **(approx) sifted all-purpose flour** | **625 mL** |
| **2 tbsp** | **baking powder** | **25 mL** |
| **2 tbsp** | **granulated sugar** | **25 mL** |
| **1 tsp** | **salt** | **5 mL** |
| **1/4 cup** | **shortening** | **50 mL** |
| **1 cup** | **milk** | **250 mL** |
| **1 cup** | **cooled mashed potatoes** | **250 mL** |
| **1 tbsp** | **milk or cream** | **15 mL** |

■ In large bowl, combine flour, baking powder, sugar and salt; cut in shortening until mixture resembles coarse crumbs. With fork, stir in milk and potatoes.
■ Transfer to lightly floured surface and knead gently 8 to 10 times, working in a little extra flour if dough is too sticky.
■ Place dough on ungreased baking sheet and pat with hands to form large oval, about 1 inch (2.5 cm) thick. Brush with milk and bake in 450°F (230°C) oven for 15 to 20 minutes or until golden brown. Slice and serve with butter. Makes about 16 slices.

# *Blueberry Buckle*

*This cake-like pudding is delectable with cream, whipped cream or ice cream. If you use frozen berries, thaw them on paper towelling beforehand, and extend cooking time to about 50 minutes.*

| | | |
|---|---|---|
| **1/2 cup** | **granulated sugar** | **125 mL** |
| **1/3 cup** | **butter** | **75 mL** |
| **1** | **egg** | **1** |
| **1/2 tsp** | **vanilla** | **2 mL** |
| **1 cup** | **all-purpose flour** | **250 mL** |
| **1 tsp** | **baking powder** | **5 mL** |
| **1/4 tsp** | **salt** | **1 mL** |
| **1/3 cup** | **milk** | **75 mL** |
| **3 cups** | **fresh blueberries** | **750 mL** |
| | **TOPPING:** | |
| **1/3 cup** | **packed brown sugar** | **75 mL** |
| **1/4 cup** | **all-purpose flour** | **50 mL** |
| **1/2 tsp** | **cinnamon** | **2 mL** |
| **2 tbsp** | **butter** | **25 mL** |

■ In bowl, cream sugar with butter; beat in egg and vanilla. Stir together flour, baking powder and salt. Stir half of the flour mixture into butter mixture; blend in milk and remaining flour mixture to make stiff batter.
■ Spread batter in greased 8-inch (2 L) square cake pan. Cover evenly with blueberries.
**TOPPING:** In small bowl, stir together brown sugar, flour and cinnamon; cut in butter until mixture is crumbly. Sprinkle over blueberries; bake in 350°F (180°C) oven for about 40 minutes or until crisp and browned on top and knife inserted in center comes out clean. Makes about 8 servings.

# CHRISTMAS AND NEW YEAR

*The busiest holiday season of the year presents us with so many entertaining occasions that we always wonder how we'll fit them all in. In this chapter, we've selected seven menus for you to choose from. All have been streamlined to make preparation and presentation easy and interesting, whether you make one or two, mix and match with your own traditions, or go for all seven! If you're in the mood for bigger parties, you'll find lots of inspiration throughout this book. Or if a calming little supper is what you're looking for in the midst of a busy schedule, we have some of those, too. Set your own pace. Take time for walks in the snow and cookie-decorating with the kids. Gather your friends around you in the comfort and joy of the season. With planned menus that you can handle easily, you'll re-discover the pleasures of the most wonderful food of the whole year.*

# A FINGER FOOD BUFFET

FOR TWENTY

*An hors d'oeuvre buffet supper is a fun and easy approach to entertaining large groups. These dishes can be eaten as finger foods or served on small plates with forks, allowing everyone to help themselves to small tastes of diverse sweets and savories. Some of the dishes are freezable; the rest are make-ahead.*

*CHICKEN LIVER PÂTÉ WITH CURRANTS

*MOSAIC OF VEGETABLES WITH ORIENTAL DIPS

*CHEESY SAVORY ROLL

*IMPERIAL CHICKEN

*ONION TARTS

*STUFFED PASTA SHELLS

*CRANBERRY CHRISTMAS SQUARES

*CHOCOHOLIC SQUARES

*CHOCOLATE TRUFFLES

**Recipes are given for menu items marked with an asterisk.*

*Mosaic of Vegetables; Stuffed Pasta Shells; Cheesy Savory Roll; Chocoholic Squares; Cranberry Christmas Squares*

## Chicken Liver Pâté with Currants

*The special flavor of this smooth pâté comes from the brandy-soaked currants that barely hint at sweetness. Serve pâté surrounded by melba toast and fruit slices. Sliced fruit will retain its color and crispness if soaked in cold salted water for 30 minutes or up to 3 hours before serving; when you're ready to serve, remove fruit and pat dry.*

| | | |
|---|---|---|
| **1/2 cup** | **currants** | **125 mL** |
| **2 tbsp** | **brandy** | **25 mL** |
| **2 lb** | **chicken livers** | **1 kg** |
| **1 cup** | **butter** | **250 mL** |
| **1** | **onion, finely chopped** | **1** |
| **2** | **cloves garlic, crushed** | **2** |
| **1/2 cup** | **whipping cream** | **125 mL** |
| **1 tsp** | **dried thyme** | **5 mL** |
| **1/2 tsp** | **allspice** | **2 mL** |
| | **Salt and pepper** | |

■ Soak currants in brandy for 1 hour. Meanwhile, cut chicken livers in half; remove any fat and membrane. In skillet, melt 1/4 cup (50 mL) of the butter over medium-high heat; cook onion and garlic for about 1 minute or until softened. Add livers; cook for about 5 minutes, turning several times, or until golden brown on outside but slightly pink inside.

■ In food processor or blender, combine liver mixture, remaining butter, whipping cream, thyme and allspice; process until completely smooth. Transfer to bowl; stir in currants mixture. Season with salt and pepper to taste.

*SERVING THE BUFFET*
***Before guests arrive, set out the pâté, vegetables and dips for early indulging. When the party gets rolling, bring out the Cheesy Savory Roll, the Imperial Chicken and the two hot dishes — Onion Tarts and Stuffed Pasta Shells. After coffee, tea and dessert, set out a cheese tray, a basket of clementines and chocolate truffles.***

■ Pack into 8-cup (2 L) crock or several smaller ones of the same total capacity. Cover tightly and refrigerate for at least 3 hours or up to 5 days. Makes about 6 cups (1.5 L).

# Mosaic of Vegetables with Oriental Dips

*Vary the vegetables as desired — cherry tomatoes add festive color — but remember to blanch broccoli, cauliflower and carrots for better taste and appearance.*

| | | |
|---|---|---|
| **2** | **bunches broccoli** | **2** |
| **1** | **large head cauliflower** | **1** |
| **3** | **large carrots** | **3** |
| | **SATAY DIP:** | |
| **2/3 cup** | **crunchy peanut butter** | **150 mL** |
| **1/2 cup** | **milk** | **125 mL** |
| **1/4 cup** | **lime juice** | **50 mL** |
| **2 tbsp** | **packed brown sugar** | **25 mL** |
| **1 tbsp** | **light soy sauce** | **15 mL** |
| **1 tsp** | **Oriental sesame oil (optional)** | **5 mL** |
| **1 tsp** | **hot pepper sauce** | **5 mL** |
| **1/2 tsp** | **grated lime rind** | **2 mL** |
| **1** | **clove garlic, crushed** | **1** |
| **1** | **green onion, chopped** | **1** |
| | **DELHI DIP:** | |
| **1/2 cup** | **mayonnaise** | **125 mL** |
| **1/2 cup** | **plain yogurt** | **125 mL** |
| **3 tbsp** | **finely chopped red onion** | **50 mL** |
| **1 tbsp** | **lemon juice** | **15 mL** |
| **1 tsp** | **curry powder** | **5 mL** |
| **1 tsp** | **granulated sugar** | **5 mL** |

■ Divide broccoli and cauliflower into small florets. Slice carrots into 1/4-inch (5 mm) thick discs.

■ In large saucepan of boiling salted water, blanch broccoli for 2 to 3 minutes or until tender-crisp. Using slotted spoon, remove to large bowl of cold water and let soak for several minutes or until cold; transfer to clean tea towel or paper towel. Using same water, repeat with cauliflower and carrots. (Vegetables can be stored in paper towel-lined bowl, covered with plastic wrap, for up to 1 day.)

**SATAY DIP:** In bowl, beat together peanut butter, milk, lime juice, sugar, soy sauce, sesame oil (if using), hot pepper sauce, lime rind and garlic. Place in serving bowl; sprinkle with green onion.

**DELHI DIP:** In small bowl, combine mayonnaise, yogurt, onion, lemon juice, curry powder and sugar; mix well. Place in serving bowl.

■ Stack vegetables in glass trifle bowl; serve with dips. Makes about 20 servings.

## Cheesy Savory Roll

*Prepare this attractive pinwheel roll the day before to allow the flavors to mellow.*

| | | |
|---|---|---|
| 1/4 cup | butter | 50 mL |
| 1/2 cup | all-purpose flour | 125 mL |
| 1-1/4 cups | milk | 300 mL |
| | Salt and pepper | |
| 4 | egg yolks | 4 |
| 5 | egg whites | 5 |
| | FILLING: | |
| 2/3 cup | cream cheese | 150 mL |
| 1/3 cup | sour cream | 75 mL |
| 1 | small sweet red or green pepper, finely chopped | 1 |
| 1 cup | shredded medium Cheddar cheese | 250 mL |
| 1 cup | corn kernels | 250 mL |
| 2 oz | smoked ham, finely chopped (about 1/2 cup/125 mL) | 50 g |
| 1 tsp | chili powder | 5 mL |
| | Salt and pepper | |
| | GARNISH: | |
| | Finely shredded lettuce | |

■ Line 17-1/2- × 11-1/2-inch (3 L) jelly roll pan with greased waxed paper or greased parchment paper.

■ In heavy saucepan, melt butter over medium heat; remove from heat. Stir in 1/4 cup (50 mL) of the flour. Return to heat and cook for 1 minute. Gradually whisk in milk; bring to boil, stirring. Remove from heat; season with salt and pepper to taste. Beat in egg yolks.

■ In large bowl, beat egg whites until stiff but not dry. Sift remaining flour over egg yolk mixture. Quickly fold egg whites into egg yolk mixture, incorporating flour.

■ Pour batter into prepared jelly roll pan; smooth top. Bake in 375°F (190°C) oven for 18 to 20 minutes or until golden and firm. Turn out cake onto clean tea towel lined with parchment paper or waxed paper. Starting at long side, roll up cake in towel; let cool.

**FILLING:** In large bowl, beat together cream cheese and sour cream; stir in red pepper, Cheddar cheese, corn, ham and chili powder. Season with salt and pepper to taste. Unroll savory roll; spread evenly with filling. Roll up and place, seam side down, on platter. Cover and refrigerate for 2 hours or overnight.

**GARNISH:** Slice roll into 1/4-inch (5 mm) thick slices; arrange in rows on bed of lettuce. Makes about 20 slices.

## Imperial Chicken

*Moist, tender chicken is nicely flavored by soy sauce and cinnamon.*

| | | |
|---|---|---|
| 1 cup | light soy sauce | 250 mL |
| 1/2 cup | granulated sugar | 125 mL |
| 1/2 cup | water | 125 mL |
| 1/4 cup | white wine | 50 mL |
| 3 | slices (each 1-inch/2.5 cm diameter) gingerroot (or 2 tsp/10 mL ground ginger) | 3 |
| 1 tsp | cinnamon | 5 mL |
| 1/2 tsp | nutmeg | 2 mL |
| 6 | boneless skinless chicken breasts | 6 |
| | GARNISH: | |
| 1 | carrot, slivered | 1 |
| 2 | green onions, slivered | 2 |
| 1/2 cup | bean sprouts | 125 mL |
| 1 | bunch watercress | 1 |

■ In large skillet over high heat, bring soy sauce, sugar, water, wine, gingerroot, cinnamon and nutmeg to boil. Reduce heat to simmer; add chicken and simmer for 8 to 10 minutes or until no longer pink inside, turning once. Let cool in liquid. (Recipe can be prepared to this point and refrigerated in airtight container for up to 3 days.)

■ Remove chicken, reserving soy liquid. Slice each breast on diagonal into 5 strips; arrange overlapping slices in circle on platter.

**GARNISH:** Scatter carrot, onions and bean sprouts over chicken. Pour 1/4 cup (50 mL) of the reserved soy liquid over vegetables and chicken. Place watercress in center of platter. Makes 16 to 20 servings.

*CHOCOLATE TRUFFLES*

*The holiday season is a time for special indulgences. And nothing is more special or indulgent than these truffles. Dusted in bittersweet chocolate or cocoa, the crisp chocolate coating encloses a velvety filling that melts luxuriously in your mouth.*

**Ganache Filling:** *In small saucepan, heat 1 cup (250 mL) whipping cream to scalding point (bubbles form around edge of pan); remove from heat. Stir in 1/2 lb (250 g) chopped semisweet or bittersweet chocolate until smooth; stir in 2 tbsp (25 mL) liqueur or 1 tsp (5 mL) vanilla. Transfer to bowl; cover and refrigerate for 1 hour or until thickened and cold.*

*Using whisk (not electric mixer), beat chocolate mixture just until creamy and lighter in color. Do not overbeat or mixture will separate.*

*Using pastry bag fitted with 1/2-inch (1 cm) plain tip, pipe filling into 1-inch (2.5 cm) diameter mounds on 2 waxed paper-lined baking sheets. Cover and refrigerate for 30 minutes or until firm.*

*Working with mounds of filling from one baking sheet at a time,*

*lightly roll in icing sugar. Gently roll each mound between fingertips to shape into ball. Return to waxed paper-lined sheet and freeze for about 1 hour or until hard and almost frozen.*
**Coating:** *In top of double boiler over hot, not boiling, water, melt 3/4 lb (375 g) chopped semisweet or bittersweet chocolate. Remove from heat and let cool slightly. Sift 1 cup (250 mL) cocoa into pie plate. Using 2 forks, dip balls from one baking sheet at a time into chocolate, letting excess drip off. (If chocolate thickens, rewarm gently over hot water.) Place in cocoa.*

*Using 2 clean forks, roll truffles in cocoa; refrigerate on waxed paper-lined baking sheet until hard. Place truffles in candy cups and store in covered container in refrigerator until just before serving. Refrigerate truffles for up to 1 week or freeze for up to 3 months. Makes about 4 dozen.*

## Onion Tarts

*The rich, mellow taste of onion is offset by a touch of Dijon mustard. Top each tart with a shrimp or smoked oyster for a festive look. The pastry dough can be rolled out or just patted into muffin tins.*

| | | |
|---|---|---|
| | **PASTRY:** | |
| **2/3 cup** | **butter** | **150 mL** |
| **2/3 cup** | **cream cheese** | **150 mL** |
| **2 cups** | **all-purpose flour** | **500 mL** |
| **1/2 tsp** | **salt** | **2 mL** |
| | **FILLING:** | |
| **2 tbsp** | **butter** | **25 mL** |
| **1** | **large onion, finely chopped** | **1** |
| **1 cup** | **whipping cream** | **250 mL** |
| **2 tsp** | **Dijon mustard** | **10 mL** |
| | **Salt and pepper** | |

**PASTRY:** Cut butter and cream cheese into 1/2-inch (1 cm) cubes. In food processor and using on/off motion, process butter, cream cheese, flour and salt until mixture resembles bread crumbs. Transfer to large bowl and gather into ball; chill for 30 minutes.
**FILLING:** Meanwhile, in skillet, melt butter over medium heat; stir in onion and cook for 1 minute. Reduce heat to low; cover and cook for 20 minutes or until onions are softened but not browned. Add whipping cream; increase heat to high and cook for about 2 minutes or until thickened and saucelike. Stir in mustard; season with salt and pepper to taste.
■ On lightly floured surface, roll out pastry to 1/8-inch (3 mm) thickness. Using 3-1/4-inch (8.5 cm) fluted cutter, cut dough into 30 rounds; fit into muffin tins. Fill with onion mixture. Bake in 400°F (200°C) oven for about 15 minutes or until pastry is light golden and filling is bubbling. Let cool slightly.
■ Remove tarts from tins; let cool on wire rack. (Tarts can be stored in airtight container in refrigerator for up to 2 days and reheated in 400°F/200°C oven for 8 to 10 minutes or until heated through.) Makes 30 tarts.

## Stuffed Pasta Shells

*These tasty shells hold a cheesy spinach filling with an interesting hint of walnut.*

| | | |
|---|---|---|
| **3/4 lb** | **jumbo pasta shells** | **375 g** |
| **2 tbsp** | **olive oil** | **25 mL** |
| | **FILLING:** | |
| **2** | **pkg (each 10 oz/284 g) fresh spinach** | **2** |
| **2 cups** | **ricotta cheese** | **500 mL** |
| **1 cup** | **shredded mozzarella cheese** | **250 mL** |
| **1/2 cup** | **freshly grated Parmesan cheese** | **125 mL** |
| **1/2 cup** | **finely chopped walnuts or pine nuts** | **125 mL** |
| **1/4 cup** | **chopped fresh parsley** | **50 mL** |
| **2** | **egg yolks** | **2** |
| **1** | **egg white** | **1** |
| **1 tsp** | **nutmeg** | **5 mL** |
| | **Salt and pepper** | |
| **1/2 cup** | **chicken stock or water** | **125 mL** |

■ In large pot of boiling salted water, cook pasta until al dente (tender but firm); drain. In bowl, toss with oil.
**FILLING:** Trim stems and coarse leaves from spinach. Rinse well, but do not dry; cook with just the water clinging to leaves until wilted, 2 to 5 minutes. Drain and rinse under cold running water. Drain again and squeeze dry; chop coarsely.
■ In large bowl, beat together spinach, ricotta, mozzarella, Parmesan, walnuts, parsley, egg yolks, egg white, nutmeg, and salt and pepper to taste.
■ Divide stock evenly between two 8-inch (2 L) square baking dishes. Stuff each pasta shell with 1 tbsp (15 mL) filling; arrange in single layer in baking dishes. (Recipe can be prepared to this point, covered and refrigerated for up to 1 day or frozen for up to 2 months. Do not thaw before baking.)
■ Cover and bake in 350°F (180°C) oven for 10 to 20 minutes or until filling is bubbly. Serve hot or cold. Makes about 40 shells.

## Cranberry Christmas Squares

*The shortbreadlike crust holds a tart but refreshing cranberry filling.*

| | | |
|---|---|---|
| | **CRUST:** | |
| **2 cups** | **all-purpose flour** | **500 mL** |
| **1/2 cup** | **granulated sugar** | **125 mL** |
| **1 cup** | **butter, cut in 1-inch (2.5 cm) pieces** | **250 mL** |
| | **FILLING:** | |
| **2** | **pkg (each 12 oz/340 g) cranberries (about 6 cups/1.5 L)** | **2** |
| **2-1/2 cups** | **packed brown sugar** | **625 mL** |
| **4** | **eggs** | **4** |
| **2 tsp** | **vanilla** | **10 mL** |
| **2/3 cup** | **all-purpose flour** | **150 mL** |
| **1 tsp** | **baking powder** | **5 mL** |
| **1/4 tsp** | **salt** | **1 mL** |
| | **Icing sugar** | |

**CRUST:** In large bowl, sift flour with sugar; cut in butter until crumbly. Pat into 13- × 9-inch (3.5 L) baking dish; bake in 350°F (180°C) oven for 15 to 20 minutes or until golden brown. Let cool on wire rack.

**FILLING:** In saucepan, cook cranberries and 1/4 cup (50 mL) of the brown sugar over low heat until berries are softened and skins pop, about 10 minutes. Set aside and let cool.

■ In large bowl, beat eggs lightly; gradually add remaining brown sugar, beating until thickened. Stir in vanilla. Stir together flour, baking powder and salt; stir into egg mixture until blended. Fold in cranberries.

■ Spread filling over crust; bake in 350°F (180°C) oven for 35 to 45 minutes or until set and uniformly browned. Let cool. (Recipe can be prepared to this point, wrapped and frozen.) Dust with icing sugar. Cut into small squares. Makes about 3 dozen.

## Chocoholic Squares

*Dark, dense and delectable, these are the ultimate chocoholic treats. To give a festive appearance, decorate with pink butter frosting and crushed peppermint candy canes.*

| | | |
|---|---|---|
| **4 oz** | **unsweetened chocolate** | **125 g** |
| **4 oz** | **semisweet chocolate** | **125 g** |
| **1 cup** | **butter** | **250 mL** |
| **2 cups** | **granulated sugar** | **500 mL** |
| **4** | **eggs** | **4** |
| **2 tsp** | **vanilla** | **10 mL** |
| **1 cup** | **all-purpose flour** | **250 mL** |
| **1/2 tsp** | **salt** | **2 mL** |

■ In top of double boiler, over hot, not boiling, water, heat unsweetened and semisweet chocolates until melted; let cool.

■ In bowl, cream butter with sugar until fluffy. Add eggs one at a time, beating well after each addition. Stir in vanilla.

■ Combine flour with salt; stir into butter mixture. Stir in cooled melted chocolate. Pour into greased 13- × 9-inch (3.5 L) baking dish; bake in 350°F (180°C) oven for about 40 minutes or until cake tester inserted in center comes out slightly moist. Let cool on wire rack. Cut into small squares. Makes about 4 dozen.

# A CHILDREN'S CHRISTMAS PARTY

FOR EIGHT

*Whether it's a holiday party for kindergarten chums or a special kids' table at a large neighborhood open house, this festive fare will delight young ones. Peppermint punch and pretty sandwiches are easy to prepare and serve.*

*PEPPERMINT PUNCH

*SANDWICH WREATH

GINGERBREAD COOKIES

## *Peppermint Punch*

*Candy canes add a festive touch to this punch that tastes like a milkshake.*

| | | |
|---|---|---|
| 4 cups | **milk** | 1 L |
| 2 cups | **vanilla ice cream, softened** | 500 mL |
| 2 cups | **chocolate ice cream, softened** | 500 mL |
| | **Peppermint extract** | |
| 8 | **small candy canes** | 8 |

■ In large bowl, whisk together milk, vanilla and chocolate ice creams, and a few drops peppermint extract to taste. Refrigerate until ready to serve. Just before serving, whisk to blend. Pour into glasses and garnish with candy canes. Makes 8 cups (2 L).

*Peppermint Punch; Sandwich Wreath*

## *Sandwich Wreath*

*For eight children, prepare about 32 round or pinwheel sandwiches (3 or 4 different kinds). Use an assortment of breads — party rye or pumpernickel, long skinny loaves thinly sliced, or thin slices of bread cut with cookie cutter rounds. For variety, use 2 different breads for each sandwich. Spread with soft butter, if desired, and filling. Cover prepared sandwiches and refrigerate until ready to serve. Place rounds and pinwheels around rim of circular plate in wreath shape or arrange attractively to fill entire plate. Decorate with evergreen sprigs, bow, radish roses or carved vegetables.*

**PINWHEELS:**

| | | |
|---|---|---|
| 1 | **sandwich loaf, unsliced** | 1 |
| | **Butter (optional)** | |
| | **Fillings (recipes follow)** | |

■ Trim bottom crust; slice loaf lengthwise into 1/3 inch (8 mm) thick slices. Trim remaining crusts.

■ With rolling pin, flatten bread slices and spread with soft butter (if using); spread with filling. Roll up jelly-roll style, starting at narrow end. Cover and refrigerate until ready to serve. Slice into 7 or 8 slices.

**FILLINGS:**

**Christmas Pinwheels:** Combine 4 oz (125 g) softened cream cheese with 1 tbsp (15 mL) maraschino cherry juice. Spread thin layer on bread slice. Place row of whole maraschino cherries across narrow end of bread (or stir chopped maraschino cherries into cream cheese mixture); roll up.

**Peanut Butter and Banana Pinwheels:** Spread bread slice with smooth or crunchy peanut butter. If desired, sprinkle with chopped cooked bacon bits. Place small peeled banana across narrow end; roll up.

**Other Favorite Fillings for the Younger Crowd:** Tuna, egg or salmon salad; chopped chicken or turkey with mayonnaise; ham and mozzarella cheese slices; devilled ham or mild salami.

# A NEIGHBORHOOD TREE-TRIMMING TEA PARTY

FOR SIXTEEN

*Share the old-fashioned spirit of Christmas with a Victorian-style tree-trimming party. Invite all the neighborhood families to come for afternoon tea and help decorate your freshly cut spruce or pine. Set up a separate little tea table laden with goodies for the children. They'll enjoy making decorations from days gone by, such as stringing cranberries and popcorn for the tree. Just don't expect them to be perfect little Victorians who were seen but not heard!*

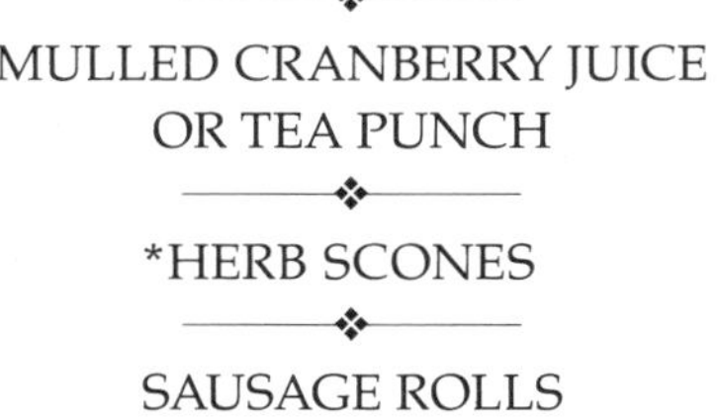

MULLED CRANBERRY JUICE OR TEA PUNCH

*HERB SCONES

SAUSAGE ROLLS

*GINGER POUND CAKE

ASSORTED CHRISTMAS COOKIES

FRESH FRUIT

TEA AND COFFEE

## *Herb Scones*

*These savory scones are perfect for a tree-trimming party. If desired, you can pat the dough into a circle and score the top into wedges without cutting through. Serve warm with whipped butter.*

| | | |
|---|---|---|
| **2 cups** | **graham or whole wheat flour** | **500 mL** |
| **2 cups** | **all-purpose flour** | **500 mL** |
| **2 tbsp** | **baking powder** | **25 mL** |
| **2 tsp** | **baking soda** | **10 mL** |
| **1-1/2 tsp** | **salt** | **7 mL** |
| **1/2 cup** | **shortening** | **125 mL** |
| **1/2 cup** | **butter** | **125 mL** |
| **1/2 cup** | **chopped fresh dill** | **125 mL** |
| **1 tsp** | **coarsely ground pepper** | **5 mL** |
| **1-1/4 cups** | **(approx) buttermilk** | **300 mL** |
| | **Milk** | |

■ In bowl, mix together graham and all-purpose flours, baking powder, baking soda, and salt. Using pastry blender or 2 knives, cut in shortening and butter until mixture resembles coarse crumbs.

■ Mix in dill and pepper. Stirring mixture with fork, gradually add enough buttermilk to make soft but not sticky dough.

■ Turn out dough onto lightly floured surface; knead lightly about 10 times. Roll out to 3/4-inch (2 cm) thickness. Using floured 1-1/2-inch (4 cm) cutter, cut out rounds; place on lightly greased baking sheet. Brush tops with milk. Bake in 425°F (220°C) oven for 15 to 20 minutes or until lightly browned. Makes about 32 scones.

*Herb Scones (top right); Ginger Pound Cake (bottom left); assorted Christmas cookies; sausage rolls*

# Ginger Pound Cake

*Currants, candied citron and ginger update the good taste of old-fashioned pound cake. If the edges of the cake are getting too brown, shield with foil during the last 10 minutes of baking time.*

| | | |
|---|---|---|
| **1 cup** | **butter** | **250 mL** |
| **1 cup** | **packed brown sugar** | **250 mL** |
| **4** | **eggs** | **4** |
| **1 tbsp** | **frozen orange juice concentrate, thawed** | **15 mL** |
| **1-3/4 cups** | **all-purpose flour** | **425 mL** |
| **1/2 tsp** | **baking powder** | **2 mL** |
| **1/2 tsp** | **salt** | **2 mL** |
| **1/2 cup** | **currants, plumped*** | **125 mL** |
| **1/2 cup** | **chopped candied citron** | **125 mL** |
| **1/2 cup** | **chopped candied ginger** | **125 mL** |
| | **Icing sugar** | |

■ In large bowl, cream butter with sugar. Add eggs, one at a time, beating well after each addition. Beat in orange juice concentrate.

■ Stir together 1-1/2 cups (375 mL) of the flour, baking powder and salt. Blend into creamed mixture.

■ Combine currants, candied citron and ginger, and remaining flour. Stir into batter; pour into greased and floured 9- × 5-inch (2 L) loaf pan or 8-inch (2 L) Bundt pan.

■ Bake in 300°F (150°C) oven for 60 to 70 minutes or until cake tester comes out clean. Let cool in pan for 10 minutes. Transfer to wire rack; let cool completely. To serve, sift icing sugar over top and cut into thin slices.

*To plump currants, cover with boiling water; let soak for 10 to 15 minutes. Drain and pat dry with paper towels.

***SETTING THE SCENE***

***To set a cosy turn-of-the-century atmosphere, cover a table or sideboard with white lace or linen tablecloth, then put all your old silver dishes into service. A silver punch bowl shows off crimson mulled cranberry juice or a deep amber tea punch, and flickering candles in silver holders immediately create an air of nostalgia. Scatter dainty touches of Victoriana — lacy potpourri sachets, white cherubic bisque angels — among pretty china dishes, and treat a white wicker basket to a garland of pink silk rosebuds.***

# A COZY FAMILY CHRISTMAS EVE

FOR SIX

*It's finally Christmas Eve and all is calm and bright. Gold, red and green balls dangle from fragrant boughs, catching the light from a merrily crackling fire. Bayberry-scented candles twinkle their welcome from the dining table and clove-studded oranges flood the air with their refreshing spiciness. With gifts wrapped and tucked safely beneath the tree, it's time to sit down to Christmas Eve supper with the family.*

*PEA SOUP WITH JULIENNED VEGETABLES

*PORK AND HAM PIE

PICKLED BEETS

*CRANBERRY CHUTNEY

CHRISTMAS FRUIT SALAD

*THREE-WAY COOKIES

## Pea Soup with Julienned Vegetables

*This flavorful soup is a light version of the traditional French-Canadian pea soup.*

| | | |
|---|---|---|
| 1 tbsp | vegetable oil | 15 mL |
| 1 cup | chopped carrots | 250 mL |
| 1/2 cup | chopped celery | 125 mL |
| 2 | leeks, sliced | 2 |
| 1 | clove garlic, chopped | 1 |
| 4 cups | chicken stock | 1 L |
| 2 cups | water | 500 mL |
| 1 cup | yellow split peas | 250 mL |
| 1/2 tsp | salt | 2 mL |
| 1/4 tsp | dried oregano | 1 mL |
| Pinch | hot pepper flakes | Pinch |
| 1-1/2 cups | julienned vegetables (carrots, leeks, rutabaga) | 375 mL |

■ In large heavy saucepan, heat oil over medium-low heat; cook carrots, celery, leeks and garlic, covered, for about 10 minutes or until softened but not browned.

■ Add stock, water, yellow split peas, salt, oregano and hot pepper flakes. Bring to boil; cover and simmer for about 1 hour and 15 minutes or until peas are softened and tender.

■ In food processor or blender, purée mixture in batches. (Recipe can be prepared to this point, covered and refrigerated for up to 2 days. Reheat before continuing.) Return to pan. Add julienned vegetables; simmer for 10 minutes. Makes about 6 servings.

## Pork and Ham Pie

*An updated variation of tourtière, this elegant savory pie can be prepared on Christmas Eve morning, then baked at dinnertime.*

| | | |
|---|---|---|
| 1/4 cup | light cream | 50 mL |
| 1 | egg | 1 |
| Dash | hot pepper sauce | Dash |
| 1 tbsp | butter | 15 mL |
| 1/4 cup | chopped shallots | 50 mL |
| 3/4 lb | ground pork | 375 g |
| 1/2 tsp | salt | 2 mL |

| | | |
|---|---|---|
| **Pinch** | **nutmeg** | **Pinch** |
| | **Pepper** | |
| **1 cup** | **finely chopped ham (about 1/4 lb/125 g)** | **250 mL** |
| **1/2 cup** | **shredded Swiss cheese** | **125 mL** |
| **1** | **hard-cooked egg, chopped** | **1** |
| **2 tbsp** | **chopped fresh parsley** | **25 mL** |
| **1 lb** | **frozen puff pastry, thawed** | **500 g** |

■ In small bowl, combine cream, egg and hot pepper sauce. Set aside 2 tbsp (25 mL) for glaze.

■ In skillet, melt butter over medium heat; add shallots and cook for about 1 minute or until softened.

■ Add pork to skillet and cook, stirring to break up meat, for 6 to 8 minutes or until no longer pink. Drain off excess fat. Add salt and nutmeg; season with pepper to taste. Stir in cream mixture and ham; let cool completely. Add cheese, hard-cooked egg and parsley.

■ Divide pastry in half. On lightly floured surface, roll out one portion until large enough to cut out 9-inch (23 cm) circle. Place on ungreased baking sheet and prick all over.

■ Mound cooled filling evenly in center of circle, leaving 1-inch (2.5 cm) border of pastry. Brush border with a little of the reserved egg glaze.

■ Roll out remaining pastry as above. Place over filling, stretching to match edges; press together to seal. Cut out steam vent in center; score top of pastry decoratively. Brush top with remaining egg glaze. With back of knife, make indentations around edge.

■ Cover lightly with plastic wrap and refrigerate for at least 1 hour or up to 12 hours. Bake in 450°F (230°C) oven for 15 minutes; reduce temperature to 400°F (200°C) and cook for 20 to 30 minutes longer or until pastry is golden brown and filling is hot. (If browning too quickly, tent loosely with foil.) Let stand for 5 minutes. Makes 6 to 8 servings.

*Pea Soup with Julienned Vegetables; Pork and Ham Pie; Cranberry Chutney*

## Cranberry Chutney

*This will fill your kitchen with a fragrance of sweet, sour and spice. Delicious with pork and turkey.*

| | | |
|---|---|---|
| 4 cups | cranberries | 1 L |
| 1 cup | sugar | 250 mL |
| 1 cup | water | 250 mL |
| 3 tbsp | finely chopped onion | 50 mL |
| 3 tbsp | white vinegar | 50 mL |
| 2 tbsp | Worcestershire sauce | 25 mL |
| 1 tsp | salt | 5 mL |
| 1 tsp | chili powder | 5 mL |
| 1/2 tsp | cinnamon | 2 mL |

■ In a medium saucepan, combine cranberries, sugar and water. Heat, stirring, until sugar dissolves. Continue cooking until berries pop, about 5 minutes.

■ Stir in onion, vinegar, Worcestershire sauce, salt, chili powder and cinnamon; simmer for 5 minutes more, stirring occasionally. Ladle into sterilized jars and seal. Makes about 6 cups (1.5 mL) sauce.

## Three-Way Cookies

*A great timesaver during a busy season, this produces a delicious variety in short order.*

| | | |
|---|---|---|
| | SUGAR COOKIFS: | |
| 2 cups | butter (1 lb/500 g) | 500 mL |
| 2 cups | granulated sugar | 500 mL |
| 2 | eggs | 2 |
| 1 tsp | vanilla | 5 mL |
| 4 cups | all-purpose flour | 1 L |
| 2 tsp | baking soda | 10 mL |
| 1 tsp | cream of tartar | 5 mL |
| Pinch | salt | Pinch |
| | GINGER COOKIES: | |
| 1/4 cup | molasses | 50 mL |
| 2 tsp | ginger | 10 mL |
| Pinch | ground cloves | Pinch |
| | CHOCOLATE COOKIES: | |
| 2 oz | unsweetened chocolate | 60 g |

**SUGAR COOKIES:** In large bowl, cream butter; beat in sugar until light and fluffy. Beat in eggs one at a time, beating well after each addition. Beat in vanilla. Sift or stir together flour, baking soda, cream of tartar and salt. Gradually blend into creamed mixture, being careful not to overmix. Divide dough into three equal parts. Wrap one portion in waxed paper; place in plastic bag and refrigerate until chilled or overnight.
**GINGER COOKIES:** Stir together molasses, ginger and cloves; blend into second portion of dough. Dust waxed paper with flour and wrap dough; place in plastic bag. Refrigerate until chilled or overnight.
**CHOCOLATE COOKIES:** In double boiler over hot, not boiling, water, melt chocolate; let cool and blend into third portion of dough. Wrap in waxed paper and place in plastic bag; refrigerate until chilled or overnight.

■ For each dough, break off small portion, refrigerating remainder. Roll out to 1/8- to 1/4-inch (3 to 5 mm) thickness between two pieces of floured waxed paper, or on lightly floured surface, or with stockinette-covered rolling pin on pastry cloth.

■ Cut out shapes with floured cutters (refrigerate dough on floured waxed paper if sticking occurs). With spatula, transfer to lightly greased or nonstick baking sheets, leaving about 1-1/2-inches (4 cm) between cookies. Bake in 375°F (190°C) oven for 6 to 8 minutes or until sugar cookies are lightly browned and other kinds are set. Remove to wire racks and let cool.

■ Makes about 5 dozen (2-inch/5 cm) sugar cookies, 5 dozen chocolate cookies and 5 dozen ginger cookies.

***SETTING THE SCENE***
***Set just the right mood for this cherished family tradition with a Canadiana theme. Be generous with pine boughs and red and green plaid — tie ribbon around cone-filled baskets, fasten bows to chunky green candles, use tartan napkins — there's never too much of anything at Christmas! Set the table with painted dishes and rustic Quebec-style woven placemats, then bring on traditional foods with an updated twist. Don't forget the pickled beets and cranberry chutney on the side. End the meal with a colorful fruit salad featuring fragrant Christmas oranges.***

# CHRISTMAS BREAKFAST

FOR EIGHT

*This year, you've got it made. Just brew the coffee, pop the frozen soufflés into the oven, then relax while you enjoy a champagne-and-orange-juice appetizer with family or guests. It's a lovely, leisurely start to the big day.*

ICY FRUIT IN SUGARED SNIFTERS

*MAKE-AHEAD THREE-CHEESE SOUFFLÉ

*POPPY SEED COFFEE CAKE

*FRUITED BRAZIL NUT LOAVES

***ICY FRUIT IN SUGARED SNIFTERS***
***The night before serving, dip rims of 8 brandy snifters into a little lemon juice and then into sugar; place in freezer overnight. Peel and slice about 6 oranges; refrigerate overnight. Just before serving, spoon orange slices and some seedless grapes into snifters; add champagne and/or orange juice.***

## *Make-Ahead Three-Cheese Soufflé*

*A baked soufflé must be eaten immediately, but this one can be assembled and frozen before baking — a nice little treat to have tucked away for Christmas breakfast. Individual ones make a festive presentation and puff somewhat better than one large soufflé.*

| | | |
|---|---|---|
| **1/3 cup** | **butter** | **75 mL** |
| **1/3 cup** | **all-purpose flour** | **75 mL** |
| **2 cups** | **milk** | **500 mL** |
| **1 tsp** | **Dijon mustard** | **5 mL** |
| **1/4 tsp** | **salt** | **1 mL** |
| **Dash** | **hot pepper sauce** | **Dash** |
| **1-1/2 cups** | **shredded Gruyère cheese** | **375 mL** |
| **1 cup** | **shredded Cheddar cheese** | **250 mL** |
| **1/4 cup** | **freshly grated Parmesan cheese** | **50 mL** |
| **6** | **eggs, separated** | **6** |
| **1/2 tsp** | **cream of tartar** | **2 mL** |

■ In saucepan, melt butter over low heat; blend in flour and cook, stirring, for 2 minutes, being careful not to brown. Remove from heat and gradually whisk in milk. Stir in mustard, salt and hot pepper sauce.

■ Return to medium heat and cook, stirring, until thickened and bubbly. Stir in Gruyère, Cheddar and Parmesan cheeses until melted. Remove from heat and set aside.

■ In large bowl, beat egg yolks until thick and lemon colored; stir in cheese mixture and let cool.

■ In another large bowl, beat egg whites until foamy; beat in cream of tartar until stiff peaks form. Fold into yolk mixture; pour into 8 ungreased 1-cup (250 mL) soufflé dishes. Cover with foil and freeze.

■ To bake, set frozen soufflés in shallow pan filled with 1/2 inch (1 cm) of hot water; bake, uncovered, in 300°F (150°C) oven for about 1 hour and 15 minutes or until knife inserted off-center comes out clean. Makes 8 servings.

## *Poppy Seed Coffee Cake*

*Here's a convenient cake you can make at the same time as Christmas dinner rolls, using half the Basic Dough recipe.*

| | | |
|---|---|---|
| **Half** | **Basic Dough for Mini-Wreath Rolls (page 238)** | **Half** |
| | **POPPY SEED FILLING:** | |
| **1 cup** | **ground poppy seeds*** | **250 mL** |
| **1/2 cup** | **granulated sugar** | **125 mL** |
| **1/2 cup** | **milk** | **125 mL** |
| **1/2 cup** | **raisins** | **125 mL** |
| **1/2 cup** | **chopped pecans** | **125 mL** |
| **2 tsp** | **grated lemon rind** | **10 mL** |
| | **GLAZE:** | |
| **1** | **egg yolk** | **1** |
| **1 tbsp** | **milk** | **15 mL** |
| | **ICING:** | |
| **1 cup** | **(approx) sifted icing sugar** | **250 mL** |
| **2 tbsp** | **milk** | **25 mL** |

**POPPY SEED FILLING:** In heavy saucepan, combine poppy seeds, sugar and milk; bring to simmer over medium heat, stirring constantly. Remove from heat and stir in raisins, pecans and lemon rind; let cool completely.

■ On lightly floured surface, roll out Basic Dough into 15- × 10-inch (36 × 25 cm) rectangle. Spread with cooled filling, leaving 1-inch (2.5 cm) border of dough. Starting at long edge, roll up jelly-roll fashion; arrange, seam side down, in greased 9-inch (3 L) tube pan. Cover with greased plastic wrap and let rise for 45 to 60 minutes or until doubled in bulk.

**GLAZE:** Stir together egg yolk and milk; brush over top of dough. Bake in 350°F (180°C) oven for 40 to 45 minutes or until golden and ring begins to pull away from side of pan. Loosen edges of loaf; remove to wire rack and let cool completely.

(Coffee cake can be prepared to this point, wrapped in foil, and frozen for up to 1 month. To reheat, remove cake from freezer and let thaw, wrapped in foil, overnight. Loosen foil; heat in 300°F/150°C oven for 20 minutes or until warmed through.)

**ICING:** Just before serving, whisk icing sugar with milk until smooth, adding more sugar if necessary to make smooth but still pourable icing. Drizzle over coffee cake.

Makes 8 to 10 servings.

*Ground poppy seeds are available in some European specialty food stores. Or, in mini-chopper or blender, process 3/4 cup (175 mL) whole poppy seeds, in small batches, to make 1 cup (250 mL) ground poppy seeds.

## *Fruited Brazil Nut Loaves*

*This hurry-up "Christmas cake" doesn't require the long aging usually needed for the traditional version. Serve in little slices.*

| | | |
|---|---|---|
| **1-1/2 cups** | **dried figs** | **375 mL** |
| **1-1/2 cups** | **dried apricots** | **375 mL** |
| **1 cup** | **candied pineapple** | **250 mL** |
| **1/2 cup** | **red or green candied cherries** | **125 mL** |
| **1/2 cup** | **chopped preserved ginger** | **125 mL** |
| **3 cups** | **shelled whole Brazil nuts** | **750 mL** |
| **1 cup** | **all-purpose flour** | **250 mL** |
| **1 cup** | **packed brown sugar** | **250 mL** |
| **1 tsp** | **baking powder** | **5 mL** |
| **4** | **eggs** | **4** |
| **1 tsp** | **vanilla** | **5 mL** |

■ Line two 8- × 4-inch (1.5 L) loaf pans with foil; grease well and set aside.

■ Pour boiling water over figs and apricots; let stand for 5 minutes. Drain and chop into large pieces. Cut pineapple into chunks. Halve cherries.

■ In large bowl, mix together figs, apricots, pineapple, cherries, ginger and Brazil nuts. Stir together flour, sugar and baking powder. Add to fruit mixture and toss to mix.

■ In separate bowl, beat eggs well; stir in vanilla. Add to fruit mixture and mix well; spoon into prepared pans. Bake in 350°F (180°C) oven for 1 hour or until tops are firm and brown and cake tester inserted in centers comes out clean. Let cool in pans for 10 minutes; remove to wire racks and let cool completely. Wrap well in foil or plastic wrap and refrigerate for up to 2 weeks.

Makes 2 loaves.

*Icy Fruit in Sugared Snifters; Make-Ahead Three-Cheese Soufflés; Poppy Seed Coffee Cake; Fruited Brazil Nut Loaves*

# CHRISTMAS DINNER

FOR TWELVE

*This big turkey-and-all-the trimmings feast is satisfyingly traditional, with some interesting updates of flavors and garnishes. It's also an ideal menu for sharing the preparation; with the host household responsible for the roast turkey, all other menu items are make-ahead and totable for re-heating or garnishing before serving.*

*CHRISTMAS SALMON

*ROAST TURKEY WITH APRICOT-ORANGE WILD RICE STUFFING

*CUCUMBER RADISH WREATH

*ONION MANDARIN SAUCE IN ORANGE SHELLS

*BRAISED VEGETABLE MEDLEY

STEAMED BROCCOLI

MASHED POTATOES

*MINI-WREATH ROLLS

*CRANBERRY TRIFLE

*STEAMED BLACK CURRANT PUDDING WITH BROWN SUGAR SAUCE

## Christmas Salmon

*Spooned onto a bed of fresh greens, this dish makes a vibrant starter that sets the holiday dinner mood.*

| | | |
|---|---|---|
| **3 cups** | **bite-size chunks cooked or canned red salmon** | **750 mL** |
| **2** | **tomatoes, peeled, seeded and coarsely chopped** | **2** |
| **1/4 cup** | **finely chopped chives** | **50 mL** |
| **1** | **small onion, finely chopped** | **1** |
| **Half** | **sweet red pepper, thinly sliced** | **Half** |
| **1 tbsp** | **lemon juice** | **15 mL** |
| **1 tbsp** | **chopped fresh basil (or 1 tsp/5 mL dried)** | **15 mL** |
| **1** | **bunch spinach or leafy lettuce, shredded** | **1** |
| | **Dill sprigs** | |

■ In bowl, combine salmon, tomatoes, chives, onion, red pepper, lemon juice and basil; toss gently to mix. Cover and refrigerate for about 1 hour or until chilled.

■ To serve, line individual salad plates with shredded spinach and spoon salmon mixture over top. Garnish with dill sprigs. Makes 12 servings.

*Christmas Salmon (on plates); Roast Turkey with Apricot-Orange Wild Rice Stuffing; Braised Vegetable Medley; Cucumber Radish Wreath*

**ROAST TURKEY**

1. Thaw wrapped frozen turkey in refrigerator. Allow 5 hours thawing time per pound (500 g).
2. Remove giblets and neck. Rinse and wipe cavity; sprinkle with salt and pepper or stuff lightly. Stuffing can be made ahead, covered and refrigerated for up to 2 days, but do not stuff bird until just before roasting.
3. Truss turkey by using skewer to fasten neck skin to back. Twist wing tips and tuck behind back. Tuck legs under skin or tie together with butcher string.
4. Place bird, breast side up, on greased rack in roasting pan. Brush with melted butter or vegetable oil. Cover loosely with foil, dull side out.
5. Roast in 325°C (160°C) oven until meat thermometer reaches 185°F (85°C) when inserted in thigh, and 165°F (74°C) when inserted in stuffing.
6. Baste turkey with pan juices 2 or 3 times during roasting. Remove foil for the last hour and baste as bird browns.
7. Let roasted bird stand for 15 minutes to facilitate carving and to retain juices.

| WEIGHT | ROASTING TIME* |
|---|---|
| 8 lb (4 kg) | 4 to 5-1/4 hours |
| 12 lb (5.5 kg) | 4-3/4 to 5-1/2 hours |
| 14 lb (6.5 kg) | 5-1/4 to 6-1/4 hours |
| 22 lb (10 kg) | 6-1/2 to 7-1/2 hours |

*Roasting time will be slightly less for unstuffed birds

# *Apricot-Orange Wild Rice Stuffing*

*Moist, fruity and colorful, this stuffing is enough for a 22 lb (10 kg) turkey. If your bird is not large enough to hold it all, combine any extra stuffing with enough chicken stock to moisten, and then bake in a covered casserole in a 350°F (180°C) oven for about 20 minutes or until heated through.*

| | | |
|---|---|---|
| **2 tbsp** | **butter** | **25 mL** |
| **2** | **onions, finely chopped** | **2** |
| **2** | **stalks celery, finely chopped** | **2** |
| **1** | **clove garlic, minced** | **1** |
| **2-1/2 cups** | **chicken stock** | **625 mL** |
| **3/4 cup** | **orange juice** | **175 mL** |
| **2 cups** | **long-grain brown rice** | **500 mL** |
| **3/4 cup** | **wild rice** | **175 mL** |
| **1 tsp** | **each crumbled dried sage and thyme** | **5 mL** |
| **Pinch** | **ground cloves** | **Pinch** |
| **1 cup** | **chopped dried apricots** | **250 mL** |
| **1/4 cup** | **currants** | **50 mL** |
| **3/4 cup** | **pine nuts, toasted*** | **175 mL** |
| **1/4 cup** | **chopped fresh parsley** | **50 mL** |
| **1 tsp** | **each salt and pepper** | **5 mL** |

■ In large heavy saucepan, melt butter over medium-high heat; cook onions, celery and garlic, stirring, for 3 to 5 minutes or until softened. Pour in stock and orange juice; bring to boil. Stir in brown and wild rice, sage, thyme and cloves; return to boil. Reduce heat to low; cover and simmer for 35 minutes.

■ Stir in apricots and currants; simmer, covered, for 10 to 15 minutes longer or until rice is tender. Add pine nuts, parsley, salt and pepper; fluff with fork to mix. Let cool completely before stuffing bird. (Stuffing can be covered and refrigerated for up to 2 days.) Makes 11 cups (2.75 L).

*Toast pine nuts on baking sheet in 350°F (180°C) oven for 10 minutes or until golden.

*LIME VINAIGRETTE*
***If you want to add an extra salad to the menu, toss a Christmassy combination of salad greens—romaine, watercress, endive and red-tipped lettuce—with this easy vinaigrette that's subtly flavored with garlic and a hint of sweetness.***

***In small bowl, combine 1/4 cup (50 mL) lime juice, 1 tbsp (15 mL) liquid honey, 1 tsp (5 mL) Dijon mustard and 1 small minced clove garlic; gradually whisk in 2/3 cup (150 mL) vegetable oil. Season with salt to taste. Cover and refrigerate for up to 5 days. Makes 1 cup (250 mL).***

# Cucumber Radish Wreath

*A colorful jellied salad in a Yuletide shape adds a refreshing taste after the main course. Guests can help themselves once they have room on their dinner plates.*

| | | |
|---|---|---|
| 2 | **envelopes unflavored gelatin** | 2 |
| 2-1/2 cups | **water** | 625 mL |
| | **Juice of 1 lemon** | |
| 1 tbsp | **granulated sugar** | 15 mL |
| 2 tsp | **Worcestershire sauce** | 10 mL |
| 1/2 tsp | **salt** | 2 mL |
| 1/4 tsp | **pepper** | 1 mL |
| Dash | **hot pepper sauce** | Dash |
| 1 | **large English cucumber** | 1 |
| 2 cups | **thinly sliced radishes** | 500 mL |
| 2 | **firm red apples, quartered and thinly sliced** | 2 |
| 1/4 cup | **finely chopped fresh dill** | 50 mL |
| | **White radishes and mayonnaise (optional)** | |

■ In small saucepan, sprinkle gelatin into 1/2 cup (125 mL) of the water. Let stand for 5 minutes to soften, then heat over low heat, stirring constantly, for 2 to 3 minutes or until gelatin has dissolved.

■ In bowl, combine gelatin mixture, remaining water, lemon juice, sugar, Worcestershire sauce, salt, pepper and hot pepper sauce; mix well. Refrigerate for about 30 minutes or until mixture begins to set and is consistency of raw egg white.

■ With sharp knife, quarter cucumber lengthwise; cut quarters crosswise into thin slices. In bowl, combine cucumber, radishes, apples and dill; toss gently. Pour in gelatin mixture; mix well.

■ Spoon into 12-cup (3 L) ring mould. Refrigerate for at least 4 hours or until set, or for up to 3 days. Unmould on serving plate and garnish with radishes and mayonnaise (if using). Makes 12 servings.

# Onion Mandarin Sauce in Orange Shells

*This tangy sauce is a perfect condiment for roast turkey. Served in decorative shells, it makes a stunning garnish for the turkey platter.*

| | | |
|---|---|---|
| 6 | **mandarin oranges** | 6 |
| 2 tbsp | **butter** | 25 mL |
| 3 | **red onions, coarsely chopped** | 3 |
| 2 tbsp | **packed brown sugar** | 25 mL |
| 1 tbsp | **grated gingerroot** | 15 mL |
| 1/2 tsp | **curry powder** | 2 mL |
| 1/2 tsp | **Worcestershire sauce** | 2 mL |
| 1 cup | **orange juice** | 250 mL |
| 1/2 tsp | **salt** | 2 mL |

■ Halve mandarins crosswise. With grapefruit knife, cut around outside of pulp and remove fruit, reserving shells. Break mandarins into sections.

■ In skillet, melt butter over medium heat; sauté onions for about 8 minutes or until tender. Stir in sugar, gingerroot, curry powder and Worcestershire sauce; cook, stirring frequently, for about 2 minutes or until onions are lightly golden.

■ Add mandarin sections and orange juice to pan; cook, stirring occasionally, for 20 minutes or until sauce has thickened. Season with salt.

■ Meanwhile, with scissors, cut edges of mandarin shells in decorative zigzag pattern.

■ At serving time, spoon sauce into mandarin shells. Makes 12 servings.

## *Braised Vegetable Medley*

*An assortment of winter vegetables is far more exciting than each one cooked on its own.*

| | | |
|---|---|---|
| **4** | **carrots** | **4** |
| **2** | **bulbs fennel** | **2** |
| **6** | **stalks celery, cut in 1/2-inch (1 cm) slices** | **6** |
| **2 cups** | **chicken stock** | **500 mL** |
| **4 cups** | **cubed peeled butternut squash** | **1 L** |

■ Cut carrots and fennel into 1/2-inch (1 cm) thick slices to make about 2 cups (500 mL) each. In large kettle or Dutch oven, combine carrots, fennel and celery; toss gently. Pour in stock and bring to boil; reduce heat, cover and cook for 4 minutes.
■ Stir in squash; cook for 5 minutes or until vegetables are tender-crisp. (Vegetables can be refrigerated in covered casserole for up to 3 days. Reheat in microwave oven at High for 6 to 8 minutes, stirring after 3 minutes, or until heated through. Alternatively, bake in 325°F/160°C oven for 15 to 20 minutes.) Makes 12 servings.

## *Mini-Wreath Rolls*

*This recipe makes enough dough for eight little dinner rolls for Christmas dinner plus one Poppy Seed Coffee Cake (page 232) for Christmas morning. If you prefer, use the whole batch of dough to make 16 rolls or two coffee cakes.*

| | | |
|---|---|---|
| | **BASIC DOUGH:** | |
| **1 tsp** | **granulated sugar** | **5 mL** |
| **2 cups** | **warm water** | **500 mL** |
| **2** | **pkg active dry yeast (or 2 tbsp/25 mL)** | **2** |
| **1/2 cup** | **granulated sugar** | **125 mL** |
| **1/4 cup** | **vegetable oil** | **50 mL** |
| **2** | **eggs, beaten** | **2** |
| **1 tbsp** | **salt** | **15 mL** |
| **6 cups** | **(approx) all-purpose flour** | **1.5 L** |
| | **GLAZE:** | |
| **1** | **egg yolk** | **1** |
| **1 tbsp** | **milk** | **15 mL** |

**BASIC DOUGH:** In large mixing bowl, dissolve 1 tsp (5 mL) sugar in water; sprinkle in yeast and let stand for 10 minutes or until frothy.
■ Stir in 1/2 cup (125 mL) sugar, oil, eggs and salt until combined. Gradually add 2 cups (500 mL) of the flour; beat for 2 minutes. Using wooden spoon, stir in enough of the remaining flour to make soft sticky dough.
■ Turn out onto lightly floured surface and knead until smooth and elastic, about 10 minutes. Place in greased bowl, turning to grease all over. Cover with greased plastic wrap and let rise for 1 to 1-1/2 hours or until doubled in bulk. Punch down dough and divide in half. Reserve one half for Poppy Seed Coffee Cake (recipe, page 232).
■ Divide remaining half of dough into 16 portions; roll each into rope about 8 inches (20 cm) long. Twist 2 ropes together and join ends to form wreath. Repeat with remaining ropes. Place wreaths on parchment-paper-lined or lightly greased baking sheet. Cover with greased plastic wrap; let rise until doubled in bulk, 45 to 60 minutes.
**GLAZE:** Stir together egg yolk and milk; brush over wreaths. Bake in 375°F (190°C) oven for 20 minutes. Reduce heat to 350°F (180°C) and bake for 10 minutes longer or until tops are golden and wreaths sound hollow when tapped on bottoms.
■ (Rolls can be cooled, placed in freezer bags and frozen for up to 1 month. To reheat, wrap frozen rolls loosely in foil; heat in 300°F/150°C oven for about 15 minutes or until warmed through.) Makes 8 rolls and enough dough for Poppy Seed Coffee Cake, or 16 rolls.

# *Cranberry Trifle*

*Tangy cranberry sauce contrasts beautifully with silky-smooth custard.*

| | | |
|---|---|---|
| | **SPONGE CAKE:** | |
| **4** | **eggs, separated** | **4** |
| **2/3 cup** | **granulated sugar** | **150 mL** |
| **1 tsp** | **grated lemon rind** | **5 mL** |
| **1 tsp** | **vanilla** | **5 mL** |
| **3/4 cup** | **cake-and-pastry flour** | **175 mL** |
| **1/4 cup** | **water** | **50 mL** |
| | **HONEY ORANGE CRANBERRY SAUCE:** | |
| **3** | **apples, peeled and finely chopped** | **3** |
| | **Juice of 2 oranges** | |
| **1** | **stick cinnamon** | **1** |
| **3 cups** | **cranberries** | **750 mL** |
| | **Grated rind of 1 orange** | |
| **2/3 cup** | **honey** | **150 mL** |
| **2 tbsp** | **orange liqueur** | **25 mL** |
| | **CUSTARD:** | |
| **2 cups** | **milk** | **500 mL** |
| **2 cups** | **light cream** | **500 mL** |
| **8** | **egg yolks** | **8** |
| **1/2 cup** | **granulated sugar** | **125 mL** |
| **1/4 cup** | **cornstarch** | **50 mL** |
| **2 tbsp** | **vanilla** | **25 mL** |
| | **ASSEMBLY:** | |
| | **Juice of 1 orange** | |
| **2 tbsp** | **orange liqueur** | **25 mL** |
| **2 tbsp** | **dry sherry** | **25 mL** |
| **2 cups** | **whipping cream** | **500 mL** |
| **2 tbsp** | **toasted slivered almonds** | **25 mL** |

**SPONGE CAKE:** In mixing bowl, beat egg yolks for about 5 minutes or until pale yellow. Gradually add sugar, beating for 5 minutes or until mixture has doubled in bulk and falls in ribbons when beaters are lifted from bowl. Stir in lemon rind and vanilla. Alternately add flour and water to yolk mixture, mixing well after each addition.

■ In separate bowl, beat egg whites until stiff but not dry; fold 1/2 cup (125 mL) into yolk mixture. Fold in remaining whites. Line 9-inch (2.5 L) square baking pan with waxed paper and grease the paper. Pour in batter and bake in 325°C (160°C) oven for 45 minutes or until tester inserted in center comes out clean. Remove from pan and let cool on wire rack. (Cake can be wrapped and frozen for up to 4 weeks.)

**HONEY ORANGE CRANBERRY SAUCE:** In saucepan, combine apples, orange juice and cinnamon; bring to boil and cook over medium heat for 10 minutes, stirring and mashing apples with fork.

■ Stir in cranberries, orange rind and honey; return to boil. Reduce heat and simmer, stirring occasionally, for 10 to 15 minutes or until cranberries pop and sauce thickens. Remove from heat; let cool slightly. Remove cinnamon and stir in liqueur; chill. (Sauce can be refrigerated in airtight container for up to 4 weeks.)

**CUSTARD:** In saucepan, bring milk and cream just to boil; remove from heat and set aside.

■ In mixing bowl, beat egg yolks for 3 minutes or until thickened. Gradually add sugar and cornstarch, beating until thickened and mixture falls in ribbons when beaters are lifted from bowl.

■ Whisking constantly, pour in warm cream mixture in steady stream. Return to saucepan over medium heat and cook, whisking constantly, for about 5 minutes or just until mixture comes to boil and has thickened. Remove from heat and stir in vanilla. Set pan in cold water to cool quickly. Cover surface with waxed paper; chill. (Custard can be refrigerated for up to 2 days.)

**ASSEMBLY:** Break cake into small pieces and place in large glass serving bowl. Combine orange juice, liqueur and sherry; sprinkle over cake. Spread one-third of the cranberry sauce over cake.

■ In separate bowl, whip cream; fold half into custard. Spread half of the custard mixture over cranberry mixture. Repeat cranberry and custard layers once more. Spread remaining whipped cream over top. Dollop with remaining cranberry sauce; sprinkle with almonds. Refrigerate until serving time or for up to 2 days. Makes 12 to 16 servings.

*SUGARPLUMS*

*After dinner, pass the port wine and set out a tray of cheeses for nibbling, mixed nuts for cracking, fresh grapes, dried fruits (some chocolate-coated) and these sweet treats.*

*In food processor or with knife, chop together very finely: 1 cup (250 mL) each pitted dates, dried apricots, dark raisins, golden raisins, pecans or walnuts and 1/4 cup (50 mL) chopped candied ginger. Add 2 tbsp (25 mL) grated orange rind and about 1/4 cup (50 mL) rum, orange liqueur or orange juice to moisten.*

*Shape into tiny balls and roll in granulated sugar, icing sugar, ground almonds or flaked coconut. Makes about 2 dozen.*

*Steamed Black Currant Pudding with Brown Sugar Sauce*

# *Steamed Black Currant Pudding with Brown Sugar Sauce*

*If black currant is not your favorite flavor, substitute another fruit jam and complementary liqueur. If you'd rather not use alcohol in your dessert, use ginger marmalade and substitute orange juice for the liqueur.*

| | | |
|---|---|---|
| **3/4 cup** | **black currant jam** | **175 mL** |
| **2 tbsp** | **cassis (black currant liqueur)** | **25 mL** |
| **3/4 cup** | **butter** | **175 mL** |
| **3/4 cup** | **granulated sugar** | **175 mL** |
| **3** | **eggs** | **3** |
| **2-1/4 cups** | **all-purpose flour** | **550 mL** |
| **2 tsp** | **baking powder** | **10 mL** |
| **Pinch** | **salt** | **Pinch** |
| **2 tbsp** | **milk** | **25 mL** |
| | **Brown Sugar Sauce (recipe follows)** | |

■ Butter 6-1/2 cup (1.5 L) mould or pudding dish thoroughly; sprinkle well with granulated sugar. Mix together jam and cassis; spoon 1/4 cup (50 mL) of the mixture onto bottom of mould. Set aside.

■ In bowl, cream together butter and sugar until light in color. Add eggs, one at a time, beating well after each addition. Stir together flour, baking powder and salt; add to creamed mixture alternately with milk, beating well after each addition.

■ Spoon one-third of the batter over jam in prepared mould, spreading evenly. Add half of remaining jam mixture and spread evenly. Repeat layering, ending with batter. Cover tightly with greased lid of mould. (Alternatively, grease foil and make 1-inch/ 2.5 cm pleat to accommodate expansion; cover mould and tie tightly with string.)

■ Place on rack or trivet in large saucepan; add boiling water to come halfway up sides of mould. Cover and steam in simmering water for 1-1/2 hours or until cake tester inserted in center comes out clean, adding more water to maintain level if necessary.

■ Unmould immediately and serve warm with Brown Sugar Sauce. (Pudding can be cooled, then returned to clean buttered mould. Wrap in foil and refrigerate for up to 2 weeks. To reheat, cover with lid or greased foil; steam for 45 minutes to 1 hour or until warmed through.) Makes about 8 servings.

| | **BROWN SUGAR SAUCE:** | |
|---|---|---|
| **1 cup** | **packed brown sugar** | **250 mL** |
| **1/2 cup** | **light cream** | **125 mL** |
| **1/4 cup** | **butter** | **50 mL** |
| **1 tsp** | **vanilla** | **5 mL** |

■ In 4-cup (1 L) measure, combine sugar, cream and butter. Microwave at High for 2 to 4 minutes or until butter is melted, stirring every 30 seconds. Stir in vanilla. (Alternatively, stir together in small saucepan over medium heat until smooth and almost boiling.) Makes 1 cup (250 mL) sauce.

*A TOAST TO CHAMPAGNE*
*Nothing says "celebration" like a glass of effervescent champagne. With a little champagne know-how, it's easy to get full enjoyment from this festive bubbly.*
- *Count on six generous glasses from each bottle. Serve in chilled, tulip-shaped glasses.*
- *All champagne sparkles but not all sparklers are champagne. The real thing comes from the cool northerly Champagne region of France. The consistently reliable house are Pol Roger, Möet, Mumm, Veuve Clicquot, Pommery, Lanson, Roederer and Dom Pérignon.*
- *When opening champagne, direct the cork away from everyone, including yourself. Holding the bottle at a 45° angle, remove the foil and wire muzzle. Grip the cork firmly with a napkin and gently twist the bottle from the base. Ease the cork out slowly, allowing just a smoky hiss as it emerges. Have the glasses ready and slowly pour a little wine into each, then slowly top up to two-thirds full.*
- *Champagne labelled brut is very dry; extra dry is a bit sweeter; and sec and demi sec are successively more sweet.*

# NEW YEAR'S EVE

FOR EIGHT

*It's time for putting on the ritz. Caviar, lobster, smoked salmon. . . just the stuff for a luxuriously memorable New Year's Eve. This menu is planned for a two-part buffet presentation: first, a trio of gorgeous appetizers for sampling with drinks during the evening; then, an elegant little midnight supper to welcome the New Year. Don't forget the champagne!*

APPETIZERS:

*BEGGARS' PURSES

*SMOKED AND FRESH SALMON PÂTÉ

*NEW-WAVE SPRING ROLLS

MIDNIGHT SUPPER:

*CAPELLINI WITH LEMON AND CAVIAR

*SNOW PEA SALAD WITH SHIITAKE MUSHROOMS

*CHOCOLATE COINTREAU MOUSSE CAKE

## *Beggars' Purses*

*Filled with sour cream and caviar and tied with strips of green onion, these little pouches make intriguing appetizers.*

| | | |
|---|---|---|
| | **CRÊPES:** | |
| **4** | **eggs** | **4** |
| **1 cup** | **all-purpose flour** | **250 mL** |
| **1/2 cup** | **milk** | **125 mL** |
| **1/2 cup** | **water** | **125 mL** |
| **3 tbsp** | **butter, melted** | **50 mL** |
| **1 tbsp** | **granulated sugar** | **15 mL** |
| **1/2 tsp** | **salt** | **2 mL** |
| | **Unsalted butter (for cooking)** | |
| | **FILLING:** | |
| **8 oz** | **cream cheese** | **250 g** |
| **1/4 cup** | **sour cream** | **50 mL** |
| **1** | **jar (2 oz/56 g) black or red caviar** | **1** |
| | **RIBBONS:** | |
| **20** | **green onions** | **20** |

**CRÊPES:** In bowl, beat eggs, flour, milk, water, melted butter, sugar and salt; cover and let stand for 1 hour (or longer in refrigerator).

■ Heat 8-inch (20 cm) crêpe or omelette pan over medium-high heat; brush with a little unsalted butter. Pour in about 1/4 cup (50 mL) of the batter; swirl to coat pan and quickly pour any excess batter back into bowl. Cook crêpe until browned on bottom, 45 to 60 seconds. Turn over and cook for 30 seconds. Remove crêpe to plate; let cool. Repeat with remaining batter, brushing pan with butter when necessary.

**FILLING:** Beat cream cheese with sour cream until smooth; set aside.

**RIBBONS:** Cut bulbs off green onions and use for another recipe. In pot of boiling water, blanch stalks for 30 seconds. Refresh under cold running water and pat dry.

**ASSEMBLY:** Place crêpes, browned sides down, on work surface; spoon tablespoonful (15 mL) of sour cream mixture on center of each. Divide caviar evenly over sour cream mixture. Bring crêpe up around filling to make little sack and tie with green onion ribbon. Makes 16 to 20 appetizers.

# *Smoked and Fresh Salmon Pâté*

*The rich flavor and smooth texture of smoked salmon comes through in this easy pâté. Pistachios and truffles add sensational color. Make sure all ingredients are as cold as possible before preparing mixture. The pâté is delicious served either hot or cold.*

| | | |
|---|---|---|
| **1 lb** | **fresh salmon fillets** | **500 g** |
| **1/2 lb** | **smoked salmon** | **250 g** |
| **2** | **egg whites** | **2** |
| **1-1/2 cups** | **whipping cream** | **375 mL** |
| **1/2 tsp** | **salt** | **2 mL** |
| **1/2 tsp** | **white pepper** | **2 mL** |
| **1/3 cup** | **coarsely chopped pistachios** | **75 mL** |
| **2 tbsp** | **coarsely chopped black truffles (optional)** | **25 mL** |
| **2 tbsp** | **chopped chives or green onions** | **25 mL** |
| | **GARNISH:** | |
| **2** | **slices smoked salmon** | **2** |
| | **Parsley or dill sprigs** | |

■ Cut fresh and smoked salmon into chunks; pat dry. Using tweezers, remove any bones. In food processor, process fresh and smoked salmon until finely chopped. Add egg whites and process until mixture is puréed.

■ With machine running, gradually pour cream through feed tube and process just until blended. Do not overprocess. Quickly blend in salt and pepper. By hand, stir in nuts, truffles and chives.

■ Grease and line 8- × 4-inch (1.5 L) loaf pan with parchment paper. Spoon in mixture and cover with buttered parchment paper. Place pan in roasting pan and pour in enough boiling water to come halfway up sides; bake in 350°F (180°C) oven for 40 to 45 minutes or until mixture is firm when touched in center. Let cool in pan for 15 minutes; invert and peel off paper. Serve hot or cold.

**GARNISH:** Curl each slice of smoked salmon into flower shape and place on or beside pâté. Arrange parsley sprigs around flowers. Makes 8 to 10 servings.

# *New-Wave Spring Rolls*

*The fabulous flavors of lobster, wild mushrooms and sun-dried tomatoes are combined in a Chinese-style spring roll, then dipped into a piquant sauce for a new taste treat. For our photograph, we garnished the serving platter with a small lobster tail, basil and enoki mushrooms.*

| | | |
|---|---|---|
| **3/4 lb** | **frozen lobster tails** | **375 g** |
| **2 tbsp** | **olive oil** | **25 mL** |
| **2** | **red onions, slivered** | **2** |
| **2** | **cloves garlic, minced** | **2** |
| **1/2 lb** | **fresh shiitake or oyster mushrooms, sliced** | **250 g** |
| **10** | **sun-dried tomatoes, slivered** | **10** |
| **3 tbsp** | **chopped fresh basil or coriander** | **50 mL** |
| **1** | **pkg (13 oz/369 g) spring roll wrappers** | **1** |
| **1** | **egg** | **1** |
| **2 tbsp** | **all-purpose flour** | **25 mL** |
| **1 tbsp** | **water** | **15 mL** |
| **6 cups** | **peanut oil (for deep-frying)** | **1.5 L** |
| | **SAUCE:** | |
| **2 tbsp** | **soy sauce** | **25 mL** |
| **2 tbsp** | **lime juice** | **25 mL** |
| **1 tbsp** | **sake (Japanese rice wine)** | **15 mL** |
| **1/4 tsp** | **sesame oil** | **1 mL** |

■ In pot of boiling water, cook lobster tails for about 8 minutes or until partially cooked through. Remove shells. Dice meat and set aside.

■ In large skillet, heat olive oil over medium heat; cook onions and garlic until tender and softened but not browned. Stir in mushrooms and cook for 2 minutes. Add lobster and tomatoes; cook for 5 minutes. Mix in basil, and salt and pepper to taste; let cool.

■ Separate spring roll wrappers and arrange on work surface. In bowl, combine egg, flour and water. Place about 2 tbsp (25 mL) of the lobster filling on each wrapper. Fold up bottom over filling; fold in sides. Spread

*(Clockwise from top) caviar on ice; Smoked and Fresh Salmon Pâté; Beggars' Purses; New-Wave Spring Rolls*

a little egg mixture on unfolded edge and fold over filling; press to secure.

■ In wok or Dutch oven, heat peanut oil to about 375°F (190°C) or until 1-inch (2.5 cm) cube of white bread turns brown in 50 seconds. Cook spring rolls, in batches, for 2 to 3 minutes on each side or until nicely browned. Drain on paper towels. (Spring rolls can be covered and refrigerated for up to 1 day. Reheat in 400°F/200°C oven for about 20 minutes or until heated through.)

**SAUCE:** Combine soy sauce, lime juice, sake and sesame oil. Pour into attractive bowl and let guests dip spring rolls into sauce. Makes 20 to 24 spring rolls.

# *Capellini with Lemon and Caviar*

*Thin "angel hair" pasta is perfect with this sauce but you can substitute fettuccine or linguine. The amount of salt you need will depend on the type of caviar you use.*

| | | |
|---|---|---|
| 1 cup | whipping cream | 250 mL |
| 2 tbsp | vodka | 25 mL |
| 1 tsp | grated lemon rind | 5 mL |
| 1/2 tsp | salt | 2 mL |
| 1/4 tsp | white pepper | 1 mL |
| 1 lb | capellini | 500 g |
| 1/3 cup | unsalted butter | 75 mL |
| 2 tbsp | lemon juice | 25 mL |
| 1 | jar (2 oz/56 g) sturgeon or salmon caviar | 1 |
| 2 tbsp | chopped fresh chives or green onions | 25 mL |

■ In deep skillet, bring cream to boil; stir in vodka, lemon rind, salt and pepper. Reduce heat and simmer gently, stirring occasionally, for 5 minutes or until sauce has reduced and thickened slightly. (Sauce can be prepared ahead and reheated just before serving.)

■ Meanwhile, in large pot of boiling salted water, cook capellini for 5 to 8 minutes or until al dente (tender but firm). Cut butter into small pieces and place in large bowl; stir in lemon juice. Drain pasta well and add to bowl. Pour in cream sauce and toss until noodles are well coated and sauce has thickened.

■ Top each serving with some of the caviar and sprinkling of chives. Makes about 8 servings.

# *Snow Pea Salad With Shiitake Mushrooms*

*The oriental flavored dressing in this salad is perfect with snow peas and mushrooms. The salad can also be made with green beans and fresh mushrooms alone. If you can't find Thai fish sauce, you can use soy sauce, but it may discolor the snow peas slightly.*

| | | |
|---|---|---|
| 1/2 oz | dried shiitake mushrooms | 15 g |
| 1-1/2 lb | snow peas, trimmed | 750 g |
| 1/4 lb | fresh mushrooms | 125 g |
| 2 tbsp | peanut oil | 25 mL |
| 1 | clove garlic, finely chopped | 1 |
| 2 tsp | chopped gingerroot | 10 mL |
| 1 | can (20 oz/567 g) water chestnuts, sliced | 1 |
| 3 | green onions, thinly sliced | 3 |
| | DRESSING: | |
| 3 tbsp | rice wine vinegar | 50 mL |
| 1 tbsp | Thai fish sauce | 15 mL |
| 1/2 tsp | oriental sesame oil | 2 mL |
| 1/3 cup | peanut oil | 75 mL |
| | Salt and pepper | |

■ Soak shiitake mushrooms in warm water for 25 minutes or until softened. Cut out and discard stems. Slice mushrooms thinly.

■ Meanwhile, in large pot of boiling water, blanch snow peas for 30 to 60 seconds or until bright green. With slotted spoon, transfer snow peas to strainer; rinse under cold running water to stop cooking and set color and texture. Pat dry.

■ Slice fresh mushrooms very thin. In large skillet, heat oil; cook garlic and ginger for 1 minute or until fragrant but not browned. Add fresh and dried mushrooms; cook for 3 to 4 minutes. Remove to bowl and let cool. Toss with snow peas, water chestnuts and green onions.

**DRESSING:** In small bowl, combine vinegar, fish sauce and sesame oil; whisk in oil, and salt and pepper to taste. Combine with snow peas and marinate for 30 minutes or up to 3 hours. Makes about 8 servings.

### *CAVIAR*

***The best and most expensive caviar comes from sturgeon. The largest eggs come from the beluga sturgeon, and vary in color from light to dark grey. Beluga caviar is the most expensive. Lower in price, but still quite expensive, are the ossetra and sevruga caviars.***

***When serving high-quality caviar, present it absolutely plain, on ice. If anything is served with it, the accompaniment should be bland crackers or bread that doesn't interfere with the caviar's taste. Some people prefer garnishes such as hard-cooked eggs, onions or sour cream, but it is generally agreed among caviar afficionados that*** **au naturel** ***with champagne or icy cold vodka is the only way to properly enjoy it.***

***Inexpensive caviar is also delicious. Salmon caviar (large red eggs), lumpfish caviar (small black or red eggs) and whitefish caviar (medium-size golden eggs) are very popular. These caviars are quite salty, have firmer eggs, but are very attractive and delicious in their own right. They make a lovely garnish on smoked salmon appetizers, cucumber slices, whipped baked potatoes or scrambled eggs.***

# *Chocolate Cointreau Mousse Cake*

*This is a sophisticated dessert that's easy to make. You can use any orange liqueur in place of Cointreau.*

| | | |
|---|---|---|
| | **CHOCOLATE CAKE:** | |
| **4 oz** | **bittersweet or semi-sweet chocolate, chopped** | **125 g** |
| **4** | **eggs, separated** | **4** |
| **1/2 cup** | **granulated sugar** | **125 mL** |
| **1 tsp** | **grated orange rind** | **5 mL** |
| **2 tbsp** | **unsweetened cocoa powder** | **25 mL** |
| **2 tbsp** | **all-purpose flour** | **25 mL** |
| | **MOUSSE:** | |
| **1** | **envelope unflavored gelatin** | **1** |
| **1/4 cup** | **cold water** | **50 mL** |
| **3** | **egg yolks** | **3** |
| **1/4 cup** | **granulated sugar** | **50 mL** |
| **1 tsp** | **grated orange rind** | **5 mL** |
| **1/2 cup** | **Cointreau** | **125 mL** |
| **1-1/2 cups** | **whipping cream** | **375 mL** |
| | **SAUCE:** | |
| **3 oz** | **bittersweet or semi-sweet chocolate, chopped** | **90 g** |
| **1/4 cup** | **whipping cream** | **50 mL** |
| **1 tbsp** | **Cointreau** | **15 mL** |
| **1 tbsp** | **butter** | **15 mL** |
| | **GARNISH:** | |
| | **Fresh strawberries** | |
| | **Sifted unsweetened cocoa powder** | |

■ Butter 11- × 7-inch (2L) baking dish; line with parchment paper, leaving overhang to lift cake out of dish. Set aside.

**CHOCOLATE CAKE:** In double boiler over hot, not boiling, water, heat chocolate until melted. Remove from heat and let cool slightly.

■ Meanwhile, using electric mixer, beat egg yolks with 1/3 cup (75 mL) of the sugar and orange rind for 2 to 4 minutes or until yolks are thickened and pale in color. Beat in cocoa and melted chocolate.

■ In separate bowl, beat egg whites until soft peaks form. Gradually beat in remaining sugar. Gently fold egg whites into chocolate mixture along with flour. Spoon into prepared pan. Bake in 350°F (180°C) oven for 20 to 25 minutes or until cake springs back when lightly pressed in center. Place pan on rack and let cool. (If cake is slightly puffier at sides, press down gently to level it.)

**MOUSSE:** In small saucepan, sprinkle gelatin over water; let stand for 1 minute. Heat over low heat just until dissolved.

■ Meanwhile, in bowl, beat egg yolks with sugar and orange rind for 2 to 4 minutes or until thickened and pale in color. Beat in Cointreau. Place bowl over saucepan of gently simmering water; cook, stirring constantly, for 2 to 4 minutes or until thickened. Beat in gelatin. Transfer to bowl set in larger bowl of ice water; let cool completely, stirring often, about 10 minutes.

■ Whip cream; gently fold into cooled Cointreau mixture. Spread evenly over cooled cake in pan. Cover and refrigerate for at least 2 hours or until mousse has set, or overnight.

**SAUCE:** In heavy saucepan, melt chocolate with cream over low heat, stirring, until smooth. Stir in Cointreau and butter; let cool.

■ To serve, run knife around edge of cake in pan. Using parchment paper overhang, carefully lift out cake and place on large serving platter or cutting board (if difficult, cut directly from pan). Cut into squares and place on dessert plates. Drizzle sauce in extended "Z" pattern over top of each square. Place a strawberry on each plate. Dust edge of plate and top of cake lightly with cocoa. Makes 8 to 10 servings.

# THE CONTRIBUTORS

**Carol Ferguson** is one of Canada's best-known food writers and is also the editor of *The Canadian Living Entertaining Cookbook*, which has become the most-used reference in Canadian kitchens since its publication in 1987. She has also played a vital role as advisor and contributor to all the *Canadian Living* cookbooks and is now a food writer, editor and consultant.

**Elizabeth Baird** is food director of *Canadian Living* magazine. She is also the author of several bestselling cookbooks and is a leading name on the Canadian culinary scene.

**Anna Carr** is on staff at *Canadian Living* and has arranged the props for many of the photographs that appear in the magazine and in this book.

**James Chatto** writes about food, wine and travel for several Canadian magazines.

**Bonnie Baker Cowan** is editor of *Canadian Living* and has been a frequent contributor to the magazine's food pages, both as writer and as editor.

**Eileen Dwillies** is a west-coast food writer, consultant and food stylist. She also teaches cooking and hosts a television program on creative cooking.

**Nancy Enright** is a food writer and the author of *Nancy Enright's Canadian Herb Cookbook*.

**Margaret Fraser** is associate food director at *Canadian Living* and is also the editor of *Canadian Living*'s Microwave, Barbecue and Rush-Hour cookbooks.

**Brian Greggains** is an established food and travel writer who has journeyed abroad extensively with an inquiring palate.

**Patricia Jamieson** was manager of *Canadian Living*'s Test Kitchen for 4 years until her recent move to *Eating Well* magazine, a publication of Telemedia (U.S.) in Vermont.

**Anne Lindsay** is a food writer, consultant and author of the bestselling cookbooks, *Smart Cooking* and *The Light-Hearted Cookbook*.

**Nancy Millar** is a Calgary-based food writer, broadcaster and cookbook publisher.

**Beth C. Moffatt** is a freelance home economist, food stylist and food writer for *Canadian Living* magazine.

**Rose Murray** is a freelance food writer, consultant and broadcaster. She is the author of several cookbooks, including *The Christmas Cookbook*, which is being published in a new edition this year.

**Ruth Phelan** is a member of the *Canadian Living* Test Kitchen staff and is also a freelance food writer and consultant.

**Iris Raven** is a freelance food writer for *Canadian Living* and also works frequently in the Test Kitchen.

**Kay Spicer** is a home economist, food consultant and journalist. Her most recent cookbook is *From Mom With Love—Real Home Cooking*.

**Bonnie Stern** is proprietor of The Bonnie Stern School of Cooking in Toronto. She is also a food writer, broadcaster, columnist and the author of several popular cookbooks, including *Bonnie Stern's Desserts*.

**Lucy Waverman** is director of The Cooking School in Toronto and is also a food writer, consultant, teacher and author of several cookbooks.

*Canadian Living*'s **Test Kitchen** developed many new recipes for this book and assisted in the selection and updating of menus which had appeared previously in the magazine.

## *Photography Credits*

**Fred Bird:** cover; title page; pages 7 (top), introduction to Evenings, 11, 12, 18, 20, 26, 29, 32, 34, 38, introduction to Daytime, 47, 48, 51, 59, introduction to Parties with a Difference, 75, introduction to Celebrating the Canadian Year, 90, 92, 96, 99, 103, 105, 107, 111, introduction to Very Special Occasions, 117, 118, 121, 124, 128, 135, introduction to The Great Outdoors, 138, 140, 141, 147, 148, 151, 155, 156, 158, 167, 168, 170, 172, 173, 174, 178, 179, 181, 184, 187, introduction to Coast-to-Coast Favorites, 199, 202, 207, 209, 211, 214, introduction to Christmas and New Year, 221, 225, 235, 243, 256.

**Frank Grant:** pages 193, 195.

**Mike Gluss:** pages 7 (bottom), 145.

**Tim Saunders:** pages 95, introduction to International Flavors, 163.

**John Stephens:** jacket/front flap; pages 71, 100, 143.

**Clive Webster:** jacket/back flap; pages 63, 65, 233, 240.

**Robert Wigington:** pages 15, 16, 23, 43, 44, 53, 56, 78, 80, 83, 85, 87, 227, 229.

**Stanley Wong:** pages 66, 67, 68, 69.

Food Styling Coordinator: **Margaret Fraser**

Props Coordinator: **Debby Boyden**

---

The publisher would like to thank the following for the use of various props for photography:

Cover: china from Villeroy and Boch, wine glasses from Bronze Dolphin, linen from Natara's Collection; title page: china and utensils from Bronson's China; page 7 (top): china from Bronson's China, glassware from Pottree & Pantree; introduction to Evenings: white wrought iron chairs and loveseat from Steptoe & Wife, tulip candleholders from Jacaranda Tree; page 38: candlesticks and glass plates from The Compleat Kitchen; introduction to Daytime: napkins, china, glasses and utensils from Bronson's China, china flower basket from Jacaranda Tree; page 51: china, glassware, linens and flower pot from Jacaranda Tree; introduction to The Great Outdoors: napkins, tin plates, sweater, tote bag and decorative baskets from Frida Craft Stores.

## *Special Thanks*

The publisher would like to thank Elizabeth How and Anthony and Augusta Adamson for their kind help during location shooting. Special thanks to Margaret Fraser for her guidance, enthusiasm and generous assistance throughout the production of this book, and to Carrie Ross for her research work and her help with food preparation on location.

# INDEX AND RECIPE CREDITS

*When a recipe appears alphabetically in the Index under its full and proper name, the name of the contributor appears in brackets beside it. Where no contributor is listed, the recipe was developed by* Canadian Living's *Test Kitchen.*

## A



## B

# D

# E



# F



# G



# H

# I



# J



# K



# L



# M



# N



# O

# P



# R



# S

# T



# U



# V



# W



# Z

| | |
|---|---|
| *Design and Art Direction:* | Gordon Sibley Design Inc. |
| *Editorial Director:* | Hugh Brewster |
| *Project Editors:* | Catherine Fraccaro<br>Wanda Nowakowska |
| *Editorial Assistance:* | Shirley Knight Morris<br>Beverley Renahan |
| *Production Director:* | Susan Barrable |
| *Production Assistance:* | Donna Chong |
| *Typography:* | Attic Typesetting Inc. |
| *Jacket Film Separation:* | Colour Technologies |
| *Color Separation:* | La Cromolito |
| *Printing and Binding:* | New Interlitho S.p.A. |
| *Canadian Living Advisory Board:* | Robert A. Murray<br>Bonnie Baker Cowan |

*The Canadian Living Entertaining Cookbook*
*was produced by Madison Press Books*
*under the direction of Albert E. Cummings.*